SAN FRANCISCO
1846–1856

THE URBAN LIFE IN AMERICA SERIES

RICHARD C. WADE, GENERAL EDITOR

SAN FRANCISCO

1846–1856
From Hamlet to City

ROGER W. LOTCHIN

New York
OXFORD UNIVERSITY PRESS
1974

F
869
S357
L67

To my father, Theodore Lotchin,
to my teacher, Daniel J. Gage,
and to the memory of my mother,
Lucile Williams Lotchin, and my
grandfather, Jeremiah Fernando Williams,
all good historians in their own ways.

Foreword

"It's an odd place: unlike any other place in creation," wrote a San Franciscan in 1849," and so should it be; for it is not created in the ordinary way, but hatched like chickens by artificial heat." In that year the California town had 1,000 people; ten years later the population exceeded 50,000. The nineteenth century had never seen anything quite like it. European visitors were always astonished to see urban growth in the New World, but not even Americans were prepared for the meteoric rise of the Bay City. All the frenetic growth of the country seemed encapsulated in a single decade in San Francisco.

In retrospect it all seems so reasonable—a city sitting on the shimmering beauty of the Bay; pastelled buildings pasted firmly on steep hills; the graceful massiveness of the Golden Gate Bridge stretching north to the green suburbs; gleaming skyscrapers nestled in the encircling mountains. Surely nature, if not God, destined a great and unique metropolis here on the Pacific. And its people, a medley of the nation's stock, seem the quintessential urbanites, while its cultural life exudes an effortless superiority over the whole West. Certainly, one would suppose, it takes no historical imagination to reconstruct the natural development of this "singular anecdote in the history of man."

Yet San Francisco's growth was neither inevitable nor tidy. Even its location was open to question and competition from the very beginning. In addition, after its regional supremacy was established, the young town suffered feast and famine economically, continuous crime and outbursts of violence, and persistent poverty and deprivation. In addition, the speed of expansion made the planting of cultural roots precarious and the establishment of congenial social routines difficult.

This volume is a study of that extraordinary first decade of an "instant city," the story of how it was possible to put 50,000 people where a short time before only a thousand had lived. What was legitimate authority? Who had the credentials to rule? Where was the repository of power that could enforce even the most modest consensus? Roger Lotchin's theme of the struggle between endemic chaos and social control provides a working framework to examine this episode in what nineteenth-century commentators called "city building."

The development of orderly growth would have been difficult under ordinary circumstances, but San Francisco was always more than merely California's major city. It was a world city from the very beginning. Set on the thither edge of continental American expansion, it was cut off from the westward-moving frontier by a thousand miles of plains and mountains; facing toward the Pacific, it was the young republic's primary contact with the Far East; only recently removed from Spanish ownership, its own past connected it South to Latin America. More than any other American city, San Francisco was a cosmopolis.

Indeed, it was built almost as an international project. Lumber came from Maine, agricultural products from Latin America, flour from Richmond, Virginia, silk from China, ice and apples from Boston, hemp from Manila, oranges from Tahiti, sugar from Hawaii, prefabricated houses from Chicago, coffee from Java. When steamboats became feasible, coal came to the Bay from England, New York, Chile, and Australia. For years San Francisco was dependent for everything on the outside world. Though it lay near some of the nation's most productive valleys, it imported nearly all its foodstuffs; its manufacturing capacity was of the most touching modesty. This dependency, coupled with a lavishly mixed population, provided from the very beginning the cosmopolitan flavor for which the city would be forever famous.

While many American cities drew people from a dozen different countries, San Francisco's Pacific orientation attracted immigrants from some new ones. The Chinese and Australians, especially, played a key role. Drawn to the port, or sometimes just conveyed there, they provided needed labor in the burgeoning urban economy. They also became scapegoats in bad times. The "Sydney Ducks," as they were called, were thought by Americans to have descended from convicts, and most were in California to escape the law. When riots and violence erupted, they were the target of mobs and police. The Chinese presence evoked a deeper bigotry and a more persistent discrimination since it coupled race and language with job competition. San Francisco was by necessity a community of strangers; but some were more strange than others.

The quick convergence of thousands of people on the young town created an almost endemic disorganization, the clearest symptom of which was, of course, the persistence of vigilantism. This phenomenon has been examined by journalists and scholars for over a century, but, for the first time, Mr. Lotchin provides the movement with an urban context and a more plausible analysis. He sees it not so much as a bout between "good guys" and "bad guys" (which side was which varies with the author's interpretation), but rather the outgrowth of a search for community. All the conflicting elements of the city—its many classes, its disparity of sexes, its various religions, its political instability—collided in a series of murders, lynchings, and reprisals. Mr. Lotchin avoids the easy judgments and glib rhetoric which has afflicted so much of the literature on the subject and sees it as an almost inevitable outcome of rapid growth.

If San Francisco was a world city, it was also intensely American. Almost all the familiar problems which characterized older Eastern and Midwestern towns were magnified in the Bay metropolis—the primacy of real estate speculation over sensible planning; public reluctance to support the most essential services while complaining of their inadequacy; the distressing incidence of poverty even in times of giddy prosperity; the uneven contest between the child population and classroom space; the Sunday observance of religious principles accompanied by weekday indifference; the heroic attempt to insinuate cultural values into a materialistic society. In short, the urban drama that took place over a span of generations in other American cities was compressed into a hasty encore in San Francisco.

Even the political patterns which took so long to develop in older cities emerged quickly in the Bay City. The conventional struggle with the state and its economic capital dominated California affairs, with San Francisco complaining of discrimination and Sacramento worried about the urban imperialism of its most populous place. Internally, too, the old conflict between boss and reformer arose early. Indeed, it appeared in classical form with a leader from New York who called his organization "Tammany" and employed the same questionable tactics that made the New York Democracy notorious. Meanwhile, the reform movement got itself characteristically close to elitism and nativism. The Rebellion of 1856, however, produced a somewhat new synthesis of the traditional encounter.

In reconstructing this founding decade, the historian is blessed with an abundance of source material. San Francisco was born in the age of both the daily newspaper and the professional photographer. In addition, as an urban phenomenon it attracted worldwide attention, with visitors swarming into the young metropolis just to see if not to stay, and many left their impressions in print or manuscript. Hence it is possible to reconstruct the original landscape as well as the physical transformation of the site. Moreover, the minutes of the council and the proceedings of the courts reveal the fitful attempt of public institutions to handle the cascading problems. And in Mr. Lotchin's skillful hands the abundant economic and social records take shape and significance.

This volume, however, has more than historical interest. The urban crisis of the last decade has led to a renewed interest in "new

towns," that is, completely planned cities of a limited size and carefully controlled population mixes. Most call for 100,000 people and
a construction time of ten years. None have been very successful,
nor are they likely to be because they lack the spontaneity, the raw
economic opportunity, and boundless optimism which made San
Francisco a going concern so quickly even under such adverse conditions. Thus, like other books in the *Urban Life in America Series*,
San Francisco: 1846–1856 illuminates a contemporary problem
while adding a fresh dimension to the past.

New York, N.Y.   RICHARD C. WADE
February 1974   GENERAL EDITOR
                                                      URBAN LIFE IN AMERICA SERIES

Acknowledgments

As is the case with all scholars, my debts are too numerous to list in any other than abbreviated form. However, certain institutions, friends, and teachers deserve special mention. The University of California at Los Angeles Library Special Collections, the University of California at Berkeley Library, the California Historical Society, the New York Historical Society, the Library of Congress, the University of North Carolina Library, the Oregon Historical Society, the Huntington Library, the California State Library at Sacramento, the San Francisco Public Library, the Western Jewish History Center, and the American Jewish Archives aided me in many ways. Dr. J. B. Tompkins and his fellow workers at the Bancroft Library at the University of California at Berkeley were helpful beyond measure. Only one who has struggled to work through the Bancroft Library Collection can appreciate the richness of its holdings. I owe further thanks to the University of Chicago Department of History for fellowships, to the University of North Carolina for a grant to support my research, to all my teachers at the University of Chicago, and to those who have preceded me in the field of history, urban or otherwise. Professor Bessie Louise Pierce introduced me to urban history through the History of Chicago Project. Zane L. Miller in particular critically discussed several drafts of the manuscript with me; and Richard C. Wade manfully battled his way through many more. Professor Wade's insistence on good style and good sense benefited me greatly, and his deep knowledge of urban history and acute sense of the important provided more insights than I can recount. I owe my wife an even greater debt for her perceptive editing, patient typing, moral support, and faith in my work, which never flagged even when my own did.

R. W. L.

Contents

Introduction

An American naval officer sat in the U.S. ship *Portsmouth,* anchored off a small hamlet in San Francisco Bay, scratching out a letter in bad English to a compatriot on shore. The epistle, which was addressed to William A. Leidesdorff, the American Vice-Consul in this nominally Mexican town, was not friendly. It warned that by the end of the morrow, July 9, 1846, the village would not even be nominally Mexican.

> At ½ past seven oclock to morrow morning I propose landing a considerable body of men under arms. And to march them from the boats to the flag staff in Yerba Buena, upon which at 8 oclock, I shall hoist the Flag of the U States under a salute of twenty one guns from the Portsmouth. afterwhich, [*sic*] the Proclamation of the Commander in Cheif [*sic*] Commodore Sloat will be read in both languages for the enformation [*sic*] of all classes.[1]

The events of the next day amply fulfilled Captain John Montgomery's threat. He landed his troops as planned, hoisted the flag, read the proclamation, and took over in the name of the "U States."

The sailors and marines had "conquered" the site of what was to become one of the world's most important and fascinating cities. It would seem only fitting, therefore, that there should have been a prolonged siege culminating in a glorious assault upon the citadel from which great heroes and timeless legends would be born. Yet, no such thing happened. There was no siege like that of the Turks at Constantinople, nor was there even any fighting. The hardest part of the "conquest" was the task of landing the boats in the mud flats and then struggling through the sandy "streets" to the Plaza for the ceremonies accompanying the transfer of power.

In the beginning, the American presence did not change the city much, although the occupation somewhat cluttered up the town. A U.S. naval officer noted in 1847 that "the beach was strewn with heavy guns, carriages, piles of shot, ordinance stores, wagons, tents, and camp equipage," while the streets were jammed with troops, "who belonged to the true democracy, called one another mister, snubbed their officers, and did generally as they pleased, which was literally nothing." [2]

The small town which had been so ingloriously occupied was no paradise for military men. It stretched for only a few blocks in each direction; it boasted very few improvements of any kind; its architecture was an undistinguished combination of adobes and rude frame buildings; and its population was small. Only its ambitions were impressive. Although the town gave some indication that it might live up to these expectations in the future, in mid-1846 it was too early to tell. Business was perking up, settlers were trickling in, and occasionally the boredom of the place was further reduced by a "cavalcade of young paisanos, jingling in silver chains and finery, dashing into town, half a dozen abreast." [3] Otherwise, the village had little to recommend it.

In 1849 the beach was still littered; but the disorder was different. Trunks and suitcases, boxes and bales, machines, shovels, barrels of flour, unassembled houses, and similar articles of economic rather than military endeavor now lined the shore. Strewn between, on, and around these tools of trade was a diverse collection of humanity from every corner of the earth. Dressed in plaid shirts and miners' boots or else their own native style, they, like the troops before them, thronged the streets; but the talk now was of gold, not war. The town was no longer like the one the military had "captured." Though not much improved physically, it was wonderfully increased in size. Now it stretched for several blocks more in each direction, and it had begun to climb the surrounding hills. Iron buildings had been added to the frame and adobe ones; and on all sides, squeezed into the streets and perched upon the hills, "were tents of every color forming an amphitheatre." [4] The harbor in front of the city was choked with what travelers almost invariably called a "forest of masts."

In 1856 the clutter was still there; but again it was different. Instead of gold mining equipment, luggage, and martial paraphernalia, there were great warehouses, extensive piers, and magnificent clipper ships. Unlike 1846 or 1849, there was hardly any beach, only a waterfront. There were no tent houses either, nor even very many men dressed in miners' habiliments. In their place stood great stone and brick piles housing large commercial establishments, banks, and factories built in Italianate, Classic, or Gothic style. Miles of streets were paved after a fashion, and the men who walked them wore the uniform of commerce—broadcloth. There was not as much excitement as in 1849, either; and what remained was the anger that men entertain when their hopes have been dashed rather than the enthusiasm of original aspirations. But if its ambitions were somewhat diminished, the place was much larger. It stretched for many blocks up the hills, between them, and beyond; and in the other direction, it extended far into what had been the harbor. San Francisco was no longer the drowsy hamlet of 1846 or the frantic, makeshift town of 1849, but a substantial, impressive city—an instant city.

Even before 1856 the metropolis by the Golden Gate had come to be a source of amazement both to its inhabitants and to visitors. That such a place could be put together in so short a time seemed incredible. "The story was told of a gentleman praising Kansas City's [early] growth who was asked when he was last there. 'Last week,' was his reply. 'Last week? Ah! but you should see it now!!'" [5] That remark applied even more forcefully to San Francisco during the Gold Rush, and some variant of this comment was repeatedly made. "At San Francisco, where fifteen months ago one found only a half dozen large cabins," wrote a French observer in late 1849, "one finds today a stock exchange, a theater, churches of all Christian cults, and a large number of quite beautiful homes."[6] "In February I had left San Francisco narrow, revoltingly dirty, its squares filled with filth and the remains of animals," noted an equally impressed Frenchman one year later. "Today San Francisco is no longer recognizable; it is no longer the old cloaca which bore that name, but the foundation of a great and beautiful city." [7] Nor did the astonishment recede much with the years. "That a city of the respectability of our San Francisco, could be raised in the short space of five or six years, appears incredible," wrote the *Golden Era* in 1856. "Possessing the appearance of an old city of a century, at the present time, it conveys to the mind the idea of being but within a day's journey to the Emporium of the Union." [8] "San Francisco, Sacramento, and Marysville, have so much of city life and character that we hardly recognize their newness," echoed the famous minister Horace Bushnell.[9] "San Francisco is unanimously declared the City of Wonders, and the Americans maintain that its rapid rise, and repeated rebuilding after the fires, are among the most wonderful things the world has seen," a female traveler noted in 1853.[10]

As the lady visitor went on to point out, the city certainly had its defects; and by the end of the period, the community was sorely distressed by the seemingly overwhelming number of these problems. The decade ended with the Vigilante rising of 1856 and an almost hypochrondriac concentration upon the maladies of the metropolis. This preoccupation with the pathological is a well known phenomenon in nineteenth-century American cities, and San Francisco's malaise fits into this tradition perfectly. Yet the pessimism of 1856 was not even typical of the city, however normal it may have been elsewhere; and it was not an accurate portrayal of the condition of the metropolis either. With all due respect to the harried urban reformers and revolutionaries of 1856, one must conclude that the important thing about the Golden Gate City was not its shortcomings but its remarkable achievements.

Given the difficulties inherent in putting together a city of about 50,000 in eight years, with a gold rush for a background, San Franciscans did extraordinarily well. By 1857 the Bay City was still disorderly; its economy was in disarray; and it was yet in large part a colonial dependency of the outside world. In fact, the protest against this subordinate status was one of the main themes of the decade as the local population tried to throw off this dependence on the outside for everything from finances to fiction, manufactures to mores. Yet the colonialism was very sequential, since San Francisco held its own tributary área in turn and enhanced its control over this hinterland at the same time that it complained of its own servitude. Despite depression, disorder, and dependency, the city had forged the dominant position on the West Coast; and it gave out orders to its neighbors as often as it received them from New York and Boston.

The pathological and the sensational, especially the search for order, nearly monopolized men's minds in 1856; and it has bewitched the city's historians ever since. Yet the concurrent search for values and rules was as important as the quest for order, and nothing better indicates the great distance San Francisco had traveled from a collection of gunslinging frontier yahoos than the impressive amount of thinking that suffused its very existence. Celebrities like James P. Casey, Belle Cora, the Emperor Norton, and others have often stolen the historical headlines; but in the background the real heroes of the community were going about the serious, sober, and tiresome task of thinking out the problems of the community.[11] In doing so, San Franciscans had to try to apportion the claims of two or more ordinarily opposite and even contradictory ideals, rules of conduct, and explanations: muckraker and booster, community and individual, law and order and revolution, competition and monopoly, otherworldliness and this worldliness, and environment and heredity. Often there was a decided preference for one or another, but hardly ever was there an absolute preference. What emerged was a kind of situational or contextual ethics which tried to reconcile the claims of competing rules and apply the one which seemed best to suit the circumstances. In short, even though it was an "instant city," San Francisco had had by 1856 a fairly impressive intellectual history, a most striking accomplishment considering its youth, and one of the most urban things about it.

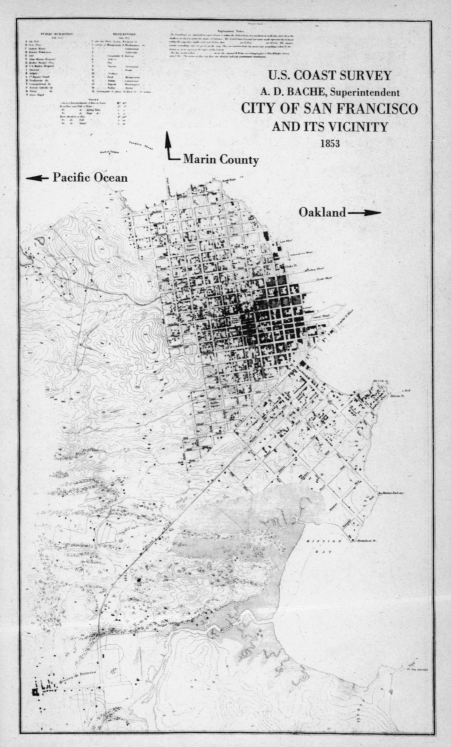

U.S. COAST SURVEY

A. D. BACHE, Superintendent

CITY OF SAN FRANCISCO

AND ITS VICINITY

1853

Marin County

Pacific Ocean

Oakland

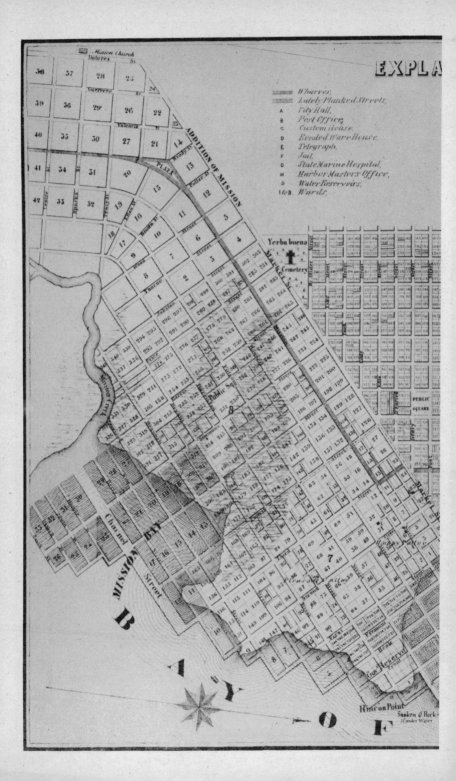

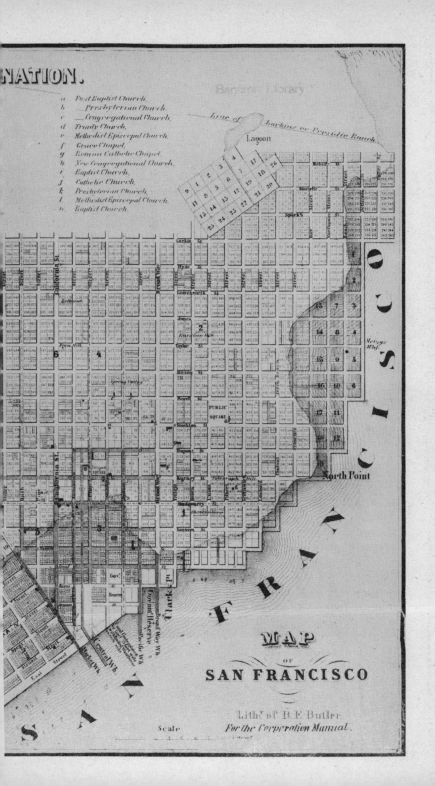

VIEW OF SOUTH PARK FROM THIRD STREET

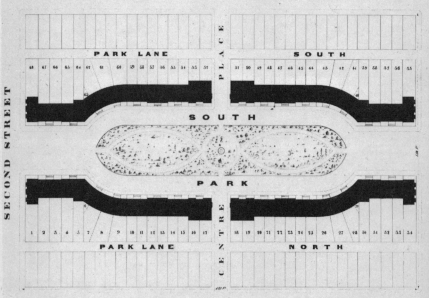

BRANNAN STREET

PARK LANE   SOUTH

68 67 66 65 64 63 61 60 59 58 57 56 55 54 53 52   51 50 49 48 47 46 45 44 43 42 41 39 38 37 36 35

SECOND STREET

SOUTH

PLACE

PARK

CENTRE

THIRD STREET

1 2 3 4 5 6 7 8 9 10 11 12 13 14 15 16 17   18 19 20 21 22 23 24 25 26 27 28 30 31 32 33 34

PARK LANE   NORTH

BRYANT   STREET

PLAN OF SOUTH PARK
PROPERTY OF GEORGE GORDON
Comprising an Area of nearly 17 Acres, between Second & Third, Bryant & Brannan Streets
SAN FRANCISCO.

GEORGE H. GODDARD. ARCHITECT

The subscriber has been for the past two years arranging for the above improvement. The object is
to construct a handsome neighbourhood, exclusively devoted to PRIVATE residences of brick or stone
of uniform design. The site chosen is almost the only suitable in the city limits. Lots will be leased
from 1 to 50 years, renewable, at 10 per cent per annum, on a floor valuation, or sold on 5 years
credits, to parties about to build   Titles Alcalde Grants, confirmed by the City together with
all pecuniary titles

Geo Gordon

LITH. BRITTON & REY SAN FRAN.

SAN FRANCISCO
1846–1856

The Patterns and Chaos of Growth

James Marshall, the partner of John Sutter, set out on January 24, 1848, to inspect the race of their primitive American River sawmill at a site called Coloma. He hoped that the current had deepened the race during the night, but his attention was soon diverted from this question to some shiny metal objects in the stream. These turned out to be gold, and Marshall hurried off to Sutter's Fort to inform his partner. For a time they shared the secret; yet the news leaked out in conversations, letters, trips, and an application for a mining lease, so that before long, an ever-widening circle of people knew. Soon after a tide of humanity changed course and coalesced into the Gold Rush.

Before its advent, the Mexican province of California, recently seized by the Americans but not yet incorporated into their territory, had not amounted to much. It had a thin and unevenly distributed population, much of which had only come into the area in the '40's. Its resources lay largely undeveloped and often unknown; its economy was pastoral and primitive and included no industry or cities. Almost overnight, the search for gold altered all this.

Those closest to the sawmill heard of the discovery soonest and responded to the news. Sutter's Fort, San Francisco, and the Bay Area generally learned of the find first and then, via ships, Hawaii, Southern California, the Pacific Northwest, China, Mexico, and

Chile. All sent adventurers to California in 1848. From 1849 on, Australia, the "States," Europe, and Asia added other significant contingents. Some came to the diggings directly up or across the Pacific, but most came by the Panama route, around the tip of South America, or across the United States. Each route had its advantages, though all involved considerable discomfort and outright peril. The Panama crossing allowed for steamer travel and shorter times on both ocean legs of the journey; but in between passengers faced exorbitant charges, jungle heat, sometimes lethal ethnic conflict, and tropical disease.[1] The trip around the Horn avoided these particular pitfalls at the risk of scurvy, storms, shipwrecks, and a voyage that sometimes took up to eight months and almost never less than ninety days. And the overland route, the most popular, had problems to match its popularity. That journey began in April or May and did not end before August or September and featured Indian troubles, heat, equipment breakdowns, seemingly endless physical exertion, and cholera.

Whichever way they came, these adventurers usually arrived ill-prepared for California. They came bringing mining equipment they could never use, wearing clothing unsuitable to the climate, bearing useless directions, banded together in mining companies that dissolved upon impact with California, and swayed by a hurricane of rumors about everything imaginable. And California was equally unready to receive them. In San Francisco and at the mines they slept in tents, "counting the stars through the roof and the wind whistling Yankee Doodle through the sides." [2] They ate in filthy "restaurants" or "Bach" quarters, crammed into small lodgings, jammed the gaming halls for want of anything better to do, and went without hospitals or medical care when they sickened from wading all day in cold mountain streams in the midst of fierce summer heat. The treasure they dug promptly caused enormous inflation; and as fast as the ore could be extracted, it went into exorbitant payments for everything. For example, desperate argonauts were forced to send their laundry to Hawaii or to throw away their dirty clothes and buy new ones to avoid high washing charges. Many hit great strikes to pay these rates, but most did not get rich and everyone worked hard.

These discomforts quickly produced a countercurrent of disillusioned California-haters, bound for the Golden Gate and passage home. Yet the influx continued to run ahead of this stream of frustration. The state census found 224,000 in 1852 and the federal count of 1860 listed 380,000 Californians. As these immigrants accumulated, the original area of exploitation quickly broadened. New discoveries and new humbugs drew the restless population northward and eastward through the Sierra Nevada into the canyons of the Feather, American, and Yuba, and still farther north to the Trinity, Salmon, and Klamath, while to the south this transient army occupied the Tuolumne, Mokelumne, Cosumnes, Stanislaus, Merced, Mariposa, San Joaquin, and even Kern valleys. Gold camps like Sonora, Mokelumne Hill, Hangtown, Jackass Gulch, Chinese Camp, Big Oak Flat, Yankee Jim's, Oroville, Downieville, and many others sprang up in their wake and cities like Stockton and Sacramento arose to supply these.

At first, California imported most of the necessities of life, even including food. However, as the wealth of the state mounted, more and more people saw the possibilities of nonmining pursuits. As John Dwinelle said of San Francisco, "My diggings are here." [3] Agriculture and commerce boomed, and industry made a good beginning. Even mining evolved from rather crude placer mining toward hydraulic and quartz mining involving large capital expenditures and sophisticated works. In fact, the entire culture became much more complex and mature, as unions, newspapers, theaters, schools, churches, homes, and clubs filled the social vacuum that had existed in '48. In short, California had evolved from a frontier area to a settled state between 1848 and 1860. It is not surprising, therefore, that this booming community produced one of America's first instant cities.

The discovery of gold guaranteed that San Francisco Bay would witness a degree of urbanization. Transportation facilities of the day and California's geography assured this outcome. The two main distributing points to the mining regions were Sacramento and Stockton, located on the Sacramento and San Joaquin rivers respectively. Both these waterways were navigable to vessels drawing up to ten feet of water. Those which drew more than that, and this group included all the clipper ships, had to reload their cargoes onto smaller boats, which in turn carried them to the interior. The transfer point was San Francisco. Therefore, the Bay City was the beneficiary of a "transportation break" in the gold mine commerce.

However, if this theory explains how there came to be cities on the bay, it does not demonstrate why urbanization began at the exact place it did. There are no convincing reasons why the metropolis of the bay area should have been situated where it is. In fact, throughout the period it was the consensus that the isolated peninsula on which the city stands was not a very eligible site. Russian, Nob, and Telegraph hills as well as numerous sand hills loomed up to complicate the development of a metropolis. There was a large mudflat immediately in front of the town but very little level ground on shore. In addition, the area had neither a good supply of water nor timber for building or shade; and its climate was less salubrious than that of other places on the bay, especially the Contra Costa. In San Francisco it was colder and the breezes blew much harder, bringing in the fog in dense clouds and filling the air with the dust and sand which abounded on the largely treeless, chaparral-choked city site. To a scientific and technological age, these disadvantages may not seem very great, and, indeed, some of them, such as the hills and mist, may even be charming. However, in an era without the means to surmount the heights easily, overcome the lack of water, cope with the pulmonary disorders caused by the winds and damp, or keep out the dust, they were much more formidable. The site did boast a good sheltered harbor, centrally located, but it had little else to recommend it.[4]

Despite the sandbar on San Antonio Creek, the Contra Costa shore, with its superior weather, level land, and timber resources, would have been a better place to situate a city.[5] So would have the Benicia-Vallejo area on the north end of San Pablo Bay. That the metropolis grew up where it did and not at one of these other spots was the result of a number of peculiar and transient developments, plus some long-range ones.

The Mission of San Francisco and the Presidio, founded primarily to promote and protect Spanish imperial interests, were established in 1776. Around the Mission of San Francisco, usually called the Mission Dolores, a town, or pueblo, arose. By 1845 this hamlet had a population of 150, though both the Mission and Presidio were virtually defunct.[6] Besides colonizing San Francisco, the Spaniards had begun other missions and pueblos around the bay: San José, Santa Clara, San Rafael, and San Francisco de Solano at Sonoma. With the passage of years, a number of ranches sprang up between these places. It was to capitalize on the commercial possibilities of this thin line of settlement that modern San Francisco was founded in 1835.

In that year an Englishman named William Richardson settled on the Cove of Yerba Buena. This inlet was on the northeast side of the peninsula and a couple of miles from the Mission Dolores in Mission Valley. Richardson chose this spot in order to trade with the Mexican population scattered about the bay. Since the harbor was less "exposed" than that opposite the Presidio, whalers and other ships often anchored there. Using two schooners belonging to the missions of Dolores and Santa Clara, Richardson carried on a commercial exchange between these vessels and the people around the bay.[7] He was soon followed by other merchants —including for a while those of the Hudson's Bay Company—and by the agents of the Boston hide traders. Thus, the future city of San Francisco had a distinctly commercial origin; but it was a commerce based on Spanish-Mexican (plus an increasing American) settlement, not on gold.

The liquidation of the Latin part of this heritage was the second critical factor in fixing the urban demography of the bay area. The years 1846–48 witnessed a war between the United States and Mexico. Although the military phase of this conflict in

San Francisco was almost comic, the event was crucial for urbanization. Since the village of Yerba Buena was the largest on the bay, the United States Quartermaster's Store, the U.S. troops' quarters, and the customhouse naturally gravitated there. This government patronage gave a decided impetus to the economic life of the town and more than made up for the wartime disruption of the hide trade.

The third development was entirely a religious matter. In the summer of 1846 a ship carrying about two hundred Mormons landed at Yerba Buena, thereby doubling the population. These people were seeking a refuge in the West from religious persecution; but instead of joining their brethren at Salt Lake, many of them stayed on at the bay hamlet.

Together, the Mormons, the Mexican War, and the desire for merchant profits caused a modest growth in Yerba Buena. In 1848 the population on the cove numbered between 850 and 1,000. Hence, by the time of the Gold Rush, San Francisco was enough of a city to attract the commerce induced by the discovery of gold.[8]

Ironically, several of the important reasons which gave San Francisco its preeminence lost their significance after 1848. The trade with the "Californios" was dwarfed by the gold commerce; the Mexican War came to an end; and the Mormons as a group were not prominent in the city's growth between 1848 and 1856. Yet from 1835 to 1848, and especially in the last two years of that period, these three transient factors were important in fixing the urban configuration of the bay area and in giving the city its main advantage—a head start. A hamlet of from 850 to 1,000 people was not very impressive compared with New York; but it was many times larger than any potential rival, and that was the crucial comparison.

When the Gold Rush occurred, still other developments combined to protect this modest urbanization. The great impetus given to economic life encouraged the appearance of rivals to San Francisco at the same time that it propelled the small hamlet into an orgy of growth. The cost of landing goods quickly rose to exorbitant levels. Because there were no wharves, merchandise had to be lightered ashore. With mining sustaining high wages and lack of space doing the same for storage costs, merchants were tempted to bypass the city and ship directly to Sacramento and Stockton. Through 1849 barks, schooners, and other smaller craft often went directly to the interior entrepôts.

This practice was abandoned, however, before it seriously cut into San Francisco's prosperity. Wildly fluctuating prices made time all important in river commerce, and the advent of steamers in 1849 offered the merchant both greater speed and carrying capacity. The simultaneous rise of the clipper ship in the California trade provided much the same advantages on the ocean leg of the journey. Because of their size, however, clippers could not navigate inland waterways, and neither could some other ocean-going boats. Therefore, a transshipment had to be made somewhere on the bay. The natural tendency was to make this transfer at the most developed spot; and as technology supplied more warehouses and wharves, planked streets, and fireproof buildings, the deterrents to the use of San Francisco eased considerably.

Thus the threat to the peninsula site receded as rapidly as it had arisen, and the chief point of urbanization on the bay remained fixed. Curiously enough, it was the introduction of more modern commercial facilities—wharves, streets, warehouses, steamboats, and clippers—which reinforced and protected the more primitive and archaic urban arrangement of San Francisco Bay. All these advantages together more than made up for the faulty geography of the site and even for the rapid destruction of its one natural advantage, the harbor. As Bayard Taylor correctly noted of San Francisco, "Whatever advantages she may lack will soon be amply provided for by wealth and enterprise." [9]

It was entirely accidental that American imperial aspirations should have coincided with the Mormon desire for religious freedom in such a way as to cast up representatives of these two ambitions on the northern end of San Francisco Peninsula at the same

time that commercial fortune-seekers located there. It was equally
fortuitous that the Gold Rush should have poured a stream of men
into San Francisco just one short year after the city had claimed
that name for the very reason of enticing settlers and before any
other town on the bay was large enough or sufficiently well known
to compete in this respect. One can also cite the almost contem-
poraneous invention of the clipper ship, which reinforced the transshipment break at the bay. The nearly exact coincidence of a war,
a religious migration, a shrewd commercial decision, a Gold Rush,
and a new discovery in ocean transport, combined with the presence of a certain level of river transportation technology and a
desire to exploit the commercial possibilities of a given situation,
are not the stuff out of which exact sciences are made. But they are
the very essence of history—novel, fortuitous, and human.

Although chance may have determined the location of the city,
historically the continued existence of cities has been dependent
upon the presence of an agricultural surplus. However, the Bay
City's sustenance, for at least half of the period, did not come
from its immediate hinterland. From 1846 to 1848 California provided much of the food and Oregon made up a large part of the
deficit. After the Gold Rush began, California was even less capable
of feeding the metropolis. The thousands of immigrants were nearly
all looking for gold to dig rather than a patch of ground to plow,
and for a time agriculture was all but abandoned. Hunting, as it had
for the cities and towns from the Neolithic Age, provided much of
the food for San Francisco's tables; and the sailing ship and the
city's oceanic location made it possible for outside sources to make
up the shortage.[10] Around 1853 the situation changed again as the
state began to produce an increasingly greater food supply of its
own. The immediate influence of this local surplus was detrimental,
but eventually the city benefited from its hinterland's potential. Yet
it was not until the close of the period that the export of California
wheat began to replace even partially the profits formerly derived
from the imports from Chile, Virginia, Oregon, and elsewhere.

Because San Francisco had access to an outside source of food, nearby rural growth was not a crucial precondition for rapid urbanization. Like a number of other American cities, the Bay City called into existence the agrarian surplus (the mines, of course, did too) by its demand for food. This pattern was especially true for the part of the peninsula closest to town, where market gardening areas grew up—at the Mission Dolores in the south and at Washerwoman's Lagoon in the north. Furthermore, urbanism had a very stimulating effect upon the agricultural potential of the entire bay area. Eventually, the metropolis provided commercial facilities for a still greater farming extension when the wheat trade arose.

Enriched by the Gold Rush and nourished by its own and the world's husbandmen, San Francisco underwent extensive physical growth. Yet most of this development was anarchic. There was little government planning for the use of land, and much of what there was turned out badly. Most of the planning, therefore, was private, individual, and small rather than public, communitarian, and large-scale. The best, and biggest, example of these private efforts was undertaken toward the end of the period at the suburb of South Park, where the promoter banned all liquor saloons, required brick buildings in the area of most congestion, and laid out the plat in an oval form surrounding a park. South Park soon became a source of considerable local pride; but there were few other examples, public or private, to match it.

The council set apart the street plat and several plazas for public use instead of speculation; and, after the passage of the Van Ness Ordinance, it reserved certain western areas for schools and more squares. In addition, this body established a master plan to regulate all grades. As the metropolis became more complex, however, the public demanded segregation or prohibition of particular activities within given neighborhoods. Though the response to these requests was minimal, the demands were significant for the future.

At first, zoning efforts took the form of nuisance indictments. Slaughterhouses, chandleries, soap and acid factories, charcoal burners, and other petty manufacturers whose trades had offensive side effects, such as odor or waste, were constantly prosecuted as

well as mauled in the press. Another deterrent was the purchase of
land earmarked for some obnoxious use. When J. Wieland proposed
to put a brewery at the corner of Folsom and Second, in an aristocratic area, the "indignant" residents "authorized fellow resident
Milton S. Latham [a lawyer and politician] . . . to wait upon [Mr.
Wieland] and make an offer of purchase for the property." Sometimes the transaction involved blackmail. In 1853 the *Alta* reported
that a speculator had purchased a lot in a respectable section for
the purpose of establishing a house of prostitution on it, knowing
full well that the residents would buy him out at an inflated price.[11]

This informal zoning soon graduated into legal banishment of
distasteful practices from certain areas. In 1852 the fire danger led
the city to the prohibition of tents and wooden buildings within the
limits of Union, Powell, Post, Second, and Folsom streets. This
ordinance also forbade or regulated the storage of combustibles
and powder within the same section. The same year saw slaughterhouses excluded from the area east of Larkin and north of Market;
and in 1854 they, along with stockyards, were driven from the city
altogether. A year earlier the hospitals had been classified in the
same category as slaughterhouses when they, too, were prohibited
within the part of town bounded by Jones, Filbert, McAllister, and
Johnson streets.

Public action sometimes took a positive turn. As early as 1853
projects were afoot to set aside certain districts for given activities.
Prostitution and gambling were two of the leading candidates for
this distinction. Though most San Franciscans did not like these
businesses, many recognized them as inevitable and gave up on
the effort to eliminate them. Instead, quarantine was hit upon as
an alternative solution; at least the evil could be put out of sight
even if it could not be put out of business.[12] Nothing formal happened, however.

The most ambitious plan for controlling land use suffered the
same fate. This was an effort by the manufacturers to protect
themselves from prosecution by establishing a "haven" and shows
very clearly the connection between zoning and annoyance prose-

cution. In 1855 various manufacturers, "having been driven from pillar to post" by their neighbors, proposed to the aldermen that a parcel of land be set aside south of Mission Creek where industry could locate with security. This section was to be situated "so remote from the inhabited part of the city that no legal question would likely arise as to what might constitute nuisances in the district, at least within the period named in the ordinances—January 1st, 1869." [13]

Zoning was, therefore, an attempt at reconciling the home-owning and the manufacturing interests while preserving the community dedication to two ideals; but after passing one board of aldermen, the proposal lost in the other. However, the proposed regulations were in no way a new departure except as to means. The normal growth of the city had encouraged a natural segregation which sorted out retail from wholesale trades, residential from both, and one kind of residence from another. Zoning would have made formal legal provision for what had already been happening informally to freeze the separation, to substitute artificial for natural parceling, to supplant individual control over the evolution of land use patterns with community, and to replace transient and changing areas with relatively stable ones.

Historically, American cities have suffered from lack of planning; San Francisco was no exception. A more flexible street plat, wider thoroughfares, and a manufacturing zone all were promising ideas, and several other improvements could have been made. Yet if San Francisco had indulged in comprehensive planning, it would have been a disastrous mistake. Many of the most elementary necessities could not have been supplied. Most importantly, no one had anything close to an accurate notion of the city's rate of growth. Even the most optimistic boosters repeatedly underestimated its development; indeed, no one knew how many people actually lived in the metropolis until the state census of 1852. And of those enumerated, it was quite impossible to judge how many were transient or permanent.

Nor was this the only information gap. Another concerned the agricultural development of the interior. Any increase in farming would throttle the city's commerce and the pace of growth. Yet when this alteration actually took place, not even the merchants most concerned understood the magnitude of it. The same kind of ignorance prevailed about the durability of the gold supply. It, too, was consistently misunderstood. San Francisco could have been better, though not comprehensively, planned.[14]

In the years immediately after 1848 the growth pattern seemed unsettled. In fact, one is tempted to conclude that there was no order at all. The shuttling back and forth to the mines, the filling of the cove, and the rapid growth created a great deal of flux.

Even religious worship reflected the problem of transiency. The Reverend Albert Williams of First Presbyterian began his meetings in the public school on Portsmouth Plaza in 1849, but for the next four years, he and his flock were in perpetual motion. After leaving the school, the assemblage met successively in the district courtroom on Dupont between Jackson and Pacific, in the second story of another structure on the latter street, and in a tent which had formerly been the marquee of a Boston military company. When the heavy rains of 1849–50 drove the worshipers from this refuge, they adjourned to the church of their Baptist rivals. Following a short tenure there, they moved to the U.S. customhouse, then to the superior courtroom at City Hall on Pacific and Kearny, and finally to a new house of worship built for them on Stockton between Broadway and Pacific. When this burned in 1851, the congregation found shelter successively in the supreme courtroom in the Marine Hospital on Stockton, in the superior courtroom in the St. Francis Hotel, and again with their Baptist competitors. Finally, in 1851 the group settled on the site where the church remained in 1856.[15]

Not everyone had the same experience as these Presbyterian nomads, yet their predicament reflected the instability that gripped the city after the discovery of gold. As each year passed, however, San Francisco settled down more and more; and under the surface of confusion, a surprising degree of order began to emerge. The expansion of the city may have been without plan, but it was not without pattern. One of the most important was natural. To a very considerable extent, the initial growth of the metropolis was decided by its geography; yet to an equally impressive degree, its geography was determined by its growth.

Throughout the years between 1846 and 1856, especially in the earlier ones, San Franciscans showed a decided preference for low ground. Both the original settlements, Yerba Buena and Mission Dolores, were situated on or near water. The Gold Rush added other low-lying colonies at Happy and Pleasant valleys south of Market Street and St. Anne's Valley and Spring Valley north of it. West of the hills, the Washerwoman's Lagoon settlement augmented this group. By 1856 a continuous line of dwellings linked these initially isolated clusters. Moreover, several new additions had been laid out, in each case avoiding the heights: Hayes Valley, just west of the present Civic Center Plaza; Horner's Addition, immediately south of the Mission Dolores; and the Potrero Nuevo, east of that. Population in the north spread westward along the foot of the range of hills fronting the bay.

Yet the low and relatively level ground soon ran out, forcing the inhabitants to eliminate those hills they could remove and scale the ones they could not. A steam shovel—known as the "Steam Paddy" or "Vaporific Patrick" after the Irishman it presumably replaced—scraped off the sand hills, and railroad cars deposited them in the cove. A similar operation was carried out at the bayward base of Telegraph Hill, where the rock of that bastion was blasted away. These projects created new areas of level land in both directions; and for a time, therefore, technology was able to ease the restraints of geography.

In the north, population flowed into the declivity between Telegraph and Russian hills, eventually flanking the heights of Russian Hill by a four-block-wide salient along the bay extending as far west as Jones Street between Union and Chestnut. To the south, settlement went down the line of Market and Mission streets, thus bypassing Nob Hill. In 1853, therefore, there was still a striking correlation between low geography and high density, with Rincon, Russian, Telegraph, and Nob hills the least crowded areas.

However, the high ground could not be avoided indefinitely; and the march to the sea was soon matched by one into the hills. "Two years ago," explained the *Alta* in 1851, "the property there [i.e., on the elevated places surrounding the cove] was considered almost worthless, as it was hardly supposed that anyone would travel up there to live so long as there were any level spaces left." However, astonishing growth and the accompanying congestion quickly caused the hills to be valued as "airy" places to settle.[16] Shortly thereafter, the city marched straight over the heights, and San Franciscans began their long tradition of cliff dwelling. Once again, technology freed the metropolis for further growth, as thoroughfares were blasted out of the high ground and plank streets were laid down to ease the burden of ascent.

In 1853 the urban frontier north of Market was about one half block west of Mason on the east side of the hills; but by 1857 the vanguard of settlement had reached beyond to Larkin, five blocks to the west, and in some places exceeded that line. The majority of residences and economic activities clustered in and around the northern part of the old Cove of Yerba Buena, while the southern part of the cove beyond Market was not yet as intensively used. The mission was still the southern outpost of the newly created urban empire, as Washerwoman's Lagoon was the northern.[17]

A number of other land-use patterns, both residential and economic, supplemented the geographic. While San Francisco was still reeling under the impact of the Gold Rush, the retail, wholesale, manufacturing, and middle-class residential sections were packed close together downtown. These were flanked by the workingmen's neighborhoods; but with that exception, there was relatively little specialization in land use. For the most part, the city was compact and undifferentiated.

Some retailing, especially grocery, was done outside the area; but most of this trade occurred alongside the others. The section of retailing, wholesaling, manufacturing, and middle-class residence was a half-moon shaped one fronting the old cove in the north part of town. The outstanding characteristic of these locations was proximity to the waterfront and to each other. Lower-class residences tended to be on the periphery of this indiscriminate grouping, although they, too, were close to the water.[18]

Much of this changed by 1857. Most of the working classes were still anchored to the outskirts of the central business district, but little else remained the same. In the interim occurred a sorting out of the various activities that had in 1850 been located contiguously. The wholesaling part of the business community migrated eastward toward the water. The middle classes erupted over the hills to the west and, to a lesser extent, into the Rincon Hill area south of Market. The retailing section tended to stay put or to spread out to the west and south, following its retreating customers. This resettling gave the retailers a position between wholesaling and middle-class residence. Unlike retailing, petty manufacturing, such as blacksmithing and coopering, did not follow the middle-class ascent of Russian and Nob hills. Instead, the migration of these artisans was north and south, away from the central position they had formerly held. In general, petty manufacturing located in the working-class districts. The lower class also tended to migrate out, though their base remained fixed.

In addition, a new element entered the picture—relatively large-scale manufacturing. This, too, was set up in a part of the working-class district, south of the original area of settlement but not in the same section as petty industry. Iron foundries, ship builders, flour and saw mills, and gas works were established either south of Market on First Street, on Market itself, or close to this part of town.

Accompanying this decentralization of economic and residential patterns came considerable specialization of land use, and hand in hand with decentralization came greater concentration of the various categories within each. For example, commission merchants were congregated on the angle of Front and California; produce merchants were segregated together on Clay Street or close by; lumber dealers were in an odd-shaped linear district along Steuart, California, and Market; clothing and dry goods merchants were on Sacramento; the lawyers, on Montgomery or Merchant; and the large-scale manufacturing, south of Market. These segregated areas were often close to each other; and the differentiation was not complete, but it was present and growing. Many of the economic spatial relationships can be explained by reference to a number of urban frontiers which delineated the areas of relative safety from fire, of high rent and land prices, of minimum drayage rates, of planked streets, of newly made land, and of accessible water supply.

It would be difficult to overestimate the influence of fire in the total development of San Francisco. Yet the impact on building location was not uniform, and sometimes it was even contradictory. One man purposely built his three buildings in different portions of town to avoid losing all of them in one blaze. Sometimes, however, fire sustained concentration. Before 1851 the town was built largely of wood; but after the terrible experience of that year, brick became increasingly popular. The practice of erecting brick structures close together grew up; indeed, before 1856 this hiving had progressed far enough to include most of the central business district.[19]

Frequent blazes also stimulated the eastward drift of the wholesaling district. "The merchant who was content to do business in Sacramento Street as long as his old building stood," explained the *Picayune*, ". . . when he was compelled to move [by being burned out], preferred the more eligible sites which the steam excavator [was] continually making in the harbor, and even at a higher rent erected his warehouse in the deep water." [20] Hence fires at once liberated the merchant from his old, less advantageous location and put him on piles over the water, where goods could be exchanged and fires combatted more easily.

The aftermath of a conflagration usually featured considerable resettlement, and one area of the city suffered drastically from it.

Long Wharf and its hinterland was originally the busiest part of the waterfront, but the holocaust of May 1851 hurt it badly. The flames partially consumed the pier itself, and the real estate in its vicinity was damaged financially.

The fires naturally put a premium on the availability of water, which in turn reinforced the bayward tendency. Since most artesian wells were located east of Montgomery and that area was also closer to the bay, this section was safer for both merchants with private supplies and those without.

The supply of land was even more influential in determining spatial arrangements. New land, lower and closer to the wharves, continually became available; and even without fires, merchants kept drifting toward the bay. Planked streets enabled them to take advantage of the new area, and proximity to the ships and wharves supplied them with a reason to do so. Yet transportation did not determine the initial pattern. It was businessmen, through financing of both street improvements and wharves, who dictated their location.

Once the original investment had been made in the planking and paving, however, the lower sites were more desirable. Thereafter, transportation became a significant variable in its own right, drawing business activity down toward the waterfront or into the planked section. In 1854, Battery Street, for example, was the only artery which connected the central business district with the warehouses in the north end of the city. Proximity to Battery thus was obviously important, and the entire area of improved thoroughfares always featured higher rents and land prices.[21]

In the beginning the very lack of street improvements affected land usage. Early in 1850 it seemed as if the city would not get its thoroughfares planked before another rainy season set in. That prospect prompted many merchants to locate on piles over "water lots," using the bay as a substitute for improved streets and leading the *Picayune* to predict that "the heavy amount of commercial and mercantile business will be likely to be done over the tide water next winter."[22]

The importance of transportation on spatial relationships appeared again in drayage rates, wharves, and harbor customs. The
teamsters, for instance, set different prices for various distances.
In 1850 the charge for anything hauled outside the territory of
Stockton, Pine, and Pacific was fifty cents to one dollar higher,
providing considerable incentive to locate inside these boundaries.
The wharves had a comparable magnetic effect. "The great strides
which business has taken towards Happy Valley within the last
few months . . . puts the success of the Market Street wharf, as a
speculation beyond doubt," explained the *Picayune*. "As is, however, always the case, the wharf will react to the improvement of
the Valley." To an extent, the docks, like the central business district, were specialized. The *Herald* noted as early as 1853 that "the
business [of the wharves] has been classified, and particular kinds
are now carried on in particular localities." That specialization, in
turn, affected what happened in their immediate hinterlands. The
Clay Street Wharf, for instance, was usually the one to which small
craft from around the bay came with produce, and Clay Street
below Front contained nearly all the commission produce merchants.[23]

The concentration of warehouses at the base of Telegraph Hill
probably owed something to the "customs of the harbor," too. The
wharves around the north part of the city were "preferred for the
accommodation of the heavy shipping from distant ports." Since
cargoes had to be landed from these ships and duty paid on them,
a storage area close to the large docks was a definite advantage.[24]

So was face to face contact downtown. "There is probably no
city in the world in which the peculiarity of the market so emphat-
ically calls for a constant and unremitted intercourse between the
merchants as in San Francisco," wrote the *Picayune*. "If a person
in San Francisco happens to become the possessor of any lot of
goods, he is obliged to traverse the whole city before he can either
determine on the state of the market, or know who is in want of
the commodity." [25] The absence of modern means of communication in part explains this necessity, but other factors reinforced

the need. Commercial exchanges, trade associations, or monopolies could have provided a central source of data; but these were ineffective. Business information remained a closely guarded secret.

The level of technology, like fire, had a nonuniform impact upon spatial arrangements. The same considerations that led the wholesalers to crowd onto the corner of California and Front persuaded retailers to scatter toward Stockton and Market. Their trade required proximity to their decentralized customers just as that of the importers and jobbers demanded mutual contiguity and access to the improved streets, wharves, and watercraft which conveyed their orders, customers, and commercial correspondence.

Others also required proximity. Though small manufacturers as a group were dispersed, they often congregated by trades outside the central business district. For example, jewelers, wagon makers, and coopers were near each other as were different but allied crafts such as blacksmiths and carriage makers. Obviously, artisans benefited from the external economies of a location close to complementary trades. Yet the placement of artisans also grew out of center city rents and lot prices, which small operators could not afford. Therefore, steadily rising real estate costs were a strong centrifugal force, expelling people and businesses from the heart of the city.[26]

Space and other resources of land, as well as its price, determined arrangements. The clay of Mission Creek soon attracted a colony of brick makers; and powder magazines left town by municipal request, since they were a menace in a thickly populated area. The ropewalk joined the suburban trek, as it required 2,600 feet of clear space without streets cutting through its operation.[27] Other activities also left the metropolis because of the deterrents of crowdedness, some by choice and others, such as slaughtering, because of pressure.

The residential configuration of San Francisco, like its economic pattern, was relatively segregated. The separation was not complete, but it, too, was growing. For the middle class, this trend implied an increasing distance between home and work. In 1850 a small vanguard had migrated as far west as Stockton and Powell, but most resided close to or in their places of employment downtown.[28] Eight years later, however, the city's bankers, clerks, merchants, and doctors looked down from the heights of Rincon (South Park), Russian, and Nob hills upon the remnants of their fellows in the central business district.

As this desertion of the center city progressed, a central phalanx of middle-class preponderance developed. Bounded by the waterfront, Sutter, Gough, and Greenwich streets at its furthest extremities, this section was based upon the central business district, from which it had grown, and ran from the harbor to the periphery. Within this part of the city the demographic mixture varied, but everywhere the working class was in the minority.[29] East of Montgomery in the central business district, that group came closest to holding its own at 47 per cent; but from there to Taylor, their proportion lessened. In the area between the downtown section and Dupont, the middle class held a lead of 65 to 35 per cent. This predominance dipped to 60 on Dupont, rose to 67 on Stockton (the most densely populated and the longest part of the middle-class section), and finally soared to 75 per cent on Powell. The next two streets, Mason and Taylor, were 60 and 75 per cent respectively.

The prevalence of the middle class in this area was striking because of their minority status in the population as a whole—39 per cent.[30] Moreover, lower-class people living amongst their "betters" were usually those closest to them in income and status—artisans and skilled workers, but few laborers.

The workingmen's section flanked that just described. It held sway north of the Jackson Street boundary of the central business district and east of the Dupont frontier of the middle class. From Montgomery to the waterfront, their lead was better than two to one; but west of that street their prevalence diminished as one neared Dupont. South of the California Street wholesaling concentration, beginning at the shoreline, and north of Howard, the work-

ing class enjoyed its greatest superiority. Closer to the bay and
downtown, that lead was longest. In the area bounded by Market,
Mission, Steuart, and Second, it was 89 to 11 per cent. In the portions of the city surrounding this great congregation, the workingmen predominated by three to one. Between Market, California,
and Dupont, this preeminence was not so great; but it still ranged
from two to one to three to one.

Thus the lower orders in San Francisco, like the upper, had
their own areas of settlement where they were an absolute majority and significantly disproportionate to their share of the population. On the outskirts of town, that is, the suburbs, beyond Leavenworth and in some places beyond Larkin, density diminished very
greatly; but the same configuration seems to have held up. The
working class lived west of its downtown concentrations and the
middle class dwelt west of its own group; yet beyond Leavenworth and Larkin, where farms mingled with city dwellings, settlement was really quite sparse and its patterns, unclear.

Within the working-class preserve, there were still other divisions based on income and employment. Artisans, for example,
tended to live farther out from the center city and the harbor and
closer to the ranks above them than did others in their group. Occupations also influenced the pattern. Carpenters, teamsters, laborers, and those whose work was not necessarily done in a particular part of town resided throughout the lower-class sections.
Machinists, blacksmiths, and water-related trades such as boatmen, sailors, shipwrights, shipsmiths, and stevedores, however,
congregated close to their jobs. In addition, the workingman generally resided in areas of petty and large-scale manufacturing or
close to the central business district and thus did not have the
same degree of separation between home and work that the middle class did.

Although these population divisions were not complete, the bulk
of the middle-class residents was clearly drifting toward the periphery and the largest concentration of workingmen was anchored near the center city. The middle class had pushed west-

ward out of their 1850 downtown location to the edge of the heavily settled section and were spreading out north and south of
there. Numerically and proportionately, the middle-class lead was
greatest in the area geographically farther from the center city,
and the working-class predominance was just the reverse. The
separation of classes was most evident where population was heavily concentrated. Dense settlement and segregation of social
groups clearly went together. It is impossible to state definitively
whether this pattern amounts to a "new" or "old" city center and
periphery pattern, but the old arrangement seems least likely. The
heaviest working-class preponderance was closer to downtown
than the largest middle-class block, and the metropolis definitely
did not break down into a middle-class core and working-class
ring. It seems possible that the new arrangement was in the process of being born, but this pattern had not yet fully emerged by
1868, almost ten years after horsecar mass transit had been introduced.[31]

The motivations that usually determined this population distribution were complicated, but those of the working class are clear.
For this group the prevailing high land and rental rates effected
both concentration and scatteration. "The laborer, at present, to
obtain a building at a rental consistent with his means," explained
the local voice of the workingman, "must either go beyond the
city limits or stow himself and family into some dilapidated building, located in one of the filthy lanes or alleys with which this city
abounds." From the beginning of the Gold Rush, Happy Valley
had been the center of working-class residence; and the avoidance
of the high ground rents downtown was a principal reason for this
development.[32]

To a certain extent, the same factors influenced the middle class
as well. Yet for those whose income afforded a choice, the matter
was more complex. Transportation contributed significantly to the
desertion of the center city. As early as 1852 there were regular,
though precarious, steamboat connections with the infant town of
Oakland; and other places in the area eventually followed this

lead. As a result, a small contingent of San Franciscans filed out of the city to these "steamboat suburbs." Plank roads and streets did for the peninsula what the ferries did for the East Bay. From 1850 on, these improvements covered an increasing number of streets, and their impact was obvious. The plank roads, especially those on Mission, Folsom, Pacific, and Brannan, together with the bridge over Mission Creek, channeled settlement toward the mission and the lagoon.[33] Beyond these points the regular roads extended development still farther south toward San José and west toward the Presidio; and these improvements, in turn, corresponded to low geography.[34] An omnibus service, beginning in 1850 and running over the first of these routes, encouraged the same demographic distribution.

South of Market, therefore, and in the suburbs, settlement was largely determined by these technological innovations. Elsewhere the sequence of events was reversed. There, population was relatively dense before any improvements were made in modes of conveyance. As early as 1847 Powell Street had its first inhabitants, yet it was not until 1852 that a limited omnibus service was inaugurated in this middle-class phalanx and 1854 before street planking was widespread. Once established, of course, these transit facilities reinforced the trend already in existence. In the distribution of population, planking was more important than omnibuses. The latter, which began in 1854 to operate between North Beach and South Park via downtown, served two middle-class areas as well as a working-class section in between. Both termini of the route were in middle-class areas, but they did not live predominantly along the omnibus routes. Rather, bourgeois residence had a much higher correlation with the street planking. Moreover, the planking facilitated and may even have been a sine qua non for the introduction of wheeled transport. As Barry and Patten noted in speaking of the Mission Dolores in 1850, "A vehicle [there] was rather a curiosity until the plank road was constructed." "The improvements in the streets that are progressing," echoed the *Pacific* in 1853, "remove the difficulty of travel in this

neighborhood, and make it far more desirable as a place of residence." [35]

Improved methods of conveyance, however, provided only the
means of migration rather than the motivation. "Status" considerations undoubtedly lured some to the outskirts of town or the suburbs, and South Park and Stockton Street both were widely
acclaimed as "fashionable" living places. Yet one should not exaggerate the significance of this factor in emptying the center city.
There were many solid, prosaic, and even more compelling reasons
for such a change. Safety was one. Some districts, such as Sydney
Valley north of the central business district, were rowdy at best
and often lethal. For a middle-class woman such as Mrs. Benjamin
Butler, who witnessed a throat slitting from her own window, this
area could be quite terrifying. "In the morning the Policemen
were up there—we were very careful not to say anything. It was
a coman [sic] occurance [sic]." So were fires. Hence people deserted the downtown section; and often their institutions, such as
the churches, went with or even ahead of them.[36]

Comfort and economy strengthened the exodus. The regions
closer to the waterfront were increasingly cluttered with the paraphernalia of commerce or manufacture. For those who left the
metropolis entirely, the attractions of the climate at other spots
on the bay were an important inducement for migration. The
Contra Costa, the Santa Clara Valley, and San Mateo, for example, each had more sunshine and less fog and wind. Moreover, the
price of downtown land, for rent or purchase, had grown enormously. Fantastic charges prevailed in the city center in the first
years of rapid growth; and though these declined somewhat, they
remained a powerful stimulus to decentralization, even for the
rich.[37]

Further motivation for this trek to the suburbs, both internal
and external ones, concerned San Franciscans' view of city and
country. Despite widespread fascination with the Golden Gate
City, there were many who were willing to praise the "rural ideal."
"It is a sententious truth that 'man made the city, but God made

the country,'" wrote the *Alta* in 1852. "The utilitarian [way] in which we live, and the practical, work-aday life which we Californians lead, do not altogether deprive us of sweet visions of green fields, wholesome country air, and retired rural homes." "With none," continued the city's leading daily, "would the change from the hustling hours of a business day in the crowded streets of a city, to the evenings and mornings of retirement in a suburban retreat, be more grateful than to the business men of San Francisco." [38]

Outside the metropolis, one could have "plenty of room without being elbowed by rude neighbors" or troubled by contact with what the *Alta* called "an accumulation of a class that always becomes numerous in every large and old city and from whose presence all who can hope to escape." Other men were fleeing different things. "Usually on Saturday I drive out to San Mateo only too glad to be under the necessity of looking after the farm, glad to be far away from the constant strife of the city life," George Howard wrote to Agnes Howard. "I picture to myself for you the life of the country that we are so charmed with among the English gentry, free from the forced, false life of the city." [39] In short, the weary metropolitan yearned for pure air, living space, beauty, trees, solitude, retirement, and a respite from the dust, bustle, conflict, crowds, artificiality, and utilitarianism of a growing city.

This set of desires cannot very well be separated into rural and urban factions, for they do not make any sense by themselves. The attractions of the country were only potent to one who had endured the city. This notion was not an argument of embattled yeoman farmers striving to preserve and extend rural values. Neither was it the construct of Jeffersonian theorists who disliked the city, nor of someone who wanted to recapture the lost "glories" of the small town. Real estate men, editors, and plain people concocted these ideas in response to urban pressures, not rural attractions. In short, the rural ideal had an *urban* origin.

As the constant hankering after solitude, retreat, and retirement indicates, the suburbs were valued as a haven from the "ceaseless

activity" of Montgomery, California, and Front streets. "Let the
Bay City keep its business, its bustle, toil, and mammon-worship,"
urged the *Chronicle,* "and [let] Oakland be an occasional refuge
for its disappointed, heart-sick workers." Yet very few San Franciscans seriously intended to take up dirt farming or even to become full-time gentry. What they wanted was a periodic break
from their urban existence. Hopefully, this trip to the country
would make life in the city more endurable. In an 1851 letter William Weston invited his aunt to take a make-believe journey with
him "out where morning breaks and look at those magnificent
flower gardens of nature—now in full bloom, and they will fill the
soul with enough of love and poetry to enable thee to withstand
the rough passes of city life, with its turmoil and vexation, for a
whole week." [40]

In other words, like many other nineteenth-century American
city dwellers, San Franciscans wanted to share the best of both
worlds. Residents of the Golden Gate City were lucky, the *Alta*
commented, to live in an area where "the commercial advantages
of the Emporium can be so readily united [with] those of the
peaceful and retired home," where one could be "removed from
the bustle of the city, and yet within a few minutes ride of it." [41]
As more and more people came to appreciate this happy combination, the separation of residence and work continued to un-
fold.

Neither this trend nor the "rural ideal" which sustained it,
however, were antiurban. From the authors of the *Annals* (the
city's first history) on down, people were endlessly fascinated
with San Francisco. Ironically enough, it was quite common to
praise those very qualities that in the context of the "suburban
ideology" were damned. When speaking of a move to Hayes Valley, South Park, or what the *Pacific,* apparently in earnest, called
"that infant queen of cities, the beautiful Oakland," the press and
people treated the bustle, confusion, struggle, crowdedness, artificiality, noise, and "ceaseless activity" as disadvantages.[42] But
when noting the splendid growth of the city, they pointed to these

same characteristics with pride. Throughout these ten years, the community's quest for wealth was accompanied by a search for values. In this effort it was typical of San Franciscans to try to reconcile different and often opposite ideals. Nevertheless, it was not inconsistent for them to embrace these seemingly contradictory attitudes, for few of the values and rules that the community admired were absolutes. The suburb was a symbol of primitivism, a residential expression of the desire for a refuge from urban progress, but only part-time, not permanent.

It is not easy to make a precise analysis of the spatial relationships in San Francisco, but at least the major themes are clear. More than anything else, these arrangements were the result of transportation and communication. The transit advantages afforded by the sheltered cove had attracted the whaling and trading ships in the first place and lured the initial landside merchants like Richardson. Once the Gold Rush set in, the later dealers naturally sought out the spot where the earlier ones had located and did so for the same reasons. Thereafter, the pattern was merely reinforced. The deep water of Clark's Point drew the warehouses; the need for face to face contact brought the lawyers to Montgomery; and that, plus the extra width of California Street, enticed the wholesalers. The waterfront attracted the heavy manufacturing, and the land fill pulled the large dealers ever eastward toward the receding waters of the cove. Even those businesses that spread out were affected by transportation considerations, since both retailers and petty manufacturers had to be near customers or others in the same trade.[43]

As downtown congestion increased, the handicaps of this area multiplied, setting in motion centrifugal tendencies. High rents and land prices, lack of space, confusion, bustle, strife, artificiality, fire, and the presence of a rough element began to drive out residences as well as some business and cultural institutions. Pushed by high density, the decentralization was channeled by transit advantages, both natural and artificial. The march of settlement was at first directed toward the more easily traveled geographic areas, such as the low places between the hills and along Mission Creek. This movement, in turn, either produced or followed other transportation advantages, this time technological ones. Planked streets and roads and steamboats even more strikingly affected the pattern of distribution.[44] Thus in one way or another transportation and communication were the most pervasive general influence in establishing the spatial relationships of the Golden Gate City in its first decade.

By the year 1856 the success of San Francisco was assured. Despite its inauspicious location, a great city had grown up on the north end of San Francisco Peninsula. Nourished by the farmers of California and the world and spurred on by competition, it had spread out over a growing expanse of land. After the initial chaos of the Gold Rush had subsided, the growth of the metropolis attained considerable order. Differentiation appeared, producing specialized areas for both business and residence. And in the few short years from 1848 to 1856, the city had grown from around 1,000 to about 50,000, from a bustling but fairly simple town to a complex city, without peer on the West Coast of the United States. What had taken New York 190 years to accomplish, or Philadelphia 120 and Boston 200, San Francisco had achieved in only eight. "There are, indeed, only two forces capable of effecting such wonders," observed traveler Ida Pfeiffer, "gold and despotism." [45]

Urban Rivalries

By 1856 the urbanization of San Francisco Peninsula had so far outstripped that of any other point that no one dared mention a West Coast competitor. The city simply had no rivals. However, this had not always been the case, though San Francisco's urban rivalry differed from the great conflicts of Eastern cities. The Bay City's struggles were neither as sustained nor as significant as those between Chicago and St. Louis; and the Pacific metropolis did not experience some of the phenomena that went along with urban imperialism in other places. The geography of California, its early pattern of urbanization, and the level of transportation technology largely explain the difference.

The other important cities which arose during the Gold Rush all were in the interior. The foremost of these, Sacramento and Stockton, could have offered serious competition by virtue of their size and wealth, but geography and the transit capacity of the era prevented their doing so. The introduction of the river steamer and the clipper ship cut out most of the direct trade between the valley towns and the Eastern United States, thus reinforcing the need for a transportation break at the Golden Gate.

Therefore, while fixing the main bay site of urbanization at San Francisco, the clipper, the steamboat, and geography also insured that the urban commercial interests of bay and valley would be complementary rather than competitive. Up-river towns could not import directly from the East and thus could not compete with San Francisco in supplying goods to the mining region. Instead, they had to cooperate with the bay metropolis. Had there been railroads to the East, rivalry might have been brisk; but these did not exist.

The San Francisco press never ceased to extol this complementarity of interest between California cities and, indeed, of the state as a whole. The assertion was not entirely valid, as the interior found out to its distress during the great San Francisco flour monopoly of 1852.[1] However, the attempt was an important part of the local ideology of concord and a way to allay interior suspicions of the city.

Yet at least one part of California did have potentially competitive interests. Several places on the bay could have provided the essential transportation break; the challenge came from this quarter. Improbable as it may seem, the main competition came from Benicia, a town speculation of Robert Semple, Thomas O. Larkin, and others, sometime residents and property owners in San Francisco. Had an untrained observer stood on the Straits of Carquinez in 1847 and viewed this venture in city building, he might well have been unimpressed. A visitor to the site in that year found its entire housing to consist of "three miserable shacks" and its transportation "network" one flatboat ferry across the straits.[2] Nevertheless, this observer could see a great urban future for the huts and the flatboat; and he was neither the first nor the last to do so.

Despite appearances, this optimism was not unfounded. Benicia lay at the head of ocean ship navigation in the bay area, many miles closer to the river than San Francisco. Unencumbered by an extensive mud flat in its front, goods could be landed at the Carquinez site more easily and cheaply, since they did not need so much lightering. Also, the ground upon which Benicia stood was less precipitous; and, with its proximity to the Napa Valley, the straits town had a much more fertile agricultural hinterland than did its rival. These advantages, plus the energetic maneuvering of its promoters, were enough to constitute a potential challenge to San Francisco, though the competition was sporadic. From 1847 to 1850, the rivalry waxed hot, at least on Benicia's part, only to cool down again until 1856, when it flared once more.

One of the earliest incidents in the struggle resulted in the re-christening of both places. In 1846 the settlement at the Golden Gate was known as Yerba Buena after the inlet upon which it stood. The bay was called San Francisco, and the official title of the mission was the same. These latter were famous, but the village of Yerba Buena was relatively unknown. The town speculators at the Straits of Carquinez made the first move in the contest by attempting to name their "settlement" Francisca, thus hoping to identify it with the widely known bay and mission.

When the promoters presented a petition "for record" to Alcalde Bartlett, an official appointed by the U.S. military who apparently had some kind of jurisdiction over other parts of the bay as well as the village on the cove, he refused to allow the new designation. Bartlett opposed the new name on the grounds that it was too similar to that of the Mission of San Francisco, and this decision was accepted. On January 30, 1847, an ordinance appeared in the *California Star*:

> Whereas, the local name of Yerba Buena, as applied to the settlement or town of San Francisco, is unknown beyond the district; and has been applied from the local name of the cove, on which the town is built: Therefore, to prevent confusion and mistakes in public documents, and that the town may have the advantage of the name given on the public map,
>
> It is HEREBY ORDAINED, that the name of SAN FRANCISCO shall hereafter be used. . . .

The identity crisis then shifted back to Francisca and soon eventuated in another change, this time to Benicia, which stuck. The *Annals* and other histories list January 30, 1847, as the date upon which modern San Francisco was retitled. However, the name had come into use nearly three months before the January ordinance made it official.[3]

San Francisco before 1850 did not seem unduly alarmed over the prospects of any number of towns that might have competed with it. Between 1848 and 1850 articles appeared in the *Alta* praising Martinez, New York of the Pacific, and even Benicia—all potential competitors—as well as Sonoma, Sacramento, and other places. In fact, the Golden Gate City was the great central realty market of the state, where promoters sold lots in rival "cities" and enthusiastically proclaimed the certainty of their success. San Francisco remained unimpressed. "God has laid the foundations of cities, and men but carry out His plans," the *Alta* assured its readers in October 1850. "Mere speculation never has and never will found a permanently flourishing city." [4] However, as the year wore on, the amusement, scorn, and even bored silence gave way to concern as the competition took a new turn.

Like San Franciscans, Benicians often appealed to what Charles Glaab and A. T. Brown have termed the "doctrine of natural advantages," stressing the favorable geographic location of their city, its more salubrious climate, and its hinterland.[5] However, they never entirely trusted in these inevitabilities. In both the economic and political spheres, the town at the Straits of Carquinez moved vigorously to overcome its late start. The Benicians' chief tactic was to secure as many cultural and economic institutions as possible and, in addition, to entice away from San Francisco everything that was not firmly committed to that city.

In 1848 it looked as if the promoters' dreams were on the verge of realization. The initial impact of the Gold Rush on San Francisco was stark, and Larkin and Semple were ecstatic. "This little town is quite deserted," observed a local merchant in his diary. "Larkin has been shaking his wise head and lamenting over the departing glories of San Francisco; and Dr. Semple is all smiles, and, in his enthusiasm over the promised success of her rival (Benicia), almost dislocates the fingers of every hand he shakes." For the next two years, Semple's bone crunching and other activities continued. Since it was taken for granted that the community needed families to assure its permanence and that families, in turn,

demanded certain facilities, Semple set aside land for a school.
This fact and other propaganda were assiduously disseminated
in the Bay City by Semple's own newspaper, the *Californian*. In
1848 he and Larkin tried to get the Golden Gate City's leading
merchants—Parker, Davis, Ross, Mellus, and Howard—and other
traders to move to the Straits of Carquinez. When the "doctrine of
natural advantages" was not persuasive, other forms of "geographic determinism" were substituted. In June 1849, a Bay City
resident was offered a lot in Benicia if he would build a house on
it; and he accepted this favor and others. In return for sending the
cargo of the *Aurora* to the straits hamlet, he calculated that "we
would have the advantage of getting land at a cheaper rate than
our neighbors in consequence of lending our aid to build up the
town." [6] Nor was this the first such favor. Writing to Semple in
September 1847, Larkin informed his partner that he had "offered
several captains, owners, and supercargoes of vessels one or two
building lots in Benicia if they would anchor their vessels at that
place, and thus prove the anchorage."

Where land alone would not suffice, the offer was judiciously
spiced up with honors. "I have concluded to give Commodore
Shubrick and others who accompanied him to Benicia my eight
lots in Square No. 44," wrote Larkin to Semple, "which in their
deeds I cal [*sic*] 'Shubrick Square.' " Whether because of this
"generosity" or out of conviction, Larkin informed Semple that
"Commodore Shubrick, and all his officers who went with him,
speak in the highest terms of our new town." [7]

Military men did not confine themselves to mere talk about the
superiority of Benicia with its advantageous site and "tastefully"
named squares. By July 1849, the headquarters of the United
States Army and "the large deposit of army quartermaster and
commissary stores," so crucially important in fixing the location of
the metropolis at San Francisco, had been moved to Benicia. In
addition, a site had been "selected by Commodore Jones for a navy
yard a short distance above the town." [8]

In 1850, Benicia—by this time a metropolis of about one thou-

sand souls—struck again. The Pacific Mail Steamship Company
established its "depot" at Benicia; and by June first, one hundred
men and one hundred thousand dollars were at work building the
"warehouses, reservoirs, docks, foundry machine shops, [and] engine manufactory" of "the first really large industrial works in
California." [9] In the same year, the Benicians added the United
States Mint and port of entry status to their imperial aims.

This new phase of the conflict centered on the attempt to elevate the straits city from a port of delivery to a port of entry along
with San Francisco. Immediately after the Gold Rush, Semple had
begun his attack on this front by trying to persuade the military
governor to allow the landing of imports at Benicia if duties were
first paid at San Francisco.[10] By 1850 that objective had been obtained and now the Benicians wanted to make their town a port
of entry. That would help Benicia's commerce by eliminating the
trouble of stopping to pay duties at the Golden Gate.

There was more at stake than just doing away with the inconvenience, however. Probably as important a consideration was the
distribution of the half million dollars appropriated by Congress
for a customhouse. The Benicians seemed to think that this money
and the officials it would support could at least be halved. These
new demands carried the battle from the Straits of Carquinez to
the flats of the Potomac.

In Washington, the partisans of Benicia also fought to reduce
the area of the Bay City's collection district so that its commercial
concerns would be even more damaged. Commodore Shubrick,
Commodore Jones (another Benicia property holder), and the
military men generally spoke very highly of the straits hamlet to
their superiors; and in addition, the Benicians solicited the aid of
merchants from Boston, New York, and other Eastern cities, who
added their praise to that of the army officers. Even non-Americans
were courted. "Arrangements with rich and important Chinese and
Russian houses to make Benicia their commercial depot are pending to be consummated on its being a Port of Entry," one of the
lobbyists wrote to Larkin in August 1850.[11]

By that month, this impressive array of "evidence" had convinced the Senate Commerce Committee; but by October the effort had also mobilized the opposition of San Franciscans. Senator William Gwin of California stunned the lobbyists when he announced his "unrelenting opposition" to their project. Despite Gwin, however, the measure passed the Senate, and, as it did so, kicked up a press furor in San Francisco.[12] Notwithstanding the claim of the *Alta* that "God has laid the foundations of great cities," it began to look as if the Benicia speculators would succeed in establishing a "permanently flourishing city." It was already prospering as a way station between San Francisco and the mines; a few steamers had been assembled there; and steam power was harnessed to its ferry. In 1850 it became an incorporated city and captured the Solano County seat, and the next year its first newspaper appeared.

Yet, despite these signs of progress, San Francisco easily prevailed. Gwin finally succeeded in defeating the port of entry scheme, and Congress decided on San Francisco as the location for the customhouse and mint. The wholesalers of the city did not desert, and two of the Benicia speculators became much less committed to the project. Larkin had much land in San Francisco, which no doubt divided his loyalties. M. G. Vallejo eventually established his own town speculation, that is, Vallejo, which had a better harbor and was closer to the Napa Valley; and its presence injured Benicia by dividing the effort to urbanize the straits area.[13] By 1850 San Francisco had simply built up too great a lead. When Benicia was incorporated, it had a thousand people, about San Francisco's size in 1848; but in the same year, the Golden Gate City's population amounted to perhaps thirty times that number.

After 1851 the San Francisco-Benicia rivalry cooled until 1856 when a new turn of events served to heat it up again. This time the struggle centered upon the newest transportation technology introduced into the state, the railroad. Oakland also participated in this new round of what the *Chronicle* dubbed "the old contest of that city with this [San Francisco] for commercial supremacy." [14] The new menace struck directly at the city's weakest spot, its isolation on a peninsula. Although one could get to San Francisco by land from the Contra Costa, the trip required a detour south for many miles. This handicap made it very likely that the hoped for transcontinental railroad would terminate in the East Bay. That placement, in turn, would divert much of San Francisco's trade to a new transshipment point. This eventuality was the ultimate problem that Benicia and Oakland posed even though the railroad was as yet only a dream.

The more immediate threat came from a projected railroad from Benicia to Sacramento to Marysville—both river ports in the San Francisco trade network. This road could obviously deflect ocean traffic directly to the railroad depot at Benicia, whence merchandise could be transshipped to the interior. On all this, lamented the *Chronicle*, "San Francisco will take no toll by the way, her jobbers no commissions, her warehouses no storage, her wharves no wharfage, her hotel keepers no way travel, and her shop keepers still less of country custom." To add insult to injury, even San Francisco's bedroom seemed disposed to enter the fray. In 1856 Oakland was projecting a railroad to San José, thus making the fertile Santa Clara Valley and the agricultural lands along the way tributary to the "City of the Oaks." Neither the dangers nor an effective San Francisco response materialized before the period ended; but their projection caused considerable alarm, with the press warning against the kind of inertia that had plagued New Orleans, while its traffic was being diverted by the Iron Horse.[15]

Actually, as early as 1852 San Franciscans moved to avoid the Crescent City's fate by chartering the San José and San Francisco Railroad. "It is very desirable," commented the *Alta*, "that while the people in Sacramento and Marysville are progressing with their railroad projects, San Francisco should at least keep pace with them." Still, the metropolis was lethargic until 1856. However, when the challenge from Benicia and Oakland arose, the San José and San Francisco project took a new start. This line, by way of the Mission Dolores, was not projected merely as a local run but was intended to guide the transcontinental around the bottom of the bay and into the city. In the bargain, it would also deflate Oakland's schemes. The first spadeful of earth was turned in 1856, on the section between the city center and the mission; but conflicting land claims, incorporation legal troubles, depression, and contract difficulties delayed the completion until 1861.[16]

Benicia included the state capital as well as the railroads in her campaign of aggrandizement, and strenuous efforts went into capturing the seat of government. It was several years before the roving legislature finally took root, and in 1853 it looked as if Benicia would be the chosen spot. Larkin's lobbyist, William J. Eames, reported that in order to get the capital changed from Vallejo to Benicia, he had distributed many town lots to the legislators plus $2,500 to a Major Graham to "bring it about." In response the Sacramentans "hired a steamer filled with provisions and liquors and kept it at Vallejo four days with the tables and bar free to all members at a cost of $13,000, but they could not succeed." [17]

The next year the Sacramento delegation did win, since Benicia did not have the facilities to accommodate the legislature and did not show promise of getting them in the near future.[18] Had the Carquinez town been able to keep the political center permanently, it no doubt would have more significantly affected the urbanization pattern of San Francisco Bay and more effectively rivaled "the city."

Statehouses have traditionally been one of the spoils over which American cities have contended, and Benicia's hot pursuit of this "prize" was typical. Yet San Francisco was an exception to the rule. The Golden Gate City was usually bored or amused by the whole question and never very interested in having the political capital of the state "grace" the commercial. For some, these attitudes arose from a desire to have the legislators as far away as possible. Conversely, others held the somewhat antiurban conviction that the metropolis would further corrupt an already frail legislature. Still others feared the reaction of the interior if the "city" captured yet another symbol of power, but for whatever reason, hardly anyone mustered much enthusiasm for acquiring the statehouse. Even the location of the capital at rival Benicia in 1853 brought only a contemptuous "Comme ci, comme ça" from the *Alta*. There were occasional half-hearted discussions about capturing the "prize" for San Francisco, but most of the time the community was unconcerned with this "honor." [19]

San Francisco's extra-California rivals were not much more menacing than the state competitors. The foremost were other seaports on the Pacific, especially Valparaiso, Chile. "It was the entrepôt," explained the *Picayune*, "from which the coasts of the continents and the islands of the Pacific had drawn their principal, and in most cases their entire supplies of European manufactures and Asiatic luxuries." [20]

The 1851 bid of Valparaiso and Callao, Peru, to buttress their commercial positions was enough to cause considerable alarm in the San Francisco customhouse. Both those Spanish-American cities were building fireproof warehouses at government expense and charging very low rates for their use. At the same time, San Francisco still lacked enough wharves, streets, and warehouses, and exorbitant land values seemed to be retarding construction. The collector thought that all this was "perfectly ruinous," since it would "prevent our control of the commerce of this ocean" by making it impossible for San Francisco to compete with its "Southern rival in this struggle for commercial supremacy." [21] Despite these fears, the threat from the south did not materialize. The bay metropolis built enough trade facilities—too many, in fact; a railroad was thrown across the Isthmus; and the Valparaiso-Callao danger faded out of existence.

Although less heralded than these external struggles, there was a similar contest within San Francisco that was important in determining the shape of the city. For the most part, the domestic contest was like that with Benicia. Just as the latter had tried to strengthen itself by luring away San Francisco's assets and securing new ones as well, the various sections of the metropolis strove to do about the same thing. These internal battles are not as easy to trace, since they were not well publicized; nevertheless, their essential outlines are clear.

Just as Baltimore and Philadelphia, Chicago and St. Louis, New York and Boston tried to aggrandize their commercial interests by throwing out transportation facilities, the most crucial phase of this intraurban rivalry concerned transit advantages. However, wharves, streets, and plank roads were the weapons used in the intracity contest rather than railroads and canals. But the aim was the same—domination of a geographic area. There were "wharf hinterlands" within the city comparable to those tapped by inter-city transportation.

Urban sectionalism appeared as early as 1847 when the city council was considering wharf construction. At that time the town extended from California Street in the south to Clark's Point (Broadway Street) in the north. The council's first appropriation for a wharf was at Broadway Street; and its second was for one at Clay, two blocks north of California. All the while, the hamlet shook with the clash between partisans of the two regions. Bancroft regarded such competition in a small place as ludicrous, but dock construction was crucial to the value of real estate around the landside terminus of the pier; and the first competitor to build his wharf, William Squire Clark, benefited immensely.[22]

After the Gold Rush, so many other portions of the city tried to imitate this success that the contest became almost street by street. Wharves projected from nearly every downtown thoroughfare north of Market and from many south of that artery. In 1851 the Commercial and Market street wharves staged a terrific display. Due to the angle of Market, the streets to its north and south would eventually intersect if extended any great length. When this fact dawned upon the wharf owners, an epic pile-driving battle ensued. Market Street began the fight when it employed a pile driver to extend its dock in front of its rival and thereby cut it off. Long Wharf called in an officer of the law to suspend this impudent proceeding and then sent its own machine to extract the offending timbers. This action brought another legal representative to the waterfront with an injunction to halt the extraction process; and after the operator of the machine had been hauled off to court, the Market Street people resumed their original effort. Again they were stopped by a Commercial Street injunction and again its machine began reversing the progress of Market Street Wharf. Still another time the removals were suspended, and finally the whole matter was compromised. Market Street was allowed to lengthen its pier, and Commercial Street was persuaded to put an angle in its own facility so that the two would run parallel.

The result of this wharf-building competition in San Francisco was very similar to that between railroads. Just as the railroads were often overbuilt and left without enough traffic, so, too, were the dock companies. "The abandoned wharves, from Clark's to Rincon's Point are rapidly falling to decay," lamented the *Alta* in 1856, "and even now present a mournfully dilapidated appearance." [23]

Long before this unhappy denouement, the competition spread from the piers to the streets. These were, of course, the land extension of the wharves and, like them, were a great stimulator to real estate values and a magnet for settlement. Almost from the beginning squabbles over street appropriations developed; and in 1851 the *Alta* revealed the sectional basis of some of this feuding. This newssheet informed the public that in order to grade and plank First Street from Mission to Market, it was necessary to compensate the northern end of the metropolis by performing a similar task on Battery Street from Broadway to Green.[24]

Other urban road building also reflected rival regional economic interests. There were two market gardening districts on the outskirts of the mission and Washerwoman's Lagoon, again in the south and north parts of town. In 1850 the area around the Mission Dolores was connected with the rest of the city by a toll plank road, and the benefit to the real estate holders and gardeners along the road was considerable. Success brought authorization in March 1853 for a second toll plank road to the same place and in July, for another to tie the mission to the southern edge of town. About a month later, the north responded with a plank road bill of its own to extend Pacific Street from Stockton on the east side of the hills to Larkin on the west. In November of the same year the new Mission Plank Road was finished, and the next month the north end of town came forth with another plank road proposal to match this southern addition. This time they asked for the right to build a plank road from Larkin, where the Pacific Street improvement terminated, to the ocean at Point Lobos. The artery in the north was clearly influenced by the example of what the mission plank roads had done for the south. In fact, the *Chronicle* argued that "its effects would be more apparent upon the prosperity of that section, than that which resulted from the first plank road to the Mission. The parties who are anxious for this measure, are all those who reside along the line." The north enders soon got their privilege.[25]

The sectional rivalry theme was not clearly stated in these plank road ventures, but the sequence of events and the logic of the situation suggest that it was there. Both the mission and Washerwoman's Lagoon areas operated in the same real estate market; as market gardening districts they competed for the same produce market; and they both were aware of the vital importance of improved transportation to their economic interests.[26]

Urban sectionalism, like the rivalry between San Francisco and Benicia, also involved the reciprocal attempt to lure away assets. "It is a bad policy," explained real estate agent Aert Van Nostrand in his 1850 reports to Rodman Price, "to drive good merchants and mechanics away, by asking exorbitant rents, especially at this time when all parts of the City are striving for pre-eminence." Two months later, after informing Price of a new renting contract to a "driving man," Van Nostrand observed that "it is necessary to offer inducements to such men now, as every portion of the town is arrayed against other sections." [27]

If one could not lure away another's landward assets, then possibly its sea-going ones might be gained. Prominent merchant Albert Dibblee described the matter to his New York partner in

1855. "There is a great effort making to take the Combination
Steamers [California Steam Navigation Company] to Market St.
wharf, and the prospect is they will go. The offer was about being
accepted when Parties at this end heard of it and got it deferred
for a few days to get up a counter offer." [28] Having the chief means
of shipping to the interior close at hand was important because it
would reduce transportation costs, increase real estate values, and
benefit boardinghouses and taverns.

Urban sectionalism was a miniature form of urban imperialism.
The means of competition were similar and so were the grand
aims. However, the outcome was not so similar. The battle between city areas was continuous and the margins, narrow, whereas
that between cities was short and decisive. By 1856 urbanization
on the Cove of Yerba Buena had proceeded so far that no rivals
had a chance to catch up in the near future. San Francisco, the
metropolis of the bay, had been founded, and the only contest left
was for place and show.

The Urban Economy

Americans are accustomed to rapid development of one kind or another. Yet even in a context of extraordinary growth, San Francisco's economic expansion was astonishing. In 1848 the town had a population of nearly one thousand people and a volume of business to match. Three years later, thirty thousand people thronged the city; and the foreign commerce of the port was surpassed only by that of New York, Boston, and New Orleans.[1] All this was caused by the discovery of gold in 1848. At first, the mining bonanza seemed to threaten the very existence of the small village, as its inhabitants streamed out in search of the precious yellow metal; but soon, the miners' need for supplies brought a wave of prosperity to the bay, and San Francisco floated gaudily on its crest.

Although this upheaval created profound changes in the city, many continuities remained, among which were its trade network and economic function. Between 1846 and 1848 the hamlet had developed a far-flung set of commercial ties with the Atlantic Coast, Europe, Mexico, Latin America, Hawaii, and the Far East, an impressive list of relationships for a town of one thousand. The articles received flowed to the interior of California, especially to the bay area and the Central Valley and up and down the coast from Oregon to San Diego. In return, local exports paid for these imports.[2] With some exceptions, these main trading areas

remained the same even after the Gold Rush; and so did the economic role that San Francisco played—"freight handler" to California and the West Coast.

Though the city's job did not change, the products it handled
did. Between 1846 and 1848 cattle provided the basic California
exports. Hides, tallow, horns, and hooves left the port, particularly
for Boston. Thereafter, the hide trade declined though it continued to be of some importance. For a few years after 1848, gold
was about the only commodity which the city had to exchange.[3]

In 1852 output in the state reached a peak of $81,000,000 and
thereafter leveled off at about $50,000,000 annually. Gold export
rose to its highest point at $54,000,000 in 1853; but in 1854 and
1855, this figure declined to $51,000,000 and $45,000,000.[4] Next
to gold, the most important item for barter was quicksilver from
the New Almaden Mine near San José.

Although the most striking development in San Francisco's out-
ward-bound trade was the rise and fall in the shipment of precious
metal, by 1855 the sale of other California products, especially
flour, wheat, barley, and oats, reached the level of 4.2 million
dollars, thus partially offsetting the fall of ore exportations.[5] Eventually this trend was important, but by 1856 it was just getting
underway.

Cargoes flowing into San Francisco were more varied. The state
of Maine provided lumber; from Oregon and the Pacific Northwest came additional timber as well as agricultural products.
Latin America, particularly Chile, supplied more of the latter,
notably flour, although the leading source of this staple came from
Richmond, Virginia. The Atlantic Coast was also a prolific source
of agricultural goods. Boston sent everything from Fresh Pond
ice to apples packed in the ice; New York and Philadelphia ex-
ported farm produce.[6] In addition, the East and England were
large suppliers of manufactured articles, while the rest of Europe
shipped wines and luxury merchandise. China sent silk; but, more
importantly, the "Middle Kingdom" was a heavy exporter of rice
for the many Chinese in California. From Manila came hemp and

sugar; from Hawaii, sugar; from Java, coffee; and from Tahiti, oranges.

Several forces combined to alter the composition of this trade. The most important was the rapid economic development of California and the Pacific Coast. In 1848 nearly all imports came from outside; but as time passed, the situation changed. For example, until 1851 the Eastern states were important exporters of lumber. As late as 1852, 8.3 million board feet was obtained from the Atlantic compared to 21.2 million from the Pacific Coast. In two short years, the figures were 9.4 and 70.2 million feet respectively.[7]

Farm products revealed the radical alteration even more clearly. Until about 1853 flour was the foremost urban import. Together with cereals and miners' provisions, it constituted the largest part of the local trade. From 1848 to 1853 nearly all the flour consumed in the state was imported into San Francisco. However, the rapid expansion of agriculture in California sharply reduced this exchange. Other agricultural imports had a similar fate. The coastal trade told the story more dramatically: by 1855 the Pacific Coast had joined the Eastern United States as the chief commercial partner of the city.[8]

Some of this reduction was caused by an oversupply of imported goods. Yet much of the surplus was obviously due to agricultural production in the interior, since the state's population increase slowed at the same time that imports suffered such a drastic decline. In the case of farm commodities, more so than lumber, the new source of supply diminished the total amount of the city's business. Much timber, whether California or otherwise, passed through the Golden Gate; but many state agricultural products did not pass through the hands of San Francisco's middlemen because they were grown in the interior rather than on the coast.

Other factors combined with the development of the Pacific Slope to effect continually less important alterations in exchange patterns. A crop failure in Java threw its coffee market to Costa Rica; the introduction of steamboats demanded the coals of Hartley, England, Lackawanna, New York, Lota, Chile, Sydney, Australia, and eventually Coos and Bellingham bays; the beginning of street lighting reinforced this demand but reduced the trade in whale oil and camphene; and the establishment of trade relations between Los Angeles and Salt Lake City augmented the flow of goods between California cities, since San Francisco was the chief supplier of its southern neighbor.[9]

The Bay City's economic life, like that of the nation at large, featured a number of fluctuations—seasonal, cyclical, and otherwise. Most important was the fluctuation between flush times and flat, but there were several other variations within this pattern. Both the larger and smaller oscillations of the economy were of enormous importance locally, but neither coincided with the national cycles. Nor did they have much connection with them.

Due to the arrival of immigrants and the military spending of the Mexican War, San Francisco had already begun its rapid climb to economic prominence before the cataclysmic year of 1848. For a time, however, its economy was disrupted by the martial operations. As William Heath Davis, a prominent merchant, explained to a correspondent, "There was [sic] no matanzas [cattle slaughterings] made about the bay this year [1846]." This cessation reduced the hamlet's trade; yet by January of the next year, the market had improved, and in late summer Davis's agent could write that "business is and has been very fair here in Yerba [Buena]." [10] Despite military activities, the Bay City enjoyed a large growth and at least selective prosperity from 1846 to 1848.

In the next eight years, the city went through two and one half more cycles of good times and bad. Ironically enough for a Gold Rush town, there were more years of bust than boom. After a short slump caused by the general exodus for the mines, the first wave of affluence commenced in 1848 after the initial gold discoveries and lasted until late 1849 or early 1850. For the next two years depression prevailed; but by the spring of 1852, a revival began which, for some sections of the economy, continued for about a year and a half. By late 1853 another slump occurred, and this one did not lift until 1858 or 1859.[11]

Declining production in the mines, a glut of goods from the East, several drastic fires, and a lack of storage facilities caused the first post-Gold Rush bust. Paradoxically, both too little and too much water brought about the drop in gold output. Initially in 1849 there was not enough water to wash the gold out of the streams; but beginning in late '49, there was so much that it washed the miners out and cut off traffic with the interior. An avalanche of merchandise from the East reduced prices just at the time that less money was coming from the mines; and, co-incidentally, the plethora put further pressure on the local specie reserve by consuming vast amounts of cash to pay for the imports.[12]

The danger of fire and the shortage of warehouse facilities added further complications. Instead of being able to store and wait for a rise, high storage rates and the omnipresent specter of conflagration forced businessmen to dispose of their holdings rather quickly, regardless of the state of commerce. That necessity, in turn, forced a horde of products onto the market and a consequent deflation.[13] Fortunately, there were some mitigating circumstances involved in these problems. Fires, for example, reduced the oversupply somewhat; the glut itself made cheap goods available for those able to buy them; and the products burned were generally the property of Eastern consigners rather than local merchants.

A superabundance of stock and a falling off of ore extraction plus a decline in immigration also contributed to the second depression. And again the reduced flow of wealth from the mountains was compounded by the massive flight of money to pay for unneeded merchandise.[14] Mineral production did not recover this time, dropping to the level of $50,000,000 per annum. A further difference between the two "busts" was in the source of the oversupply. In the first, the excess came almost entirely from "abroad"; but in the second, California played a very significant role. Oddly enough, the development of an agricultural surplus in the city's hinterland, an event much ballyhooed in the press, was the downfall of many local businessmen, who had formerly imported for the interior what that area now produced itself.

Within the larger economic cycle, the most important fluctuation was seasonal. From the very beginning of the Gold Rush, the commerce of San Francisco fell into a spring-fall trade pattern, with the liveliest traffic taking place during these periods. Several circumstances, largely climatic, produced this result. Summers in the interior brought a significant reduction in ore production. The dry months of July, August, and September were the sickly season when heat and disease took a high toll and the shortage of water became progressively more acute, thus hampering mining operations. As fall approached, the dullness receded, usually even before any significant rainfall. Wet weather seriously damaged California's primitive road system; and in order to avoid the resulting enormous freight charges, interior merchants bought heavily at San Francisco sometime before the rains and snows began in earnest. Thereafter, they purchased only necessities until the roads improved. The quickening of business caused by the expected arrival of the wet season, however, was further accelerated by its actual advent, which revived mining and thereby augmented the flow of gold to the city.[15]

Yet the same weather that reinvigorated commerce eventually almost completely throttled it. When snow and rain fell in the mountain areas, many men were idled, and the roads were rendered less usable. As the waters in the rivers rose, others left the stream beds; and at the same time the flow of population from San Francisco to the mines halted. All these developments greatly reduced demand.[16]

When the rains ended, local commerce again picked up. At the moment the interior merchants needed to replenish their dwindled stocks, dried roads allowed them to do so. As the river waters receded and the snow melted, miners once more hustled to work. Ultimately, however, this bustle gave way to the summer lull and the entire cycle began anew.

This pattern persisted even in periods of depression, but its advent was always unpredictable. "The fall trade appears to have commenced, and indeed it is time it should," commented the *Alta* in 1855. "Its inception appears to be later, by nearly a month, than in 1853 or '52, although it is somewhat early [*sic*] than in '54, when it continued longer, after a late commencement, than was to have been expected." [17] To an extent, the seasonal character of commerce was reduced by good roads and water-carrying works in the interior; but even these improvements did not alter the fundamental pattern.

Within this spring-fall trade cycle, there were both bi-weekly and weekly fluctuations. Every two weeks a steamer left for Panama; and at this time, businessmen settled their balances abroad and wrote their official correspondence. These duties consumed a couple of days before the ship left and also exhausted the supply of spare money. Therefore, finances were tight and business was dull just before and after "steamer days." [18] Moreover, it was customary for country buyers to come into San Francisco to make weekly purchases; but they usually did not arrive until Tuesday and left on Saturday, thus compressing local business into a Tuesday through Friday span.[19]

Another trade cycle involved individual goods. The Gold Rush created dramatic shortages that encouraged dozens of merchants to order large quantities from the East, each man hoping to make a killing. A few did, but the inevitable outcome was an over-supply, which in turn led to low prices and few buyers. Then the surplus wore off and higher prices returned. This scarcity-glut cycle sometimes engulfed the entire market, but even in good times individual products were subject to it.

Often individual businesses departed from the larger patterns. Since dry weather was necessary for building, construction boomed in the "dry season," while trade languished. Gas, camphene, and whale oil concerns also prospered at a time of general commercial dullness, as the longer winter nights sustained a high demand for their products. Finally, commercial doldrums due to an overstocked market meant a lively time for warehouse-men, who stored goods being held for a rise.

Even in businesses that went with the larger trend, there was not always an exact coincidence. General commerce, for example, lagged from the beginning of the spring of 1853; but real estate hit its peak at the end of 1853, some nine or ten months after commerce slumped. The construction "industry" held up until the summer of 1854; and the banking panic was delayed until February 1855. When the banks folded, however, everything else turned sour. Much of the explanation for this disjointedness probably lies in the dynamics of the local commercial economy. Merchants were accustomed to a summer lull and did not realize that they were in a depression until the fall trade of 1853 faltered. In bad times traders usually resorted to selling real estate to get money. Moreover, in recessions, banks had to extend more credit; and it took time for this extension to reach its limits.

As would be expected in a great "commercial emporium," economic activity was highly specialized. Before the Gold Rush, of course, this was not so. Traders were at the same time importers, exporters, jobbers, retailers, wholesalers, and bankers. In some cases there was not even a differentiation between the transporter and the merchant, since ships anchored off the hamlet were often equipped as stores as well as freight carriers. After 1848 specialization, both within and between occupations, quickly developed. "We will do business in San Francisco as well, and with as much system as anywhere," said a local editor. "Bankers are merchants no more; commission houses are ceasing to be jobbers; furniture warehouses no longer sell anchors and chains; silks and ribbons are no longer found forgotten under piles of overcoats." [20]

In commerce, the division of labor was especially evident, running from importers at the top to peddlers at the bottom of the scale. The first handler of goods was the importer. Usually he was an agent of someone else, that is, a commission merchant handling consigned goods, as well as an operator on his own. In some cases this dealer would sell directly to the "country trade," but ordinarily he would dispose of his stock to a jobber who performed that function. It was to him that country tradesmen came to receive their stores.

Market conditions produced a fairly constant struggle among merchants to "break each other down." When prices were low, goods in "first and second hands" (importers and jobbers) could either be sold for a loss, for cost and charges, or for a small profit. If the holder preferred not to "submit," he could store his stock in hopes of a rise.[21] The interior trader and urban retailer had a similar set of options. If the market fell, they could buy heavily or purchase small lots in anticipation of a greater decline. When inflation occurred, the opposite choices appeared. Usually when prices were very high, retailers and interior merchants bought just enough to satisfy their immediate needs and waited for the upward trend to abate.

When the local retailers and country operators got the best of their city counterparts in this contest, still another urban merchant entered the picture. Importers and jobbers usually disposed of their merchandise at private sales. However, when economic activity was sluggish or one product too plentiful, the public auctioneers were called in to get rid of the surplus. These dealers were always important, but their greatest business normally came on a falling market. In 1856 "property . . . worth perhaps 50 millions of dollars" was disposed of under the gavel, prompting the *Alta* to claim that this activity took "precedence over all others." [22]

The amount of urban commerce was considerable. Between April 1, 1847, and April 1, 1848—the last year before the Gold Rush—the *California Star* reported eighty-four vessels entering the port. In 1855, despite the panic, the number had risen to 1,250. Since many more of these were clippers, the total increase was much larger than the figure of ships alone reveals. Tonnage advanced from 50,000 in 1848 to a high of 550,000 in 1853, though it then sagged to a depression low of 425,000 in 1857. But by 1859 this index had risen to 596,000.[23] At the end of the period, by far the largest number of bottoms entering and leaving the Golden Gate were engaged in the coasting trade, with the total for the Eastern domestic ports holding second place; but the amount of carrying capacity employed in the two runs was nearly equal, since boats trading with the East were much larger. Statistics on the interior trade are scarce, yet enough exist to suggest a large-scale exchange. In 1855, when flour imports, the main article of commerce in earlier years, were no longer important, the traffic to Sacramento and Marysville alone amounted to 320,000 tons.

The trade continually vacillated between systems of cash and credit. From 1848 to 1850, the latter was in effect on a grand scale, resulting in considerable losses to the lenders and, therefore, a return to cash. Pressure for credit usually rose from the same two sources that brought the depression of 1853–58. When gold production fell, country traders had to trust the miners for their supplies. This extension of credit generally set off a chain reaction which ultimately ended up on Montgomery Street in San Francisco, since interior dealers passed along the pressure to city merchants and they, in turn, to the banks. A surplus of goods in the Bay City could also stimulate the demand for credit, as businessmen turned to the bankers for money to pay for shipments and to cover storage costs until the glut wore off. The amount of commerce done on faith was often no small affair. In 1855 the jobbing firm of Brewster and Company alone had $350,000 owing them from the interior, $250,000 of it from Marysville.[24]

The great majority of ships leaving San Francisco were nearly empty. Gold took up little cargo space, and there were not many other exports. A few vessels carried bulky California products such as wheat, and a larger number obtained charters to pick up guano at the Chincha Islands on the way home. Most of the others made the trip "in ballast." This article often consisted of the rock of Telegraph Hill, which was ultimately used to pave the streets of various exotic places.

The conditions of doing business in San Francisco were often extremely difficult and always very demanding. In 1848 there were no wharves, scarcely any warehouses, and very bad streets, producing exorbitant charges for lighterage, drayage, and storage. Until 1851 fires were a great threat, compounded by the absence of fire insurance. Gradually these physical obstacles were overcome, but others were not. The general uncertainty was so profound and tenacious that there was a widespread conviction that business in San Francisco was as much a game of chance as any played in the gaudy saloons on the Plaza.

Probably the greatest single difficulty in the city's mercantile activities arose from the lack of information. Newspapers from abroad, from the interior, and from San Francisco supplied business news and views, many of them from special market reporters and analysts. In addition, each merchant had his own correspondents and other informants. Ship manifests, which arrived via the Isthmus and, therefore, before the vessel itself, offered further knowledge. Both papers and manifests were kept at the commercial exchanges, where men congregated daily to trade items. Businessmen's messes and other face to face contact provided still more facts.[25]

In the aggregate, these sources may seem ample, but in fact they were not. Mercantile information and rumor in the press or on the street were frequently wrong and often "inspired." There was a large amount of smuggling that did not get into the commercial news; and increasingly, men hid their dealings. By 1855 the practice of shipping goods under the label of "unspecified merchandise" was widespread, largely veiling the nature of commercial cargoes.[26]

This defect was compounded by the almost total lack of statistics on what was being produced in California and on the Pacific Coast. This lack was especially evident in 1853 and 1854. City and country cooperated very effectively to glut each other's markets, as too many agricultural products were imported and too many grown. The local ignorance of gold output was equally profound. Historians have shown that after 1852 the amount of gold mined in the state declined. However, from 1852 through 1856 the press teemed with claims that mining yields were as good or better than ever.[27] This information gap remained throughout the period, and business calculations suffered accordingly.

Economic decisions were hampered further by multiple control of shipping orders. Much merchandise was only consigned to San Francisco traders, and many firms had Eastern owners or partners. According to the highly respected *Chronicle*, 90 per cent of the city's commercial activity was controlled by parties outside the state. The *Annals* indicated that this extralocal power was present even before the Gold Rush. These arrangements left much decision-making to parties far away. With a commercial scene as volatile as that of the bay metropolis, such a situation was unsatisfactory and led to almost continuous friction between correspondents over commercial instructions. Local merchants sent out instructions, but they were often ignored or doubted; and Easterners sent what they saw fit.[28]

Not surprisingly then, Atlantic shippers were usually blamed for an overstocked market. However, San Franciscans had a very considerable hand in conjuring up the oversupply. Merchant Albert Dibblee, who for months had been condemning the stateside shippers for creating a surplus, wrote to his partner in 1856, "I have written my ideas—if incorrect, why in Heaven's name go in; if there are *very few* shipping—if you are sure of it—then there is a chance to do well." Since so many at this time were hoping to "do well," very few of them did. Moreover, despite all the complaints about the "insane" course of Atlantic and foreign merchants, San Franciscans often followed the same policy in the interior. As Dibblee angrily acknowledged, "Some parties here have pursued a reckless course in sending lots of goods to the interior on consignment to be forced off, the most certain way possible to break down the market and stop trade here." [29]

Even when businessmen had full control of their own operation, there were many frustrations in dealing with outside parties. The agent might wait too long to send the products; he might try to get in on a good thing in the California market by dispatching a lot of goods on his own, thereby competing with his own corre-spondent; or he might ship the order on a slow boat. Clipper ships, though speedy, were given to sweating, that is, giving off moisture from their green timbers, which damaged merchandise; and the Panama and Nicaragua routes involved frequent handling and much hot weather, resulting in broken, rusted, or molded cargoes.

The extreme volatility of the business situation added uncer-tainty to these annoyances. However natural it may have been in Gold Rush circumstances, this was small compensation for the harried trader trying to operate with at least a minimum of rea-soned calculation. The introduction of a shallow draft steamer could open new areas to low-cost transportation; a steamboat rate war could also cut these costs; storms at the Golden Gate could halt business for fear of water damage while handling; a flood or fire at Sacramento could create massive new demand by wiping out much merchandise and many buildings. When Sacramento was largely destroyed by fire in 1852, San Francisco boomed be-cause it had to replace the entire stock as well as many of the buildings of its hinterland partner. These rapid changes repeatedly made merchants' conclusions obsolete while rendering speed cru-cial, for without it the terms of trade might have changed before a man could complete his dealings.

Nowhere was the instability of the market more in evidence than in the city's price index. In the years 1848–50, the fluctuation was enormous; but even in the relatively more stable years that followed, prices were very volatile. Flour, the leading staple for most of the period, reached a high of nineteen dollars per barrel in 1850, forty-seven in 1851, forty-two in 1852, thirty-one in 1853, thirteen in 1854, and fourteen and a half in 1855. However, these were only the highs. The lows for the year were frequently under ten dollars. These "California prices"—often very high, always un-stable, and universally deplored—included nearly all goods at one time or another.[30]

Part of the specialization of business involved the evolution of banking into a separate occupation. Until 1849 a man with money or gold dust to deposit could leave it with a tradesman or saloon keeper or anyone else with a strongbox. Initially, miners or merchants often kept their own money, and this practice did not completely die out until after 1856. From 1849, however, the tavern keeper's safe gave way increasingly to the banker's vault, though the custom of keeping one's own money was partially revived in 1855 due to the financial and commercial panic of that year. James King of William, a local banker, estimated that in 1849 only the agent of the Rothschilds had a capital over $100,000. A year later twice that amount was considered a "fair share of the deposits." "Yet so great was the change . . . ," King editorialized, "that the same banker who in '50 and '51 considered himself tolerably well patronized with $200,000, found himself in '52 with nearly $600,-000 far behind Page, Bacon and Company who had three times that amount." Paralleling this increase in deposits came a proliferation of financial institutions, which by 1853 had already reached a total of nineteen.[31]

In time, bankers developed the usual kinds of business. They accepted deposits, paid out checks upon them, sold exchange, made loans, traded in gold dust, collected notes, and invested in whatever seemed profitable. The buying and selling of notes was small when compared to Eastern firms, as was trading in stocks and bonds. Gold dust, which in the beginning was bought and sold by all men in the business, gradually became a specialty in itself. Private coiners, the United States Mint, and assay offices offered miners an immediate way to realize on their dust; and after a time, only the very expert could make money at buying and selling gold.[32]

Some of the prominent firms were also express companies. Both Wells Fargo and Company and Adams and Company doubled as such, as did Page, Bacon and Company originally. Others—like Lucas, Turner and Company and Drexel, Sather and Church—were strictly banking concerns. These lending institutions varied in size all the way down to the Miner's Exchange Bank and the pawnbroker. Though poor men patronized banking establishments of all sizes, the pawnshop was known as the "poor man's bank." (The interest rates belied the appellation.)[33]

None of these local money changers were burdened with an excess of governmental regulations. The California Constitution forbade joint stock banks, and it prohibited the issue of paper money. After the panic of 1855, other regulations were suggested but little was done. With the exception of the constitutional prohibitions, men in the money business were free to do pretty much as they pleased.

The financial panic of 1855 demonstrated conclusively that they had done so. There had been failures in 1850–51 and there had been other runs, but no general collapse. The year 1855 added this dimension. The panic began in February, though there had been ominous signs for some time before the crash. From the end of the spring trade of 1853, San Francisco's merchants were in a depression; and in the fall of 1854, a local businessman, politician, philanthropist, and patron of good music, Henry Meiggs, fled the city indebted to nearly everybody. Meiggs's resort to "French leave" hit the city's financial structure hard. So did a near-fatal run that fall on Adams and Company. These developments set the stage for the drama of February.

When the Panama steamer brought the news that the parent firm of Page, Bacon and Company had had its commercial paper protested in New York, long lines of angry men formed along Montgomery Street, demanding their deposits. While customers besieged the front doors, fellow bankers, "fearing the consequences of a panic, lent them [the hard-pressed and vulnerable firms of Adams and Company and Page, Bacon] enough money to carry them through" a part of the run; but even this was not enough to fend off the inevitable.[34] After the run subsided, Page, Bacon and Company, Adams and Company, Robinson's and Wright's Miners' Exchange were ruined; Wells Fargo and Company was temporarily suspended; and every other financial institution was shaken. Page, Bacon and Company was ruined by overremitting to the East to sustain its ailing parent branch. Eventually this company paid its creditors about thirty-seven cents on the dollar; but Adams and Company and others paid hardly anything except to their defense lawyers.

Contrary to the claims of those who thought the economy was better off for having been tested by fire, the effect of the panic was disastrous. When the banks gave way, dozens of merchants fell with them. In 1855 there were 197 bankruptcies with liabilities of $8,377,827 and assets of only $1,519,175. Time proved even these assets to have been overestimated. The Reverend T. D. Hunt, writing from the interior, noted "the intense excitement here in consequence of the bank failures in San Francisco. Men have seemed to be holding their breath as if waiting and watching to see what next would come." What came next came very quickly, as the panic that began in the city soon engulfed the state hinterland.[35]

Enormous rates of interest revealed further difficulties of banking. In 1850 money was bringing 10 to 12 per cent a month. The figure had declined to 2 per cent by 1855, but that still amounted to 24 per cent a year.[36] Many factors kept the interest rate high. One was the great transiency, which might put the borrower in New York when his note was due. Since land titles were insecure, banks also charged higher rates on loans which had land for collateral, especially if the borrower was a stranger. Moreover, since men were in a hurry to realize, they borrowed for short terms and the banker had to charge more because the loan was not out for very long. The state law of escheats also encouraged this inflation. If a foreign financier died, his money invested in California and his property escheated to the state rather than his next of kin. And finally, despite the fact that San Francisco was a Gold Rush town, it suffered from periodic acute shortages of capital. These difficulties combined to increase the lender's risks; and he, in turn, demanded more compensation. Predictably, the high interest rates lured in large amounts of capital and helped lower charges somewhat.

The sources of investment capital were three-fold. There was no special stock exchange until 1861; but city and state bonds, mining stocks, and other municipal issues—those of the wharf, gas, and water companies—were sold at the various merchants' exchanges by brokers and bankers and, periodically, at auctioneers' sales. Outside sources supplemented this supply. California issues were quoted in New York City and other Eastern markets; and much money came from England, France, and Germany. It was usually managed by resident foreigners such as B. Davidson, the Rothschilds's agent.[37]

Though certainly considerable, the exact amount of these extra-local sources is unknown. In 1853 a reported $2,000,000 of foreign capital was present; in 1855 there was supposedly $11,000,000 from "abroad" sunk in real estate alone; and it was claimed in 1854 that "most of the buildings" in the metropolis were "put up" with funds "borrowed in the different states of Germany, France, and England; and some in our Eastern states." [38] Whatever the exact amount, it was enough to keep the local press very anxious about the "investment climate." The city's financial system, however, was not so tied to that of the East and Europe that San Francisco was pulled down in the panic of 1857.

The outside world also provided a large part and at times nearly all of the city's usually inadequate currency supply. When the Gold Rush hit, very little money was in circulation; and circumstances combined to prolong this situation. Both the United States customhouse and Eastern and European shippers required payment in specie. In order to meet these obligations, without which there could have been no trade, businessmen hoarded coin. The ensuing scarcity in turn encouraged the importation of foreign money, the establishment of coining businesses, and the widespread use of gold dust as a circulating medium.

Coinage companies began operation in 1849 and continued through most of the ensuing decade. When money was short, businessmen generally petitioned manufacturers like Moffatt and Company for a new issue; and many firms imported foreign currency. The result was a most varied medium of exchange, including Prussian florins, Indian rupees, California coins, French francs, English pounds, Spanish American money, and gold dust.

Gradually this motley system gave way. Both foreign and California pieces passed about at inflated values, which brought them into disrepute even when they were indispensable. The provision for United States money from the San Francisco Mint (1854) and U.S. Assay Office and a campaign by the press and business community were forcing foreign and California coin out of the market by 1856. For most of the period, however, the diverse, confusing system prevailed; but it does not seem to have hampered economic development. In fact, the era when money was less uniform was more prosperous than after it became standardized.

Banking and commerce were prominent businesses, yet real estate was as important and perhaps even more so. In 1854 the city's first history claimed that "the richest men in San Francisco have made the best portion of their wealth by possession of real estate," and many in the community agreed.[39] Real estate was a less specialized occupation than either commerce or banking because everyone, from bankers to bartenders, indulged in land trading. Even so, realty was a fairly separate pursuit; and the largest dealers were those who concentrated on it rather than dabbled.

San Francisco's realty boom, like its commercial prosperity, began before the Gold Rush. In 1846 William Heath Davis wrote to H. D. Fitch that "land speculations have been brisk at this place. Most of the lots . . . have been taken up." The next year Governor Stephen W. Kearny released the government's claim to beach and water real estate and the market surged again, with beach and water property reaching six and seven hundred dollars an acre. Some "lots in San Francisco of 50 varas granted by the Alcalde in '44 for $15" were "worth $1000." Yet even this increase was insignificant by comparison with advances stimulated by the Gold Rush. In December 1849, Thomas O. Larkin sold eight water lots and one other for $300,000.[40] However, late 1849 marked the termination of the first "flush times" in real estate as speculation grew rife and a deflationary reaction set in.

A second great rise reached its peak in the December 1853 city sale. Lawyer John McCrackan wrote, "Our city just at this time is dull except [for] Real Estate Speculations, upon which our people seem crazy. I drew papers of a piece of property today for my friend 'Hood' which in 1846 cost him five dollars. It sold today for sixty thousand." Cheap land was plentiful—ten to five hundred dollars—during both periods of real estate highs, but such bargains were not available in the built-up portion of the city. Yet after December 1853, values declined by 75 per cent; and it was not certain that the retreat had been halted as late as 1856.[41]

These cycles were very different in one respect. The advance ending in 1849 was almost entirely speculative, since there were few improvements to give added value to land. In 1853, however, streets, wharves, brick buildings, and other works provided very legitimate cause for enhanced prices, though speculation was also influential.

Perhaps no other part of the local economy was more frenzied and unsettled, even in later years. The experience of artist William S. Jewett was common enough. In January 1850, Jewett bought a lot for $200 and sold half of it a few months later for $250. "It was all cash transaction," wrote the painter, "no sham at all about it except I have never seen the lot nor don't know where it is . . . but it is a certainty that I have $250 on it and that I honestly believe it to be in existence and above water." [42]

The dizzying ups and downs of the market left behind a trail of human wreckage. Many, like William Squire Clark, made thousands without doing anything very brilliant; but many others were wiped out. As the *Alta* sadly acknowledged in 1855, "Nearly all the prominent operators of 1852–53 are now bankrupt, and the mass of smaller men are utterly ruined." [43] Among the former was Joseph L. Folsom, once reputed the city's richest man.

The vagaries of the market were not the worst problem to be faced. Land titles were extremely insecure, since there was considerable doubt that American alcaldes in California had had power to grant certain kinds of land, and many false Mexican

claims had not yet been exploded. All this led to endless court
battles and sometimes "compromises." If someone wanted land
badly enough, he simply bought up all opposing titles. In the case
of the fraudulent Limantour Claim, $100,000 ultimately changed
hands in these "settlements." [44]

It was sometimes argued by contemporaries as well as by later
historians that these shaky titles deterred investment in real estate.
In some cases this was true; but, despite all the insecurity, when
prosperity prevailed realty transactions boomed into the millions.[45]
In fact, land drew off large sums necessary to more lasting improvements.

One very important influence upon this market was the condition of commerce. During a slump when money was short, men
usually preferred selling lots to borrowing at "California prices."
Or if there was an overstocked market, potential real estate funds
were drained off to pay for the excess. In both cases, land prices
fell. Affluence had the reverse effect, as did other urban developments, especially transportation. Street grading and planking, as
well as private commercial improvements, always enhanced values. On the day the first ship tied up at the first wharf capable of
serving sea-going vessels, "real estate went up one hundred per
cent in the business part of town." Neighborhood building, legal
or not, also boosted prices. "There is no better way than to build
myself," McCrackan explained to his family, "form a respectable
neighborhood, and then sell out to best advantage." "Rincon Point
is covered with houses," Van Nostrand informed his boss, "many
erected by squatters but all occupied and tending to increase the
value of lots adjacent thereto." Obviously, simple population
growth had a like effect as did the advent of horse-drawn omnibus
service.[46]

Industry developed much more modestly than the realty business, its tardiness in some degree linked to the latter pursuit. Speculative land prices and the resulting high rents increased the expenses of manufacturing, and realty and commerce, with their
more dramatic opportunities, drew off potential investment. High

wages, insecurity of titles, Eastern competition, the relatively small domestic market, scarcity of resources such as coal and iron, the transiency of the population, lack of capital, and several lesser problems further retarded manufacture; but even so, industrial development was by no means negligible.[47]

The most important factors in this rise were the expanding population and economy of the Pacific Coast. Yet even when these two conditions disappeared in the slump of 1853, the growth of industry was not halted. Deflation curtailed demand, but it also reduced wages, rents, land prices, and commercial investment possibilities, further expanding opportunities for manufacturing.

The main industry, iron foundering, was born in a commercial depression and prospered from 1850 on. The bottleneck in this business was the high price of iron, and it was broken in a typically odd San Francisco fashion. In 1850 and 1851 a series of disastrous fires severely injured local merchants, yet the resulting mass of scrap iron—ruined safes, hinges, stoves, and walls of iron buildings—was the making of the foundries. The demand for repairs on steamers, ship construction, steam boilers, quartz mining machinery, castings, fittings, and gas company equipment immediately provided a market for this curiously acquired supply of metal.[48]

The pioneer and ultimately leading iron works was the Union Iron Foundry, built up from the Donohue brothers' blacksmith shop. This business was a good one. Scrap metal cost three-fourths to one cent a pound and when finished, sold for twenty. These profits soon generated competition; and by 1853 the Eagle, Alta, Vulcan, Pacific, and Sutter companies shared the field with the original firm. In addition, by 1856 the city had two brass foundries, at least one sizeable boiler works, "a number of establishments . . . where metals are extensively worked but which may not be properly denominated Foundries," and numerous shops that processed gold and silver.[49]

Closely dependent upon the "metallurgical" industry because of its need for parts was shipbuilding. At first this trade consisted in large part of assembling dismantled boats sent out from the East.

Gradually, however, the Happy Valley and Steamboat Point yards began producing their own steamers, scows, schooners, and other sailing craft. In 1850 the *Alta* claimed that thirty-seven steamboats had already been built on San Francisco Bay. Yet it was 1853 before the first steamer made entirely "upon the Pacific" appeared; and after the advent of the California Steam Navigation monopoly, construction of these craft largely declined. Up to 1854, the largest sailing ship manufactured was the 200-ton *Theodore Allen,* much smaller than the 2,000-ton clippers or a San Francisco-built steamer like the *Queen City.* Along with this boat building went ship repairing; and before the end of the year 1856, the city boasted a dry dock on which to do this job.[50]

Food processing was another important industry. Flour milling was not pursued from the Gold Rush until 1852, when the "City Mills" opened. Until that time Californians raised little wheat and imported most of their flour. Milling depended on farming, but the reverse was also true. In 1850 the scarcity of milling facilities caused less wheat to be grown. City industry called agriculture into existence and vice versa. By 1856 the shortage of mills had ended. San Francisco alone had ten in 1853. Meat processing existed before the Gold Rush; and, unlike flour, the slaughterhouses never suspended. Packing, however, got a much later start. Lack of refrigeration and relatively mild weather made it impossible to drive the animal heat out of meat in order to preserve it in salt. One Joseph Steinberger solved this problem in 1856 by building his packing house on a wharf at North Beach. Being over the water reduced the temperature enough to salt the meats. Other manufactories processed coffee, spice, vermicelli, macaroni, beer, whiskey, sugar, soda, starch, mustard, crackers, and candy.[51]

A broad number of individual or small groups of industries rounded out the manufacturing development of the city. A stone dressing mill, several brick yards, and a number of sawmills operated to satisfy the needs of the construction trade. Several sewing shops existed, some producing bags and others, clothes. In addition, there were many hatters. Tobacco processing had already begun, as had camphene and whale-oil refining, rope making, hide curing and processing, gas manufacturing, and the production of furniture and farm machinery.[52]

These enterprises ranged in sophistication from the Union Foundry with its factory size and division of labor all the way down to the blacksmith shop without either. Many of the local industries used steam for power, though windmills supplied some.[53]

Despite the modest character of industrial growth, the press ecstatically welcomed each new manufactory as a means of reducing San Francisco's "dependence" on the outside world. At times, local products belied this optimism. For example, the *Sagamore*, the "finest" steamer built in the city up to July 1850, was also one of the first to explode. San Francisco boilers were just as unstable as California prices, and its bricks were often a synonym for mud. Nevertheless, industry was important. "The inhabitants are generally employed in commercial pursuits," claimed the *Alta*; "but all the ship building and repairing, iron casting, and several less important kinds of labor, for the whole state, are done here." [54]

Yet the extent of manufacturing was certainly not sufficient to explain urbanization as a "response to industrialism." Urbanization and industrialization came almost simultaneously, but the city clearly came first. Industrialism was more a response to urban growth than vice versa; but more importantly, both were a response to commercial development.

The city quickly developed an ample transportation system to handle both its manufactures and imports. The two crucial events in Pacific navigation both came in 1849. The first ocean-going steamer, the *California*, arrived early in that year. This boat belonged to the Pacific Mail Steamship Company, which held the government mail contract and was the leading ocean steamship company. Many "opposition" lines rose to compete with it, however, such as the Nicaragua Steamship Company of Commodore Cornelius Vanderbilt and the Independent Opposition Line. These ships plied between San Francisco and Central America, stopping at both San Juan and Panama. At first, service was monthly; but it soon became bi-weekly. In 1855 the Isthmus-Bay link took on added importance with the completion of the Isthmian railroad. This road, plus faster steamers on both the Atlantic and Pacific sides, reduced the traveling time to New York to about twenty-four days. The railroad diverted some freight traffic from the "Horn," but most of the passengers had already abandoned the Cape Horn route. After 1850, regular service was established to Oregon, San Diego, Los Angeles, and coast ports in between; but efforts to forge similar links to Hawaii, China, and elsewhere were not successful.[55]

As important as the advent of steamships to the California trade was the simultaneous appearance of the clipper ship. Though a few of these had been constructed before 1848, the Gold Rush greatly increased demand for them. The biggest advantage of these vessels was speed; the *Flying Cloud* arrived from the East in eighty-nine days, whereas it took older, smaller ships up to eight months. This crucial superiority quickly gave the clippers the largest portion of the city's ocean freight.[56]

A combination of greater space and speed gave the steamboat a comparable victory in California's river trade. In 1847 a small steamer, the *Sitka*, navigated the bay and Sacramento River, but it ultimately proved unseaworthy; and until 1849 the schooner and smaller craft held sway on the bay and rivers. At the end of that year, steamers began to contest both the freight and passenger trade and soon won both. Their triumph was very lucrative; the *Senator* alone earned $600,000 during its first year's work. Sacramento and Stockton were the main termini of steamboats from San Francisco; though several lesser places, especially on the bay, also were connected to the city by steam.

The ocean and river steamers were similar to Eastern "floating palaces," but their service did not always live up to the grandeur implied by that name. There was always plenty to drink, often a good race to participate in, and sometimes a snagging or explosion to enliven the trip. However, the boats were chronically late; they were often grossly overcrowded; service was bad; charges, high; and waiters, surly. Ordinarily, service varied according to the amount of competition present, as "opposition" speedily improved steamship company behavior.

Nevertheless, the public was probably better off under monopoly. One of the things that boat owners tried to improve during periods of competition was speed, and racing invariably resulted. By 1856 the trip to Sacramento was reduced to just over six hours by competition between the monopoly and the "Opposition." Accompanying this time saving was a reduction in the number of prows, paddle wheels, boats, boilers, and people occasioned by collisions, explosions, and other picturesque occurrences. The owners and captains were obviously to blame; but steamboat racing was a very democratic sport, in fact, a kind of social compact. "It is a tacit agreement that if they [the passengers] will travel on his boat, he shall blow them into eternity sooner than see his boat left behind. They understand it, and he understands it; in accordance with the implied contract, he ties down the safety valve and they all go into eternity together." [57] "A horse has been stolen: so lock the stable door," needled the *Alta* at the usual belated reaction. "Captains quit racing till this disaster is less fresh in the minds of the people, and then . . . rush in as recklessly as ever." [58]

Faulty steamboat inspection laws and the absence of even one instrument in the state to test the safety of boilers further emphasized this indifference. Even worse, there was little or no effort to remedy these defects. Yet, even though these liabilities were much more dramatic than the improvements in water travel, they were far less important.

The stagecoach and, to a lesser extent, the railroad rounded out the external transportation system. From 1850 on, the bay metropolis was connected by stage to San José, Monterey, Santa Barbara, Los Angeles, San Diego, and other California cities. In addition, with the completion of the Sacramento Valley Line from Sacramento to Folsom in 1856, San Francisco gained a direct boat and rail tie all the way to the mountains. Since its officers and directors were mostly local men, it was very much a Bay City enterprise.

Urban carriers, in contrast to clipper ship, steamer, and stage, were very prosaic, but just as adequate. There was certainly no transportation "crisis." People got around as well as or better than their modern counterparts despite their primitive means of loco-motion—human feet, horses, carriages, hacks, and omnibuses. The latter two were entirely commercial, but horses and carriages were both commercial and private. Privately owned transportation, whether horse or carriage, was not as prevalent as in our automo-bile age. In fact, the balance between personal and public means of transportation seems to have been about like that recommended by twentieth-century critics of the automobile.[59] The former were usually employed on special occasions, such as a moonlit night or the Fourth of July or a theater date, and for long-distance trips out into the country.

Within the city, hackneys, coaches, pedestrianism, public con-veyances, and boats took care of passenger travel.[60] Omnibuses were the closest thing to a "mass" transportation system, but the resemblance was not very great. Crim and Bowman initiated the pioneer line in 1850 between the Plaza and the Mission Dolores and eventually extended service to the Presidio, North Beach, and South Park. As with steamships, there was an alternation between competition and combination. Since these vehicles did not explode, competition was most beneficial, at times drastically lowering fares. Hotels often provided omnibuses to convey patrons from and to lure them to their places of business. Other lines specialized in transporting steamer passengers or their luggage to their urban destinations. A ferry traversed Mission Creek; and for a time at least, one could travel from downtown to the mission in a rowboat on the bay and Mission Creek.

Water transport, drays, and railroads conveyed most of the freight about town. From 1848 until about 1851, there were too few wharves; and this defect created a large lighterage business.

But as the docks advanced, the lighterers retreated; by 1856 their importance was considerably diminished. Drays, the other main reliance for transporting goods, remained crucial. By 1854 there were 1,047 of these licensed in the city.[61] Railroads were used almost exclusively for hauling fill to the bay, and railroad building within the corporation got little farther. Some work was done on the projected San José road, but it was not finished; and the Market Street horse railway did not even reach the ground-breaking stage.

Whether transit companies or otherwise, older business forms outnumbered modern ones in San Francisco; yet the drift toward newer kinds of economic structures was already under way. Single proprietor institutions or partnerships continued to be numerous after the Gold Rush. Often there were several "partners," thereby combining more resources.[62] Next up the ladder were the joint stock corporations, and though relatively few in number, they played a disproportionately important role. Perhaps the first corporation was the Central Wharf Joint Stock Company. Established in 1849, this group built the famous "Long Wharf," the first really good dock in the city. The Pacific Wharf Company also was a joint stock endeavor, as were the gas works, the San Francisco and Mission Dolores Plank Road, California Steam Navigation, Sacramento Valley Railroad, California State Telegraph, Clay Street Wharf, Broadway Street Wharf, American-Russian Commercial, Bellingham Bay Coal, Saucelito Water and Steam Tug, and Northwest Ice companies.

To an extent, the governing bodies of these corporations were linked together. These directorates were not centralized in the style of J. P. Morgan, but they did provide some overlapping control of the city's generally anarchic economy, as many businessmen served two or more corporation boards.[63] This trend toward collective action also represented a significant countertendency to the growth of specialization, since success in specialized pursuits brought money to invest in other enterprises.

The standards that governed the conduct of these businesses

varied considerably. Ethical conduct did not attract the headlines or become the subject of remark as frequently as its opposite, yet the community certainly had its good men. As one of them wrote, "We have confidence in ourselves, and a firm belief that honesty, sobriety, industry, and energy will finally, under the blessing of God, carry us forward and crown our efforts with success at last." [64] The panic of 1855 revealed that many conducted their affairs upon these principles. Wells Fargo and Company, Lucas, Turner and Company, John Parrott and Company, and Drexel, Sather and Church all weathered the crash and paid their depositors. The city appreciated this kind of conduct, and the press was often full of praise for this or that "highly respectable" businessman. However, many of these ultimately turned out to be dishonest, and those that did not were in a minority. It is difficult to escape the conclusion that economic ethics were generally malodorous.

The field of transportation provided many examples of the majority ethic beyond the collisions, races, and bad service. By listing passengers as crewmen and by legal quibbling, "vessels and steamships which arrive at this port, are constantly in the habit of carrying more passengers than the law allows," despite federal laws, public opinion, and frequent tragic consequences. In fact, "so much suffering, misery, and mortality have been caused by the cupidity of owners and agents of vessels engaged in the California trade" that the *Herald* was moved to call it the "middle passage." The companies argued that the extra passengers were picked up "as an act of humanity" after being abandoned by unscrupulous sailship captains, but this allegation was often not true. Sometimes miners were lured down from the mountains by low fares which were raised just before the steamer left. Worse yet were the sailingship speculators, who sold cheap tickets but failed to put adequate water and provisions on board vessels bound for Panama. This arrangement necessitated intermediate stops where more money was extorted from passengers for supplies. Discriminatory freight rates, later made famous by the railroads, were already present in the clipper trade.[65]

Commerce was equally riddled. Merchants proved themselves every bit as ingenious at smuggling as their Revolutionary fore-fathers. The transfer of goods at Bodega Bay to a coasting vessel which then entered San Francisco duty-free, the introduction of foreign merchandise into American packages in transit across the Isthmus, false manifests, containers with fake tops, passengers' luggage, and crews' bunkrooms provided ample means of illicit importing.[66]

Malpractice did not end at the shoreline. "All [the flour] that inspects bad is worked up with sweet flour, packed in sacks, and sold as superfine sack flour at full rates," explained a merchant of a widespread and notorious practice.[67] William Tell Coleman noted some equally dubious uses of commercial information. The marine reporter of the day was paid by the Merchants Exchange to bring news of cargoes just in. Coleman gave the man $50 a month to report to him "privately before he did anyone else," after first asking him "if in his conscience he could do it." Other abuses of commercial information were equally popular. "The daily papers publish large sales of Flour . . . , but all those I have con-versed with on the subject consider them sham sales, made and reported in order to bolster up the price," wrote Alexander Grogan in 1856.[68]

The notoriously corrupt insolvencies of the panic of 1855 ex-posed even greater shortcomings. "Scarcely a day passes," la-mented the *Alta,* "that does not chronicle one or more applications for the benefit of the Insolvent Act; and what is still more deplor-able, these failures are, many of them, without assets." False credi-tors were widely used to avoid payment. The first attachment served was the first paid, and often not much was left after that. There were nearly 200 insolvencies in 1855 with liabilities of over $8,000,000 and hardly any assets. This appalling state of affairs moved the *Chronicle* to charge that "the name of a San Francisco businessman will be no better than that of a 'Sydney Duck,'" a conclusion the *Era* had already reached.[69] After Adams and Com-pany closed its doors, their books were found floating off North

Beach (a place they could scarcely have reached by chance); mutual recriminations among employees abounded; and large sums remained unaccounted for.

Page, Bacon and Company paid more—to the wealthy. "At 5 A.M. [hardly a normal business hour] they paid off the attachments in full, and made a pretended opening of their doors at 9 A.M. but let deuced few outsiders in," wrote a witness. "It was a planned thing, and while a man every 5 minutes was let in, they were paying off the large depositors by some back door contrivance." [70] While this alley "contrivance" provided relief for the rich, the street was a combination of pandemonium and pathos. Depositors besieged the stable houses while the defaulting institutions "were surrounded by hundreds of anxious looking men, mostly miners and laboring persons, who gazed most wistfully at the barred doors and windows that separated them from the fruit of years of toil and privation." As the *Pacific* noted, "There were some apprehensions that efforts might be made by desperate losers, to break open vaults and be their own paymasters,—a strong police force was in attendance to prevent such occurrences." [71]

The cut-throat rivalry that underlay these ethics was another of the local patterns that were not ushered in by the Gold Rush. In 1847, Talbot H. Green wrote to Larkin that "the traders [here] are a sharp set, dog eat dog." The Gold Rush both intensified the economic struggle and stimulated a search for ways to avoid it. As the *Alta* commented, "Competition is the life of trade, but . . . there may be too much of a good thing." [72]

The most important means of escaping this strife was combination—monopoly, duopoly, and oligopoly. Commercial combines were organized either to end a downward spiral of prices or to exploit or create a scarcity. Using borrowed capital, the dealer or group "cornered" a product, raised the price, pooled their stock, and waited. If buyers failed to appear or a sudden glut developed, the ring lost out. However, if only a few goods appeared, the speculators offered a price for them and threatened to flood the market if refused. This maneuver generally "convinced" the holder of the coveted lot.[73] If successful, the pool raised profits, prices, and prayers of relief from an anguished community.

In order to get in on the "better feeling" in the monopolized sector or to save money, someone generally tried to break the corner. If the opposition was strong enough, they shattered the cartel or were invited to join it; and monopoly prevailed again until the next challenge. Moreover, when prices went up, many other merchants sent for some of the hoarded product; and when these orders or news of them began to arrive, the combination folded. Such an outcome did not occur in transportation and some other fields, however, because not everyone could order a steamboat, plank road, or gas factory. Besides being less enduring, trade monopolies differed from other combines in another way: the commercial cartels were often undertaken by speculators who were not regular operators in the business they were cornering.

There were mercantile pools in a number of staples, but those in flour were the most spectacular. Supposedly, the monopoly of 1850 "involved . . . at least 1 million of dollars"; but the year 1852 witnessed the most dramatic and tragic combine. When a "corner" appeared in the fall, buyers were wary. "Ever since the rise last spring Merchants up the River, and Traders to the mines, have avoided buying goods ahead—getting the supplies from hand to mouth," wrote Albert Dibblee. Moreover, in 1850 and 1851 country traders had laid in large supplies at high prices in anticipation of the annual decomposition of the roads. When the roads held up relatively well, many were caught with a lot of high-priced supplies. These various experiences, therefore, encouraged cautious purchasing. When bad weather hit in 1852, however, the roads did deteriorate; and extreme shortages resulted along with some starvation in the mines. Though not as unfortunate, such speculations were frequent enough to cause the *Chronicle* to charge in 1856, "There is probably no other city in the world where this kind of gambling is carried on to a greater extent." [74]

The noncommercial combinations generally occurred in city

services and transportation. The California Steam Navigation Company was undoubtedly the most famous. From its advent in 1854, the new alliance overwhelmingly dominated steamer traffic between the Central Valley and the city, despite attempts at competition. The omnibus service in San Francisco was another, as were the plank roads to the Mission Dolores and the Presidio, the gas company, the Contra Costa ferry, and the water cartmen. The grandest combination of all was the one that failed—the bulkhead scheme to control the entire waterfront.

These alliances were sometimes not complete. "California Steam" had competition from sail even after the merger of 1854, and the gas company had to battle the camphene and whale-oil dealers.[75] Though the monopolies may not have been total, they were close enough. The people considered them as such and suspected them accordingly. Yet it is important to note that most areas were free from such combinations. Banking, construction, newspaper, retail, hotel, restaurant, most commercial, and many other significant enterprises had nothing analogous to "California Steam." Neither did the real estate business, despite much talk of land monopolists.

The problem of these combines plainly illuminates the city's search for values and rules. There was a general prejudice against monopolies in San Francisco, but no absolute opposition. Since everyone believed in liberty, it was admitted that men had the right to form combinations in pursuit of their own interests; and these were not invariably considered bad. Yet alliances were not always beneficial. As a contemporary letter to the editor put it, "When it [speculation] is unsuccessful, the loss is limited to a few; when it is successful, as in the case of flour two years ago [1852], the loss falls upon the community, and is a very great evil." "A land monopoly is vastly more injurious to cities than to rural districts," echoed the *Golden Era*. "An avaricious man may own half the area of a city, and while he refuses to sell his waste land at a purchasable price, citizens are compelled to purchase in inconvenient places, or to rent at ruinous rates." "It is a social necessity that laborers have a home of their own." [76] These collisions between principles usually forced a painful choice.

"We are not in the least disposed to advocate an interference in business transactions," wrote the *Herald* of the great flour cartel of 1852, "having always been of the opinion that trade will best regulate itself without intermeddling, but in all ages and in all countries attempts to create an artificial scarcity in bread, by monopolising and raising the price of breadstuffs, has been regarded as a speculation wholly illegitimate." Obviously, the editor was about to make an exception to his general rule as his preference for freedom weakened in the face of its abuse. Where the problem of land monopoly was concerned, the *Golden Era* advocated government intervention; and even in an anarchic city, it was probable that a majority favored legal action against the gas company and the plank roads because they had become burdensome and the bulkhead scheme because it was feared that it would also.[77]

This same practicality was equally visible in regard to the universally accepted and oft-repeated cliché that "the world is too much governed." Yet that sentiment did not imply an absolute opposition to state participation in the economy, particularly monied intervention. In fact, with regard to financial "meddling," especially federal, San Francisco felt positively neglected. It was part of the local "rhetoric of martyrdom" to charge that the government had done next to nothing for the Bay City. This accusation was hardly accurate. Washington's many favors to the city never seemed to be enough.

The San Francisco economy was partially linked to the national and world business structures and partly independent. The money market was closely tied to New York and London, and the ocean transportation companies were entirely Eastern enterprises. Many of the businesses, especially banks, straddled the continent, having partners in the "States" who were often the dominant party. Moreover, much business was done on a consignment basis, and the outside world supplied the bulk of the city's merchandise.

Yet San Francisco's business cycle did not correspond to the
national one even though the panic of 1855 was touched off by
the Eastern involvements of Page, Bacon and Company. There
was no comparable occurrence in the East to cause that firm's
troubles; and, more importantly, their failure would not have
had wider repercussions if local business had not been so over-
extended. This vulnerability was due to California conditions: the
decline of gold production and the rise of farming. Moreover,
when the "national" panic hit the East in 1857, it was not like
1929 when the whole country went down together. The worst was
over in the Bay City at the time New York collapsed. It is difficult to say whether this noncoincidence was due to the lack of a
national American market in the 1850's or whether it was caused
by the unique economic specialization of California; but whatever
the reason, the independence did exist.[78]

That was exactly the way the people wanted it. Their ideal
seems to have been economic *autarky,* and nowhere else was the
anticolonial theme more persistent. Time and again the newspapers bemoaned the export of gold, the remittance of rent and
interest money, the departure of citizens, and the unwillingness
of stateside shippers to share commercial power.[79] Every new
"manufactory" built, each packaging innovation and product introduced, and every virgin acre of land tilled was hailed as a means
to diminish California's bondage. Paradoxically enough, however,
the city was the leading supporter of every one of the measures
that would ultimately bring the local economy into unison with
the rest of the nation and world: clipper ships, outside investment,
transcontinental wagon or rail roads, overland telegraphs, and
steamship subsidies.

This program indicated the incipient independence of the San
Francisco economy. By 1857 gold was still the "cornerstone," but
the metropolis was no longer merely the "warehouse" for the Gold
Rush.[80] That event was essentially a massive redistribution of the
wealth of the Sierra, and in this reorganization no other California
locale fared as well as "the City." It transformed quickly the gold

of the mountains into resources of its own—buildings, factories, dry docks, banks, chambers of commerce, workingmen, lawyers, and merchants. This aggregation was still dependent upon the multi-million dollar flow of minerals from the interior, but the assets of San Francisco increasingly took on a life of their own as the depression of 1853 clearly dramatized.

American cities have traditionally responded to their economic crises with measures of defense.[81] San Francisco in the 1850's was overly dependent upon a few businesses; and when these threatened to collapse, its role as the state's chief booster took on increased importance. Individually and in groups, men began taking steps to protect the aggregation of urban resources.

Activities to roll back the depression more often than not centered around immigration, the supposed key to prosperity. The city implored steamship companies to cheapen their fares and the federal government to build a transcontinental railroad, or at least a wagon road. If these latter things could not be done, the authorities in Washington should provide protection from the Indians on the California and Oregon trails. To coordinate all these efforts, an Immigration Society was established in 1855 by George Gordon and others. Moreover, those already in the city or state were urged to stay put, and the verbal onslaught on transiency escalated as the economic curve plunged. Even the Vigilante uprisings of 1856 were related to this desire to strengthen the attractions of the community. As the *Pacific* put it in 1855, the metropolis must be "morally inviting" if it expected to attract immigrants; and the campaign of '56 against gambling, vice, and political corruption was not unrelated to this overriding community necessity. Neither were other "reforms," ranging from the demand for cheap rents for workingmen to more difficult divorce procedures to the exclusion of the Chinese.[82]

Still other projects supplemented these. The local railroad-building schemes suddenly became much more important, and San Franciscans actually began to worry about Oakland's and Benicia's ambitions for track. Concurrently, they urged the national govern-

ment to subsidize a steamship line to the Far East so that when
the transcontinental arrived, the city would be in a position to
act as transshipment point for the China trade. That aspiration
complemented the desire to find a market for the oversupply of
merchandise and for the burgeoning agricultural surplus in the
interior.

Along with this drive for export and re-export markets came
a passion for developing the interior. This was the chief reason
that population was in such demand; and to insure greater agrarian
yields, urban leaders founded the California Agricultural Society
in December 1853. This first important organized attempt to promote scientific agriculture in the state was almost entirely an urban
project; its first executive officers all were San Franciscans, and
"few actual farmers" attended the convention that organized the
new institution. The driving force behind the society was James
Warren, an urban nurseryman, who became the long-time editor of
"a weekly paper which . . . for the early years virtually constituted
the agricultural journalism of California." [83] Finally, a drive for
greater urban productivity buttressed that for larger rural output.
Industrialization became a much more important topic in the
press, and eventually the Mechanics Institute staged an Industrial
Exposition to dramatize the potential for manufacturing on the
coast.

The thrust of these measures was obviously toward diversifica-
tion, recovery, and economic independence from the outside
world. Yet the decision to promote the interior also grew in large
part out of the conviction that urban development in California
had far and away outstripped rural growth. The city was much
too big for the hinterland that it possessed, and, therefore, the
tributary area must be increased by stimulating immigration.
"Not more than one half the population of San Francisco have
permanent and profitable employment in their various occupations. . . . All sorts of pursuits incident to city life, are suffering a
plethora," noted the *Golden Era* in 1855. "Thus it is, while the
number of persons to do the business of the country has increased

tenfold, the population of the state has failed to keep pace." This maldistribution explains the urban conviction "that our chiefest need is the steady influx of an industrious and moral population" as well as the frequent advice to the city's unemployed to resort to the interior because town trades were definitely "overdone." [84]

What had happened in the few short years since January 1848 was a partial reversal of roles. San Francisco had been forced into cityhood mostly because of the needs of the Gold Rush and was, therefore, a product of the interior. Yet by 1857 the city of about 50,000 was already becoming the promoter rather than the step-child of the interior, largely due to urban needs.

In less than ten years, the metropolis of San Francisco had fash-ioned an economic structure which even the most ardent booster of the town of Yerba Buena could not have envisioned. It was the "Great Commercial Emporium of the Pacific" just as its admirers claimed, and its economic ties circled the globe. The state's most important form of transportation, the steamboat monopoly, was based and owned in the city and fanned out up the rivers from its wharves. Connected to this system was California's only railroad, which was built and controlled by San Francisco capital-ists. The telegraph, the most modern form of communication, radiated into the interior from the city center and deposited its profits in the same place.[85]

California's gold, gathered from the gulches and streams of the Sierras, flowed into San Francisco via the express companies, which, like the other instruments of commercial dominance, were headquartered there. For those who did not want to ship their gold home in the form of dust, the city housed a mint for the con-version of the ore into currency. It also had the state's most sig-nificant financial institutions in which to deposit the newly minted money. In addition, the financiers of the city provided the fore-most California capital market. When that urban structure col-lapsed in 1855, it dragged the entire state into financial panic. In good times or bad, the long wharves that stretched into the bay from the ends of Clay, Broadway, and California streets handled nearly all the state's imports and exports. And when California manufactures began to encroach upon the importer's market, many of the factory goods were fashioned south of Market Street.

In short, the urban role in the California economy was striking. Historians and other social scientists are generally given to the practice of emphasizing the year 1920 as the great watershed, when the rural nation became an urban one. However, if things other than population statistics are taken into account, the year 1920 means a great deal less. With approximately 56,000 people, San Francisco had 14 per cent of the population of the state in 1860.[86] The prominence of the city, however, was way out of proportion to its numbers. The 14 per cent of the population living in the metropolis dominated the business of all the rest and did so in a convincing fashion. San Francisco may have sounded the anti-colonial alarm against its Eastern urban masters, but its power vis-à-vis the interior must have made that area feel like a tributary state.

Labor

Throughout the period under discussion businessmen dominated San Francisco's economy, but that preeminence was often challenged by their employees. It was customary in the Bay City during the 1850's to speak of capital and labor, yet to define the words was less common. Some jobs—such as boss carpenter, stevedore, drayman, lighterman—were located in a no man's land between the two spheres, and it was not always easy to discover the boundary. However, it was agreed that a line did exist. If "working man" is not a wholly satisfactory definition to the scholar, then it is best to leave the category undefined and simply write about those people who considered themselves, and were thought by the rest of the community, to belong to the ranks of labor.

The fate of this group was intimately bound up with the business cycle. From 1848 to 1850, therefore, the worker enjoyed great prosperity. So much money was being earned that many people considered becoming what might be called "downwardly mobile." "I thought quite seriously of going into it [draying] at one time myself," wrote John McCrackan, the New England lawyer. "They pay a man to drive a cart fifteen and twenty dollars a day. . . ." [1] In 1850 and 1851, the toiler suffered somewhat along with the rest of the community; but 1852 and 1853 were good years. After that, however, depression set in.

Despite periods of unemployment from 1848 to late 1853, this

was generally considered a golden era for workers. The words of
James Collier, collector of the port, written in 1849, expressed a
conviction that was widespread. "Here, *Labor* controls Capital,"
he said. "In other words, the Mechanic and Artisan fixes [*sic*] his
own prices, and the Capitalist is compelled from *necessity* to submit." So independent had workers become that many of them refused ordinary employment on any terms.[2]

Long before 1853, however, well-being had become far from
universal. In January 1850, R. R. Taylor wrote, "Thousands roam
the streets without employ, and every shift is resorted to to avoid
actual starvation in the 'golden land.' " In May an Irishman and
his friend "nearly walked the shoes off our feet looking for something to do, but in vain, there are too many seeking employment."
In September 1852, Stephen Woodin witnessed the same thing:
"There is [*sic*] more people in this country that is [*sic*] out of
money and destitute than any country I was ever in." In March
of the next year the *Herald* wrote, "This latter class . . . in San
Francisco [the unemployed] is daily on the increase."[3]

The widespread idleness coupled with the persistent assertions
that labor was well off should amply demonstrate the truth of the
current saying that "it has always been a mystery to one half of
the people in the world how the other half lived." After 1853, however, even the most ardent booster knew. In September 1856, the
Alta estimated that there were 3,000 men out of work in a city of
about 50,000. Until this time, unemployment had often been
blamed on laziness; and San Francisco clearly had an oversupply
of "gentlemen" waiting for "something to turn up." However, the
number who were conscientiously trying to find work was much
greater.[4] When jobs were available, as in the summer of 1853,
there was little idleness.

Unemployment was cared for, if at all, by private and public
agencies. All the city hospitals, including the State Marine, doubled as makeshift poor houses. The British, French, and Sardinian
consulates helped their citizens; and other consuls may have aided
their own nationals. Besides government relief, there were private

hiring exchanges, known as intelligence offices; but these had an unsavory reputation for collecting fees much faster than they supplied jobs.[5] Both the Ladies Relief and Protective Association and the Y.M.C.A. maintained employment agencies, as did the various foreign benevolent societies. Besides these, a few unions and some clubs offered help to their needy brethren.

Wages, in periods of adversity and prosperity, were closely dependent upon the mining region or frontier. "Wages here are ruled by the price in the mines," wrote a San Francisco merchant. "If a man can get in the mines $5.00 per day he is unwilling to work here for less." The same attraction gave the metropolis a notoriously unstable labor supply, especially in 1848 and 1849. "It is easier to keep 50 men at work in cities at home, than to keep two men agoing here," noted another observer, "and so uncertain are men here that one day you have more than you want and next, none." [6] It was particularly difficult to keep sailors from going to the mines, a fact to which the hundreds of deserted ships in the harbor bore eloquent testimony. "Sailor jumping," it was widely feared, would ruin commerce by deterring captains from calling at San Francisco. In fact, from 1848 to 1853 so many vessels brought so many goods that a depression was caused by the oversupply.

This relationship between city and frontier worked conversely as well. "Business in our line is very good," wrote a laboring man in 1853. "So much so that everybody in my class has been on strike for higher wages. . . . The miners began to flock in from the mountains and *damned glad to gain employment* at the former rates. . . ." Even without a boom, many miners wintered in San Francisco; and others came there throughout the year to recoup their fortunes or health.[7] In summer, when commerce was not brisk, the dry season in the diggings dumped excess men onto the San Francisco labor market. Thus the frontier was a kind of safety valve for the city, but the reverse was also true.

The mining industry was the most important factor affecting the scale of wages, though there were some other significant influences

as well. The periodic oversupply of merchandise in the local market had the same effect. So did chance occurrences, of which fire
was probably the most frequent. Since the city was seriously
burned on so many occasions, artisan, mechanic, and laborer all
profited by the recurring opportunity to rebuild.[8]

Sometimes men doing the same job got widely divergent rates
of remuneration, depending on the skill of the worker. In addition,
wages were very unstable and irregular even in the best of years;
and in 1848–49 they often reached remarkable heights. Before
the Gold Rush, laborers received from one to three dollars per day.
In 1848 the going rate was six to ten a day, and other wages
climbed in proportion. The next year some seamen were offered
$300 per month; servants, from $100 to $300; teamsters, fifteen to
twenty dollars per day; and journeymen carpenters, sixteen. The
battle to maintain these rates seesawed through 1853; then wages
declined. In 1856 compensation for sailor, servant, and carpenter
had fallen to thirty, forty, and three to five dollars respectively.[9]

It is impossible to tell whether they were representative, but
there were many workingmen who, like their capitalist employers,
charged "all the traffic would bear." A female observer noted that
"it is really wonderful to witness the avidity and eagerness displayed by all, from the merchant down to the lighterman, of taking advantage of making money." The same fact came out in other
ways. The Typographical Union refused to lower wage rates during 1850–52 even though the flush times were long gone. City
hackmen had a notorious reputation for overcharging and abusing
their patrons—especially strangers in town. And the "custom
among the draymen to rush headlong, at the first tap of the bell to
the scene of disaster," impeding the work of firemen and charging
outrageous prices for removing threatened goods, earned the teamsters a similar image.[10]

The length of the working day did not vary as much as the compensation. In 1853 a state law recommended a ten-hour day, and
supposedly this provision was widely honored. However, many
toiled at least eleven a day, while others worked less than ten.

During the "militant" summer of 1853, the longshoremen struck
for nine hours and won; and in 1855 they were still working that
amount. In some instances the eight-hour-day was already present: the city council provided in late 1852 that this should constitute a day's effort for work on the city streets.[11] But for most workers, this shortened time remained an aspiration rather than a reality. Yet whatever the duration of the hours, the working week was
always six days.

From the remaining evidence, the nature of the tasks performed,
the primitive labor-saving equipment available, and the hours put
in, it is safe to assume that labor was hard. "Well what shall I
write I am well and busy, plenty to do. If I dont make much I am
not lonesome unless on *Sundays* and then I am so damned tired
I sleep all day to prepare for the next brutes' task," wrote a laborer.
"I sometimes think to myself and dam [*sic*] a working man any-
how, and think him no better than the meanest brute, and but little
more his advantages truly, labour, eat, drink. And at last go to the
D——l—as the good folks say—" [12] Fortunately, not many of the
"brutes' tasks" had to be performed at night, although printers did
form an exception to this rule; and on occasion other trades did,
too.

Job hazards did exist. Several men were injured at Henry
Meiggs's saw mill, one of them losing a hand. Distilleries, either
camphene or alcohol, were prone to catch fire; and at the Novelty
Distillery conflagration of 1855, two employees lost their lives.
Two others were killed in 1854 when a raised house fell on them,
and in 1853 a well digger was crushed to death by an improperly
secured windlass. Injuries from windmill machinery, from runaway drays, and from unloading ships added further casualties to
the list. Very little, if any, compensation existed to offset these
dangers, although seamen had the privilege of full treatment at
the U.S. Marine Hospital, which opened in 1854.[13]

Since most businesses were small, separation between employee
and employer was not great. Even in the largest "factories" such
bosses as the Donohues had working-class beginnings. Teamster-

ing and lightering firms were modest; and journeymen carpenters
and bricklayers, longshoremen, and others worked in close contact with their superiors. Yet this intimacy does not seem to have
mitigated working conditions. Greater contact certainly did not
prevent the recognition of class distinctions between labor and
capital; neither were workers deterred from agitation, sometimes
violent, on behalf of higher wages. Nor were employers any less
demanding because of having had a turn at the work themselves
or on account of knowing the laborer by his first name. The *Alta*
in 1853 stated the matter quite explicitly: "The employer as a general rule, taxes the laborer to the utmost limit. . . . Wherever we
may turn we find that capital takes advantage of its power, and labor is obtained at the lowest rates at which it can be procured." [14]

The attack on salaries was continual, especially that mounted by
the city's "ladies," who also had most intimate contact with their
employees. "There is a class of people who . . . come destitute
of money and friends and offer their services at the low price of
25 or 30 dollars per month," lamented an unemployed female.
"This class is preferred by those who wish to hire, and this causes
a continual reduction of wages." [15] Sometimes these efforts were
organized. Housewife Chastina Rix noted indignantly in her diary
"a certain call of the *Ladies* of San Francisco for a meeting to reduce servants wages." [16]

Other employers had similar schemes. "The tenacity which some
people have manifested in their efforts to effect a reduction in the
wages of labor and to lower and degrade it by bringing in . . .
inferior races [Asiatic, Negro, and Kanaka] is really marvelous,"
complained the *Alta*. One of these attempts was the Contract Labor Act unsuccessfully introduced into the state legislature by
prominent San Francisco attorney Archibald C. Peachy. The *Alta*
itself imported some "inferior races," that is, white scabs, or "rats,"
from New York. Leasing state prisoners to businessmen was yet
another low-wage device. According to the *Call*, the practice "em-
braces boot and shoe-making and repairing, brick making, ship
building, the repairing of machinery and perhaps other pursuits."

In addition, there was at least some resort to child labor, though this custom was not widespread.[17]

The most nefarious method of depressing wages was shanghaiing. In the early days crews deserted for the mines *en masse,* encouraging kidnapping in order to secure men. Seamen were available for coast or Hawaiian voyages, since these trips did not take the mariners too far from the gold fields and provided welcome work during the slack season in the mines. Voyages to Shanghai were less popular, however, because they usually continued all the way around the world. Therein lay the origin of both the coercion and the name of the custom. Shanghaiing was generally carried on by sailor boardinghouse proprietors. Although the procedure continued for ten years after the Gold Rush, mariners were not so scarce after 1851; and thus there was less necessity to employ the "press." However, sailors were not any less in the grip of the city's most oppressive economic cartel.

The lodging homes, numbering twenty-three in 1855, were part of a monopoly that controlled the labor market for mariners. Captains had to get their crews through shipping agents. These latter, in turn, allied themselves with the boardinghouse operators, or "landsharks," and therefore signed up only those men staying at an approved hostelry. The seamen fell into the hands of the "landsharks" by shanghaiing, by necessity, or by sailor thieving. Each house had a "runner"—such as the notorious "Cock Eyed Patsy" —whose job was to entice Jack Tar to jump ship, usually plying him with liquor and promises of better wages. Once inside the hotel, the sharks threatened the sailor with a return to his vessel if he did not cooperate. Sometimes, in the bargain, a confederate lawyer even sued the deserted shipmaster for the seaman's back wages; and San Francisco juries were often very sympathetic to such pleas. The mariner was usually soon indebted to the boarding master, and the lion's share of his back pay as well as his advance for signing on anew went to the crimping brotherhood.[18]

The press took considerable notice of both shanghaiing and sailor thieving. In fact, the custom of trying such cases in the dis-

trict court or before the consuls of the nationals involved dealt a
severe blow by 1856 to the pettifoggers who specialized in disputes between captains and crews.[19] Yet the boardinghouse monopoly remained.

To counter these and other pressures, the laboring men had
weapons of their own, the most important of which was cooperative action. This could be either political or economic, but the
latter—"pure and simple" unionism—was usually preferred. Although these joint efforts sometimes resulted in the formation of
permanent alliances, the cooperation generally was ad hoc and
ephemeral even when unions did grow out of it.

In spite of the frequent bad treatment, the community had a
relatively favorable opinion of the laborer and his cause. At times
the press complained that high wages hampered the economy, especially when they had to pay them; yet the newspapers never
ceased to praise every evidence of the well-being of the mechanic,
artisan, and laborer and to deplore conditions—such as expensive
housing, the lack of savings banks, or costly justice—that might
prevent the immigration of workers into California. Current economic theory buttressed this solicitude, since it was held by many
that labor was the sole, or at least the most important, producer of
wealth. Moreover, in common with other parts of America, San
Francisco believed in the dignity of toil and glorified it accordingly. "Walk though our streets and have reverence for labor," the
Alta directed. This respect was forthcoming because "every industrious laboring man, good mechanic, or artisan, is a valuable acqui-
sition to a young and growing city," as the *Chronicle* argued.[20]

It was natural, therefore, that the people generally agreed that
labor had certain prerogatives in the community. And it was usually conceded that the freedom to organize and to strike, the crucial ones so far as labor was concerned, was among the workingman's "rights and privileges." "It has been held by some authority
that combinations to raise wages are contrary to justice and to the
policy of our laws," noted the *Alta* in an article upholding the liberty to both organize and strike, "but that proposition can never be

maintained by any person who has a clear idea of justice or of the spirit of American institutions." "Let the laboring classes, then, of every kind unite and sustain each other," encouraged the *Chronicle*.[21]

In urging a policy of mutual aid, both the labor spokesmen and independent journals were keenly aware of the example of their employers. A "journeyman" wrote to the *Herald* in 1853, "It is sufficient for us to know, that by a systematized organization of wealth and talent, the mechanic and laborer . . . are made subservient to a very small fraction of the human family." "Every class of society are compelled by circumstances to combine for mutual protection," a printer argued at an 1854 union meeting; ". . . and the history of every nation and of every calling shows that those who have maintained their union have reaped the richest reward." [22]

Though labor enjoyed general community recognition of its legitimacy, the particular privileges of workingmen, beyond that of unionizing, were vague. In effect, therefore, labor had the freedom to contend for as much as it could get, using the accepted methods of the day. How much that would be was generally determined by the degree of prosperity and the organization present. In 1848–49, good times were enough to insure ample remuneration to most men; but in 1853 it took both economic well-being and cooperation. Most of San Francisco's labor activity consisted of prosperity rather than adversity strikes, with the majority occurring in the summer of 1853. However, the city's workingman, like his business counterpart, turned to mutual aid in times of both opportunity and crisis.

In unionization, as in the business arena, San Francisco's leadership was quite evident. In fact, the history of labor organization in the state throughout the fifties is little more than the chronicle of activity in San Francisco. There the initial labor legislation in the state passed; an organized body of workingmen made the first demands; the original union organized; most of the subsequent organizational activity centered; and the first national charter was granted.[23] The labor market was often glutted and its businesses

"overdone." Nevertheless, the imperative needs of the instant city
—the state's largest—for buildings, transportation, food, clothing,
and other services gave unions more "openings" than any other
place in California, rural or urban.

Probably the first instance of joint cooperation among California
workers to raise wages occurred in late 1849, when the journeymen
carpenters struck and won a daily wage of sixteen dollars. By the
summer of 1853 a number of other crafts had followed this lead.
The printers formed the West Coast's first union, the San Francisco
Typographical Association, in 1850; and the coalheavers, teamsters, bakers, tailors, musicians, steamboat runners, bricklayers,
and sailors all engaged in some sort of collective effort. As much
unionization occurred in July and August of 1853, however, as
throughout the remainder of the ten years. During these two
months, Carpenters' Hall, the Mountaineer Saloon, and other
workingmen's gathering places hosted constant meetings of laboring men, mostly skilled. At least sixteen crafts—journeymen carpenters, journeymen house and sign painters, teamsters, firemen
and coalpassers, riggers and stevedores, longshoremen, journeymen blacksmiths, hod carriers, journeymen oak coopers, shipwrights and caulkers, journeymen stonecutters, steamboat and
steamship waiters, journeymen tinsmiths, plasterers, journeymen
bricklayers, as well as laborers—undertook some kind of union activity. Of these, eleven actually went on strike, several successfully.[24]

Very little organizing succeeded the active summer of 1853.
Many of the groups formed during the decade were ephemeral,
though a few did have some permanency. The Eureka Typographical Union lasted at least six years, and the Riggers and Stevedores
Union Association endured until 1919. Both were founded in 1853.
At least eight and probably more unions still existed in 1856. How
many men were in the various associations is impossible to say,
but probably most did not belong. In 1854 the Riggers and Stevedores had 300 members (this included some sailors); but the print-

ers, a trade that had a union throughout the period, were over-whelmingly unorganized in mid-1854.[25]

A further organizational development, one that was to be more important in the future, had its origin in this period. Not until the '80's did San Francisco's workingmen succeed in establishing a confederation; but as early as 1853 the subject was bruited. The suggestion coincided with the rash of disputes of that summer and reappeared in succeeding years. "The remedy we suggest is a Trades Union," urged the *Call* in 1856. "In San Francisco, the printers, the carpenters, hatters, tinners, painters, stone cutters, shipwrights and caulkers, and a number of other trades, have so-cieties for the protection of their separate interests. If they were to combine their forces and work in concert—induce other classes of mechanics and laboring men to organize also—they would be the most powerful body in the community." [26] Unfortunately for labor, the *Call's* suggestion remained only that.

Several circumstances retarded unionization, but government hostility was not one of them. In cases where strikers were ar-rested, it was often only after disorder had provoked a reaction. Even so, labor violence did not always bring arrests. Moreover, law enforcement capability was weak. At 300 members, the Rig-gers and Stevedores had from four to ten times as many men as the city had police. In addition, judicial injunctions had not yet become important; and a powerful, relatively unified employer opposition was also absent.[27] The lack of opposition from capital and government distinguishes San Francisco's labor relations in the 1850's from those of later years.

Transiency, one of the most significant problems in the city, hampered efforts at organization. Probably the most crippling agent, however, was oversupply. Nearly every passenger entering and leaving California stopped by the Golden Gate, and many tarried before moving on. The mines also dumped their excess upon the metropolis; and in good times miners came there in search of high wages. These extra men were the self-imported

"strike breakers," more effective in keeping labor in check than all
the devices used by businessmen. Finally, it must be mentioned
that the associational impulse throughout San Francisco was still
relatively weak. Not only were there few labor unions, but most
other nonbusiness groups had a difficult time getting a foothold
there.

Unions sought much the same goals as today. Above all, they
claimed the "same legal and equitable right to regulate the value
of labor, that the merchant has to place a value upon his merchandise, or the banker to fix his rates of exchange." The organizations
also desired to standardize wages, to insure their prompt payment
on the date due, to regulate hours and work rules, and, in short, to
control as completely as possible the conditions of their work.[28]

Some of the tactics used to secure these ends are familiar
enough, but there were more unusual methods as well. If the
typographers found someone working for nonunion rates or an
office paying them, the offending party was tried before the union
and his name published in the community press as a "rat" (their
word for scab). On one occasion, the boat owners on the Stockton
route had agreed to dispense entirely with their steamboat runners, who were universally considered a bad lot. In keeping with
the cleverness that won them acclaim as the city's most accomplished swearers, the runners banded together and tried to throw
all of the Stockton passenger traffic onto one boat. Another atypical maneuver was suggested at an 1854 meeting of the Eureka
Typographical Union when it was proposed that a "secret order"
be established which would "have all the powers usually bestowed
on 'Rat Committees' and . . . exercise such supervisory control of
the trade as may be consistent with the Constitution of this Union." The main reliance, however, was on negotiation and the
strike. Often these were very colorful affairs. With fife, drum, and
American flag, strikers carried the battle to the community, usually ending with a rally at the Plaza.[29]

Some unions—notably the teamsters and stevedores—like the
guilds before them, included employees and employers.[30] How-

ever, most alliances were made up of unskilled laborers and journeymen, of which the latter were most numerous. Some groups,
including the stevedores and possibly the printers, carried on welfare activity in addition to their work on behalf of wages and working conditions. Others also had a recreational function, such as getting up a teamsters' parade in 1852 and the Riggers and Stevedores
Ball of 1855. On occasion, too, they turned out for each other's
funerals.

The surviving minutes of the Eureka Typographical Union provide some insight into the inner workings of at least one organization. It was a regularly organized body complete with constitution
and rules. Any printer (though no employers) could belong in return for paying dues and an initiation fee. The typographers held
regular meetings, which were orderly and to the point, and conducted business fairly democratically. Officers were elected every
six months, and they shared power with the membership both in
theory and practice. Like any other group, the Eureka on occasion
showed some institutional tension, especially on the matter of
granting wage reductions, their principal concern.

The experience of the Eureka Union reveals a further matter of
importance, common to the entire labor movement. It was obvious
that an individual man could not by himself secure his "rights" if
his employer was not disposed to grant them. Yet organization did
not solve the problem of minority rights. The single printer was
caught between two centers of power, both often unmindful of the
difficulties of his position. Printing establishments could and did
fire men for demanding union wages. On the other hand, the
Eureka could and did "rat" laborers for accepting less. "The Association of Printers, in accordance with republican principle, have
established equitable laws for the equal members of their own
body," explained the Eureka president in 1854. "Those who except
themselves and refuse to move with the generality, are naturally
subjected, it is true, to inconvenience and opprobrium. But this is
a just consequence of lawful organization, whether of societies or
of entire states, a voluntary outlawry brings its own affliction." [31]

The violence that frequently accompanied working-class disputes demonstrated the truth of this statement. The waterfront
had more than its share of rough-housing. In 1852 sailors attacked
and damaged the rigging of a ship, and in 1850 striking seamen
forcibly removed some of their number who had agreed to sail
for less than the strikers. Three years later striking firemen and
coalpassers executed a similar removal from a Panama steamer
and, in addition, carried out a forced examination of all passenger's tickets to be sure no coalpassers had been smuggled
-aboard. During the same summer, riots erupted between rival
teamsters and between the employees of the Mountain Lake Water
Company and some other employees, who were trying to get up
a strike. The next year "a number of laborers and cartmen employed in excavating on Francisco Street, for some reasons which
could not be ascertained, engaged in a tremendous fight." This
labor violence generally grew out of some competitive situation
within the working class and was usually intramural.[32]

These working-class rows were rough affairs, but they did not
always produce serious casualties. An attempted seamen's strike
in 1855 degenerated into a potato-throwing contest; and the
1853 teamsters' free-for-all was cooled off when the California
Street Wharf, upon which they were contending, collapsed,
plummeting the furiously battling draymen into the waters of
the bay.[33]

The strikes that often accompanied this violence were much
more important than the union vote, yet the latter had some significance. In 1850 the teamsters nominated two men and elected
one, James Grant, to the city council. In 1853 there was a
"Regular Mechanics and Workingmen's Ticket" made up of candidates from the regular slates endorsed by a labor meeting; and
the next year an organization of boatmen, called the "Turn Out,
Turn In Club," was active in the election.[34] In addition, in most
years all the parties in the city were zealous in wooing the workingman's vote.

Of all San Franciscans, the laboring class was among the least articulate; yet they did convey some idea of what they wanted from the government. In general, they asked the politicians for the same thing that capital did—help whenever it was needed. The teamsters were the first in politics, and in 1851 they secured the introduction of an ordinance forbidding aliens from engaging in trades such as draying and lightering. Within three years the cartmen petitioned the city to "prevent the accumulation of too many carts and horses by any one person." [35] The mechanics' lien law and the ten-hour-day law of 1853 were other labor desiderata.

With the establishment of the *Daily Morning Call* in late 1856, workmen secured a newspaper ally, though the *Fireman's Journal* had previously played this role to a certain extent. Most of the efforts of the *Call,* however, were directed against the state prison contract which allowed the leasing of prisoners to businessmen. It also advocated the building of a bulkhead along the waterfront to provide jobs and protested vigorously against a federal tariff and California's attachment law.[36]

Immigration was a concern that lay both within and without the sphere of government jurisdiction. Part of the anti-Oriental feeling in San Francisco after 1850 stemmed from the laborers' resentment of Chinese competition. The legislature even adopted a couple of proposals to deter this immigration. Yet the teamsters' and lightermen's attempt to ban all foreign rivals is proof that the Chinese were not the only foreigners under attack. The *Call* noted another dimension of the problem in 1856.

> Cannot some of those "first citizens" who were so anxious to increase immigration into California . . . devise measures to procure employment for the thousands of unwillingly idle men who are now in our midst? . . . We say, let the unemployed who are already here be the objects of our solicitude first. These provided for, we may take into consideration the expediency of extending assistance towards our trans-montane friends.[37]

San Francisco's exclusionism, therefore, was not simply antiforeignism, or "nativism," but part of the intramural struggle among workingmen and their intramural one with capital.

In other matters the workers were not so anxious for government interference. They opposed bitterly any attempt to regulate exorbitant hack charges and teamstering rates during fires.[38] Yet both passed, and these actions merely strengthened the conviction of the *Call* and others that the politicians neglected labor concerns. The governor, however, did throw workingmen a sop in January 1857 by urging modification of the state prison contract. A trades union confederation was advocated primarily to end this indifference to "the rights of the mechanic," but neither this threat nor any other show of unity forced the politicians to take a more lively interest.

Accompanying the economic and political struggles of laboring men was a rhetorical battle aimed at justifying themselves in the eyes of society and asserting their own importance. They usually expressed this prolabor argument in a theory of class reconciliation rather than in one of class struggle, holding that there was an identity of interest in the community. The phrase "United We Stand; Divided We Fall," the strike slogan of the oak coopers in 1853, expressed this notion at one level; the demands for a trades union of all workers took the identification of interests one step higher.[39] The broadest assertion of the interdependence came in the *Call* in 1856.

> In advancing the interest of the working man, we add to the prosperity of all. The scientific, the commercial, and the mechanical interests are so blended . . . that to improve the condition of one enhances the other, and to strike a blow at either affects the whole connection. Thus by adding our mite towards the elevation and protection of the working class . . . we . . . assist in elevating the interests of every portion of the community.[40]

Though the economic community was divided between capital and labor, these two groups did not necessarily have antithetical interests. To be sure, spokesmen often noted that the concerns of these two did in fact often clash. "Since the earliest period," complained the *Call*, "the usurpations of capital upon the interests and the rights of labor, are palpable to every intelligent citizen who examines our statutory enactments." Yet even where such opposition occurred, it was held to be a "false antagonism." [41] The workers of the Bay City wanted to join rather than overthrow those above them. The specter of communism may have been haunting Europe, but its existence was not recognized in San Francisco.

Even though the laborers' spokesmen saw the harmony of interests, they did not think the two groups were equally important. "All members of society are consumers of wealth, but all are not wealth producers," proclaimed the *Call*. "Consequently the producers are the sustainers, the feeders, the educators and supporters of all the rest; and whatever decreases the powers and means of the producers, is an additional burthen thrown upon the shoulders of the producing classes. . . ." [42] Thus, the labor theory of value was both an economic theory and an argument of class justification.

Whether this assumption was more a matter of conviction or merely "vocational chauvinism," it is certain that it was widely held.[43] Nor was this self-esteem markedly different from the businessmen's belief in the superiority of their own group in society. Yet the laboring man's claim to preeminence was hollow, for the great disunity among workingmen rendered them much less powerful than the business community.

A Transient, Urban People

There has probably never been a more thoroughly "uprooted" city population than that of San Francisco of the forties and fifties. It had its foreign population; but unlike many other American cities, it had very few long-time "native" residents. At the most, about one thousand people were on hand when the Gold Rush struck, three-fourths of whom had not been there more than two years. Yet even these, like the smattering of "older residents," the mining fever soon rendered transient. Therefore, after 1848 San Francisco was a totally rootless community—in a sense, even the Americans were immigrants. What is more, most men intended to remain that way.

Nobody referred to San Francisco as "home," observed the Vigilante C. J. Dempster. That was some place east of the Rocky Mountains, below the Equator, or across the Pacific to which one longed to return. Moreover, the mines, not the city, were the California destination of most men. "San Francisco is now in many respects like a railroad depot," explained the *Californian* in 1848, "hundreds are continually going and coming, while but a few remain permanently. . . ." What kept people at the Golden Gate even temporarily was the same thing which had attracted them in the first place. "Don't think because I am getting a little property here that I am going to make it my home," wrote a native of New Brunswick. "It is all for the hopes of gain; for I should not spend my life here unless it be very short for [all] Caly and her gold." As another resident put it, they all were "birds of passage." The press repeatedly announced the decline of this transiency, but even at the end of the decade it was a widely acknowledged reality.[1]

The home ties seemed to pull all the harder because of the lack of local ones. "I cannot stay here with . . . those four dear children so far off constantly sighing for me to be with them," one resident lamented. "How I dread being left here in this forlorn place," protested a second. "You don't know how homesickly it is," bemoaned a third. For some, the longing was even more overwhelming. "In this land of strangers, where nothing but the merciless grasp of the money getter greets you on every side . . . when business hours are over, I often stroll away into the world of spirits," William Weston wrote to his father, "to my own dear home, with wife and little ones hold sweet communion, to the home of my childhood. . . ."[2]

The loneliness was especially visible on "steamer day," when the boat left with its load of homeward-yearning letters and departing "Californians." Masses of San Franciscans, many with tears in their eyes, invariably bid it farewell. When the steamers came in, the scene was even more poignant. People jammed the wharves hoping to greet a loved one or friend, and the boats in the harbor were often packed with a curious humanity trying to catch a glimpse of the arrival.[3]

Even those who had no one to greet hoped for a letter. From the moment the mail arrived, both eager residents and miners temporarily returned besieged the post office. Standing in lines sometimes six abreast and several blocks long, men waited for hours and often camped out all night to keep their advanced places. Ingenious inhabitants turned the occasion into a money-making affair, standing in line in order to sell out to someone farther back in the column or peddling snacks and sweets up and down the ranks of weary waiters.[4] From the "Californians," in their turn, there flowed a stream of brave letters, daguerreotypes, Chinese shawls, mini-nuggets, and other mementoes to keep the home ties alive. The loneliness, like the transiency rate, continued well into the fifties.

With many, these emotional bonds prevailed. Thousands simply packed up and made their way back "home"—to New York, Boston, New Orleans, Paris, Dublin, or Newburyport, Massachusetts. However, "California fever" claimed a steadily growing number, often very quickly. "There is a charm connected with a life in California, that every day becomes more and more binding, in proportion as our conveniences and refinements increase," wrote McCrackan to his family in mid-1850. "Were it not for you all, my dear family, I should be perfectly content if I . . . would end my days here," he assured them in 1851. "I am almost convinced that the taste of California life is fatal." [5] McCrackan finally returned to his native New Haven, but the weakening of old ties proved decisive for thousands.

Despite their original intentions, a considerable number made their "homes" in San Francisco. In addition, many others stopped there temporarily, and its population spurted. The Gold Rush gave the greatest impetus to growth; yet here again, the trend was already underway. In 1844 only about fifty people lived in the future city; but from that point on, the figure quickly increased. In 1846 the total was between two and three hundred, and the town's first census in 1847 found 459 persons. The second count, taken in 1848, revealed another doubling.[6]

This growth abundantly impressed early residents, but what happened thereafter stunned even the most sanguine boosters. The population skyrocketed to 34,000 by the state census of 1852 and climbed to about 56,000 by 1860. No scientifically accurate figure for 1856 is possible, but around 50,000 would seem to be correct and matches contemporary estimates.[7]

The city's growth had important seasonal variations. Since mining could not be carried on as extensively in colder weather, many left the mountains for San Francisco and other favorite wintering places. In addition, the inclemency made the placers inaccessible to the often unknowing newcomers, who were forced into a temporary sojourn at the Golden Gate. Eventually, however, the storms abated; and then the papers, letters home, and diaries were filled with the news that "the fine weather has cleared off a large portion of our surplus population . . . and people are . . . seen hurrying to the landing places, armed with picks, shovels, and frying-pans, bursting with anxiety to get a peep at the 'elephant.'" [8]

Those who stayed were a diverse group, making San Francisco "the most curious Babel of a place imaginable." Again, this was a characteristic that the Gold Rush accentuated but did not inaugurate. The first census showed a marked variety of people; and though there were some shifts in the proportions over the years, the basic pattern of heterogeneity remained. In 1847 about half the population was American, a balance that was relatively unchanged in 1860. At 50.09 per cent, San Francisco had the third highest proportion of immigrants among American cities. It was slightly ahead of Chicago, behind Milwaukee, and nearly 10 per cent behind St. Louis. Even New York City, the great receiving center for Europeans, was less populated with aliens than the Golden Gate metropolis. The ratio was also considerably higher than that of the state as a whole which was only about 39 per cent, though several areas in California had a heavier concentration of immigrants than the city.[9]

Throughout the period, young men not burdened by the care and counsel of their elders nor comforted by the presence of their wives and children peopled San Francisco. It was continually announced that more and more women were arriving, but there were never enough to balance off the male sector. The 1847 census already showed a masculine predominance of more than two to one and an even greater prevalence of youth. Nearly everyone in the city was under forty years of age. By 1860 the female imbalance had been slightly redressed to 39 per cent of the total; but in the interval, the disproportion was outlandish. The state survey of 1852 put the ratio at six to one, and earlier post-1848 estimates ran as high as ten to one.[10]

Among these youthful males there was racial as well as ethnic variety. The 1847 census showed that about one-fifth of the city's population was non-Caucasian—Negro, Indian, and Hawaiian. By 1860 this proportion had dropped to less than 10 per cent. Moreover, the Indians and Hawaiians, who had originally been the bulk of the nonwhite population, were almost entirely replaced by Negroes and Chinese, who made up respectively 1,176 and 2,719 of the 56,000 residents.[11]

The "motley" array of humanity that was San Francisco came from almost everywhere. There were the usual European groups prominent in the Atlantic migration. In addition, the heterogeneity was enhanced by large contingents from non-European lands and by the diverse origins of the Americans themselves. Among the "natives," the largest numbers came from the Middle Atlantic states and New England respectively. New York provided the greatest contribution, followed by Massachusetts. The Midwest, the South, and California supplied the next largest group, but their proportion was much less. Moreover, to a disproportionate degree these people were former urbanites. The Negro part of the American immigration came from the same areas as the white. Some runaway slaves were among the black population, but most were free Negroes from the large cities in the New England and Middle Atlantic states.[12]

To this American mélange was added an even greater foreign one. By far the greatest single contributor was the British Empire, within which Ireland was the most prolific source, followed by England, Australia, Scotland, Wales, and Canada. The other large European suppliers were Germany and, even though not usually given to relinquishing her sons to lands outside the Empire, France. Switzerland, Poland, Sweden, Belgium, and Italy also contributed a small number of their young men to San Francisco. Much more significant donors to the local melting pot were the nations of

Latin America, especially Mexico and Chile; and about equally important was China's Pearl River Delta.

The majority of foreign residents embarked directly from their homelands, but a substantial number, chiefly the Germans, Irish, and Italians, did not. More than half of the former came from a country other than Germany, usually somewhere in the United States. Nearly half the Irish came from the British colony of Australia; and most of the rest were resident in the "States," especially New York, before they packed their bags for the golden land. Most of the Italians hailed originally from Liguria and Genoa in northern Italy, but many had previously lived in Latin America.

The presence of gold and so many "indirect" immigrants makes any explanation of foreign migration somewhat different from that for the East. Agrarian distress and the first pains of industrialization in Europe were generally displacing large segments of population and propelling them toward the United States. The Germans and Irish, however, who were among those Europeans hit hardest by the modernization of economic life, were the very ones who often came to San Francisco after first having lived somewhere else. Agricultural and industrial modernization undoubtedly influenced the English and French to come to San Francisco, and distressing conditions also explain in part the arrival of Latin Americans and Chinese. The revolutionary politics of 1848 likewise contributed something as did the Tai Ping Rebellion. Yet for foreign and American immigrants alike it was the lure of the city and its golden hinterland rather than economic and political adversity that was the most important factor in bringing newcomers to the metropolis.

The people who were tossed up on the shores of San Francisco Bay by the Gold Rush were endlessly amazed at the ethnic variety in which they found themselves. That astonishment was true of foreigners and Americans alike, despite the fact that the United States had always been a nation of immigrants. Many were from places like New England and the South, which had not yet come in contact with the extreme mixture of peoples that was to mark

the later nineteenth century. Even more hailed from European
lands which had less ethnic diversity. Few, indeed, failed to express their astonishment. "It is perhaps the most perfectly cosmopolitan city on earth," noted the *Alta*.[13]

Milton Gordon has distinguished three ways in which Americans
have traditionally viewed this ethnic variety. "Anglo conformity"
demanded adherence to the "Anglo-Saxon standard"; "cultural pluralism" urged each group to maintain considerable distinctness;
and the "melting pot" invited all to contribute to a new nationality.[14] San Francisco natives voiced all three approaches on occasion; but their dominant thinking most closely approximated the
philosophy of the melting pot. The exact position of the immigrants is less clear. In the beginning they, like everybody else,
intended to return "home"; but as their residence lengthened, they,
too, became willing to accept considerable ethnic modification.
This spirit of assimilation was by no means universal in either
group, however; chauvinists and cultural conservatives contested
the field with ethnic accommodationists. Both had their triumphs
as urbanism nurtured the seemingly contradictory tendencies of
contact and exclusiveness. Sometimes clannishness seemed to be
increasing as the number of "ethnic" institutions proliferated. Yet
behind this superficial façade of nationalism lay the more powerful realities of a new urban experience common to all. By 1856 a
synthesis was emerging, not yet a "new nationality" but certainly
on the way to becoming one.

The natives, by and large, welcomed foreigners to San Francisco
and, in doing so, put forward the familiar arguments about asylum,
the melting pot, and cosmopolitan nationalism that were common
to the nineteenth century. Yet immigrants were expected to conform to certain American standards and values. What the natives
insisted upon was revealed in their praise for some foreign groups.
"We know of no class of our citizens who display more enterprise
or industry . . . than those . . . of *la belle France*," said the
Picayune. "A French loafer—a Gallic idler, is an anomaly in San
Francisco. They mind not what employment they get, . . . and

go on the sterling principle that no one need be ashamed of his work, if he be honest." They applauded the same qualities in the Jews and something else as well. "The Hebrews of this city are very numerous, possess much wealth, and many of them rank among the most energetic and influential of our citizens," the *Chronicle* wrote. "Their religion is certainly in many respects practical. . . . They never let their brethren become charges upon the public. They are industrious and thrift of course attends them." "We personally have met many Jews, and found some of them the very spirit of honor, educated and accomplished men, polite in manner, and kind and generous in deed and sentiment." "It is said that not one Jew, during the revolutionary war, took part against the liberty party," agreed the *Herald,* "and that the Jews have always taken the side of freedom against oppression." The Germans, noted a Prussian resident, "have obtained the good will of the natives by their soberness, honesty, and industry, which qualities the real Yankee the more admires, as he sees in them the fundamental principles of a great nation." "They are an orderly and intelligent people," added the *Annals,* "and show fewer criminals than a proportionate number of any other class of citizens. They learn the English language very readily, and many of them are naturalized citizens." [15]

Some of these characteristics, such as industriousness, love of work, energy, business acumen, and progressiveness, were thought by all to be disproportionately American. Yet the natives usually rather carefully avoided the smug assumption that they had all the virtues necessary to make a good community. It is quite clear that Americans thought of themselves as the dominant group in the city, but they also retained considerable respect for other cultures and much willingness to learn from them. "Of all the arts, music is the one most universal and most powerful in its influence," the *Herald* wrote in an editorial thanking the "French Emigrants" for introducing Sunday morning concerts. "Of all others it is the best calculated either to wean man from an overintense pursuit of wealth or to refresh him in the intervals of commercial cares and business anxieties." "The Germans are a people who are worthy of all respect," argued the *Bulletin*. "They possess many admirable and estimable qualities which Americans would do well to understand and imitate." The natives, for example, were quite dedicated to the doctrine of hard work, but they depended upon the Europeans to help offset this preoccupation by teaching them something about pleasure and the art of living. "We are too much a money seeking and money making people," said politician-editor Frank Soulé; and he welcomed the German emphasis upon friendship and "social amenities." The *Annals* also expressed this rejection of Yankee all-sufficiency, even in the midst of a fulsome tribute to him, when it referred to the Americans as "the national lords of the soil, the restless and perhaps unhappy people of progress." [16]

As each group made its contribution, San Franciscans hoped that all would eventually merge into a new nationality, exemplifying the good qualities of each. "From thirty-six German Governments you came, from thirty States we came," commented Frank Soulé in a speech to the Turnverein. "Yet freedom has established here her temples of worship, where many nationalities, like the rain which falls upon the earth, percolates through the sand, supplying the fountains, flowing into rivers and rolling out into the ocean and becoming one great and harmonious flood of pure transparent water, form a unit of civilization." [17]

This statement did not mean that all were welcome.[18] There was a hierarchy of esteem in which the dominant native whites held their diverse neighbors. They hailed the English, Scots, and Germans, almost without reservation; and they cordially received other residents of northern and western Europe. But they had less enthusiasm about immigrants—usually Irish—from Australia because so many of them were thought to be ex-convicts. Somewhere in the middle of the spectrum came the French, and at the bottom, the Negroes, Chinese, and Latin Americans.

To a significant degree, the natives' estimate of other groups was sheer prejudice. The *Annals'* argument that depravity was less vile when practiced by Caucasians was typical. "The lewdness of fallen white females is shocking enough to witness, but it is far exceeded by the disgusting practices of those tawny visaged creatures," wrote the city's pioneer historians. Yet there was much more to the matter than bigotry. San Francisco's welcome was contingent upon the immigrants' supposed ability and willingness to contribute to the community. Even the French, who were moderately well liked, were not totally accepted because of their lack of dedication to the city. The French ostentatiously clung together, learned English grudgingly, and were quite transient. The Latin Americans and Chinese were similarly transient and uninterested in learning the language, and the latter were linked in the minds of natives and many foreigners alike with a servile status. Most of the Chinese came to California as indentured servants, and many resented the labor market's being flooded with such competitors. In addition, comparatively few middle- and upper-class representatives of the other two outcast groups lived in the city; thus, fewer of their members could contribute anything beyond their brawn to building the metropolis.[19]

Despite the obvious prejudice which often laced ethnic discussions and the truth of Moses Rischin's comment that the host people were committed to an "Anglo-Saxon manifest destiny," that commitment did not exempt them from searing self-criticism nor blind them to their own failings. "The best evidence we have of the Chinese of our city becoming *Americanized,* is the fact that fights and quarrels are of very frequent occurrence among them," needled the *Era* in 1853. "There are in the world no more adroit thieves,—more enterprising free booters, more daring villains, more ruthless assassins, than those in whose veins flows our boasted Anglo Saxon blood," the special pleader for the New Englanders agreed. "It is just like an American," complained the *Pacific* of the destruction of Sacramento's "noble oak trees." "He has no love or regard for an aged tree, or any thing else venerable in the past." [20]

Conversely, with the exception of the Spanish Americans, the merits of the outcasts were not ignored. These Latins seem to have impressed no one, and the community unfairly dismissed them as

"Greasers"—shiftless, dirty, cruel, and lazy; but it praised both
Negroes and Chinese on many occasions. For example, it was almost invariably pointed out that the Chinese, for all their supposed
opium smoking, filth, and servility, were also industrious, peaceful,
and thorough.

Even groups that had no defenders elsewhere in the nation had
numerous supporters in the city. In the rest of America, the fate
of the Indian was practically ignored in the 1850's for the slavery
question; but in San Francisco, the situation was reversed. Unim-
portant after the early years when they helped Richardson man
the boats used to collect hides and tallow from around the bay,
the red men were nevertheless not forgotten. And not only did the
Indians receive sympathy, but the dominant whites came in for
blistering criticism from their own kind. "WHITE BARBARISM,"
screamed the heading of an 1852 article. "The red man is not the
only savage. The white man is his brother. . . . Indeed when in
desperate pursuit of some sensual or ambitious end, the superior
knowledge of the white man makes him the greater savage of the
two," asserted the *Pacific*. "Fate cannot lighten the guilt of [the
Indians'] murderers. He who has shot an Indian has shot a man.
And he who has done it for a reason that would not justify him
had he killed an American, is by human and Divine laws worthy
of death." The *Golden Era*, though sometimes expressing hostility,
also defended and explained Indian culture and ran articles by the
Cherokee, "Yellow Bird," which did the same.[21]

The foreigners were equally willing to give and take. "There
were many things of German origin which were good and ought
to be maintained," which should be woven "into the civilization
of our new fatherland," wrote the editor of the *German Journal*.
Others "ought to be abandoned for those of foreign origin. The
attempt to draw the line necessarily created difficulty." Yet the
immigrants usually drew "the line" between Americanism and for-
eignism in the same place as the natives. "In so far as the methods of getting along in practical life were concerned [he] . . .

was willing to confess the inferiority of the Germans to the Americans," admitted a German editor to the Turnverein in 1855. "But there he insisted that the inferiority ceases. Physical freedom and plenty of food and drink are not sufficient to satisfy all the wants of man." [22]

Even the French, never much given to self-denigration, admitted the advantage of certain native habits, especially the Americans' "general business talent, spirit of enterprise, facility in forming associations and working in union, bold and decisive spirit, and esteem in which they hold labor." [23] As the superpatriotic future French consul, Patrice Dillon, put it, "I made painful reflection regarding the conduct of France, . . . we fight for philosophical or political formulas while the two great nations [Britain and the U.S.] who alone march equal with us in the world of ideas and facts everywhere extend and develop their influence and their commerce." He noted that "true liberty consists in the eyes of every American, not in spreading with impunity philosophic extravagances to an audience starved for material luxuries, but in devoting himself without trouble or hindrance to the occupations for which each feels a special aptitude." [24]

Group realities of San Francisco followed the recommendations set forth by its ethnic theorists. Contact and cooperation were fairly widespread, and some modification took place. This assimilation was both structural and behavioral. The degree of this change varied, however. In business, the immigrants very quickly learned how to stay afloat in the treacherous currents of the city's economy. In politics, change was also visible. Here the Irish became important, as did both Jews and the natives of despot-ridden Germany. Language was another area of accommodation, especially by the Germans. In both language and religion, the Jewish community was beginning to transform itself. By 1856 Beth El Congregation had adopted English-language prayers. They expressed a willingness to adopt the "*Minhag America,*" whenever it would be published" and to move "towards moderate reforms, as advocated by the *Israelite*" of Isaac Mayer Wise, the "Americanizer." At the same time, a choir of mixed voices appeared at Emanu-El.[25]

The melting pot also bubbled in the schools. "You will perhaps be amused to know how many nations were represented by the children and their Parents," wrote John McCrackan of a school examination, "viz, Americans, French, Spanish, Irish, Scotch, English, Italian, . . . Californians, and one Kanaka boy." [26] Even when foreign and native children were not mixed, the "ethnics" went to school with other aliens unfamiliar to them previously. And even in the American schools, children found themselves next to students from other parts of the United States—Yankees with Southerners and both with Midwesterners.

While the newcomers struggled with American English, Yankee commerce, politics, and the public schools, the natives took the advice that they should imitate foreigners in cultivating the amenities of life. Very early, they wisely acquired a taste for exotic cuisine, especially French and Chinese; and the frequent presence of Americans at German lager beer saloons as well as at Turnverein Mai Fests and other ethnic fêtes indicated a further appreciation of foreign pleasures. They patronized some of the higher manifestations of immigrant culture, too, such as the French theater and the Germania Concert Society. The music of the latter was a bit heavy and often the natives were found to be dozing, but they gamely continued to attend. The *Annals*, at least, was convinced that the influence of the French, Germans, and Hispanic Americans was responsible for the fun-loving character that the city had already assumed. "The grave national character of United States men was converted into levity and cheerfulness by the example and sympathy of their merry neighbors." [27]

Other areas of urban life witnessed the same integration. Parades commemorating some American event became an area of multi-national contact, and even the Chinese turned out for them. The attendance of the California Guards at the funeral of a noted "forty-eighter" indicated that tokens of respect flowed in more than one direction. Ethnic and religious balls and banquets almost always featured some mixing, since it was customary to invite representatives of many groups to each affair, where they toasted each other ad infinitum. One could even find an institutionalized aristocratic melting pot "at the Pacific Club, where gentlemen of fashion and position of all nations congregate." At the other end of the social spectrum very intimate association occurred in Pacific Street dives where "you may find congregated together the Negro, Mexican, and white of both sexes." The press thundered against these places, but their expressions in no way embarrassed the customs of the vice district. And, of course, contiguous living encouraged social intermingling, since as yet the various peoples had not sorted themselves out into distinct ethnic neighborhoods. Other exchanges likewise existed: the fire department had foreign members (some 200); the Masons had immigrant clubs which on occasion met with the rest of the order; and many city functions, such as fund-raising committees, were heterogeneous.[28] So was the most tumultuous episode of the entire era, the Vigilance rising of 1856, which threw together all kinds of ethnic groups.

The *Annals* noted the subtle modification of cultures that these diverse contacts produced.

> The presence of the French has had a marked influence upon society in San Francisco. Skilled workmen of their race have decorated the finer shops and buildings, while their national taste and judicious criticism have virtually directed the more chaste architectural ornaments, both on the exterior and in the interior of our houses. Their polite manners have also given an ease to the ordinary intercourse of society which the unbending American character does not naturally possess. The expensive and fashionable style of dressing among the French ladies has greatly encouraged the splendid character of the shops of jewellers, silk merchants, milliners and others whom women chiefly patronize, while it perhaps increased the general extravagance among the whole female population of the city.[29]

An even more striking example was the suburb of South Park. This most fashionable American residential area was copied from English models, supplied by a British developer.

Among foreigners, this modification of cultures progressed at varying rates. It was easiest for the British to fit into the life of the city, though the English and Scotch adjusted more easily than the Irish. Among non-English speakers, the Germans were by far the most adaptable. They readily learned the language; they were republican in politics; they hastened to become citizens and, in general, convinced Americans of their willingness to identify themselves with this country.[30] The other large European group, the French, was consciously resistant. The Spanish Americans and Chinese were even more so.

The explanation for this resistance is not hard to find, for a considerable amount of chauvinism and cultural conservatism coexisted with the spirit of ethnic accommodation. As befitted the host country, the Americans often assumed bumptious airs. Sometimes these took the form of overwrought praise for the Yankee and all his works; in other cases, Anglo-Saxon superiority was uncritically extolled. The *Alta* noted in 1851 that even those immigrants who returned to their homes "will carry back with them a knowledge of the English language, an idea of the American institutions and liberties, a portion of the energy and order [this was the year of the first vigilance committee] of the great Anglo-Saxon race, and an understanding of the blessed principles of Him whose precept will yet spread peace among the nations, and make the 'wilderness . . . blossom as the rose.' "[31] In its less assertive forms, this nationalism was not intolerable, but it was wearisome. Fortunately, however, the anti-foreign element in local Know Nothingism was not very strong.

Often the sense of native superiority found vent in humor at the expense of the Irish. For example, there was the mythical "Mike O'Nale," who claimed to be "an Irish man shure from ould ireland" who "kim to Calerforna in 1850 to make the honest penne and . . . had bad luck entirley, but . . . made a pile an lost it evry happenny by the fires bad luck to em." Yet this sort of ethnic condescension was also intranational. The analogue to the stage Irishman among the Americans was the Pike County Missourian, who also was given to queer expressions sometimes used to disguise editorial comment. "Is thar any god in California that commands the wimmen to go undressed?" queried the nonexistent John Scroggins. "If thar be Ile give up sending for Sukey, sure, for me and her and all the little Sukies is going to go in for the fashions of old Pike and *nothing shorter*, we are. . . ." The "Pikes," as they were called, "more or less derisively," and the Emerald Islanders shared their role as the butt of urban jokes with the blacks, who were endlessly parodied by the minstrel shows. Yet the whole community enjoyed laughs at the expense of the "Stage Yankee," also a perennial subject of some uproariously funny literary and theatrical performances.[32]

Less amusing were occasional American expressions of anti-Semitism. These were not frequent, however; and by and large, as Jewish resident Henry J. Labatt noted, his coreligionists were relatively immune from such attacks in the metropolis. In fact, insofar as public statements are concerned, it is clear that philo-Semitism easily outweighed hostility. For example, in 1855 when the Speaker of the California lower house castigated the Jews over the problem of Sunday closing, several Golden Gate newspapers responded with support for the aggrieved and so did a San Francisco legislator, E. Gould Buffum of the local Know Nothing Party! A foreign traveler, I. J. Benjamin, even went so far as to state that "nowhere else are they [Jews] regarded with as much esteem by their non Jewish brothers." [33]

French chauvinism was at least equal to American. "Most Frenchmen here cannot live on friendly terms with the Americans, whom they consider a savage, ignorant people," noted a Gallic nobleman in 1851. "Repelled by the difficulty of learning English and unable to communicate with the Americans, they live entirely among themselves and do business with each other." Until the end of the period, naturalization remained a burning question among the French, with the French language press split over the issue. The opposition of the leading Gallic journal, which was the mouthpiece for the French Consulate, was so pronounced that it was driven into support for the American Party, an incongruous position even for San Francisco. "For ourselves, secretly, we are not sorry to see the Know Nothing tendencies exposed, particularly if the effect is to preserve to our country the large number of citizens carried off every year by naturalization," the *Echo du Pacifique* admitted. "The Know Nothings hate foreigners, and wish to oppose their naturalization—so much the better. The prodigal sons of France undeceived will remain faithful to the mother country." [34]

On occasion this love of France was expressed in the "spread eagle" style for which contemporary Americans were supposedly noted. During the Vigilante uprising of 1856, a correspondent for the *Herald,* itself an ethnic baiter, attacked the Gallic residents for remaining stubbornly revolutionary. A French newspaper answered with considerable irritation and more than a little condescension for several nationalities. "Though other tongues be not barbarous," wrote the journal, "yet it is difficult for them [the French] to substitute for their own pure, simple and flexible language, the hard and guttural sounds of the North and West." The same response was forthcoming to the charge that the French "would not lose that name to acquire the title of Americans. . . . We know that the Danes, and even some Germans, do not deserve the like charge," wrote *Le Phare,* "but the French esteem nothing higher than this very reproach." [35] And as for revolutions,

Well, and who has made that a crime in them? . . . When France struggles, almost single handed, against the demon of tyranny, for the profit of all, at one time superior to its enemies, at another time yielding to their accumulated forces, does it become the cold inhabitants of the North to throw defiance upon a herculean nation, which has killed more tyrants than other people have offered homage to? France revolutionary, France the pioneer, France the apostle and martyr—you dare to insult her.

> Frozen Northmen, stunted Laps, you would insult the sun that melts your snows and annihilates your icebergs! [36]

The "Frozen Northmen" and "Stunted Laps" resented this nationalism, and it no doubt contributed to the momentary popularity of the American party. Yet the natives did not oppose foreign patriotism per se, just excessive amounts of it. "The occasional devotion of Germans to the old Fatherland does not so fill their hearts that they become insensible to the numberless political and social blessings which they receive in their adopted country," explained the *Annals*. "But the wild glorification of Frenchmen to every thing connected with their beautiful France, is often a neglectful insult to the land that shelters them, and which they would ignore, even although they seek not to become its permanent citizens." [37]

The Americans and French had no monopoly on chauvinism, however. "The foreigners have not demoralized the natives. On the contrary, . . . how is it that the thousands of innocent, simple minded foreigners have changed upon these shores? They were inexperienced, almost helpless creatures," wrote the *German Journal* in a counterblast at Know Nothingism that sounded very much like it. "They had their faults, but they were not criminals; and criminals they have here become. There is a portion of the native population which soon brings the harmless immigrant to be ashamed of his old fashioned European morality, and to consider his sense of duty as folly." Thus it was the natives who had corrupted the "helpless" newcomers; and moreover, according to the *Journal*, all of Europe (which would have included Tzarist Russia and Bourbon Naples) did not contain as much corruption "as one single State of the Union." [38]

Almost every group of which there is any record was capable of this unpleasant ethnic assertiveness. Jews resented comparison to Mormons and Chinese. Negroes described "the Chinaman" as "filthy, immoral and licentious," with a face "expressive of nothing but stupidity," and asserted their own superiority to "three fourths

of the foreign population in the country." And the Chinese went
them one better, arguing that as inhabitants of the "Inner Kingdom" they were superior to the rest of the world.[39]

Accompanying this chauvinism was mutual ignorance which insured reciprocal incomprehensibility. A young bank clerk was appalled at the masculinity of the French women who sold vegetables
in the metropolis and amazed at their queer, Medieval-looking
carts. The "China Boys" were just as stupefied when advised of the
Christian belief in an afterlife. Their amusement at this notion was
only exceeded by the *Alta*'s surprise at their laughter. That paper
was forced into the sad admission that it would take a few years
to teach them "divine truths." [40]

The various groups did not invariably respect each others' customs even when they were acquainted with them. Americans continually tried to pass Sabbath laws despite the popularity of the
"continental Sunday" amongst immigrants. However, those who
pursued their recreation on Sunday were not uniformly thoughtful
of churchgoers. For several Sundays in 1854, the Turnverein, on
their way to their weekly outing, marched past the doors of one
congregation "to the sound of martial music, with drum, fife, and
horn in full blast." This eventually brought an outraged protest
from those who wanted to "have a quiet day in all the seven" to
worship.

Much ethnic discord did not involve Americans at all. The foreigners imported many of their quarrels and often enlivened San
Francisco by them. Irish nationalism found frequent expression
and, on at least one occasion, eventuated in an attempted ransom
kidnapping of a British sea captain. Continental European hatreds
paralleled the insular ones. "The Alsatians are claimed, and sometimes rejected by both Germans and French," observed the *Annals*.
"There does not seem much sympathy between the rival races,
less a great deal than is between either of them and the Americans. The French complain that they are not treated so kindly
by the last as are the Germans." The same discord showed up in
1856 when the editor of a German journal, in defending the partic-

ipation of the Germans and French in the Vigilance Committee, referred to the prominence of the "low Irish" in the opposition Law and Order Party.[41]

Events in Europe such as the Crimean War further fed animosities in San Francisco. When the Panama steamer arrived with the news that Sebastopol had fallen, Allied nationals were overjoyed and their navy made the hills reverberate with salvoes in honor of this victory. The news was premature, however, and it then became the Russians' turn to rejoice; but, lacking a navy, the best they could manage was a thirteen-gun salute fired off an old, rented ice ship. When Sebastopol really surrendered, the French, British, and Piedmontese organized one of the largest celebrations in the city's history. Aside from a brawl between an Englishman and some Russians, the "War" passed without casualties.

Both the intramural antagonisms and the often touching determination to preserve some of the "old ways" found expression in a number of national organizations and practices. The Hebrew Benevolent Society, begun in 1850, was the first of these institutions in the city; and similar Jewish agencies eventually joined it. The Chinese, Germans, Irish, and French got started somewhat later; but by 1856 each had at least one thriving association for the aid of its fellows and sometimes others.[42] These societies provided relief, established hospitals, found employment, supplied transportation, and performed various other good works on a fairly significant scale. The origin of these institutions was urban as well as ethnic, for San Francisco simply did not supply many of the services that its people needed, especially medical ones. The complaint that foreigners were not allowed into the city hospital was not true; but they, along with everybody else, got pretty mediocre care. Sometimes the language barrier further compounded their discomfort, and these deficiencies encouraged the founding of new establishments.

Almost every traveler's account of the Bay City noted the constant contact among nationalities in the streets, yet ethnic neighborhoods appeared. Although not monolithic, the concentrations were sufficient to give certain districts the tone of a particular people. For the most part, these ethnic aggregations were the result of income and conscious choice. Segregation was advanced as a "solution" to the "Chinese problem," but it was not adopted by the city council. In the early days, the French congregated on Commercial Street around the Polka Saloon, a gaming house run by a conational; later, they shared the "Latin Quarter" in North Beach with Italians and Spanish Americans, though the latter had another colony at the Mission Dolores. The Irish were spread out but were most numerous on Market Street around St. Patrick's Church; and the Chinese were also dispersed, though they had a large grouping, "Little China," around the intersection of Sacramento and Dupont and, for a time, settlements of fishermen and launderers at Rincon Point and Washerwoman's Bay. The greatest concentrations of Negroes were in the first and second wards, but they lived in nothing resembling a ghetto.[43]

Most of the groups had some kind of newspaper to express their interests and supply them with news. These sheets were often ephemeral; but for varying periods of time, some kind of paper existed for nearly every race and nationality, with the French *Echo du Pacifique,* established in 1852, the most durable of the foreign journals. Since so few of these newssheets have survived, their exact role in the life of the immigrant is difficult to gauge. The *Echo* and the French column of the *Picayune*—probably the most complete of the remaining foreign language newspapers—undertook activities whose impact was no doubt ambivalent. They reinforced their readers' Frenchness by keeping them posted on happenings both in the homeland and among that nationality in California. Yet they purveyed American news to the Gallic community which was calculated to weave them more intimately into the fabric of their new country rather than to strengthen their bonds to the old.[44]

Both the ethnic theater and school were well suited to this latter task, but neither had a very secure existence. The French Adelphi Theater, started in 1850, and the Chinese playhouse maintained their place in the entertainment world; but German and Spanish theaters failed to gain a firm foothold. The drama of other nationals did not even get started. In education, still less progress was made, with only the Germans and Jews managing to found schools, both affiliated with churches or synagogues.

Churches were more durable and numerous and, therefore, more prominent in defending the immigrants' heritage. In the beginning, the city's Hebrews all worshipped together, but so much ethnic tension appeared in their community that they could not coexist within the same synagogue or benevolent society. By 1856 there were no fewer than four religious congregations, one each for Germans, Poles, Russians, and Anglo-Americans. The Polish synagogue even carried out a purge of its English officers comparable to the Know Nothing efforts against foreign officeholders in the city. The Jews, so often considered a monolithic group by their enemies, did not usually intermarry because the Bavarian Jews looked down upon their Polish brethren. During the early years, many Catholics met in one parish, St. Francis, located in the north end of town. To cope with the national variety of Catholicism, the clergy conducted services in various languages at different hours. However, by 1856 the Irish were worshipping at St. Patrick's and the French at Notre Dame des Victoires. The first German Protestant church did not appear until 1856, by which time it could take its place alongside the Welsh Presbyterian Church, which had peacefully seceded in 1852 from First Presbyterian in order to enjoy services in its own language and according to its own national usage.[45] And, of course, the Chinese established their own houses of worship.

Though more important than theaters and schools, national churches in San Francisco did not necessarily play the most crucial role among immigrant institutions.[46] The Jews founded their synagogues and benevolent societies almost simultaneously in 1850; but other aliens were not so zealous in transplanting their faith. Germans and French, possibly the two largest ethnic units, did not establish religious organizations until 1856, after associations of almost every other kind had been founded. Mutual aid, pleasure, culture, and even lager beer were supplied first. Other groups, including the large English one, did not even bother to found a church of their own.

Ethnic pastimes paralleled other activities. The Germans were the best organized, with the German Club, the San Francisco Verein, and the Turnverein, the latter being the most active recreation alliance in the city. It held frequent celebrations and outings, and its Mai Fest was an especially important event for foreigner and American alike. The St. Andrews Society of the Scotch performed many similar services. Fire companies doubled as social groups, with the immigrant community represented by the Lafayette Hook and Ladder Company. The French and Hebrews had their own Masonic Lodges, and the Sons of the Emerald Isle and the Hibernian Society provided a similar outlet for the Irish. Many of the other pleasures were more informal, but they still were carried out on an ethnic basis. For example, the Verandah and Schuppert's saloons were German haunts and the Polka, French.

What was true of play was also true of work. As Russailh indicated, the French often tended to "do business only with each other." The Italians, according to one of their historians, would also "invariably" trade with one another because of the convenience of language and because they preferred dealing with their countrymen. The panic of 1855 revealed the same custom even more clearly. At the House of B. Davidson, agent for the Rothschilds, there was a long line of angry depositors, just like those at the other Montgomery Street banks. Yet at Davidson's, the men in the column expressed their anger in foreign tongues rather than in English.[47] With the Chinese the practice of trading with one's own kind was even more pronounced.

The commemoration of some national holiday was one of the most important activities of the various ethnic organizations. What the Mai Fest was to the Germans, St. Patrick's Day and St. Andrew's Day were to the Irish and Scotch. The Swiss celebrated

both the independence of Switzerland and, as Genevans, the "esca-
lade"—which marked the failure of the Duke of Savoy to scale the
walls of that city in 1602. Polish nationals gathered to toast the
"expulsion of the Russian Grand Duke Constantine and his army
from Warsaw."⁴⁸ On occasion, too, the observances were sad, as
when the British solemnly marched the streets of San Francisco in
a last tribute to the Duke of Wellington or when the Belgians did
the same for their deceased queen.⁴⁹

The American attitude toward these alien manifestations in their
midst was generally friendly.⁵⁰ Moreover, the same respect was
forthcoming for any reasonable exhibition of foreign culture. About
the only unwelcome ethnic institution established by Europeans
was a proposed repatriation society. When the sponsors of Société
Mutuelle de Répatriement claimed that it was impossible for
Frenchmen to "live happy at a distance from or without the hope
of returning to their country," the *Bulletin* entered a strong dissent. "As Californians, we do not like the idea of losing our French
population," protested that paper.

> We believe that many excellent traits have descended to the
> American character from the Huguenots. We have no objec-
> tion to a person loving his native land; we recur to the scenes of
> our own childhood with the most heartfelt emotion; but we
> brought our "penates," our household gods, with us, and have
> established them in a new home. . . . So far as the benevolent
> purposes of the new Sociétié Mutuelle de Répatriement is [*sic*]
> concerned, we wish it all success; but so far as it fosters and
> encourages the purposes above referred to, we sincerely hope it
> may fail entirely. . . . Let them [the French] live their lives
> under our banner; let their bones repose under our sod, and let
> their names go down to posterity with those of the pioneers who
> have founded and cherished the nationality of California.⁵¹

The major exception to American tolerance and even support
for ethnic life and practices came in regard to the Chinese. This
group was at the same time the most exotic, most transient, least

free, most brutalized, and most clannish nationality in San Francisco. This combination of qualities insured Caucasian resentment of them.

The "Celestials," as they were called, came directly from the Pearl River Delta of China.[52] The early immigrants and significant numbers thereafter were merchants. Though not held in high esteem in the Confucian scheme of values, these men dominated the San Francisco Chinese community and were generally respected by Americans.[53] However, the mass of Orientals were different. Nearly all were men, the few women usually being prostitutes and semi-slaves at that. Most sought a small fortune that would enable them to return home to a life of ease and honor, and none had the slightest interest in assimilation. As Gunther Barth puts it, until the '70's they were "sojourners" rather than immigrants. The Chinese also differed from other aliens in that they were not free; most were indebted to their merchant conationals in the Bay City for their ticket to the "Golden Hill," as they called California. Until their obligation was paid, they remained under the supervision of this group.

A number of organizations, generally based on a home region within the Pearl River Delta, exercised control. The merchant guilds, which totaled about five by the end of the period, were the principal Chinese associations; but secret terrorist societies dominated a part of the community. Whether in San Francisco or Chinese Camp, these Bay City alliances governed the Chinese labor force and almost everything else in the state from the Middle Kingdom. The dominance was nearly complete and almost entirely extralegal. Kinship and regional loyalty bound the "Celestials" together; but when these did not suffice, force and intimidation did.

Whatever the case may have been legally, in fact the Chinese demanded and exercised a kind of autonomy.[54] In their relations with the rest of the community, the Asians were dealt with under American law; but among themselves, they settled matters without resort to the legal system. Several attempts were made to bring Chinatown within judicial purview; but these invariably failed, as the terrified Orientals refused to cooperate for fear of reprisals.[55]

The exotic area around Dupont and Stockton was the center of what Barth calls "Chinese California," more so even than San Francisco was the center of "American California." In addition, it was the most successful attempt among foreign groups to duplicate the cultural forms of their homeland. Chinatown literally became a bit of the Pearl River Delta, with gambling halls, opium dens, restaurants, temples, theaters, brothels, and lodgings. According to Barth, this district functioned as a safety valve, providing an environment similar to the home that all longed for. After a night in Chinatown, the immigrant could again face up to the unremitting and often unrewarding toil that was his lot in the Golden State.

American reaction to this fragment of the Pearl River Delta varied. There seems to be little doubt, however, that the Chinese were considered the lowest order in the city. "The truth is evident," wrote the *Chronicle,* "Americans generally in California, look upon the Negro as a superior race, as they appear here to the Celestials." [56] Nevertheless, there was a good deal of ambiguity in Caucasian attitudes.

Initially, these Asians were welcomed; but around 1852 hostile opinion began to crystallize. The merchants' control of the mass of Chinese, which made them something close to slaves, was especially objectionable. Too, the rest of the community found Chinatown's filth, disease, opium dens, vice, fire hazard, and crowding to be obnoxious. In addition, Chinese laborers came into competition with whites in at least one sphere, holding nearly a complete monopoly on laundering, a rivalry that caused some bitterness. The violence that accompanied Chinese quarrels, the large influx of "Celestials," their unwillingness to be governed among themselves by American law, their practice of trading mostly with each other, and their extreme transiency all added further irritations. Teasing, bullying, and humiliation by town toughs and even little children soon followed dislike. On several occasions, however, the courts sent someone to the station house for as much as ninety days for this brutality; and despite the general prejudice, the press and others opposed maltreatment.[57] Yet the image of the industrious, harmless, law-abiding, cooperative Chinese who took care of his "own" and whose presence was needed to develop the state economically was not enough to overcome the stereotype created by Chinatown.

Neither the friends nor the foes of the Asians accomplished much. A Protestant mission was established which did a lot to introduce an exotic culture to the white inhabitants of San Francisco but did not make much headway with the Orientals. Nor were the efforts at "reform" very successful. People talked of segregating the Chinese outside of town, of "cleaning up" the district, of bringing the area under the control of American law, and of restricting immigration, but without result. The closest anyone came to cleansing Chinatown was when the fire companies, by way of nasty but petty harassment, washed down its tenements. Chinatown remained a despised, quasi-autonomous, exotic district in the midst of the city.

American organizations did not play as important a role as the immigrant ones, nor were they as highly visible. They existed nevertheless and were in many respects strikingly similar to the foreigners' associations and customs. With the Americans, however, there were both racial and former residence divisions.[58]

In fact, the first resource the newcomer from the "States" had to draw upon in this new environment was his credit in the old. The editor of a French-language column of a local paper noted that he was constantly sought out by his newly arrived countrymen for advice and tips. The natives, too, usually came bearing letters of introduction or verbal messages to some person already established, just as European immigrants were directed to the address of one of their relatives or local villagers. Letter or no, it was customary to seek out people from familiar places. A young resident noted in his diary that the first thing his company did when a Boston ship came into the harbor was to send over several boats to see if it carried "any Rhode Island boys." [59]

Although San Francisco was only a small place, old acquaintances turned up with remarkable frequency. Argonaut R. R. Taylor met so many Eastern friends that he was moved to write that "the only question now is who is *not* here." [60] This experience was common enough, especially in the early days, to give the city a very definite "old home week" quality. If the alien, no matter how obscure his country, could always find someone who could speak his tongue, so the American immigrant could always meet someone who spoke English with an accent he knew.

The longing for familiar faces found expression in distinct native residential "hives" just as it did among foreigners. "I lodge . . . with a number of other Boston people," wrote a New Englander in 1850. "Holden and Reddington of E. Boston live next door so that we have a regular Massachusetts neighborhood." "The Rochester Lodging house is doing well," a former citizen of the "Flour City" noted. "It is the regular Rochester Headquarters and there is [*sic*] from 10 to 15 Rochester men here all the while. So that I hear from every Mail from Rochester . . . and Lewis Kenyon takes two Rochester papers which he brings right here so that I have the general news." Sometimes the group grew beyond the size of a boardinghouse, which collected and disseminated information about "home" while housing the homesick. Press employee William Herrick, formerly of New England, remembered that in 1853 "Happy Valley was a region in the neighborhood of Second and Howard Sts., most/ly/ dwelling houses, inhabited chiefly by New England people." Nearby Rincon Hill, with its "families of sea captains and shipping merchants," had a "flavor of Nantucket and Martha's Vineyard," remembered a resident. "On Green and Vallejo Streets above Kearney, were the homes of many of the Southern families." [61] Thus, like the mountain people from Appalachia of a later day, the American migrants to San Francisco tended to stick together.

The natives also had their own peculiar societies based on former residences. From 1850 on, there was a Knickerbocker Society and a New England Society, thus providing "ethnic" organizations for the representatives of the two largest American groups in the population. Sometimes the basis of the alliances was urban rather than state or regional. Men from particular Eastern cities usually staffed the various fire companies. Empire Engine Company was of New York origin; Monumental was from Baltimore; Howard, from Boston. In 1850 "the shore-ship THOMAS BENNET . . . was headquarters for the Baltimore boys"; and in the office of W. D. M. Howard, "and about its entrance, the old pioneers used to congregate." [62]

Just as immigrant associations kept up the old ways, so did the native. The New England Society very early began celebrating the landing of the Pilgrims at Plymouth Rock and observing Thanksgiving. Indeed, this group fought to make the latter a recognized state holiday, which it was from 1849 on. Beyond that, the descendants of the Puritans boasted about their role in founding the public school system, Sunday schools, and democracy in America, urged the foundation of colleges and measures of moral purification to attract immigrants from east of the Hudson River, and in general praised the virtues of what they called the "Fatherland." "Sons and daughters of New England! . . . *Preserve your birth-right*," exhorted T. D. Hunt. "No higher ambition could urge us to noble deeds, than . . . to make CALIFORNIA THE MASSACHUSETTS OF THE PACIFIC." [63] The *Pacific*, organ of the Congregational and Presbyterian churches, was the "ethnic" paper which disseminated these sentiments and carried news and stories of New England doings at home and in California.

New Yorkers commemorated St. Nicholas Day; and they, too, tried to perpetuate their own peculiar customs. "Let us plant in this virgin and fruitful soil the germs of those good old Knickerbocker principles and virtues," resolved the Knickerbocker Society, "whose growth and development will produce so abundant a harvest, and add so greatly to the dignity, glory and permanent prosperity of our State." [64]

Even the statuary of distant cities revealed the loyalty of San Franciscans to their former homes. In 1850 residents from Baltimore combined to raise money for a statue commemorating two Baltimoreans who fell in battle in the War of 1812. They did so in language intelligible to any immigrant banquet. "Desirous of promoting this object as well as to show, though absent in far off climes, we cherish for our native city a patriot's love, and a feeling of pride to know she is deservedly styled the Monumental city we tender the amount of five dollars each," resolved the "uprooted" Marylanders.[65]

Death and tragedy occasioned banding together, too. Vermont had no Iron Duke to mourn; but when local merchant Bezar Simmons passed away, the Vermonters were out in full force, marching the streets in honor of his memory. Even such an unlikely place as Chenango County, New York, had enough citizens to pay similar respects to one of their deceased brothers. And during the New Orleans epidemic of 1853, San Franciscans from that place raised a relief fund for their old home in the same fashion as French and German residents were to do later during the Franco-Prussian War.[66]

"Society" revealed the same pattern. Social lion John McCrackan observed in 1853 that there was "already a set formed almost exclusively of Southern people." He feared that this clannishness would divide San Francisco into Northern and Southern "circles." "I dont think they will allow politic or sectional feelings to influence them, still the Southern and Western people are queer and will more readily assimilate than those from the East." [67]

Finally, affairs of both church and state reflected the divisions amongst the natives. The Southerners, like the Bavarian Jews, French Catholics, and Welsh Presbyterians, set up their own church in 1855; and the calling of the Reverend Dr. Scott to Calvary Presbyterian Church had sectional overtones. So did First Congregational, which was known as "the New England Church." [68] Politics witnessed the same thing. Former New Yorkers, for example, originally founded one wing of the Democratic party.[69]

Negroes were not a group based upon their former homes, nor were they residentially segregated; but they had their own separate ethnic institutions and customs. There were two Negro churches, one Masonic Lodge, and a cultural and literary association called

the San Francisco Atheneum. Blacks also had their day of solemni-
ties, the "anniversary of the final abolition of slavery in the British
West Indies Colonies." [70]

For Negroes, separate development was not entirely a matter of
free choice. Prejudice was neither total nor as bad as in the South,
but it was nevertheless considerable. Many people did not even
want Negroes to come into California, and no one favored assimilation. That meant discrimination, though the matter is often poorly
documented. John Henry Brown noted that before the Gold Rush,
a colored man could get a drink in his tavern, provided he did not
come too often; but in another tippling house, the mere request led
to a beating. Ultimately, Negroes gained their own institutions of
this kind or shared them with other outcasts. The city provided
separate schools, and blacks had to sit in the balcony of the Jenny
Lind Theater and even inspect the Vigilante quarters on a segregated basis. In 1856 a white crowd forcibly prevented a black
grandmother from reclaiming her runaway half-white granddaugh-
ter because they could not believe the maternal relationship. Other
evidences of "amalgamation" were equally discouraged, but they
continued to appear.[71] Spanish Americans and Negroes mixed most
frequently, though others did, too.

From time to time racial violence occurred, although there is
no record of any lynching. In 1850 a mob tried to eject a number
of Negro residents from their homes near Clark's Point because
they were thought to be too noisy. The press did not note whether
the black people offered any resistance on this occasion, but they
did not always respond passively to hostility.[72]

Native prejudice against blacks is much more easily documented because very little immigrant source material has survived. Yet there is enough foreign evidence extant to indicate
that the use of the term "Anglo-American racism" implies a
monopoly on racial bigotry that did not exist. "Tis but a few
months since a negro was stabbed in the streets of San Francisco,"
said a delegate to the convention of blacks in 1855. "The murderer
was a Spanish man," and "on the day of his trial his counsel

ridiculed the idea of his being punished, and said he had 'only killed a nigger.'" "The Spanish race" in America had continually "adulterated its purity by constantly, and without the lest repugnance or prudence, mixing with races of inferior blood, Indian or black," noted a French consul in 1856. "By these regrettable crossings they are hardly distinguishable in so many localities today from the Indian and black races, and are scarcely superior to them either in manners, industry or intelligence." A similar, though not so blatant, statement appeared in 1854 after a physical encounter at the local auction house of Newhall, Gregory, and Claghorn. A large group of merchants, "chiefly, if not altogether, of Jewish firms," resolved "that whereas one of our fellow citizens has been grossly outraged by some of the members of the above firm, in aiding and abetting their negro servant in abusing and insulting one of our citizens," they were determined to boycott the firm and urged others to do so as well.[73]

Thus it is clear that San Franciscans shared the general white American prejudice against Negroes. Yet the hostility was always ambiguous, and respect and support coexisted with antipathy. In 1856, when someone tried to get up a fuss because Negro educators from San Francisco had attended a school convention, the *Chronicle* poked fun at the troublemakers. The local black school was segregated, but a white school board had recommended its establishment in the first place at a time when it was illegal in the South to teach slaves to read and when "proposals to educate Negroes invariably aroused bitter controversy" even in the North; and in 1856 a Caucasian Grand Jury urged the founding of a second institution of learning to accommodate the growing black population. Education was the second most crucial question before the Colored Citizens Convention of 1855 (see below); and as one delegate said, "In one locality only in the State—San Francisco—a school is established for colored children, which is sustained by the liberality of that city's government."[74]

The foremost Negro grievance was that they could not testify on their own behalf in court cases involving whites. The *Herald* supported this exclusion; but by 1857 the black drive against this law had picked up white allies—the *Call*, the *Alta*, the *Pacific*, prominent Republican Frank Pixley, and the Grand Jury —due to sympathy or self-interest. Sometimes the ban was not rigidly enforced. On one occasion, a man who was supposedly one-eighth black gave evidence when he assured the court that he had never seen his father. In 1854, using equally curious reasoning, the bench allowed a native of Goa to testify when it ruled that "the word black was intended to apply only to the negro race, and not to Asiatics or other white men who might happen to be black." [75]

San Franciscans feared abolitionism because it might rend the city as it had the Eastern states, but they encouraged other Negro activities. The white press praised every indication of church building or the establishment of institutions such as the Atheneum as it did individual blacks themselves. The same papers which thought nothing of using the word "nigger" could also argue that "the great majority of the Negro people in San Francisco are industrious and engaged in those manual and mechanical labors, which have a strong influence to preserve the hopes of self-reliance, and morality of the laborer." [76]

None of these civilities made the metropolis a utopia for Negroes, but urban life did provide them important leverage. San Francisco Negro residents dominated "Black California" just as Bay City Orientals did "Chinese California." San Francisco was the main center of religious activity in the state, and the churches there supplied much of the leadership among Negroes. San Franciscans were overwhelmingly dominant in the fight against the testimony ban. They organized a pressure group, the Franchise League, which spearheaded the drive against this prohibition; they dominated the state-wide black conventions of 1855 and 1856 which were called to agitate the question; and they launched the only black newspaper in California, the *Mirror of the Times*, to promote this end and other racial interests.

Economic success and point of origin explain this San Francisco black leadership. Rudolph Lapp has noted that California Negroes had more wealth than their brothers elsewhere in the union. Indeed, their ability to "accumulate material goods in spite of handicaps . . . lay behind the testimony controversy, since the rights they sought were valued as a means to protect their wealth." Because San Francisco was so overwhelmingly preeminent in this as in other black endeavors, it is realistic to assume that Bay City blacks were wealthier than their brothers in other parts of the state. The Negroes of the Golden Gate City were from Northern cities rather than from the Southern countryside as were the blacks in the interior, and this familiarity with city life plus the greater opportunities that existed there for blacks as well as whites probably explains the importance of San Francisco Negroes.[77]

Ironically, these urban advantages often passed unnoticed. The Committee on Agriculture and Mines at the remarkable Colored Citizens Convention of 1855 resolved that "facts are abundant, going to prove that agriculture, as a pursuit, is the road to wealth, honor and independence; the time has come when we must become owners and cultivators of the land." [78] The facts of black life in California belied this claim, but the agrarian myth could still obscure the opportunities of urbanism.

If these American and foreign ethnic institutions expressed a longing for separation, then it seems clear that the melting pot was considerably more effective in the beginning, especially for Europeans. As time passed, each segment of the population received reinforcements and set about establishing their own clubs, schools, churches, benevolent societies, and national observances. Originally, nearly all intended to make their fortunes and go "home"; but as the "fatal" taste for California life grew, more and more decided to become immigrants instead of "sojourners." But as this transformation progressed, they tended to congregate as New Englanders, Baltimoreans, Frenchmen,

Bavarian Jews, Germans, and Southerners. It is ironic that at
the very time their attachment to their new home grew, so did
the outward manifestations of loyalty to their old. Yet the old
ways gave the uprooted the comfort, stability, and continuity
necessary to face the uncertainties and novelties of city living.
Ethnic life was really a vehicle to ease the transition from one
culture to another.[79]

It seems fair to claim that San Franciscans lived two lives, or
even several. What took place thereafter was a battle between
present and former homes. In the short run, urbanization tended
to preserve diversity by concentrating large numbers of similar
groups within a small area, thus providing a base—a sufficient
market—for group life. But in the long run, the city also provided
the many common currents necessary to erode the loyalty to their
former "homes." European and other ethnic and subethnic groups
were born of long cultural processes which produced a shared
language, folklore, mythology, poetry, and history. Yet their
presence in San Francisco cut the foreigners off from their former
ethnic experience and enmeshed them in a new one. However
strongly the traditionalists may have deplored the fact, the old
group identities became increasingly anachronistic and irrelevant.
The new focus of their lives was San Francisco and no amount
of hankering after the past could repel its demands. Urban contacts were too frequent, urban complexities, too numerous, and
urban instability, too profound to allow any but the most tenacious and rejected—the Chinese—to avoid an increasing participation in the common life of the metropolis. The narrow streets
jumbled people up together; business, pleasure, educational, and
ceremonial life multiplied their contacts; decentralization repeatedly uprooted them residentially; and the growing use of
English gradually wiped out the main European criterion of nationality.[80]

What stands out above all in San Francisco's ethnic experience is its complexity; and any attempt to capture the essence
of group life in simple labels and phrases like "nativism," "alien-

ation," "filiopiety," or "Anglo-Saxon racism" is doomed to failure. There was an immigrant-native division within the city. All the foreigners were less familiar with American culture and all the natives were more accustomed to it. Americans obviously considered themselves a part of a distinct group, and so did immigrants. Yet in many respects, this immigrant-native dichotomy obscures more than it reveals.

Both groups were internally fragmented. Natives were often as much Baltimoreans as they were Americans; and Frenchmen and Polish Jews obviously identified more with their own cliques —and sometimes subcliques—than with other immigrants. Moreover, the tensions and chauvinism that in part produced these alliances radiated in all directions. The French may have thought that Americans were savages, but they were "alienated" enough from others to refuse to worship with their fellow immigrant Catholics. What is more, loneliness was common to all. Americans understood fully as well as Europeans what it meant to be "uprooted"; and they, like their foreign counterparts, instinctively grasped for whatever was familiar. In short, the ethnic experience of San Francisco revealed a common humanity as much as it did the differences between foreigner and native.

Government in San Francisco

The problems of governing an instant city were staggering. When rapid urbanization overwhelmed the tiny hamlet, it had hardly any government at all. No tradition of municipal affairs guided the city fathers; almost no political structure eased the pain of fearfully fast growth; and even fewer civic facilities existed. Streets, wharves, hospitals, city halls, administrators, charters, ordinances, firehouses, and schools had to be conjured up overnight in the midst of seemingly utter chaos. What had taken other cities years to collect San Francisco created almost instantaneously. In addition, the metropolis had to achieve these things in spite of the massive indifference of its gold-crazed, transient citizens, most of whom did not wish to cooperate or to be taxed and agreed with such time-worn phrases as "the world is too much governed" and "that government is best which governs least." Given these physical and attitudinal handicaps, government compiled a mediocre record.

The form of government remained constant for most of the period, but the constitutional basis was altered. Before 1850 a body of tradition (Spanish and Mexican) plus the instructions of the United States military governors comprised the legal framework; when the Yankees occupied the state, they decided to retain local law until after the conflict. The changeover to

American law occurred between the drafting of the first state constitution in 1849 and the achievement of statehood in 1850.

On April 15, 1850, the city received its initial charter; and three new ones followed before 1856. The first granted considerable authority—the power to build streets, wharves, hospitals, market houses, waterworks, and workhouses; to exercise the right of eminent domain; and to establish a police force and fire department and appoint other necessary officers. The government could also tax, spend, and borrow; hold, acquire, and sell property; and even regulate certain economic activities. Furthermore, the charter contained an omnibus clause allowing the mayor and common council the "power within the city . . . to make by-laws and ordinances not repugnant to the Constitution and laws of the United States or of this state." [1]

After 1850 the fundamental law evolved in contradictory directions. On the one hand, it gave the municipality wider authority, an expansion that came about partly because its original prerogatives, especially in regard to streets, were challenged in the courts and, therefore, had to be buttressed and clarified. In addition, new grants implied in the omnibus clause were made explicit. The corporation could establish schools and a House of Refuge, fix safety regulations for the erection of buildings, prohibit wooden structures, and enclose and improve public grounds. The 1851 charter even contained a kind of "home rule" referendum provision which allowed basic amendments to be made by a three-fourths vote of the aldermen and approval by the people. Moreover, this procedure did not require legislative confirmation.[2] On the other hand, the city's competence was curtailed in different ways. For example, fiscal extravagance led to spending limitations. These stipulations did not come from state meddling in municipal affairs, for local citizens drafted charters and the financial restrictions were popular with the home constituency. Yet, until 1855 administrations ignored debt restraints and avoided other provisions as well.

The charters of 1855 and 1856 contained strong economy

clauses including penal and personal liability sections for waste-
ful officials. Beginning in 1855, spending plummeted from a decade high of $2,646,190 in 1854–55 to $856,120 in 1855–56. By
1856–57 the corporation could disburse only $40,000 for the indi-
gent sick and $8,000 for the fire department. It could impose a tax of
$.35 per hundred dollars for schools and only $1.25 beyond that for
all purposes and could, in fact, spend only for such things and in
such amounts as the fundamental law allowed. These restrictions
rendered the municipality less able to provide the services authorized by expanded legal clauses in its charter.

However, the document did not enlarge all of these provisions.
It either reduced or removed several. The 1856 charter eliminated
the omnibus legislative power and made absolute the antidebt
provision. The common council could no longer sell land or
lease public property for more than five years; it could erect
buildings but could not buy land. In general, the government
could wield only those powers minutely prescribed by the charter.
Hence the collection of "prohibitions" clearly offset increased responsibility.

San Francisco thus inched toward government by charter.[3]
The Consolidation Act of 1856 was clearly a self-denying ordinance with slight overtones of a penal code. After 1856 the
metropolis tried to get back the lost privileges, but in that year
the people preferred a legal straitjacket to involvement in the
affairs of state.

The form of government established under the charters reflected that already in existence. When the Americans arrived in
1846, the legal arm of Yerba Buena was the alcalde, who had
wide judicial and executive powers. Upon landing, the military
appointed naval officer Washington A. Bartlett to this office; and
later in the year he won the office by election. In the summer of
1847, the military governor named a legislative body to aid Bartlett's successor; and in the fall another referendum chose a council by popular vote, thus at least half way supplanting the Mexican
system with the American. The Spanish titles of alcalde and

ayuntamiento continued in use with the former remaining as executive and judiciary with power to grant land; the latter exercised legislative authority and appropriated money. In August 1849, more Mexican elements (and more confusion) accrued in the form of prefect and judge of the first instance.

The 1850 charter completed the transition to the American system by establishing a mayor and council. It replaced the unicameral legislature of 1847–50 with a bicameral one, though the number was again reduced to one in 1856. The year 1849 had seen the enlargement of the executive by the election of heads of departments of streets, police, and finance. Like the national system, San Francisco's provided for only partial separation of powers. The mayor participated in the legislative process by virtue of his veto; and the aldermen had a hand in executive matters by their right to appoint administrative officers, such as policemen, and by their authority to create new offices, distribute funds, and impeach. When it came to a direct confrontation, the council had more legal power; but a mayoral veto backed by an aroused public opinion remained a formidable deterrent.

The judiciary and executive began to separate in 1849 when a judge of the first instance took over the alcalde's civil cases involving sums over $100 and in 1850 when the Recorder's Court, Justice of the Peace courts, and the County Court of Sessions jointly assumed his criminal jurisdiction. In the same year, the Justice of the Peace courts and the Superior Court replaced the Court of First Instance. There were unsuccessful attempts to abolish the Superior Court (mostly by defeated parties), but little change occurred in the system. From 1850 through 1856, San Francisco County shared the responsibility for governing, often supplementing and duplicating the efforts of the city and providing for roads outside the corporation limits, a prison, and a hospital.

With the exception of Bartlett and the first council, all the city and county officials were elected legally by white males twenty-one or over who were citizens and residents (and illegally by many who were neither). Elections took place at least once a year and frequently more often. State, national, and local contests were sometimes staggered so that campaigning took place annually; but other circumstances produced further elections. In 1848–49, for example, several disputed canvasses required an encore; and a mistake in the 1851 charter led to two municipal races.

Though previewed in 1851 and 1855, the major governmental innovation occurred in 1856. The Consolidation Act, one of the first in the nation, merged the city and county, mainly for reasons of economy. To a certain extent this merely extended the existing arrangement, since the two legislatures already intertwined, being made up predominantly of aldermen. In the 1856 act a single, twelve-man Board of Supervisors replaced the one county and two city bodies. In addition, the executive and judiciary joined, thus eliminating further overlapping offices such as tax collectors, assessors, and surveyors.[4]

The 1856 reform also divided San Francisco County, greatly extending the city and drastically reducing the county. Heretofore, on the north and east the metropolis had the same boundary as the county, which was an imaginary line in the bay. The 1851 charter extended the southern and western limits to two and one half and two miles respectively from the city center, and the charter of 1855 kept them there. In the Consolidation Act, the county and city lines came to rest in the same place (the present location); and the remainder of the territory became San Mateo County.

This truncation had the support of both urban and rural districts. Since many parts of the area lacked regular rapid transportation facilities, a trip to the county seat sometimes took two days for traveling and one for business. Outlying residents resented paying the same tax rate as the municipality, since they did not receive equal services. Nor did they approve of San Francisco's monopoly on state representatives and senators. The "Southerners'" demands met little opposition in the metropolis. The press argued that it would be too costly to extend services to such a large district and agreed that the county should be divided.[5]

It is not unusual for American cities to limit their own expansion to avoid the expense of providing additional services. Moreover, for the 1850's, the decision was not at all irrational. The city had enough room to expand, and even its most ardent boosters did not foresee that it would outgrow its new corporation line. In the long run, however, the self-denying action of 1856 contributed to the "Balkanization" of San Francisco Peninsula and thereby added significantly to the problems of governing.

Yet for the time being, consolidation had the opposite effect. Putting the city frontier so far in advance of settlement established a "reservation." Within this preserve, independent suburbs could not arise to block the metropolis's growth or force it into expensive and vexatious annexation battles. In short, in facing the perennial planning dilemma of reconciling the demands of the present and future, San Francisco limited its right to expand in the future by making this right more secure for the present.[6]

With one exception, therefore, expansion conflicts did not occur; but this lone struggle demonstrated the value of the Consolidation Act. Initially more important than Yerba Buena, in 1839 the "center of local government," the Mission Dolores was a separate settlement.[7] In 1850, while the state legislature designed the first San Francisco charter, the residents of the mission petitioned to be excluded from the city limits. They wanted their own administration so that they could improve transportation facilities on Mission Creek and into the interior of the peninsula. In addition, their request amounted to an attempt to zone that part of the county for farming and to protect the rights of those who claimed their land under preemption laws instead of under Mexican grants. Nature had set that area apart for agriculture, it was argued, and the scheme to include it within the corporation was the impudent effort of real estate developers to defy this geographic imperative. Fortunately, the charter of 1850 included most lands contiguous to the mission and that of

1851, the rest. Thus, before more local vested interests could grow up to block the path of urban development, the area of the present city was put off limits to suburbs.[8]

The other significant modification of the structure of government was the introduction of the autonomous agency—a familiar panacea of later urban reformers. The Funded Debt Commission grew out of financial policies that by 1851 had nearly bankrupted San Francisco and was given complete power to handle the resulting indebtedness, bypassing the council entirely. It had authority to care for, sell, or rent most city property, including land, wharves, and buildings; and it handled the payment of interest on the municipality's obligations. Similar, but less independent, agencies came in the wake of the county and new city debts run up by 1855.

Popular attitudes and habits largely determined how the structure of government worked in practice. The predominant feeling about government was probably one of dislike and suspicion. Few eagerly volunteered to serve the people or to exercise civic virtue. Most had come to get rich; and unless government contributed to that end, they ignored it, even when its actions were potentially crucial.

The ideal of nonpublic service reinforced the habit of nonparticipation. Popular sentiment held that government needed good men; but contradictorily, municipal service did not receive the public recognition that would attract them. Furthermore, any political ambition was positively suspect, and professional politicians were anathema. With local government held in contempt by so many, its decisions were never considered sacrosanct; therefore, noncooperation and outright obstruction abounded. Finally, the public tolerated considerable corruption. These attitudes obviously discouraged the development of the civic consciousness that so many paid lip service to.

A good part of the time, therefore, the contents of the public till were under siege by those demanding ordinary services, such as street building and fire prevention, and others not necessarily governmental. For example, charitable organizations like the Protestant and Catholic orphan asylums sought subsidies from the town and state. Other parties followed their lead, urging a public grant for a savings bank to attract workingmen to San Francisco, a gift to the Mechanics Institute for the same purpose, a bulkhead around the waterfront to provide work for the unemployed, subsidies to the San Francisco dispensary, and monies to the volunteer military companies because they supposedly protected the Republic.[9] In addition, people begging for contracts and other plums abounded.

To pay for such projects, the city and county had three main sources of revenue: the sale of real estate; taxes, including licenses on occupations, real and personal levies, and street assessments; and the printing press. However derived, finances provided most of the abuses and headaches of government.

The dispensation of land afforded a large supply of funds, but nothing else that the corporation touched yielded as much frustration. Popular insistence led to the rapid alienation of the public domain; yet that action induced squatting, violence, and court cases without end. Under Mexican law the municipality could dispose of all its land except beach and water lots. General Kearny, the American military governor, soon granted this latter privilege to the town so that it could finance port facilities with the proceeds. This sale took place in 1847, and several others followed before the Gold Rush. Disputes over titles had occurred before this, but until 1848 there seemed to be little doubt of the city's authority to hold and to dispose of realty. However, soon after the Gold Rush, those rights were questioned. The majority of old residents believed that San Francisco owned the usual amount of land granted to Mexican pueblos; therefore, the possession of real estate could come only through purchase. Yet a minority of the settlers argued that there had been no pueblo and that, therefore, the city territory was open to preemption.[10] According to their reasoning, no legal dispensation of the public domain had occurred since no one had the authority to carry out the operation. This argument proceeded throughout the period while both sides behaved as if the issue had already been settled. Squatters descended en masse upon unoccupied or undefended lots while purchasers carried on a lively traffic in real estate and pressured the corporation to sell even more of its holdings.

The preemptionists suffered more condemnation from contemporaries, but considerable chicanery also attended the course of their opponents. Henry Haight, future partner in the banking house of Page, Bacon and Company as well as eventual governor, described the situation to his father.

> Another class of titles are private grants from the Alcaldes under the military regime subsequent to the conquest of the country. These grants were made many of them to the Alcalde himself. The grantee being a man of straw. They were made indiscriminately, often, always in fact, for a trifle and to persons already large holders of real estate. The validity of these grants where no previous grant had been made will we suppose be confirmed notwithstanding the frauds and corruption by which they were obtained.[11]

Mexican law limited the number of lots any one person could buy and required certain improvements upon the land. The American city council repealed the latter requirement, and speculators circumvented the purchase limit by employing "men of straw" to buy property on their behalf. As late as the great sale of public slips in December 1853, "front men" still plied their trade.

To make matters worse, in 1849 G. Q. Colton was appointed justice of the peace; and he claimed the right under Mexican law to distribute property. This "official" gave out plots (many of which had already been sold) at a very nominal sum and then absconded to the East with the money. However, the Colton Grants remained in San Francisco, often in blank form and ready to be filled out by their owners and distributed to potential allies. In fact, according to lawyer John McCrackan, "the fact of every lawyer in town being a grantee, and consequently interested in having them sustained" considerably enhanced the chances of the Colton lands.[12]

As if all of this were not scandalous enough, the state also claimed a share of the San Francisco land pie. Supposedly, it had the legal right to relinquish property to the city, getting a large percentage in return. Matters stood this way when the contest over titles reached the courts.

The squatters won the first round in November 1850. In the case of *Fourgeaud* v. *Chapman,* Superior Court judge David O. Shattuck ruled that under Mexican law alcaldes could not grant beach and water lots because these could not be owned by private parties. Therefore, Governor Kearny did not have the power to authorize the sale of these lands. On January 18, 1851, the press reported an even greater squatter victory in the case of *Selim E. Woodworth* v. *William Fulton and David Hersch.* The State Supreme Court ruled Woodworth's title invalid, stating that American alcaldes and town councils had no power to grant any land, not just beach and water lots.[13] As most owners had received their realty since the "conquest," these decisions rendered worthless nearly every deed in the city.

Both sides redoubled their efforts. The squatters stepped up their occupations, while the holders of municipal titles, beleaguered on their own lots, simultaneously laid siege to the legislature. It was hoped that if the state relinquished its "rights" to San Francisco lands, the lobbyist's city titles would be that much stronger. These "Leavenworth grantees" established a command post at San José, the "Water Lot Rancho," where they wined and dined the representatives of the people. Though charges of bribery were denied, $75,000 was spent on the operation; and if this did not go for graft, then it is eloquent testimony to the lawmakers' appetites. In any case, the First Water Lot Bill relinquished for one hundred years (later permanently) the state's interest in return for 25 per cent of the sale price.

Then came the usual complication. The Colton grantees also took the steamer to San José; and they, too, secured a law. This

Second Water Lot Bill offered to forego the state's 25 per cent if the metropolis would confirm the Colton grants. Eventually this bill was repealed, but only a mayoral veto prevented the city council from accepting its provisions.

While the Leavenworth and Colton men were in San José, the preemptionists built fences, shacks, and associations to enforce their "rights"; but the worst troubles arose between 1853 and mid-1854. Sometimes the contest came before the courts, but law was expensive and often might was preferred. Large landowners like Joseph Folsom hired gangs or personally forced the squatters off their property, exchanging lethal and nonlethal shots and blows in the process. Sometimes "owners" compromised; in other cases, they leased at low rents to have the lands occupied (occasionally the lessees then claimed the properties themselves under preemption rights) or built shanties or stored lumber on the lots to fend off potential occupiers.

Despite the rash of squabbles, 1853–54 marked the high tide of squatterism. In 1854 the property owners established the one-thousand-man People's Organization for the Protection of the Rights of Property and Maintenance of Order. This group pledged to defend large and small landowners who held a title recognized as good, "such as Alcalde grant, city title, title under judgment against the city and such titles as the law has held valid." Thereafter, the disturbance subsided.[14]

Even before this extralegal victory, the titleholders had won a lawful one in the case of Cohas v. Legris and Rosin. On October 13, 1853, the State Supreme Court reversed itself and ruled that San Francisco was a Mexican pueblo, entitled to pueblo lands which the alcalde could dispose of. In October 1854, the Board of Land Commissioners, set up by the United States government to pass on property titles in California, reinforced this judgment. As early as 1851 the city had begun pressing its claim to four square leagues of pueblo lands, and the Board's recognition of San Francisco's pueblo status legalized the holdings of those who had purchased their property from the municipality.[15] The Commissioners' decision was appealed to the U.S. courts, and it was several years after 1856 before Congress and the Judiciary definitively confirmed San Francisco's title. The discovery in 1856 of the Pueblo Papers, hidden by a Mexican resident, and their purchase by the Vigilance Committee—one of their few constructive acts —from a speculator who had fraudulently acquired them helped the city's claim considerably.

In 1855 the council added its own weight to that of the Commissioners and courts. The "Mexican" lotholders had made good their titles against squatters, the state, and some other grantees; and now they sought to eliminate all possible corporation claims. Alderman James P. Van Ness, eighth ward Democrat, proposed the necessary statute as early as March 1854; the Know Nothing government passed it in June 1855; and their Democratic successors supplemented it. This ordinance relinquished all city titles to lands within the 1851 charter limits "to such persons as had been in actual bona fide possession thereof from the first of January 1855, to June 20th of the same year, or could show by legal adjudication that they were entitled to such possessions," except those lands set aside for public purposes.[16]

According to People's party mayor H. P. Coon, real estate speculators contrived the Van Ness Ordinance; but in the long run, it benefited all by reducing the insecurity of titles. At the time of its passage, however, the *Chronicle* charged that the law was an attempt to get land without paying for it. The *Alta* admitted that the ordinance would legalize some "notorious frauds," a charge which Van Ness's own testimony confirms.[17]

The final threat to the "Mexican" and city titles came from other Mexican grants, supposedly made previous to rather than during the American military rule (1846–50). The largest of these claims was that of José Y. Limantour, who alleged ownership to much of the built-up part of town. Many settled with Limantour by paying literally thousands for his titles to their lots; and when the Land Commissioners confirmed his grant in January 1856, these compromisers seemed wise. However, the gloom of the first month of that year faded before the developments of the last when Limantour's claim was declared a forgery.[18] After 1855–56 the Land Commissioners settled several similar cases, most of which further buttressed the legality of municipal titles. Some claims remained undecided until after the period, but several of the main encumbrances to city titles had been removed.

In regard to land titles, the city had a legitimate grievance against the national authorities. The slavery struggle postponed the admission of California to the Union and thereby delayed the clarification of property questions. Then the government set up a long and involved procedure for settlement which kept the validity of titles uncertain for years. It may be true that this process merely followed long-established precedent, but the practical result in San Francisco was disorder and vexation.

None of these problems deterred San Francisco from rapidly selling its holdings or dissuaded people from buying them. Large sums of money derived from the council auctions, if not always from the alcalde sales. That of January 3, 1850, for example, brought $635,130. The next year, control of city lots passed to the autonomous Funded Debt Commission; and thereafter, sales dwindled. The aldermen had one last fling, however, in 1853 when it disposed of the public "slips" adjacent to Central, Clay, and California street wharves, which had not been conveyed to the Commissioners. The property sold for about $1,200,000, ostensibly to eliminate the floating debt and the scrip system of finance. What happened next was typical. The wharf companies received an indemnification of $185,000; the state took its interest; and the depression quickly reversed the realty market. Many could not or would not remit their installments, and some began suit to recover their down payment. It was easy to find a legal flaw in the ordinance authorizing the sale that most everyone had originally wanted, and court cases and attachments on city funds followed. Final adjudication was delayed until the sixties; and, in all, $257,-135 was not paid.[19]

San Francisco's real estate produced much more trouble than money. The city realized large sums, but not as much as it should have. Moreover, the land available for sale rapidly diminished through auctions, court judgments, theft in the form of alcalde "grants," the Van Ness Ordinance, and the trusteeship of the Funded Debt Commission. The people justified this alienation on the grounds that private parties would improve the properties, thereby producing more taxes. Yet the loss of the public domain was much more striking than the augmentation of revenue.

Taxes caused almost as many headaches as real estate. The Court of Sessions set the first county tax rate; and thereafter the Board of Equalization—the Supervisors in a different guise—did. For the city, the council committee on equalization carried out the same function some of the time and a joint session of the ward assessors, the rest; ordinances established corporation licenses upon recommendation from the committee on license and excise. Each unit of government had its assessors, and the sheriff and tax collector respectively gathered in the amount due. Reductions in rates could be had by appearing (with a plausible case) before the County Board of Equalization or the equivalent municipal body.[20]

The city and county derived money from four different taxes. The first, established in 1847, came from licenses on occupations. For part of the period 1850–53, this levy was progressive, being geared to the quantity of business done. This feature did not apply universally, however. In December 1853, for example, auctioneers, among the largest businessmen, and hawkers, among the smallest, bore a graduated tax. Yet merchants bought no license at all, though they formerly had been charged progressively. Hawkers were commonly discriminated against. Under the 1853 law they paid $100 per quarter, the same as a theater and four times as much as a butcher or a fruit and candy stand operator.[21] The tax on real and personal property, levied by both city and county (the county's only tax), followed licenses in time but not in monetary importance. Between 1850 and 1857, the property levy, especially on realty, produced the most revenue for the city; and its relative significance increased with the years. Street assessments were the fourth and final source of public funds.

Contemporaries repeatedly claimed that these assessments constituted an onerous burden; and they obviously took a large portion out of local incomes. If a merchant owned his own store and lot, he very likely paid all four charges, three of them annually and the property taxes to both governments. However, the demand for services always outran revenues.

Moreover, it is clear that taxes were hardly oppressive. In his annual message of 1853, Mayor Cornelius K. Garrison, agent for the Nicaragua Steamship Company and banker, bluntly informed the aldermen that the city assessment of twenty-eight million was too low and should be closer to forty million. "Here where the revenue from money and property is five or six times as great [as in other cities], and the tax levied only double per cent, the common and popular cry of onerous taxation is not certainly founded on fact or good reason." [22] In the year Garrison spoke, Sacramento paid $5.35 to San Francisco's $3.85½.

This evidence deterred neither complaints nor more forceful opposition. Licenses, for example, caused continual difficulty; and popular resistance actually defeated the laws introduced in 1849 and early 1850. Licensing legislation finally passed; but at best, residents paid their fees reluctantly. At least once this tax was refused and tested in the courts; and every excuse imaginable was used to avoid payment.[23]

Street assessments told the same story. As late as 1852 large amounts remained outstanding for work done in 1850, and new charges brought the delinquency to $500,000 in 1855. According to the Board of Assistants' committee on streets, this sum could not "be collected without a process of law." [24] The courts repeatedly upheld the city's right to sell property to satisfy unpaid street assessment, but injunctions continued to be issued against the practice. A list of nonpayers in March 1855 included J. L. Folsom and Sam Brannan, the two largest landowners in town; James Lick of

the famous Lick House, a '60's landmark; merchant Selim Woodworth; the Methodist Church; Grace Church; ex-sheriff John C.
Hays; Alfred A. Cohen, a partner in Adams and Company; Henry
Meiggs; B. R. Buckelew, large real estate owner and developer of
Clark's Point; merchant J. B. Biddleman; and Charles Minturn,
member of the California Steam Navigation Company monopoly
and long-time agent of the steamer *Senator* and Cunningham's
Wharf. Arrears ranged from a few hundred dollars to $3,400 in the
case of Brannan.

The collection of real and personal taxes ran into similar trouble.
Between 1850–51 and 1854–55, the city took in close to 90 per cent
of what was owed it, with one year showing collection of 106 per
cent, the surplus probably being back taxes. In 1855–57, however,
the percentage slid; and 1855–56 witnessed a concerted effort to
avoid payment altogether (see below). Then, as earlier, it was
urged in defense of this "tax strike" that the money simply went to
enrich corrupt officials. Yet, as the *Alta* pointed out, the new charter
strictly limited spending; and, indeed, the administration of 1855–
56 was the most frugal in four years. However, people like Brannan
preferred to withhold payment until the new Vigilante-sponsored
People's party took over. This perennial Vigilante finally forked
over his arrears, but many others did not. The percentage of collection for real and personal charges dipped from 66 per cent to 59 per
cent in 1856–57, the lowest figure in the decade. This decline occurred despite the reduction of assessed valuation from 32,000,000
to 30,000,000, the lowering of the city and county rate from
$3.15 5/6 to $1.60, and the advent of the Vigilante government. Apparently citizens were just as averse to paying during the reign of
virtue as during that of vice.

"We confess that . . . we desire to see valid and conclusive tax
sales and an end to all this dodging which has been going on for
several years," complained the *Chronicle* of this rich man's game.
"The great majority of poor men always pay their taxes," this paper
stated in January 1856, "but it is the rich who grumble and refuse to
pay and the richer they become, the more they grumble, and the

more stubborn they are." [25] "Their alleged excuse is, that to pay the taxes would only be to encourage the rascality of men in office, such an excuse is very easily made," continued the same paper. "But the refusal to pay taxes strikes at our good officers as well as our bad ones. Without . . . taxes we will have no grand juries, no roads, no schools, no courts; and the public business will fall into a disorder which will be far more costly, in the end, than an extravagant . . . government."

Since expenditures often exceeded income, the printing press frequently made up the deficiency. In the summer of 1850 the municipality tried to provide services, especially street paving, in part by a license tax. Land sales had raised large amounts, but the merchant-businessman council had squandered much of this money. Moreover, the government wanted to save its remaining realty, hoping for a rise in value. But the revenue bill that carried the license provisions also provided a salary for the aldermen (rather liberal it was supposed); and, for the fourth time since the beginning of 1849, popular clamor defeated the city fathers' attempt to tax the population.[26] On July 17, 1850, the *Alta* remarked acidly, "In the meantime those who should be contributing their mite, and who should have been doing so for the last year, have been chuckling behind their bags of gold dust, and thinking what a 'great country' this is, where they expect their lives and property to be protected and yet do not have to pay for it." [27]

Unable to raise sufficient money by taxes and unwilling to waste its real estate, the government turned to scrip in July 1850. These promises to pay bore an interest of 3 per cent per month (not unusual interest with California prices), and nearly one million were issued. By the time the necessary financial crisis forced a funding scheme, the principal plus interest amounted to almost two million.

First proposed in the fall of 1850 but not enacted until the spring of 1851, the funding scheme exchanged city stock bearing interest of only 10 per cent per annum for the scrip. In addition, a sinking fund to pay off the stocks at maturity and the Funded Debt Commission were created. Though generally overshadowed by the corruption that caused it, this institution provided the only efficient and nearly honest management of city revenues.

The failure of the first scrip policy did not prevent a second. Soon the city began dispensing more promises to pay (warrants), though this time without any interest; and once more dangerously mounting indebtedness forced a funding. An honest Board of Examiners sifted through more than two million dollars in warrants and finally allowed over $400,000. A new, separate debt commission ensued, this time made up entirely of city officials. The county followed the metropolis's debt-ridden ways, issuing scrip in 1850–51 (eventually declared illegal), warrants thereafter, and funding as the town had.

A final, though minor, source rounded out the city's income. As early as 1850 a half million dollar loan to finance urban improvements had been suggested, but issuing scrip proved easier. In 1854–55, however, the metropolis borrowed $200,000 for the fire department and $60,000 for the schools.[28] Before this source of funds could be exhausted, the 1855 charter initiated the crackdown on San Francisco's prodigal ways.

Widespread repercussions grew out of this financial weakness. It forced the government into a number of fiscal expedients which merely compounded its problems. This helplessness, in turn, left San Francisco vulnerable to the attacks of its more rapacious citizens and partially defeated its attempt to serve its people. In snowball fashion, each failure made the next more likely.

The scrip-warrant system of finance revealed this process very clearly. The pre- and post-1851 issues depreciated to as low as thirty-five cents respectively. Contractors, victuallers, and others getting these depreciated monies charged according to their market price; but when they presented them for redemption, they demanded and were given full face value. Since the government could seldom cover all its outstanding warrants, politicians could decide which scrip to honor. As middlemen, they turned a nice profit by purchasing depreciated warrants and cashing them in at face value. The politicians bore the blame for this lively traffic, but they had many accomplices.[29] In the case of the 1850–51 scrip, the city paid three dollars for one dollar's worth of services received, plus the 3 per cent interest per month for about one year and the 10 per cent per annum at which the debt was funded.

Some of the most unsavory devices, after that of scrip, were measures to collect money due the city. Year after year the government unsuccessfully threatened the many delinquents with penalties. When threats failed, the corporation usually tried "compromise," a euphemism for lowering the holdouts' obligations. In one year, the "compromise" amounted to a reduction of 74 per cent. "I scarcely know whether to blame most," said a disgusted letter to the editor, "the city that yields to and encourages such a course, or the delinquents who have forced and who profit by it."

Services suffered immeasurably from the perennial financial crisis. The police had to be supplemented by private officers; and rather than deriving revenue from its own wharves, the corporation had to let private parties build them. It then lost its share of the proceeds through fraud. The waterworks, gas works, streets, plank roads, and, on occasion, hospitals, operated in the same manner. Often the government "farmed out" the collection of delinquent taxes for a percentage because it could not manage the task itself. Nearly every one of these "bargains" eventually produced legal headaches and financial loss. Moreover, in the case of hospitals, juvenile delinquency, and criminal rehabilitation, the city violated its ideals of humane treatment because it could not afford to finance them.

Lack of money also crippled the corporation's defense in the numerous damage suits. Often the metropolis frustrated the rapacity of its tormentors, but the scarcity of funds made the effort difficult and provided fresh grievances which eventually found their way into court. Lawsuits, in turn, further aggravated the financial problem, for win or lose, lawyers' and court charges had to be paid. Legal fees alone in the years 1850–53 were $200,000, just slightly less than the entire amount expended for schools in 1854–55.[30]

The most famous of these cases illustrates perfectly both the folly of a private-public approach to urban problems and the reinforcing nature of financial weakness. Peter Smith, the former operator of the city hospital, had a bill of some $60,000 for which he had received the usual promissory notes in payment. Upon the town's adoption of the funding scheme in 1851, Smith demanded cash for his scrip instead of 10 per cent bonds. The courts initially ruled in his favor, but the government had no money. To satisfy the judgment, the sheriff began selling municipal assets; the buyers—working in league—kept the bidding low. Therefore, it took an enormous amount of property, including all the city wharves, to compensate the good doctor. The Smith claimants eventually lost, but not before much expensive legal battling and inconvenience.[31]

Another series of suits brought the metropolis equally close to disaster. During the "great" fires of 1850–51, numerous properties were dynamited to contain the blaze. In the path of the flames those buildings had very little value; but the owners sued for full compensation just the same. In 1850 damage suits worth half a million dollars stood before the courts. Most lawyers felt the government was liable; but one, John W. Dwinelle, correctly believed its case could be won. For his services in saving the $500,000, however, Dwinelle turned in a bill for $25,000, although it was later reduced. Even a successful defense could be very costly.

So numerous were these cases that frequently the understaffed city attorney or county district attorney had to call in expensive outside legal talent to stave off catastrophe. Like any other article of commerce, these judgments changed hands on the open market, where speculators bought them at a discount and sued to collect. In late 1854 a quarter of a million dollars in such claims was before the courts. Anyone who won attached urban property or funds; and in 1855, at a time when the police and teachers had not been paid in months, all the money in the treasury was attached, including the fire department and school loans. The *ne plus ultra* of fiscal weakness came in 1855, when the mortgage on the city hall could not be paid and for a time its "repossession" seemed imminent.[32]

By 1856, then, the financial prospects of San Francisco looked bleak. That year found the metropolis with one source of revenue, land, largely exhausted; its people unwilling to contribute the other, taxes; its charter prohibiting both scrip and loans; and its treasury besieged. Given this situation, the penny-pinching policies of the People's party are quite understandable.

From at least as early as 1851, a provision required budgeting the city's resources; and the second charter made annual appropriations mandatory. Yet until the crackdown of 1855–56, the amount authorized never very closely approximated the figure spent. The 1855–56 charters banned special accounts, procedures, and other limitation-evading devices; but before this legal straitjacket was slipped on, much careless handling and leakage of money occurred, especially from the contingent fund. Actually, the charter of 1856 took the function of budgeting, except for a $70,000 "surplus fund," almost completely out of the hands of municipal government.

San Francisco's budget received very considerable sums, which point up again the disproportionate importance of that place. From October 1849 up to mid-1855, a total of $4,597,251, excluding scrip and loans, flowed into the city treasury compared to $3,333,947 collected by the state. If the $1,426,003 taken in by the county from 1850 to '55, is added to this figure, local revenues almost doubled those of the entire state government, to which the metropolis contributed $835,341.[33] San Francisco may have been the legal creature of the state with a mere 14 per cent of the population, but its revenues exceeded those of California, even after it paid 25 per cent of the state budget.

Before the fiscal year 1853–54, itemized figures on municipal and county disbursements are spotty; yet it is safe to say that transportation costs, such as streets and wharves, claimed the greatest expenditures before and after this period. From 1853–54 to 1856–57, the streets and Plaza received $1,415,660, most of it in 1853–55. Thereafter, the new charters put the entire burden upon adjacent propertyholders. Salaries, care of the sick, police pay and prison maintenance, the fire department, old debts and sundries, and education followed streets in order of importance, ranging from $884,-579 to $415,838. Education expenses rose to the head of the list in 1856–57, but the total amount allotted did not reach $100,000. Other large sums went for legal aid, advertising, stationery, street lighting, and elections.

The anatomy of an ordinance or administrative decision reveals how government allocated these resources. A new law usually began as a petition to the council or board of supervisors. The plea was then referred to one of the various committees, which were important units of government. This body then investigated the request and, if necessary, called upon city officers, lawyers, teachers, engineers, surveyors, and others to testify. Occasionally, these private persons drew up laws, charters, or reports. If the measure received the committee's recommendation, it might be passed by the boards and, in the case of the municipal government, signed by the mayor. Other services came directly from executive departments. The street commissioner, for example, could supervise the construction of thoroughfares, let the contracts for some street work, and remove obstructions.

Institutional tension within the administration stalled many measures; and rivalries between the mayor and council, the two boards of aldermen, aldermanic committees, and the Funded Debt Commission frequently enlivened the government proceedings. These latter, however, were by no means dull. Council debates on important measures often featured a noisy gallery; a mass meeting of the citizenry hissing and groaning beneath the chamber window; the brandishing of aldermanic canes, pistols, and knives; and the exchange of some extremely frank sentiments or even material objects, such as inkwells, among the city fathers or between them and the crowd. The amount of money available and the degree of civic pressure usually determined whether the act passed, though obnoxious measures triumphed over public opinion and the mayor's veto if aldermen considered them "popular" enough.

Officials rendered some services free; but under the prevailing fee system, the aid of the sheriff, court clerks, county clerk and surveyor, and coroner came very high. Sheriff's dues, for instance, were estimated at $75,000 to $100,000 per annum. Fortunately, the Consolidation Act reduced these charges, except those of the sheriff, to reasonable amounts. Some city officers—the tax collector, comptroller, and treasurer—took a percentage, usually one to one-half, of all monies that passed through their hands, which offered them a fairly satisfactory return. The mayor, marshal, recorder, city clerks, and others received salaries. When paid in cash, this remuneration was adequate; but often scrip substituted for currency. The aldermen, deprived of any stipend at all except in 1855–56, when they earned $1,000, constituted a special pariah class. The "salary grab" controversy of 1850 insured the nonpayment of these men. Their lack of pay could hardly have induced the solons to live down the accusation that they got ample "compensation" on the side, even if they had been so inclined. Some functionaries had to give bonds to guarantee their good conduct; but before 1855, many behaved badly anyway.

Services rendered by these officials, except that by several judges and several mayors, hardly ever repaid the citizens. Ordinances were vague, badly drawn, and full of expensive loopholes. Even extraordinarily important records often simply vanished. In 1855 the bonds of contractor William A. Dennis, given to guarantee his construction of a horse railway down Market Street, inexplicably disappeared, along with those to secure the building of several wharves. And if the desired document remained on hand, locating it could be difficult. In 1856 the clerk of the common council informed the *Alta* that he found the papers of the last six years piled in a single heap and that after six months he had still not been able to sort them out.[34]

Corruption in part explains this inefficiency; but political appointments, some of whom had no qualifications—such as the ability to read and write—augmented the bungling. Absenteeism was rampant, since many regarded their positions as sinecures or neglected them for politics or business. A resident noted in 1856 that he could not even locate the tax collector during election time. This custom, not confined to election periods, surely did not improve the collection of taxes, as hardly anyone anxiously sought this officer in the first place.

Individuals did not necessarily regard these local government decisions as final. Failing in the metropolis, the petitioner often tried the state government. If the request had already been granted at the bay, the seeker would frequently make doubly sure by securing confirmation from the California legislature. These appeals explain a significant portion of the cases of state interference into San Francisco matters. They were often desired and actively solicited by "home" interests.

The final fate of a law or executive decision hinged on its enforcement. It usually took a combination of public opinion and power to secure popular acquiescence. Many people obeyed without being dragged before a judge, but numerous prerogatives had to be tested in the courts—the right to tax, to empower certain officers to collect these levies, to sell private property for delinquent taxes, to dispose of land, and to establish a Funded Debt Commission. How the judiciary decided these cases mattered tremendously on the local level, much more so even than national decisions. In effect, an individual with the price of a lawyer held a suspensory veto over the community's law where he was concerned. Moreover, anyone who refused to be bound by the statutes, whether a reluctant taxpayer like Brannan and Folsom, a swindler like Argenti, a litterbug, a speeder, or a Sydney Duck like James Stuart, could force one of two unpalatable alternatives. Either the aberrant behavior had to be tolerated or money had to be spent on legal fees, police, and inspectors. San Francisco's law-giving ability rested upon popular acquiescence in large part, but also in significant measure upon its willingness to sacrifice economy for justice. The law carried a price just as surely as flour, lumber, and nails.

Often the mere threat of legal confrontations deterred the community from trying to enforce its rights or forced it to accept an expensive "compromise." In 1853, for example, the municipal government wanted to sell the Central Wharf slips to bolster its finances. The dock company threatened suit to recover damages even though the city owned the area and had only granted its use —free at that—to the wharf corporation. To avoid ruining the sale by injunction delays, the council decided to pay off the latter even though the maneuver was recognized as blackmail by the councilmen. This deal alone cost the metropolis $185,000 on a sale of land worth $1,200,000.

The expansion of government and law is proof that frequently the city chose prevention over economy. In addition, the need for services and spoils added policemen, health inspectors, fire wardens, meat inspectors, clerks, wharfingers, plaza keepers, sextons, and other officials to the public payroll.

Benevolent operations further augmented the corporation's role. The city eventually assumed or subsidized the schools, orphan asylum, industrial school, hospitals, and several other projects founded or conceived before 1856. In these areas the initiative of private enterprise was considerably greater than that of the public authorities; but unlike wharves, gas, water, plank roads, and other money-making ventures, philanthropy usually could not raise enough capital. That brought requests for public intervention. All this temporarily raised the total number of city employees to 200, making the government one of the largest local employers. Thus, somewhat reluctantly, San Francisco rapidly acquired a bureaucracy—notwithstanding the popular conviction that the world was too much governed.[35]

By any ideal standards, the overall efficiency of government in San Francisco would not rate very high. However, if one discards perfectionist criteria as inapplicable to a gold rush city and judges the performance by other measures, the metropolis comes off better than generally admitted. Compared to the success of other urban areas, the Bay City was not so ineffectual. The same conclusion is warranted if one compares the management of public and private business.[36]

Both the corporation and the county accumulated huge debts; yet nearly every kind of institution in the community shared that dilemma. Though not overrun with politicians, the churches, too, stayed almost universally in the red, some of them dangerously so. What is more, even the most superficial examination of the insolvency calendars of the years 1853–59 reveals rampant financial mismanagement in the private business world. In 1855 alone, liabilities in the economic arena amounted to $8,377,827 with assets of only $1,519,175. The politicians never failed quite that badly. In fact, unlike private enterprise, the city did not repudiate any of its legal monetary obligations. Despite charges that the funding of 1855 constituted such a maneuver, the corporation paid most of what it owed and, for that matter, much that it did not owe. Moreover, the same incompetence showed up elsewhere in the private sector. Locally manufactured bricks, steamboat boilers, and buildings often proved worthless. The periodic collapse of the latter provided one of the continuing sources of minor excitement in the city, as shacks, merchants' stores, and bonded warehouses disintegrated into their component parts. The same fate overtook several wharves, one of which fell into the bay under a load of rioting teamsters and another, in 1851, with several warehouses.

These private failures could be very serious. One evening in 1855, Thomas Benson drowned by falling through a hole in Davis Street, which at that point stretched over the water. The street had been provided with sidewalks behind and in front of this gap, but the property owner at that point refused to mend the sidewalk. The charter made him responsible for repairs, and the street commissioner had "repeatedly requested" him to undertake them. A

resident Italian living next door informed the *Chronicle* reporter
that "he and his partner have rescued more than a dozen persons
from that hole, and . . . the neighbors had rescued others." [37]

The press and public often magnified government malperform-
ance. City Hall received the blame for not fixing the streets in
cases where legal responsibility clearly rested with property owners. All kinds of unnecessary projects, like reimbursement for the
militia companies' armory, came forward for subsidies; and the
press called the government parsimonious when it did not pay
them. The newspapers hammered away at the bad condition of the
Plaza until it caused the expenditure of $33,000 to beautify this
square, despite the fact that the corporation had to borrow several
hundred thousand dollars to equip the schools and fire departments. Even soundly conceived city projects faced ridicule if they
failed. In 1850, when the mayor's well diggers did not hit water
under the Plaza, the whole affair was contemptuously dubbed
"Geary's Folly." However, within two years the feasibility of artesian wells had been fully demonstrated. The corporation, being
among the first to drill, understandably did not know where to dig.
They had made their attempt one block west of Montgomery
Street, east of which many wells subsequently appeared.

In other cases, the news media failed to notice the bad luck of
the government or to recognize its achievements. It was practically
a reflex action with the newspapers to ask rhetorically what the
people had derived from their taxes and answer that they had received nothing. Obviously, the populace did get something for its
money; and some of the waste had nongovernmental causes. In
1851, for example, fires consumed the city hall, city hospital, and
many feet of street planks, inflicting a loss of at least $200,000. The
guilty parties in this case were those who had built a tinderbox
town as well as those who had fired it rather than the city fathers
—no matter how corrupt—who tried to govern it.

Moreover, the press and citizenry often did not "discover" the
flaws in government projects that turned out badly until after the
event, even though the whole affair might have been carried in

the papers. This happened partly because the journals had often approved of or acquiesced in the initiation of schemes that went awry. They also publicly commended office holders or candidates who subsequently involved themselves in shady dealings. Henry Meiggs, before his abrupt departure in the fall of 1854, had an extremely good reputation; and the press had repeatedly lauded him for his dedication to the public interest and urged his election. Many others received the same ballyhoo and eventually served the community badly.

Between the years 1846–56, San Francisco was a noncooperative community, governed just about as well as it deserved or could have expected to be. Many refused to be taxed, to obey the laws, to fix the streets, to serve on juries, to participate in politics and government or even to vote, or to deal honestly with the corporation. In these circumstances, the level of achievement could hardly be impressive.

Urban Problems

Late in 1847 the *California Star* carried the news that a Russian sailor had tumbled into a water shaft and drowned. The city council ordained "that from and after the twelfth of November, 1847, all property owners desiring to dig wells upon their premises; or who may now have them dug, shall under penalty of fifty dollar fine, carefully close and box them up." [1] All too often during the remaining years, the community repeated this crisis response. Besides being too late, efforts to provide streets, wharves, fire prevention, water, hospitals, and police protection always fell far short of the demand. In addition, the services were generally maldistributed. Even so, the government needed considerable assistance from private enterprise. However, few contemporary muncipalities labored amidst comparable difficulties. The frenzied excitement of a gold rush did not provide the ideal circumstances for orderly urbanization.

Fortunately, a plan had been laid out prior to the Gold Rush. In 1839 a survey had been made; but in 1846 Alcalde Washington A. Bartlett ordered a new one. Finished in 1847, this latter plat, apparently based on the model of Philadelphia with some modification, straightened out and extended the original one. It employed the right angle pattern, but in two different sections. North of Market, streets ran approximately north and south, east and west;

but to the south, they pointed northeast, northwest, southeast, and southwest.[2]

A common complaint in later years was that the streets were too narrow and did not conform to the hilly nature of the site. Jasper O'Farrell, who carried out the 1847 survey, tried to modify it to allow for the heights and to provide wider streets; but the alcalde and property owners overruled him. According to the *Alta*, "To sell a few more feet of lots, the streets were compressed like a cheese, into half their width." The plat was changed south of Market by pointing that artery toward the mission and enlarging the blocks, probably as bad an error in the long run as choosing the square plan, for it created a number of triangular blocks and "T" intersections and did not match up the streets from the two different sections.[3] The traffic nightmare of contemporary Market Street is the direct result of this alteration. The city ended up with the wrong plan modified in the wrong way.

Whatever its defects, the mere existence of a plat prior to the Gold Rush was a godsend. The gridiron pattern was one of the few elements of order in an initially anarchic situations. San Francisco had quite enough trouble over land titles; and if the O'Farrell survey had not reserved at least the streets from squatting, the confusion would have been much worse. Actually, given the fact that William Eddy, an early surveyor who laid out much of the city, stayed drunk a goodly portion of his working day, it is a wonder that the matter turned out as well as it did.[4]

The attempt to better the "avenues" came on the heels of the second survey. In September 1847, a new council began the improvements by filling a small salt lagoon which covered Montgomery between Jackson and Washington. Done to facilitate travel between the best landing site and the main part of town, this first street construction was carried out to serve the interests of business, a pattern that was adhered to fairly closely thereafter. Besides this work, a little grading and filling took place elsewhere in the city; but when the Gold Rush arrived, the streets were very largely in a state of nature.[5]

For two years this primitive condition prevailed. The relatively mild winter of 1848–49 allowed the community to avoid much building, but the heavy rains and immigration of 1849–50 turned the streets into virtual swamps. "Yet we must pick our way! pick, jump, stride and totter and we got somewhat into some thing that no doubt looks very like a street on a map but it was not recognisable [*sic*] in its natural form although they called it 'Broadway,'" wrote an argonaut of a crossing; "it proved so to us for . . . all succeeded in getting stuck." [6]

This crisis precluded further delay; and from December 1849 on, the government began to alleviate it.[7] Yet the inundation that goaded the council into action prevented any significant attack on the mess until things dried up in the spring. Thereafter the work went forward; and by the fall of 1850, the main part of town was ready.[8]

If two-thirds of the property holders petitioned the council, the city repaired the thoroughfares; and until 1851 the owners generally paid two-thirds of the cost. Thereafter the municipality contributed progressively less and after 1856, none at all. Even earlier, however, the lot owners sometimes covered the entire expense. Interested businessmen entirely financed Commercial Street, pushed through to give the Central Wharf Company more direct access to the main artery, Montgomery, in violation of the original plat.[9] The street commissioner usually supervised the improvements, but private contractors did the work.

Construction took the form of grading, planking, and sewering. The plentiful supply of wood from Oregon and California largely excluded stone or other paving materials.[10] Redwood, considered more durable, was sometimes substituted for pine; but since planks quickly wore out, the city tried cobblestone and Russ pavements, with the inventor himself present to install the latter. By 1856 paving covered several city blocks, but planks were still the rule.

In terms of money spent and distance built, though not durability, the record was impressive. Streets were usually the most expensive item in the budget, and improvements soon reached a total of many miles. Yet enormous difficulties accompanied this only partly successful effort. During the two great holocausts of 1851, for instance, many planks burned, thereby ruining the avenues as well as spreading the blaze. Even without such an extraordinary test, wood wore out quickly; and the installation of gas company pipes and other construction caused considerable further damage. The individualistic approach provided other embarrassments. For example, in lieu of uniform specifications for building sewers, each property owner provided his own. Therefore, a drain might suffice for the builder's lot but not be adequate to carry off the water from geographically higher areas. The downhill owner was often loath to build a bigger and more expensive work to accommodate his neighbor's drainage. Financing improvements was one of the most stubborn and dramatic problems facing the government.[11]

Grades were a special headache, since rapid and unpredictable growth made it difficult to plan for drainage. In 1850 the city established a system of gradation, but by 1853 the steady advance into the cove made it anachronistic. Alderman J. P. Haven underlined the need for drastic alteration, claiming that two-thirds of the buildings in the lower part of the city had flooded basements. The Hoadley grades, adopted by the Whig government in 1853, provided a comprehensive program to carry off the water and enabled property holders to build with some assurance that the incline of the streets would not be altered thereafter.

Much raising and lowering of thoroughfares and buildings ensued, sometimes with comic effect. Lydia Rowell Prevaux noted that to get into her house, "we had to come up a ladder twenty feet high. We drew up our wood and water with a rope. . . . We are not troubled with callers or with a desire to go out or rather down." For the businessmen east of Montgomery, however, the matter was not so funny. Damages to them caused by the alteration amounted to $3,000,000. Eventually the outcry against the Hoadley system led to its modification in 1854, thereby easing the financial burden and saving much of the city's hills, which were earmarked for extensive trimming.[12]

Because of such handicaps, the quality of the streets usually ranged from moderately good to miserable. Fires and the cessation of new construction and repairs soon nullified the vigorous beginning. By the winters of 1851–52 and 1852–53, San Francisco had reverted to a "wading city," whose streets were described under "MARINE INTELLIGENCE." Despite resumption of patching and building, especially in 1853 and 1854, the avenues in many parts of the city remained in a "shocking condition." [13]

This dilapidation was more than just an amusing matter of local color. Several miles of thoroughfares stretched over the bay on piles, and these were especially dangerous. In January 1856, a leading paper commented, "Since the present City Charter went into force it is said that fifty-seven men have lost their lives in consequence of the wretched condition of our streets, chiefly those leading over the water." [14] If one compares this with the fifteen homicides in the city in 1856, a crime much complained of then and later, the magnitude of the problem is clear.

The government received frequent censure for this inadequacy; but with the power to initiate enhancements and the responsibility for financing them, the lot holders must be blamed for whatever defects existed. "On my return from the East, I found the street before my door unfathomable and the plank all gone," wrote William Rabe, a doctor and politician. "I have tried to get Clay street merchants to subscribe to replank the street, but they *all*, except Saroni, Archer and Co., flatly refused to pay one cent. . . . I am afraid that those who complain are the least willing to pay." Not until the Consolidation Act of 1856 provided for the sale of property whose owners refused to pay and also established their personal liability in case of accident, did many—though not all—come around. [15]

The arrangement for financing assured that some quarters would be neglected. By 1854, when most grading and planking ceased, the improved section included the downtown portion, the economically important Market Street, and much of the western residential area. Working-class districts saw less construction, which came only after other places had been provided for.[16]

Plank roads, somewhat analogous to suburban freeways, were an important supplement to the streets. Lacking the money to build for itself, the city contracted with the Mission Dolores Plank Road Company in November 1850 for the first wooden highway. The company was responsible for maintenance and could collect tolls for seven years after completion. At that time, the property reverted to the city.[17] Running from the Plaza down Kearny and Mission, this thoroughfare proved so crucial that the council awarded a parallel route on Folsom to the same company in 1852 and granted two similar franchises in 1853, from the mission to the south edge of town and from Stockton to Larkin on Pacific. The new road contracts resembled the initial one, except that the pioneer company received the additional privilege of operating the only plank road to the mission. The city reserved the right to regulate tolls on all of them.[18]

Beyond the corporation limits, the County Board provided for the extension of the highways. By 1853 the way south via the mission was graded and provided with bridges. Known as the San José or New County Road, for the most part it followed the older trail as far as the Abbey House.[19] In 1854 the board let another contract, this time to provide an improved connection to the ocean by a plank road from Larkin and Pacific.

The metropolis's record of keeping its avenues clean was not as impressive as its history of building them. Many mistook the thoroughfares for a dump and ornamented them with refuse and junk. Sometimes the street commissioner removed a part of the filth, and occasionally the city council took a hand. During the cholera epidemic of 1850–51, the council provided a garbage scow and fined people for discarding waste. Eventually, public scavengers were appointed; but by October 1856, they had quit because of the government's inability to pay them.[20] Altogether, the scavengers, street commissioner, and people did only a mediocre job.

An "expert" realistically portrayed what the enfeebled forces of cleanliness had to contend with. "Allow me to name some nuisances that exist which are very annoying and exceedingly dangerous to the public," wrote an angry drayman to the *Chronicle*, "viz: the throwing of glass bottles, iron hoops, tin lard cans, tin cheese boxes, tin egg cans, wooden hoops with nails in them, besides any quantity of nails and all sorts of old rubbish, into the streets." "The custom of throwing slop water into the streets from chamber windows is a filthy nuisance," he continued. "These things are practiced every day." Other correspondents pointed out that Washington Square had become a trash and waste "depot"; that Market and First served as a similar repository; that the gas company was polluting Beale between Mission and Fremont; that people dumped garbage into the bay at Clay and Drumm; and that at Jackson and Front, "the night carts are fast filling up with an abominable compost the great holes in the street." [21] In terms of cleanliness, San Francisco in the 1850's was much more akin to colonial cities than to the modern bay area metropolis.

Keeping thoroughfares clear and safe seemed equally impossible. Merchants, builders, teamsters, and others violated ordinances by cluttering sidewalk and street with the paraphernalia of construction or commerce, often making the parking problem acute long before the automobile. Frequently pedestrians could not get around these nuisances without venturing into the chaos of the avenues, where traffic jams, "furious driving," and "drunken riding" by draymen and horsemen often endangered life and limb. "A man was knocked off his horse in Kearny Street, yesterday, merely for undertaking to ride over a fellow who had no horse," needled the *Alta* in 1851. Yet neither the papers nor the punishments authorized by the council availed. As late as 1854 the *Chronicle* lamented, "Our city is a race course." [22]

Anyone walking through San Francisco, therefore, had to wend his way carefully through numerous obstacles; and from 1846 to late 1850, the nocturnal pedestrian had to perform these feats in the dark. The lurid glare from gaming houses, bars, hotels, and other establishments furnished some illumination; but for the most part, the gloom was unbroken. After late 1850 this situation improved, but never very much.

In October 1850, J. B. M. Crooks, a whale oil dealer, began supplying outside lanterns for merchants; and numerous others put up their own.[23] The council hired Messrs. Perry and Dexter in 1851 "to light the city"; and in late 1851 these contractors were superseded by Crooks, who was to illuminate the area between Battery, Kearny, Jackson, and California. The *Alta* commented that the contract went forth in "true San Francisco style": there were not enough fixtures, burning for too short a time, giving off too few rays.[24] It was just enough "to render the darkness visible," quipped the *Herald*.[25]

In the meantime, the government arranged with James Donohue and Company to introduce coal gas. This franchise, which was to replace that of Crooks upon its completion, gave a fifteen-year monopoly of streetlighting privileges, and thereafter the municipality had the option to purchase. The company and the council each named one man to the rate board, and the third was nominated by these two. For the first five years, however, the city had no representatives at all. The aldermen ratified the agreement in September 1852, and all of the company's stock had been taken up by December. Despite problems and the prediction of camphene dealer Alexander Stott that "San Francisco cannot be lighted with gas in the next twenty five years," the first illumination occurred in February 1854.[26]

Originally, the lights went on from Dupont to the water and from Jackson to California, which meant the down town section and little else. Private service was more extensive, since it "so delighted" people that they "permitted the company to lay their pipes through all the principal streets" and "into almost every dwelling"; but the public imbalance remained a sore point. "Some portions of the city thickly peopled and much traveled at night are

not lighted at all," complained the *Chronicle* in January 1856.[27]
Finally in 1856 extension into Happy Valley evened up the service
somewhat.

Besides the maldistribution of services, the contract had other
flaws. The lamps generally were not turned on all the way (sometimes not at all) and then only for part of the night. Most controversy, however, arose over the extortionate monopoly rates; and
in 1856 this matter came to a showdown. In an effort to secure
more reasonable prices, the Board of Supervisors turned off all the
fixtures except those at intersections, and public San Francisco left
the period pretty much as it had entered it—bathed in moonlight.[28]

Even during the day, the task of finding one's way around often
proved difficult, since the avenues were not numbered until 1856
and then only partially. "It is only recently that the principal business streets have been numbered, and of those running north and
south none appear to be generally thus favored above Montgomery," complained the *Evening Bulletin.* "At present, it is necessary
to draw a small map of the residence of the person it is proposed
to visit without a guide, accompanied by some such direction as
'St. Ann's Valley, third house northwest from the grocery, alongside of sandbank, small yard in front, stairs leading up to second
story, bulldog chained in the back yard.'" [29]

The harbor was the seaward extension of the streets and therefore a part of the same transportation problem. Several attempts
to build wharves in 1846 and early 1847 produced minor landing
facilities but nothing substantial. In the latter year, however, discussion of a wharf to accommodate sea-going vessels at low tide
—one from which the city would derive revenue—got under way.
After the new council was elected in September, it allocated $10,-
000 and $2,000 for docks at the foot of Clay and Broadway streets
respectively. The first of these was completed (by whom is not
clear) and in use a year later; but a storm soon destroyed it. The
other proposed structure remained only a plan.[30]

With a liberal grant from the municipality, private enterprise
succeeded where public had failed. On May 3, 1849, the Central

Wharf Joint Stock Company obtained the right to build a work, and the city reserved for it the use of certain lands between Clay and Sacramento. Money was quickly raised; and by August 31, 1849, the famous Long Wharf neared the low water mark.[31] Eventually it extended several blocks from its starting point on Leidesdorff.

Similar construction, private and public, soon followed. The council initiated a plan in 1850 to put piers at the foot of each thoroughfare, beginning with Market, Broadway, and Pacific. As usual, the city ran out of money, and private parties obtained the right to finish the docks and operate them for a term of five years in return for a percentage of the wharfage. At the end of that time the property reverted to the municipality. This same formula was followed in letting contracts in 1851 for piers at Folsom, Washington, Vallejo, Jackson, and Clay streets. In the meantime, several entirely private works had been built: Law's, Cunningham's, Buckelew's, Howison's, and Meiggs's. By 1857 the city had at least seventeen of these major landing facilities.[32]

The harbor, like the streets, supplied a number of vexations. Many piers were poorly built and were made from materials for which certain seagoing worms had an insatiable appetite. A series of spectacular wharf collapses beginning as early as 1851 resulted from these circumstances.

While sea creatures nibbled away at the docks, the town continually encroached upon the old cove, transforming water and wharves into land and streets. This process, in turn, forced the piers out of the sanctuary of the inlet and into the more open waters of the bay. Some citizens would have continued this procedure indefinitely, but a line drawn in 1851 finally stabilized the city front. This halted further expansion, but not before the cove was mostly filled in and the original harbor ruined. In 1856 a bulkhead to stay the further ooze of land into the bay came under consideration, but the political excitement of that year plus a desire for a thorough investigation led to postponement.[33]

For whatever order existed amidst the shipping, the harbor master—a kind of seagoing street commissioner—was responsible. He saw that boats were properly moored during bad weather, found berths for incoming ships, guarded against fire, and in general, looked out for the interests of the port.[34] His task proved a very difficult one. For several years after the Gold Rush, barks, brigs, steamers, and other craft—a large number of them abandoned by runaway sailors or shattered mining companies—literally jammed the landing area. Many of these broke their moorings during storms and collided with other vessels, causing great damage, which the destruction of the inlet and consequent loss of shelter did nothing to abate.

The sale of water lots provided added and endless troubles, for purchasers wanted to fill them in despite wharf owners' opposition. As a result, a species of guerilla warfare ensued, featuring court injunctions, midnight and Sunday pile driving and extracting, the sinking of sand-filled hulks by sea-borne squatters, and even armed clashes between claimants to the same property.[35] A ship-master anchored in a legally assigned berth might wake up to find a pile driver noisily surrounding his vessel with structural timbers at the behest of a supposed water lot owner.

The introduction of fire into the crowded shipping loomed as a constant menace, since the wharves connected to the planked streets. The harbor master often got the very minimum of cooperation from ship captains, warehousemen, or merchants in his attempts to impede conflagrations or maintain order.[36]

Yet those protecting the anchorage from fire were magnificently successful compared to their counterparts on shore. The era of flames came to the city before the epoch of gold. Between 1847 and 1849, blazes swept through the chaparral that closely invested the city, a house, the ship *Philadelphia*, a warehouse, and the "Shades" Tavern. On December 24, 1849, however, San Francisco had its first extensive holocaust, which consumed an entire block. Several months elapsed before the destroying element struck again in force—on May 4 and June 14, 1850. The first of these disasters razed only three blocks, but the next was more serious. September 17, 1850, witnessed the loss of another four squares; but the next large outbreak was delayed until May 4, 1851. Eighteen blocks and parts of seven others—perhaps one-fourth of the city—were destroyed and over thirteen more razed on June 22, 1851. A final holocaust struck on November 9, 1852, the least serious of the large conflagrations.[37] There were fairly destructive fires thereafter, but nothing approaching the 1849–52 tragedies.

Collectively, the visitations of the 1850's were just as dramatic, destructive, and possibly as important to the earlier city as the much better known earthquake and fire of 1906. Like their descendants who lived through the latter, the spectacle fascinated and terrified San Franciscans of the fifties. The archaeologist Heinrich Schliemann described the night of May 3 and 4, 1851.

> I arrived here last night and put up at the Union Hotel on the Plaza. I may have slept a quarter of an hour, when I was awoke [sic] by loud cries in the street: "fire, fire," and by the awful sounds of the alarm-bell. I sprung [sic] up in all haste and looking out of the window I saw that a frame building only 20 or 30 paces from the Union Hotel was on fire. I dressed in all haste and ran out of the house, but scarcely had I reached the end of Clay street when I saw already the Hotel on fire from which I had just run out. Pushed on by a complete gale the fire spread with an appalling rapidity, sweeping away in a few minutes whole streets of frame buildings. Neither the iron houses nor the brickhouses (which were hitherto considered as quite fire-proof) could resist the fury of the element: the latter crumbled together with incredible rapidity, whilst the former got red-hot, then white-hot and fell together like cardhouses. Particularly in the iron houses people considered themselves perfectly safe and they remained in them to the last extremity. As soon as the walls of the iron houses getting [sic] red-hot the goods inside began to smoke, the inhabitants wanted to get out, but usually it was already too late, for the locks and hinges of the doors having extended or partly melted by the heat, the doors were no more to be opened. Sometimes by burning their hands and arms people succeeded to open the doors and to get out, but finding themselves then surrounded by an ocean of flames they made a few

paces, staggered and fell, rose again and fell again in order not
to rise any more. It was tried in vain to arrest the progress of
the fire by blowing up of houses with gunpowder. Wishing to
avoid dangers I went up Montgommerry [sic] street and as-
cended "Telegraph hill" which is a mountain about 300 feet
high close to the city. It was a frightful but sublime view, in
fact the grandest spectacle I ever enjoyed. The fire continued to
spread in all directions sweeping away the whole of Washington
street, Kearney street, Montgommerry [sic] street, California
street, Sansome street and many others and except a few houses
on Battery street, Bush street and on the Hillside, the whole
beautiful city was burned down. The roaring of the storm, the
cracking of the gunpowder, the cracking of the falling stonewalls,
the cries of the people and the wonderful spectacle of an immense city burning in a [sic] dark all joined to make this catastrophe awful in the extreme.[38]

Foremost among the causes of these events is the fact that until
after June 1851 the city was a perfect tinderbox. Most brick and
iron buildings constructed before the 1851 tragedies were not fireproof and wood predominated as building material. Moreover,
canvas was widely used for tents as well as for walls and ceilings.
As the Reverend Samuel H. Willey said in 1851, everyone knew
one match could reduce the whole city to ashes, "and yet every
man was acquiring with such rapidity that all hoped to complete
a fortune ere such a disaster should occur." [39]

The summer dry spell and the accompanying high winds made
the cloth and board town even more vulnerable, and widespread
carelessness and maliciousness contributed further to this result.
Faulty chimneys protruding from canvas walls and piles of combustibles abounded. Time and again, bursting camphene lamps,
candles falling against curtains or fabric walls, or discarded "see-
gars" started fires.[40]

Incendiarism received the blame for many of the worst conflagrations, and it was argued then and later that the 1851 Vigilantes
squelched this activity. Yet the Committee did not catch a single
incendiary nor did they deter the commission of that crime after
their summer interlude was over. Arson remained common be-

tween 1851 and 1856. Of 253 fires reported by the *Alta* over this period, 31.6 per cent were attributed to this cause. Moreover, both press and fire bugs usually tried to commemorate the anniversary of the great May 1851 disaster—the former by warnings to the community and the latter by an encore. On May 4, 1852, for example, there were three separate attempts to burn the town.[41]

The second popular uprising in 1856 had no more success in quenching the incendiary's torch. As late as 1856–60, arson still made up 25 per cent of the causes of fire, enough to demolish the city many times over.[42] This eventuality failed to occur because there was less flammable material and a greater preventive capacity, not because of the lynching deterrent.

Yet this relative immunity was achieved in a curiously spasmodic fashion. Immediately after a blaze, the council and citizens actively conceived protective measures; but as the crisis receded, "their ardor cooled, even more rapidly than the burning timbers and smoldering ashes."[43]

The cycle of progress and apathy appeared in the wake of the first serious conflagration. On December 24, 1849, despite previous attempts, not even one fire company operated in San Francisco. On December 25, however, men began organizing. By the time of the May 1850 fire the several volunteer groups had not banded together into a unit; but even before the debris was cleared, they began forming one. Shortly after the destruction of June 14, 1850, the city council passed an ordinance creating a fire department; yet not until October 1850 did this institution assume some semblance of order (there was another major conflagration on September 17). In the meantime, the council built four cisterns; but when the holocaust of June 1851 occurred the reservoirs were empty and remained so two months later. The events of May and June 1851 finally completed popular education; and thereafter the work of protecting the city went ahead much more steadily. A paid board of inspectors faithfully scoured the community for inflammable material. The cisterns multiplied from four to sixty by 1855, and the fire chiefs made certain they were filled. Authorities established a district within which cloth or canvas shanties could not be thrown up nor combustibles stored in careless fashion; and in 1853, they proscribed new wooden structures from that area.[44]

A new and energetic head, George H. Hossefross, tightly structured the volunteer and largely unpaid fire department. The whole membership chose department officers, and government consisted of a board of elected delegates representing the various companies. The city and men divided expenses, with the former contributing the major portion, thus adhering to the usual pattern of public and private sharing of municipal services. New York served as the model for the San Francisco organization; but many individual companies copied their regulations from other cities, including Boston, Baltimore, Philadelphia, and, in the case of the French Lafayette Company, Paris.

Most important, building habits changed. After the May and June occurrences razed over thirty square blocks, the preference for masonry and stone marvelously increased, as San Franciscans grimly set about putting up thick-walled, iron-shuttered, tile-roofed brick fortresses (which often had their own water supply), determined not to be victimized again.[45] All these developments together, rather than lynching, finally provided relative immunity from fire.

These public or highly visible private measures were the first line of defense; but a great number of smaller precautions supplemented them, since conflagrations were a very personal matter. The alarm bell usually emptied the populace into the streets; and from there they dashed off to help, to watch, or to save their own goods—and sometimes to do all three. McCrackan kept his law books in crates upon his shelves, and merchant J. D. Farwell parked a scow under his store to allow immediate evacuation. Others located their structures on the outskirts of town, to windward, or as William Weston, "in three different quarters of the city, in order to lessen the chance of loosing [sic] all at one fire." Even so, the blaze of May 4, 1851 "made a clean sweep of his property."[46]

Altogether, these precautions were a great improvement, but glaring weaknesses remained, particularly carelessness. In 1855 the Grand Jury reminded the wardens of the "vast number of stove funnels passing through wooden tenements," which the *Alta* said rendered "the building/s/ liable to take fire at any moment by a spark or two lodged in a dry spot." Residents refused en masse to correct this difficulty or to be careful on the Fourth of July. In addition, the streets were often blocked or broken, so much so that in October 1855 the volunteers refused to "roll their machines below Davis Street, on any occasion of fire, until the streets were repaired." People persisted in building wooden structures in violation of the ordinance; and in 1853 a minor furor arose over an inhabitant who had powder illegally stored within a few feet of a serious blaze, thus endangering the firemen. Naturally, the city promptly passed an ordinance prescribing heavier fines.[47]

The economy drive of 1855–56 further reduced the department's effectiveness. In those years, nearly half the cisterns were out of repair; most of the hose was defective; Howard Engine Company was actually evicted from its headquarters; and the Consolidation Act reduced funds to the absurdly low figure of $8,000 per annum. In addition, only one watch tower, no fire coroner (building inspector), an occasional shakedown of businessmen, and considerable drinking at fires complicated the situation.[48]

The close connection between the fire companies and politics also hampered efficiency. In 1855 the council Democrats and Know Nothings deadlocked over appropriations to their favorite companies, endangering everyone. The continual struggle of the volunteers to increase their independence of both politicians and government paralleled these problems. Finally, there was a growing number of "kid glove" members of the department, usually merchants or politicians, who bought their way in to secure exemptions from jury or militia duty and to gain prestige, but avoided fires.[49]

Perhaps more serious yet was the maldistribution of services. Most of the volunteer units and cisterns concentrated in or close to the business district in an area bounded by Bush, Stockton, Front, and Broadway, with only two companies outside, one at the Mission Dolores and one south of Market.[50] Since the majority of brick buildings were located downtown, the greatest protective capacity was at the least flammable place. The department's democratic organization hampered the attempt to correct the imbalance. Companies refused to move to areas of greatest need and blocked the entry of new companies from an ill-protected district, and the chief was powerless to force these necessary measures.[51] The faulty distribution remained into the sixties, even after the advent of the reforming People's party.

A tragi-comic incident in 1856 when flames were detected at a suburban slaughterhouse strikingly demonstrated the consequences outside the center city. To reach this part of town, firemen had to haul their engines to the top of California Street Hill and down to Larkin at the bottom. On the descent, the exhausted men could not keep their engines from running away. As a result, the equipment was damaged, the men narrowly missed a similar fate, and both reached the scene just in time to poke around in the ashes.[52]

Despite its defects, the department received and deserved high praise from the citizenry. It performed with relative efficiency in much, if not all, of the town; it had good morale and courage; and it was usually free from the rowdyism that plagued its Eastern counterparts. "After it [a fire] is over, instead of stopping a while to have a fight—as they [firemen] file past one another on their way home," wrote volunteer Robert S. Lammot, "you hear such cries as Hurrah for the 'Howard'! She's always the first in service —Three cheers for the 'California'—she is *some* at a fire—There comes the 'Monumental'! good for the Baltimoreans. . . ." The community realized that almost any undetected spark might jeopardize the entire town and esteemed the defenders accordingly. Ironically, in a place universally admitted to be glutted with selfish individuals, the most highly respected set of men least embodied this egotism. It is obvious that in defending the town, self-interested and altruistic motives intertwined closely. Yet the latter were admired. "Their voluntary occupation was a good and grand one, and required much skill and courage," wrote the *Annals* in a typical tribute, "while it was pursued under circumstances involving great personal danger, and often much inconvenience and pecuniary loss to individuals, who, at the call of duty, cheerfully forsook their own private business to save the community from a terrible calamity." [53] Once again, the duality had to be worked out, this time between individual and community.

The *Annals* rightly considered these conflagrations disasters. Yet one of the odd features was their ambiguous effect. For the burned-out trader who owned his goods and store, the fires were tragic; but for the commission merchant who had an oversupply of Eastern goods, the possessor of construction materials, and the mechanic who would use them to rebuild, the searings often turned into windfalls. Likewise, as Alexander Stott noted, "Fires here have covered up the rascalities of many /a/ one. . . ." Whether or not he was referring to such knavery, Jonas Winchester wrote to his wife of the fire of September 17, 1850, which burned out his *Pacific News*, "I am confident my prospects are improved by the disaster." [54]

The community benefited also. Fires razed the city hall, streets, and hospital and promoted vigilantism; yet they had a curiously constructive influence as well, forcing preventive measures, clearing out bad housing, and replacing it with better buildings, all of which lent permanency to urban development. Businessmen either had to abandon or to increase greatly their stake in San Francisco by erecting expensive, fireproof structures. Multi-thousand dollar investments in brick buildings thereafter bound those who stayed to the city; whereas before, a canvas and board shanty had been an evanescent commitment.

This positive effect helped solve an allied urban problem. During the entire period, springs, wells, cisterns, and shipments from Saucelito (spelled Sausalito today) supplied water. Initially, the city slaked its thirst from the first of these sources; but artesian wells, mostly located east of Montgomery, soon replaced the springs. By 1855 there were 175 artesian wells, some driven by windmills. Water drawn from these or brought by tug from Sauce-lito sold at five to twelve cents a pail from wagons or stationary tanks. In 1856 the carters, not to be outdone by other enterprises, formed themselves into a monopoly. Though the Marin County product was better, its distributors found it increasingly difficult to compete with the local article; and the Saucelito Water Com-pany's share of the market declined markedly.[55]

This system proved inadequate, especially during fires. The cis-terns had to be filled by dray and hose with salt water from the bay, a costly, time-consuming, and unhandy process. In addition, a desire to share the large profits of the cartmen supplemented this initial impetus.[56]

The corporation began by drilling an artesian well in the Plaza, but this effort encountered no water. In March 1851 Azro D. Mer-rifield requested permission to provide public and private needs by piping water into the city from a lagoon near the Presidio. Since the council was about to step down, the Englishman's peti-tion was laid on the table. However, the fire of May 4, 1851, got it off again; and the proposal passed unanimously in early June. A companion measure by C. K. Hotaling, involving a reservoir atop Telegraph Hill, steam engines to fill it, and gravitational dis-tribution, cleared the council and then went straight into limbo.[57]

The final contract with Merrifield's Mountain Lake Water Com-pany contained a twenty-year grant with an exclusive privilege for the first five. In return, the city received free water and the right to appoint three of the five-man rate commission. Yet the works did not ultimately revert to the corporation as originally provided. This system, supposedly patterned after the Croton Aqueduct of New York City, was to include storage reservoirs and redistribution facilities.[58]

When Merrifield left town in the summer of 1851, a local group bought his franchise but accomplished nothing until the city agreed in 1852 to make the grant a monopoly. The promoters said that otherwise they could not raise the capital. Difficulties plagued the company from its inception. The presence of several politician-speculators in the organization made investors suspicious; and labor troubles and a trade depression followed a late ground breaking in May 1853. By mid-1854 these obstacles had halted the project and necessitated an extension of the completion deadline. But in 1855 the *Alta* eagerly looked forward to having running water as well as gas in the home. "The comforts of life could then be said to have arrived nearly at perfection." Unfortunately, the amenities remained only half faultless because the company finished no more than one-third of its aqueduct. Its deadline was extended until January 1, 1857, but not thereafter.[59]

The San Francisco City Water Works then acquired the grant. By fluming the contents of Lobos Creek, which emptied into the Golden Gate, around the top of the peninsula and into a reservoir on Greenwich, this company finally succeeded in introducing a large-scale supply of water, but not until September 1858.[60] To contemporaries the whole affair seemed inordinately drawn out; but when compared to the efforts of more venerable Eastern cities, San Francisco's record was good.[61]

The inadequate artificial water supply as well as the super-abundant natural one aggravated the problem of health. Especially in the years 1848–50, the damp, cool climate was one of the foremost circumstances which combined to make the Bay City a center of sickness. The Gold Rush introduced large-scale tent living; and when the rainy season came, particularly that of 1849–50, widespread illness ensued. The scarcity of good drinking water increased the incidence of poor health. Furthermore, as the transportation center of the state, San Francisco received the afflicted from the mines, especially during the "sickly" season of July and August, when the heat in the diggings was greatest. Ocean vessels added more patients who had contracted fever on the Isthmus, scurvy on the trip around the Horn, or some other illness.[62] Finally, the city was often crowded and always very dirty and its people frequently ill housed.

The most common complaints between 1848 and 1850 were dysentery and diarrhea; some medical observers claimed that at times five to ten deaths per day followed from these and other causes. These maladies continued to be important, but consumption and other pulmonary disorders subsequently replaced them as the foremost killers. Scurvy, cholera, typhoid, and various fevers also took a large toll, although they came irregularly. Venereal disease, though not a leading cause of death, resulted in the largest number of hospitalizations.

For nearly half of its first decade, San Francisco was ill equipped to handle these infirmities. Commodore Shubrick of the U.S. Naval Forces commandeered one of Thomas Larkin's sheds for a hospital as early as April 1847; but not until late 1849 did the common council take an interest in the mounting illness. By November, the storms that forced the aldermen to undertake street construction also created a health emergency which goaded them into naming two doctors "to establish an outdoor practice among the indigent sick townsmen." In December a local hospital was paid to care for them, and this contract came into the hands of Dr. Peter Smith on February 5, 1850.[63]

This pattern usually prevailed through 1856, but the price varied as did the party to whom the patients were "farmed out." Private secular individuals, the state, secular individuals again, and, finally, a Catholic sisterhood successively tried the job with varied results. These arrangements raised objections throughout the decade. The sisters were opposed as Romanist, the politicians as careless, and the private contractors as self-interested and therefore tempted to abuse their trust. As it turned out, these latter fears were often realized; but the aspiration to get the indigent sick under direct municipal supervision was not.

The only municipal clinic opened in the Waverly Hotel late in 1850 and burned in the summer of 1851. Thereafter, as formerly, the contract system prevailed. Smith's hospital had preceded the Waverly into the flames; so after mid-1851, San Francisco paid the state to care for its patients. The State Marine Hospital was established in 1850 (reorganized in 1851) and supported by the state because the transportation hub of California always had an undue number of ill nonresidents on hand. The city relied on this institution until 1855, when a political scandal destroyed it. During 1855–56, Dr. Gibbons and the Sisters of Mercy held the "franchise" successively.

Besides the usual facilities, special ones appeared in 1850 for cholera victims and in 1854 for smallpox patients. These were "pest houses," kept separate from the regular establishments in order to prevent contagion. Another important facility for caring for the sick, the U.S. Marine Hospital at Rincon Point, completed in December 1853, provided service only to sailors.

Private arrangements supplemented these public ones. The Odd Fellows and the Masons actively aided their sick members; and in 1854 a group of Americans founded the San Francisco Dispensary, which gave medical care and prescriptions to the needy. In addition, both the British Consul and the United States Customs Collector paid for treatment of their nationals, especially sailors, in the years just after 1848. The French, Swiss, Jews, and Chinese had their own "hospitals" or other provisions for helping their countrymen, and the Germans were building theirs as 1856 closed. From 1849 several other private hospitals functioned in the city, but how much use they got is not known. From the surviving letters and diaries, it would appear that private physicians, of whom there were many in San Francisco, usually treated noncharity patients at home. San Franciscans, like all other mid-nineteenth century Americans who could afford to, generally shunned hospitals.[64]

After 1850, therefore, numerous facilities alleviated suffering; but public facilities remained crowded and, with the exception of the Rincon Point institution for mariners, improperly housed. "The building occupied for this purpose is a miserable apology for a house, and is totally unfitted as a hospital for the sick," stormed a Grand Jury in 1853. "The want of room [there were 300 patients in 1853] is so serious an evil that the visitor becomes indignant at a policy which, by retaining this collection of sheds, must entail upon the poor patient additional suffering, and check both the efforts of nature and the physician in affording relief." [65]

Within these flimsy walls, efficiency varied. The Waverly Hotel hospital of Dr. Edward Chapin and that of the Sisters of Mercy were exemplary. The conduct of Dr. Smith's hospital stirred considerable controversy, with Whigs and friends upholding him and Democrats attacking. However, the first female nurse, Sophia A. Eastman, found the hospital "in a deplorable state, filled with the scourings of creation." Smith's predecessor had done little better, for a time even refusing to feed some of his patients during a contract dispute with the city. [66]

The State Marine Hospital generally received praise from the press and grand juries, but the establishment had its troubles. [67] It survived an investigation in 1851 into charges that it demanded excessive fees and took in boarders, but a later inquiry proved fatal. In 1855 the institution was found to have political and social as well as medical functions. The facility was under the guidance of Ned McGowan and James Claughley, two wheelhorse politicians in the San Francisco "Tammany" Democracy. Moreover, these worthies used the money to furnish gifts to prostitutes and mistresses, whose frequent presence may have enhanced the esthetic dimension of the place though probably not the sanitary. In addition, the entire medical staff, as well as the movable patients, was required to vote "the ticket"—as many times as they could—on pain of dismissal. Resident physician of this charity hospital, S. B. Mills, had luxurious quarters in the building, complete with shooting gallery. To add a final gruesome touch, dark hints that rotten eggs were served to the sick and that corpses remained unburied till the rats had chewed the flesh off their faces circulated about town. Though the directors claimed that these activities did not interfere with the mission of the hospital, the state legislature apparently concluded that the pleasure provided by this achievement in medicine did not offset the accompanying political and social pain.

The "insane" probably got worse care than any other group. The corporation housed them initially in the old prison brig, but by 1852 the state had established an asylum at Stockton and sent San Francisco's patients there.[68] Yet because the security at the state institution was on a par with that of the city jail, the inmates were soon back at the Golden Gate. The government made further provision in 1852 by farming them out to a private individual. Lodging in the station house was the attention given to those not sent to Stockton or to this local party.

A number of other steps helped safeguard the community's well-being, mostly after 1850. The habit of leaving animal carcasses around the town brought forth the Bay City's first sanitation regulation. In 1847 the council prohibited the shooting of any carrion-eating fowl, thereby making these creatures the official city scavengers. Thereafter, the protective ordinances increased somewhat in sophistication. In 1850 the instrument of progress was an epidemic and its symbol of achievement, a Board of Health, replete with resident physician and assistants. First suggested by the San Francisco Medical Society in a report on the cholera menace, this body organized shortly thereafter on November 5, 1850. Abolished in 1851 and re-established in 1852, it again became defunct, only to be called into service once more by a supposed epidemic threat from several hundred sick Chinese. The cholera outbreak of 1850 further prompted the city to crack down on refuse dumping, provide a garbage scow, and begin agitation for the creation of a meat inspectorate—born four years later. Other ordinances regulating privies, refuse dumping, livery stables, and wastes from chandlers and distillers followed in time. A kind of negative zoning ultimately banned slaughterhouses from the city limits and prohibited the erection of hospitals within certain sections.[69] The municipality even hired human scavengers to replace the birds, though these fowl plus dogs, rats, rains, and tides probably reduced the mess as much as the council's appointees.

Altogether, men, animals, and nature were not very successful. An 1852 description of a North Beach block revealed the level of achievement. "In the square . . . persons have for a long time been in the habit of emptying cart loads of garbage until the space is by this time lined with an immense pile of rubbish and filth of the worst description." In itself, a refuse-filled block in a dirty city is not so alarming, except that the area was "opposite the State Marine Hospital." [70]

All in all, San Francisco became considerably more healthy after 1851, but it is not likely that its precautions were the most important cause of the improvement. In an age of medical practices such as bleeding, leeching, and cupping, their ineffectiveness was perhaps to be expected. Good housing and water, increasingly present after 1851, probably had more influence in reducing illness than all other city and private efforts combined.[71]

Before 1851 the community's sick suffered greatly; and like many human situations, this one showed the best and worst in men's nature. Touching stories of friend nursing friend back to health abound, but so do tales of indifference. "The unsheltered sick have been inhumanly neglected during the excitement created by the gold discoveries, and many have died who with proper attention . . . might have survived," the *Star and Californian* complained in 1848. "We think the demand for a public hospital at San Francisco is urgent." [72]

The struggle for law and order in the metropolis, like so many other themes in its history, did not begin with the Gold Rush. In the year before the advent of the argonauts (during which time the town grew from 459 to about 1,000), the bay hamlet witnessed at least one murder, several duels, a couple of jailbreaks, several robberies including one large one, a mutiny in the harbor, many desertions, some squatting, and instances of drunkenness and rioting in abundance. "Street turmoils are almost a daily occurrence," the *California Star* lamented in December 1847. "We have among us a most finished set of scape graces, and unscrupulous knaves, well fitted for any lawless and violent work whatever." [73]

In the years after 1848 the rascals multiplied and the notoriety of the city grew apace. Much of its ill fame represents press exaggeration, but a large part of its reputation was well deserved.

Many influences contributed to the unfortunate prevalence of law-lessness, not the least of which was the continuation of very weak urban government. Law enforcement was not one of the matters upon which the community lavished money. Moreover, until 1850 the city and county judiciaries were inadequate, and the United States courts did not even open until 1851. In the beginning some bad men occupied the bench; and even when good ones presided, a tremendous backlog of cases initially delayed, if not thwarted, justice. The courts improved markedly; but even so, many crim-inals escaped punishment.

Into this situation, which combined minimum restraints with maximum temptations, came people from all over the globe. Many were scoundrels, especially those from the British penal colonies in Australia, but also some from the Eastern United States. Most residents paid scant attention to government, law enforcement in-cluded, until something went wrong. Not that crime failed to elicit enormous dissatisfaction. But legal remedies bored the citizenry. They expected the police and courts to protect them and to curtail lawlessness, though they frequently settled their own grievances.

This dependence on personal violence was pervasive. The squat-ter difficulties were often settled without resort to legal procedure, and men quarreling over the use of buildings did the same thing. On one occasion, lawyer McCrackan of staid New Haven found himself wielding a Colt's edition of the law to dissuade a hired gang of sailors from evicting him from his office. Rival steamboats rammed each other; their captains exchanged shots "in passing"; hostile bands of teamsters beat up on one another; crimps shang-haiied sailors; competing confectioners fought; and lawyers, jour-nalists, politicians, theater managers, actors, sporting men, and most anyone else with a grievance also "had it out"—quite often in the very midst of town.

Supporting such habits must have been profitable to the many downtown weapons dealers. "The most of our citizens if not all go armed," clergyman Francis Prevaux informed his parents in 1851. "I myself do not go out evenings without a cane which though it looks perfectly harmless . . . will be found to contain a sword two and a half feet long." [74] Other men went about with leaded canes, bowie knives, cowhides, and pistols. These were justified in the beginning as necessary to fend off "Sydney Ducks" (supposed criminals from Australian penal colonies); but the practice of carrying concealed weapons for use in personal combat outlived the downfall of the Australians and, in fact, survived both Vigilance Committees.

Fortunately, these "affairs" often turned out in opera bouffe style. In 1855 Frenchman J. Alexander Briant, pressed for payment of his obligations, decided to settle the debt, debtor, and creditor definitively. He walked into his tormentor's store carrying a carpetbag full of gun powder, pointed a pistol into it, and fired. Despite the grave possibilities of such an act, the angry Gaul only succeeded in singeing off one beard, rendering himself sans culottes, and blowing the pool cues out of the hands of the sporting men across the street.[75] Many of the "affrays" did not end so amusingly, however. Occasionally the "duello" caused some stir, especially after a sensational killing, but not enough to curtail the custom substantially.

The universal transiency that rapidly shuffled witnesses, prosecutors, and criminals in and out of town and the general lack of restraint typical of this new community further encouraged illegal activities. Finally, the poverty which prevailed in spite of the Gold Rush supplied further reasons for the decided increase of lawlessness. From 1847 to 1856, however, the cycle of crime fluctuated considerably.

The papers bemoaned the amount of iniquity from June 1847 to January 1848; but not much was heard thereafter about wrongdoing until the summer of 1849, when a band of rowdies provoked the first and mildest of three outbursts of vigilantism. The gang, called the Hounds, or Regulators, included primarily disbanded veterans of Stevenson's Regiment of New York Volunteers. According to a local tavernkeeper, John H. Brown, businessmen

San Francisco in 1847.

San Francisco in January 1849.

Panorama of San Francisco's waterfront in 1850.

View down Sacramento Street, 1856.

San Francisco's first high school graduates, December 15, 1859.

Sansome Hook and Ladder Company, 1856.

Pacific Engine Company Number Eight, 1856.

Execution of James P. Casey and Charles Cora by the Vigilance Committee of San Francisco on May 22, 1856.

Fire of June 22, 1851.

(Above) Assassination of James King of William in 1856.

(Left) Portrait of James King of William.

Suburbia, South Park in 1856.

Outskirts of the city, Washerwoman's Lagoon in 1856.

At the edge of the city, Mission Dolores in 1860. This settlement was established in 1776.

(Left) The Miners Exchange Bank in 1856. (Right) First Baptist Church on Washington Street between Dupont (Grant Avenue) and Stockton in 1850. This church, completed in July 1849, is said to be the first Protestant house of worship erected in California.

First state celebration, held October 29, 1850, in honor of California's admission to the Union.

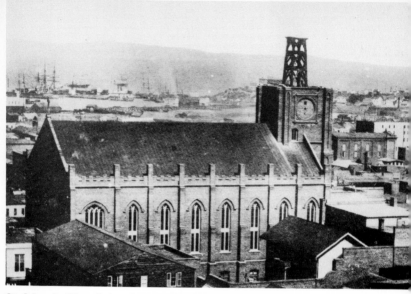

St. Mary's Church in 1856, with unfinished spire.

The El Dorado and the Jenny Lind Theatre (City Hall) in 1856. Portsmouth Square is in the foreground.

hired the Hounds to catch runaway sailors at $25 a head. The group also had some duties as agents of the government, at least in the beginning of their career. At first, they did good service to both port and city; but later they degenerated into a "plunder-bund." [76]

As one of the few organizations in the anarchic town, the Hounds were a formidable challenge. Though most of their victims apparently were foreigners, especially Spanish Americans, they harassed and bullied others as well. The reign of lawlessness came to an end on the night of Sunday, July 15, when the gang attacked a group of Latin Americans living in a tent colony on Telegraph Hill. This incident, in which several "Chilenos" were wounded, a few robbed, and all roughed up, provided the crisis that finally roused the community from its lethargy. "There is great excitement among property holders and organized parties patrol the town nightly under arms," Charles Winslow wrote to his wife on July 19. A volunteer police force (there was no regular one) of 230 organized, which promptly rounded up the Hounds. A jury trial, at which two citizens supplemented distrusted Alcalde T. M. Leavenworth on the bench, condemned the troublemakers to banishment, imprisonment, and fines. The law did not generally carry out these sentences, however, because of the lack of facilities—such as a prison. [77]

With the elimination of the Hounds, lawlessness declined; but civic interest in preventive measures decreased proportionately. [78] Not until September 1850 did crime once more reach alarming proportions; and the robberies, assaults, and some murders continued into the new year.

In late February, the dramatic beating and robbing of a merchant named Jansen again generated great excitement. Two suspects were caught and a lynching narrowly avoided. The people in mass meeting appointed a jury which, on February 23, four days after the robbery, heard the case. No lawyer would consent to prosecute; so a merchant, William T. Coleman, undertook the task. At the trial, the bench refused one of the prisoners, Thomas Berdue, the right to face his accuser and gave him only twenty minutes to produce certain witnesses. Moreover, as his lawyer, David Shattuck, pointed out, the prosecution based its case upon the testimony of Jansen, who was still in a stupor from his pummeling and not even present to be cross-examined. Both the press and citizenry remained convinced that the defendant was guilty and that he was not Berdue at all but the notorious Australian criminal James Stuart. The jury stood nine to three in favor of this opinion; but lacking unanimity, they turned the suspects over to the constituted legal authorities.[79]

Coleman tried again to get the residents to take the case into their own hands, but he failed; and the regular courts convicted Berdue.[80] As it turned out, the inhabitants, press, and courts all had been wrong. It was doubly fortunate, therefore, that they had not applied the later suggestion of reformers like James King of William that a majority rather than a unanimous decision be sufficient to convict, for the "people" certainly would have condemned an innocent man.

Whether because of or in spite of the actions of February, the crime cycle again dipped precipitously; and by the end of April, the leading newspaper speculated that the villains must have withdrawn. The large number of thefts that accompanied the fire of May 4, 1851, and continued thereafter demonstrated the incorrectness of this thesis.[81] As San Francisco neared mid-year, a crisis brewed once more.

On June 8 two separate meetings considered the disasters of fire and crime that had overtaken the city. At the Howard Street Presbyterian Church, the Reverend Samuel H. Willey told the congregation that the trouble was largely inherent in the situation. The difficulty of founding a new town under trying circumstances, one of which was enormous indifference to the public welfare, must be blamed for the ills which had beset the metropolis.[82] Far from thus sharing the guilt as Willey urged, the second gathering chose to level the finger of accusation at the "Sydney Ducks" or "Coves," the courts, and the lawyers. This conclave decided that the solution was a Committee of Vigilance.[83]

At its height, this group numbered about 500 and was led by the merchants. Apparently the Committee purposely excluded the working men; yet in all probability, they supported the extralegal actions as did most of the city press and a majority of everyone else, foreigners included.[84] In the course of its vigorous and highly organized activities, the Committee established patrols against fire and theft and deported numerous persons. Its members also asserted the right to search without a warrant, though they subsequently dropped this claim; and they denied the right of habeas corpus, forcibly entered and searched the house of a man accused by one of their members, the banker Felix Argenti, of stealing from his mistress, and assaulted a ship captain who refused to have his longboat searched. But hanging was the activity for which the Vigilantes were most noted.

Three days after its founding, the citizens' body had its first "triumph" when a Sydney man named Jenkins was caught stealing a safe. The Vigilance Committee condemned him after a closed trial, without a lawyer, and carried out the sentence immediately on Portsmouth Plaza amidst a tumultuous midnight scene. The police and others tried to rescue the robber; but after much struggling, the "people" got him aloft.

The second victim was James Stuart, caught between the mission and the Presidio. After some days of confinement incommunicado, he confessed to numerous crimes and was hanged. Stuart, like the final two recipients of Vigilante justice, Samuel Whittaker and Robert McKenzie, was a "Sydney Duck." These latter two had not committed murder as had "English Jim," but they were lynched anyway.[85] Before they breathed their last, they were rescued by the sheriff and governor only to be recaptured by a squad which swooped down upon the county jail, whisked off the prisoners, and seventeen minutes later helped dispatch them amidst another scene of frenzied excitement.

Though never formally disbanded, the organization ceased active operations after September. For about two months after the final hangings, crime subsided; but between late October and June 1852 a new outbreak became so serious that the Vigilantes threatened to swing into action again in May. Yet not until November 1852, did large-scale lawlessness begin anew, and it persisted well into 1853.[86] In 1854, 1855, and early 1856 there were once more widespread complaints about waves of lawbreaking.

The last one of these helped revive the Vigilantes. This movement was touched off by the dramatic killing of two prominent people. General William H. Richardson, U.S. Marshal, was shot by a gambler named Charles Cora after a disagreement in a saloon. Despite widespread outrage, the citizens made no extralegal moves. Instead, two hearings followed: the trial in the press returned a verdict of murder, but the one in court hung between murder and manslaughter. The slayer, therefore, was languishing in jail when the next killing occurred. This time the lethal bullet struck James King of William, a crusading reform editor of the *Evening Bulletin,* who was locked in a newspaper squabble with James P. Casey, a political brawler. The martyred journalist fell on the fourteenth of May, and the Vigilance Committee immediately began enrolling several thousand men into military companies. As in 1851, the movement had the support of almost every class or division and was led by merchants. The opposition "Law and Order Party" also included many group representatives but not very many total followers.

The first move, a descent on the county jail, netted Casey and Cora. When King died a few days later, the two prisoners—after a secret trial which the Vigilantes claimed to be fair—were hanged before a huge throng of men, women, and children. The Committee then proceeded to other things, mostly the deportation of those supposedly responsible for political corruption. They exiled about twenty more before the rising subsided and probably scared many others out of town. One captive, Yankee Sullivan, the pugilist, committed suicide in custody. Before the citizens group disbanded at the end of the summer, its rope was again called into use. One Joseph Heatherington, undeterred by the two previous lynchings, shot a Dr. Randall in an affray. He and a convicted murderer named Brace were hanged.

Although the 1856 institution was better organized than its predecessor, it nearly came to grief when some of its members tried to arrest a State Supreme Court Justice. David S. Terry, a very tough man, stabbed his would-be captor; but luckily, the arresting "officer" lived and the judge was eventually "acquitted." Had the wounded man died, Terry reportedly would have been hanged.[87]

The incursion of an armed citizenry into the process of law enforcement was, on the whole, unfortunate. Yet most contemporaries of the committees defended them.[88] The essence of this defense was that the situation was so bad and the legal authorities so incompetent that the people were justified in taking the law into their own hands. The Vigilantes were supposedly sober, moderate, fair men, not a wild lynch mob; and their work was relatively effective. Many admitted that popular indifference encouraged lawlessness, but this side of the controversy got decidedly less emphasis. It is beyond cavil that the Vigilantes reduced the criminal population by the number hanged and deported. In doing so, they eliminated a gang of robbers in 1851 and a bevy of political bullies in 1856. Yet the deterrent soon wore off.

On October 10, 1851, a bare six weeks after the hanging of Whittaker and McKenzie, the *Herald* reported a brutal murder. Eleven days later the *Alta* added the depressing intelligence that "within a short time past a gang of miserable, thieving, scoundrels have entered our city." Nearly the same thing happened in 1856. The Vigilantes disbanded on August 18; yet by October 22 the *Alta* admitted that "crime, vice, dissipation still rear their hydra-heads in our midst—evil-doing of every description is still practiced; and although more cautious and circumspect in their operations, offenders against law and the public weal are scarcely less numerous or successful than of old. In both 1851 and 1856, therefore, the Vigilantes achieved at best only a six-to-eight-week respite from the usual amount of criminality.[89]

Even in their heyday, the committees did not deter the most serious crime. On the day after "English Jim" was hanged in 1851, Francisco Guerrero was clubbed to death in broad daylight on the Mission Dolores Plank Road. Another murder followed the lynching of Jenkins by a scant two weeks.[90] The year 1856 witnessed the same scene. On May 30, one Chinese resident stabbed another; and two days later, another knifed a man on Jackson Street Wharf. One Frazier attacked George H. Rhodes at Hillman's Temperance House on June 6; on June 24, an unknown assailant shot William Ford; and on July 6, two Chinese were murdered at the Lagoon. Three days later a certain Slater stabbed one McLaughlin at the fashionable Rassette House; on the fourteenth, Mrs. Jordan did the same to ex-police officer Henry Darling; on the eighteenth, there was an infanticide; and one day later, Jacob Levy killed a thirteen-year-old boy, Jacob Spiegelstein, by clubbing him over the head with a brick. On July 24, Thomas Turner shot Luke Pierce; the next day Heatherington killed Randall; on August 1, one Mexican knifed another; and on the sixth, ex-policeman Jameson wounded James Gordon and George Russel in a similar fashion. Proving that nothing was sacred, one Stevens attacked a Vigilante on the 27th with a slung shot; on September 2, there was a "deadly assault" by Edward Travis; and on September 19, a "SHOOTING AFFRAY" in a lager beer saloon.[91] Sandwiched between these more violent crimes were several large robberies and numerous "ordinary" assaults and batteries.

Obviously the reign of virtue was punctuated by frequent backsliding, yet all the while the press claimed that perfect order prevailed. Even if the necessary statistics existed to prove the decline of lawlessness, such words as "cleansed" and "purified"—so frequently used by Vigilante defenders—would be wholly unjustified.

The same thing was true of fire. It was generally agreed that incendiarism caused nearly all the city's terrible fires. Allegedly, the 1851 Vigilantes abolished this threat, yet the crime of arson remained common in subsequent years. Even at the height of its power, the Vigilance Committee did not do away with incendiarism. On June 11, they hanged Jenkins as a deterrent; and on June 22, more than thirteen squares burned. Since arson was generally held to be the cause, the death of Jenkins made no more impression on the fire bug than the hanging of Stuart had on Guerrero's murderer and the later lynchings had on the cutters, shooters, and robbers of the summer of 1856.

It seems clear, therefore, that the Vigilantes' effectiveness has been overrated. So has their moderation and fairness. It may be true that the San Francisco committees were a far cry from those in the mines; yet incommunicado jailings, secret trials, denial of the right of habeas corpus, refusal of legal counsel, arrogation of the power to search without warrants, condemnation to death without appeal, and extralegal deportations do not constitute anything close to the American ideal of moderation and fairness.[92]

The execution of Cora was particularly unfair. The slain man was a popular United States marshal, the accused, a gambler and the paramour of a prostitute. The papers promptly labeled the killing murder. On November 11, 1855, James King called Cora "a dastardly assassin" and charged that the victim had been "*shot down* in . . . cold blood, unarmed, and without a moment's warning." The entire press adversely discussed the character of the supposed murderer, especially the fact that he was a gambler, and hinted darkly that his mistress was mysteriously moving to secure his acquittal by infamous means. "Little Richie," on the other hand, they pictured as a respectable family man.

With these preconceptions drummed into its head, the town sat back to watch the trial. After the usual jury-dodging, of which even King complained, a panel was selected; but upon hearing the case, it could not agree. Immediately the press cried that justice had been perverted again. "Hung be the heavens with black!" cried the *Bulletin*. "The money of the gambler and prostitute has succeeded." [93]

Cora subsequently fell victim to "Vigilante justice," and very few
tears were shed in his behalf. Yet they should have been, for his
whole case was grossly unfair, starting with the prejudicial newspaper comments. His jury was a good one, not the usual set of
courtroom loafers who presided over the majesty of the law in the
Justice of the Peace courts. Far from letting him off, that group
agreed upon punishment but not on how much, since the penalty
for manslaughter was so lenient that some of the jurors held out
for murder. The lesser verdict could have been reached then and
there but for this intransigeance. Moreover, the prosecution refused
to allow the introduction of evidence that Richardson was a violent man while the press made his antagonist's background notorious. Yet witnesses testified that the marshal had come to the
saloon where the shooting occurred in search of the gambler on
two different occasions in a state of inebriation. Stranger still is
the fact that he came in the company of two politicians, one of
whom was Vi Turner, a prominent "sporting man." The prosecution itself admitted that the deceased had threatened to slap the
accused's face on several occasions. In an age of the "duello," the
possible consequences of this menacing gesture were obvious, especially to a Southerner like Richardson. In fact, as his own press
supporters willy nilly pointed out, he was the aggressor throughout.

The whole unseemly fracas began in a theater when the dead
man's wife objected to being stared at by several men. The general told them to avert their gaze, but they were looking instead
at another woman, supposedly Belle Cora, sitting close by. The
marshal thereupon tried to have her put out; but since there was
no law against a prostitute's presence, he failed. This ill-conceived
attempt to protect frail womanhood from what King called "the
breath of the harlot" put the two men on a collision course.

It was averred, quite possibly accurately, that Cora's friends
tried to influence the jury. However, that was no more reprehensi-
ble than the newspapers' effort to prejudice the whole town against
the gambler. At worst, Belle's supposed attempts could only be

considered as "equal tampering." Yet even if this meddling did occur and it had secured the reprieve, that does not prove the charge of murder. As a matter of fact, the Vigilante court, presumably uninfluenced by the friends of the accused, divided in the same manner as the legal panel. Both were hung juries; but in the case of the former, the rule of the majority prevailed rather than that of unanimity. It must have pleased the newly departed shade of James King of William for Cora to be condemned in this manner, for "majority rule" in jury trials was one of his pet "reforms." In effect, the "people" intervened to avenge the aggressor in an affair of honor similar to dozens of others it had tolerated for years. That was partially true of the Heatherington case as well.

The Vigilantes strongly emphasized that the authorities remained either unwilling or unable to establish law and order. Profligate lawyers defended criminals with legal quibbles and delays; the courts were inefficient if not corrupt; the police were likewise wanting; and juries were easily packed. Though the situation was a good deal more complex than this, the indictment was true. Yet the lynchings did nothing to correct these defects. The despised politicians, however, did. In February 1856, Frank Tilford, Broderick's lieutenant, carried through the legislature an important legal reform which increased the maximum sentence for manslaughter from three to fifteen years and provided a punishment for meddling with juries. This lack of a tough penalty was exactly what had temporarily saved Cora.

What is more, by 1856 the judiciary was much superior to that of 1851, and a backlog of cases did not delay justice. San Francisco in 1856 was not a raw frontier town without a government, and thus the Vigilantes were not filling a legal vacuum as they certainly had in the Hounds affair of 1849. To find a man guilty of murder was difficult, but the citizenry had made next to no effort before the crisis of 1856 to procure better legal procedures.

The people themselves enormously complicated one aspect of the problem. The imperfections of the jury system were especially flagrant and particularly relevant to the issue of crime. "Jurying" was, for some, a way of making a living and not necessarily an honest one. Yet one of the hardest tasks involved getting a "respectable" person, especially a businessman, to neglect his store for a judicial panel.[94] People excused this notorious reluctance on the grounds that it took only one rascal to pack the panel and therefore disrupt the processes of justice. That may have been true in some cases, but leaving the field to the scoundrels could not have helped matters. Moreover, the tampering issue was never a key one on which the people demanded reform until the end of the period. Citizens stubbornly refused to serve the courts and just as obstinately neglected to regenerate them.

Neither the first Committee nor the citizens attempted to do much about the widespread personal violence. For example, during the first uprising, one of the Vigilantes, William Graham, and another man shot it out in the bright light of day on Portsmouth Plaza in the heart of town. Graham, as well as two bystanders, was wounded. In 1851, at the very climax of the extralegal activities, the passion for personal encounters apparently increased rapidly. "I told you in my last that the 'Duello' was becoming all the rage, and last week we had three more," wrote McCrackan to his family in September.[95] Of the four men hanged in 1856, three came to this end by their attempt to settle grievances in the long-tolerated style. It is to King's credit that he inveighed against the "code," but his death by a variant shows how strong the habit was and what price the community paid for its inaction.

In fact, the citizens' organizations were always quite selective in deciding what crimes they would consider. At the fire of June 1851 a mob killed two innocent men thought to be stealing. Neither punishment nor inquiry followed this deed.[96] The fate of Yankee Sullivan was especially preposterous. He was charged only with ballot box stuffing, which makes his confinement-induced suicide even more outrageous, though hardly anyone noticed. In another case, the community protected a ship captain, later convicted in court of having brutally mistreated his men, from a gang of sailors. Vigilante defenders saw this incident as an example of their fairness, but the failure even to investigate the charges is better proof of a double standard.

Of the many violent crimes that occurred during the movement in 1856, only that of Heatherington was punished. Moreover, a man named Rod Backus, who had been legally found guilty of taking a life, was passed over for Cora, who had not, and for Brace, who had. The '56 group saw fit to deport politicians accused of ballot fraud, but not corrupt businessmen such as Felix Argenti, who had tried on one occasion to steal several hundred thousand dollars worth of corporation real estate. How the Committee chose the recipients of their "justice" is indeed an intriguing matter.

The extraordinary emphasis on vigilantism has meant that the sensational and atypical aspects of law enforcement have nearly crowded out the ordinary in the city's histories. The committees that usurped part of this duty in the summers of 1849, 1851, and 1856 and whose tenure "in office" did not amount to nine months in all, have received endless attention at the expense of the police who held the job most of the time. Yet their everyday exertions reveal at least as much and probably more about the struggle for order as the periodic uprisings of lynch-minded citizens. In fact, the normal efforts tell much about the irregular.

The origin of the police force goes back at least to 1847, when the council appointed two constables to keep the peace. Later in the year they halved this contingent; and to make up for the deficiency, the councilmen became jointly responsible to aid in the maintenance of law and order. The alcalde also served as something of a law enforcement officer, as did the sheriff and, for a time, even the Regulators. Not much is known of this system except that it was inadequate, as the subsequent Hounds' episode indicates. In the wake of that crisis, a regular police force organized in August 1849 (and the first militia company in late July), and reorganized several times, in fact, almost yearly.[97] The annual shake-up markedly affected pay, numbers, and political composition.

On the whole, the city took very little notice. The government never had a very clear commitment to the establishment of wise and workable police regulations, and the people had even less. Despite all the excitement over the Vigilantes, the public sustained no significant pressure upon the municipality to deepen its interest in its permanent law enforcement capacity.

Most of the time, the police department was caught between crime wave-generated emergencies and economy drives. The first of these came in February 1850, when Alderman Samuel Brannan, a prime mover in each Vigilante uprising, unsuccessfully urged a drastic reduction of the force. Instead, the manpower level remained at about seventy-five until after the 1851 Vigilante upheaval. The false security induced by that occurrence plus the perennial demand for frugality pared the number to thirty by January 10, 1852. Later that year the total climbed to fifty; and in 1853, to fifty-six. A crime wave in 1854 spurred a further increase to eighty, but the retreat of the menace and the budget axe again halved the ranks. At the time of the 1856 Vigilante outburst and even after, the police force for a city of 50,000 was down to thirty-four, approximately half as large as that of 1849, which had served a much smaller population.[98]

As with other services, the center city received better coverage and the outlying districts worse or none at all. In February 1857, the chief of police reported that he could not "extend the regular beats beyond Stockton, Pacific and Market streets." Periodic protests from the press and the unprotected North Beach and Rincon Point areas indicate that this maldistribution was a matter of long standing. Even downtown was ill protected. When the department had fifty-six officers in 1854, for example, only fifteen were on the streets at any one time. The remainder were off duty or assigned to the Recorder's Court, the Mission Dolores, the marshal's office, the jail, or the chain gang. Less than twenty men on foot, stationed within the district enclosed by Market, Stockton, Pacific, and the water did not insure "saturation" coverage.[99]

Occasionally, as in 1854, the council took up the problem but decided that an adequate force was a luxury that the municipality could not afford. A group of privately paid special police generally supplemented the regulars. These men often numbered as high as thirty and were subject to the orders of the city marshal; yet even so, man-power remained insufficient. Moreover, since they were employed by businessmen, the special deputies sometimes served to protect illicit activities rather than to detect them.

Remuneration was as inadequate as the numbers. Financial crises before both outbreaks of vigilantism found pay in arrears. In 1856 the police had not received their wages in eight months! Even when pay was regular, they received it in scrip, which was always depreciated. Ordinarily officers made about $100 per month, which in 1854 was less than a clerk at a local store, who brought home $131. Moreover, the latter did not have to face the unpleasant prospect of breaking up a drunken row in a saloon whose patrons were probably better armed than the United States soldiers at Fort Point or of patrolling the gloomy streets. The low and infrequent pay could not have encouraged much zeal, especially in protecting men like James King, who was leading a tax strike at a time when the men had not been paid in months. The papers constantly speculated on whether the patrolmen supplemented their inadequate incomes by the traditional payoff; and in several instances, they seem to have done just that.

From 1850 to 1855, the guardians of the law were nominated by the aldermen, mayor, and marshal with the councils naming most. This arrangement made the jobs a part of the patronage pie purchased by the highest bidder, thus sacrificing the ideal of security of tenure to the Jacksonian principle of rotation in office.[100] A large annual turnover resulted, therefore; but many men held over, even when the People's party carried out a considerable purge in 1856. The Charter of 1855 provided for a Board of Police Commissioners, consisting of the mayor, city marshal, and presidents of both boards of aldermen, who made appointments and presided over disciplinary hearings. Instead of being subject to removal every year, men could now be deprived of their posts only for just cause, thus hopefully eliminating partisan control.

Since the new institution was exactly divided between Democrats and Know Nothings, a deadlock over the nominations developed immediately. This impasse continued for several months, during which time the mayor swore in twenty officers on a special basis every three days, and the city could not even pay them.

Character references supposedly were an important safety device against the entry of bad characters into the department. The *Herald* described how the theory worked in practice in 1851 less than a week before the Vigilantes hanged Jenkins. "Men come to the Marshal recommended by leading merchants and property-holders, relying upon which he gives them a place only to find when the mischief is done, that they are worthless and faithless . . . ," complained the editor.[101]

However, the ten-year period witnessed a number of familiar reforms in law enforcement techniques. The department divided the city into separate beats, established a chain of command, kept criminal information records, and provided for a detective force from 1853 (they apparently were so efficient that they left hardly a trace of their activities except their expense account). Law enforcement officials neglected such suggested technological innovations as a daguerreotype file on criminals, but they did employ interurban telegraphic communications.

A major innovation came in January 1857, with the introduction of uniforms, which had been delayed by the policemen's protest that requiring standard dress constituted a financial hardship when their pay was low and irregular as well as "a badge of servitude." Heretofore, a badge comprised the only identification, and that could easily be concealed under a vest or collar or even counterfeited. With the police standing out, they could not duck out on riots, frequent low gaming halls except on official business, or politick while on duty. Moreover, citizens would ostensibly have a greater sense of security and the criminals a larger respect for the law if the police were highly visible.[102]

The efficiency of the department varied. Until about the fall of

1850 the press filled columns with paeans to the cops and their chief, Malachi Fallon, an ex-keeper of the Tombs Prison in New York. By the time of the hempen summer of 1851, the praise had turned sour; but the new force of the post-April Whig government won back the laurels. Until about the time of the 1856 lynchings, several more cycles of praise and blame succeeded, usually following the crime rate.[103]

The kinds of illegal activity detected remained relatively stable throughout. For the years through 1856, the Recorder's Court statistics exist for at least twenty-nine months. These show that the majority of offenses in the city were drunkenness, violence, and theft. The exact count is as follows: drunk and disorderly, 2,560; assault and battery, 1,249; larceny, robbery, and burglary, 1,227; violating city ordinances, 953; breach of the peace, 367; assault with a deadly weapon, 227; nuisance, 185; threats against life, 141; fighting, 134; vagrancy, 133; and malicious mischief, 121.[104]

Especially controversial was the number of murders. In December 1853, the *Chronicle* quoted District Attorney Byrne that "1,200 murders had been committed in the city and county within the last four years and there had never been but one conviction before the courts." [105] The estimate of condemnations was about right, but that of homicides was probably a ten-fold exaggeration. Even though incomplete, the extant crime register shows that only forty-seven murder cases appeared in the Recorder's statistics, that is, less than two a month. Twelve hundred murders would have been almost one per day, yet nothing close to that many were reported by a press that did not make a practice of overlooking any sensational occurrences.

Moreover, three papers supplied very different versions of this "horror story" within six months of its release. The *Chronicle* referred to the 1,200 *violent* deaths within the last four years, of which it speculated 150 to 300 were murders; the *Alta* carried a Grand Jury Report alluding to "the one hundred or more cold-blooded murders" in the last three years; and the *Pacific* had run the same story earlier. Despite these corrections, contemporaries frequently cited the 1,200 figure to show how unsafe the city was and therefore how necessary the resort to vigilantism.[106]

Just as there were special economic districts in the Bay City, so were there certain areas more prone to criminality. Prior to 1851, Clark's Point (called Sydney Town after the numerous Australians) and North Beach had already acquired unsavory reputations. Long Wharf, especially the Whitehall portion, shared this notoriety, as did Pacific Wharf and Street, usually referred to as "that classic neighborhood." [107] The wharves and waterfront in general abounded in tough sailor taverns, small-time gaming houses, and "Peter Funk" (phony) auction houses. Illegal, though quite genuine, sales of another kind occurred in the many houses of prostitution of Washington, Clay, Pacific, and Jackson near Stockton. From time to time, various subdistricts, such as "Cat Alley" on Pike or "Lansquenette Row" on Commercial vied with these better known sections for the attention of the police.

The rowdy parts of San Francisco, especially those which housed gambling and prostitution, were a growing concern to the residents. In the beginning they tolerated these pastimes because of the lack of recreation and women. By 1856 both deficiencies had been greatly ameliorated. Therefore, toward the end of the period, municipal and state governments passed laws against these pursuits. Yet the prohibitions merely proved what some had said all along, that is, that these customs could not be suppressed. Failing this, the community was moving toward another solution when the period closed.[108]

Many argued that in Eastern cities vice was not as openly practiced and that it was generally segregated in its own special district. This recommendation gained great popularity because of the spatial relationships in San Francisco. In order to get from the Stockton-Powell-Mason residential area to the shops on Montgomery, women and children had to pass down streets populated with courtesans. Virtuous females resented this contact and dis-

liked the influence that the harlots and their allies were thought
to have.[109]

These objections were decidedly environmentalistic. The *Alta*
explained that the Latin and Chinese ladies of pleasure contributed to the problem; but "the principal offenders, and those whose
example is the most dangerous to the public morals are the Americans, who dwell in splendid houses in the principal streets of
the city, and endeavor to attract attention by sitting before their
open windows and doors." Instead of relying upon personal
strength of character to save the individual from the attractions
of gambling or prostitution, people argued that it was "the duty
of the law makers to drive all such practices into the dark recesses of night, where the young and unsuspecting will not find
them, unless they seek them out. Those who wish to gamble will
find an opportunity," continued the *Chronicle*; "but the law should
remove the temptation from those who have not yet fallen into
the fatal passion." [110]

By 1857 the environment between Stockton and Montgomery
had been substantially improved, despite the failure of both segregation and suppression. The prostitutes and gamesters were made
to operate under cover even though they remained on the main
thoroughfares. Just as the slaughterhouses, candle makers, and
hospitals had to leave the city, the trollops were harassed out
of its sight and the gamblers, into back rooms or upstairs in a
kind of vertical zoning.[111]

A concern for the youth of the city motivated the vice district
proposal in large part, and this fear seemed justified. In 1856 the
Chronicle complained, "The evil of juvenile delinquency has been,
and is, growing formidable in our midst"; and from at least 1853
on, the city council, grand juries, and press groped for a solution.[112]
The community's favorite panacea, considered but not yet adopted
by the government, was a House of Refuge.

This scheme, like the segregation of sin, was based on environ-
mentalist thinking in its rehabilitory if not its punitive aspects.

By isolating the juvenile offender, he could be surrounded by constructive influences which would at the same time prevent him from corrupting innocent children by association, reform him, and keep him away from his usual bad environment or incarceration amongst hardened criminals.[113] The role of one's "surroundings" in the development of young personalities, delinquent or otherwise, the community clearly understood.

> We should remember that those little boys whom we see wandering about the streets ragged and dirty, spending the day time in watching opportunities for theft, and at night coiling themselves up in barrels, or among bales and boxes upon the wharves; it should be recollected, we say, that those drinking, swearing, loafing children, most of them, become so from the force of circumstances, and that society at large is, to a great extent, responsible to itself for the amount of evil they may do in the future, as well as morally responsible to the children themselves.[114]

This same explanation applied to other groups. Citizens commonly remarked that San Francisco with its numerous temptations, its relative absence of traditions and restraints, and its concentration of often discordant nationalities was morally a very dangerous place. The unwary might easily be swept away into iniquity by the force of these peculiar local circumstances, and only the re-establishment of clubs, churches, and, above all, the family presided over by women—"God's own police"—could provide the necessary "wholesome influences" for improvement. Before the rising of 1851, the *Herald* even argued that skyrocketing lawlessness resulted as much from economic problems as from an influx of Sydneyites. "High rents, . . . as well as dear provisions, may lead to the increase of crime," argued the editor; for if honest men could not make a living working they would make it stealing. Sometimes "natural depravity" was stressed instead, but the environmental interpretation predominated.[115]

Despite the wide recognition of extenuating situations, all agreed that society had the right to protect itself against those "either by nature or circumstances inclined" to lawbreaking. One often heard it argued that the certainty rather than the severity of punishment was the ideal; that vengeance would make the offender an even more embittered outlaw; that reformation should be striven for; and that "the great desideratum" was "prevention instead of . . . cure." Yet it was agreed that nearly all wrongdoing deserved some kind of chastisement, including in some cases the most extreme one, and, moreover, that these penalties were an effective deterrent. The bad luck of the transgressor might elicit the sympathy of the city, but it did not excuse him.[116] As was so often the case, the community found itself trying to square the contradictory principles of societal responsibility and individual accountability, neither of which worked as absolutes. Nor did reformation without retribution.

In most respects, the actual treatment of convicts fell far short of the theory set forth. The chain gang remained the most popular panacea and existed (sometimes only on paper) throughout the period, though the prisoners lost their shackles late in 1856.[117] Since it was widely believed that many stole to avoid work, they considered the chain gang the ultimately effective deterrent. Moreover, exposing the criminals to public view would shame them further and identify them to the community for future caution. And, of course, the prisoners paid their own way; they could either work on some public project or be hired out to businessmen.

Conditions inside the jail left much room for improvement. Whipping was common, and no sort of reformatory training or trade mastery was encouraged. Young and old, alcoholic and insane, sick and well, men and women often shared the same prison, with the latter doing the cooking and washing. Prison routine for 1856 provided for two meals a day on one pound of beef, one-fourth pound of bread, and half a gallon of water; a daily sweeping of the rooms; and a half bucket of water every other day in order to keep the men and their clothes half as clean as their cells. How strictly the contract was enforced is dubious. The year 1856 found the prisoners without bedding or beds and

only blankets and a prison floor on which to retire. In the same
year, the chain gang, one of the city's few racially integrated institutions, contained fifteen men in rags who on occasion got poor
and scanty fare, including bread that "had been gnawed by rats."
In November 1853, the judiciary committee of the Board of Aldermen inquired "whether the City Marshal could not afford by the
terms of his contract, to supply the city prisoners with better diet
than bread and water." [118]

The physical accommodations for prisoners were as bad or
worse than their food and treatment. San Francisco had a cala-
boose when the Americans acquired it, but only in late 1851 did
the city erect a substantial building. From 1846 to 1851, various
structures—including for a time the schoolhouse—and the prison
brig *Euphemia* (until it was "repossessed" by a creditor of the
city) did the job; but these were insecure and escapes were frequent. "San Francisco's jails are very much like the one we read
of at Nantucket," needled the *Alta*; "a prisoner sent the sheriff
formal notice that if he did not repair the jail and keep out the
sheep, he, the prisoner, would vacate the premises." Even in a
secure jail, favored prisoners were allowed to sit about the office
or take an occasional night out on the town. A committee of the
common council aptly summed up the internal condition of the
early bridewell in 1849 when they "found it the most awful and
filthy den, perhaps ever beheld by any human being." The *Courier*
stated in 1850, "Our prisons, from the number in them, are regular Calcutta holes." [119]

In early 1851 the county began to build a prison which, after
much corruption and delay, was finished late that year. Raising
$4,000, a small part of the structure's price, was one positive con-
tribution of the Vigilance Committee. More secure as well as more
comfortable than its predecessors, the county jail remained the
city lock-up through 1856. It also stayed overcrowded. In October
1853, the Grand Jury reported that six men occupied each of the
thirteen eight-by-twelve cells. The cleanliness varied as did that
of the station house under the city hall, which the Grand Jury,

in October 1856, described as "a disgrace to any civilized city." [120]

The many flaws in San Francisco's system of law enforcement prevented the realization of the ideals for either reform or retribution. Few violators were taught a good lesson by chastisement for the simple reason that few were caught. And those apprehended the city could hardly afford to feed, let alone rehabilitate.

The pattern of public and private cooperation in the solution of urban problems followed largely from financial exigency. Volunteer fire departments were customary; but the shortage of money dictated the policy of cooperation in providing streets, plank roads, wharves, hospitals, gas works, and a water supply system. Usually, however, this collaboration called for a public voice in the regulation of rates and ultimate public ownership. This "municipal socialism" was taken for granted, though never labeled.

Certainly not all of San Francisco's responses to urban problems were born of crises, but many were. Residents knew full well about the high incidence of crime in port cities, about political corruption, about sickness, and about fire hazards. Both the logic of the situation and the experience of other urban areas strongly indicated that certain challenges would arise, but it took the sad experience of the San Franciscans themselves to initiate responses to them. The lessons of the past seemed irrelevant to the Golden Gate metropolis, yet the price of relearning them was very high.

Since the city so often learned to solve its urban problems the hard way, the overall record of achievement was ambiguous. Measured by any ideal yardstick, the accomplishments were puny. Yet if other, more realistic, standards are applied, the Bay City's performance must be rated much higher. San Francisco had many troubles and failures in meeting its responsibilities, but few nineteenth-century American cities did a brilliant job in this respect and fewer still had to make the attempt under more trying conditions. And if compared with pre- and early post-Gold Rush conditions in the town, the improvement was enormous. Anyone who had plowed on foot or horseback through the sand to the mission or from Clark's Point to Clay and Montgomery, had stumbled about at night in the gloom, had landed goods by lighter from the ships at Clark's Point, had witnessed the city in flames on the night of May 3–4, 1851, or had seen men withering away, unattended, in their tents in Happy Valley in '48 and '49 could tell that by 1856 there had been tremendous advances. The same person would also have admitted that there was still room for many more.

The Structure of Politics

"The complaint is universal that San Francisco is unheeded in the State Legislature," wrote the *Herald* in a typical lament. And San Francisco *was* over-represented on the California tax ledgers, under-represented in the capital, and periodically victimized by interior legislators. Yet behind this façade was a quite different reality. "Each party is confident of being at least equally strong with its opponents outside the city," the *Chronicle* wrote of the 1855 election. "They look to San Francisco to decide which shall be victorious. This city contains one eighth of the voters of the State. It is a center whence the parties are managed. It is the residence of the leading politicians, and the chief font whence money, the great means of supporting political war, is drawn." [1]

So intense was the "lure of the city" on weekends that politicians frequently did not get back to Sacramento until Tuesday. This problem became so serious that one legislator urged, only half in jest, that the capital be removed to San Francisco, since only at the Blue Wing, Union, or other political saloon could a quorum be obtained on Monday.[2] And it was in the metropolis that these weekending politicians and their urban allies concocted the great majority of measures affecting the city.

Yet the feeling of oppression was an important part of a developing urban consciousness and was, in turn, the most significant unifying theme in San Francisco's political history. In time, this feeling

matured into a kind of city-state nationalism. Eventually it sparked
a reform crusade which ended in an urban revolution and, in its
extreme form, even gave rise to demands for political autonomy
or independence from the United States. It was in the midst of
this unfolding local attachment and loyalty that the eternal struggle to reconcile individual and community interests was most
clearly revealed.

If the Emporium was the de facto capital of California, "during
election time, Montgomery street may be considered San Francisco," observed the *Chronicle*. "There are all the bankers' offices,
which supply the true 'sinews of war,' . . . there are the newspaper establishments, whose employees are ever going stealth-
ily about, 'taking notes,' " [and the lawyers' offices also]. "There,"
continued the same paper, "are unnumbered bar and billiard rooms
—and *there* our host of gentlemanly and seedy loafers, the two
hundred candidates and their multitudinous friends." Throughout
the day, they "drink and smile, chew and spit. . . . There 'everybody' speculates on the chances; while nearly everybody belches
forth perpetual volleys of oaths, which, like the discharge of
shotted guns, mean nothing, save impotent fury, noise, smoke
and stench." [3]

Politics always suffered from enormous apathy, but thanks to the
activists, never from any lack of color. "I have never seen so much
excitement in the States," wrote McCrackan of election day.
"Everyone seemed perfectly wild" when the *Brother Jonathan*
steamed in with the 1856 election returns. "Ministers, judges, lawyers, merchants, clerks, cobblers, and market women, all rushed
in one dark mass on towards the wharves to learn the news." "Political fandangoes day and night for the last three days," noted Milo
Hoadly. "Beats all to pieces and no mistake." [4]

Before the vote, politicking was continuous. "The friendly salutation, the warm grasps of the hand, and the earnest enquiries
[sic] after one's health . . . are really delightful," wrote the *Alta*.
"And what scheming, wire pulling, maneuvering, and humbugging
always exist." During the balloting, candidates went from ward to

ward beseeching support, followed by often tipsy hordes of the faithful. "Candidates for office must treat every one out of ten," Hoadly wrote in astonishment.[5]

A grand parade generally marked election eve. A fireworks display and an enormous bonfire on Telegraph Hill were clearly visible to the ranks on Montgomery waiting to pass in review. The mile-long spectacle "presented in a close built street, in a dark night, a most imposing sight," marveled William Weston. "I never saw it equalled before, dense crowds of men throng the sides of the streets," amused, appalled, or outraged by the slogans, chants, or floats.[6]

"Happy Valley Iron Against Custom House Gold," "Whigs Tremble and Obey Your King!" screamed the Democratic illuminations in 1851. "Africa for the Africans and Their Sympathizers," "No Extension of European Dominion on This Continent," "No Religious Tests," "We Will Not Let the Union Slide," proclaimed the same party in 1856. "Free Soil, Free Men, Fremont," "Young America *versus* Old Fogy," "Democratic Courtesy—Caning Senators & Shooting Irishmen," "Fremont and the Pacific Railroad," replied the Republicans. "Some of the transparencies were the richest and most expensive I ever saw; all kinds of devices and shows, which the ingenuity of man could devise were executed," noted William Weston in 1851. "On the sides of one was a noted member of the old Council caught fast in a *huge trap*, while *stealing city lots*. On another was the *old mayor* pocketing city scrip. . . ."[7]

Next day activity redoubled. Wagons, gaily bedecked with banners and posters, dashed about transporting voters to and from their homes. Others waited at the wharves for the Sacramentans, in town for the day to vote the San Francisco graveyard, fully assured of reciprocity. Bands passed to and fro; lines of men stood before each poll distributing and urging their tickets; and "window committees" peered into the polling places to guard against or, as the case may have been, promote irregularity.[8]

The institutions of which all this colorful activity was a by-product formed slowly. Until 1849 no parties existed; therefore, most

political desires were expressed through the press and public
gatherings. These, in turn, represented the wishes of pressure
groups, cliques, and city sections.

Once begun, the mass assembly remained a significant institution throughout, featuring parliamentary organization and procedure, debates, resolutions expressing the consensus of the group
and sometimes the community itself, and committees to carry
out the intent of the body. This direct democracy gave birth to
the first school in San Francisco, numerous protests against corruption, the People's party, various economic regulations, and a
demand for a state constitutional convention and civil government.
These forums (called indignation meetings after 1849) had no legal standing, but their advice was often considered binding upon
the ruling bodies. Even when ignored, these assemblies provided
an important political outlet. Although usually unorganized, pressure groups also continued to be important after 1849. Some structured institutions—such as the Teamsters Union, the Chamber of
Commerce, and the churches—sought to wield influence; but the
rule was the ad hoc alliance, formed for an instant and abandoned
as quickly. Economic self-interest served as the ordinary cement;
but ethnicity, morality, religion, and political ambition provoked
an endless variety of alignments. The press, like the town meeting,
usually spoke for some pressure group.

After 1849, all these institutions had to share the field with political parties. Popular meetings, pressure groups, and the press
were enough for Yerba Buena; but as that hamlet became the city
of San Francisco, parties grew up to broker the greater complexity
of interests and to promote their own. In fact, the major party developments in California through 1856 began in urban areas,
usually in the Bay City. One of the most significant of these was
the transplanting, between 1849 and 1851, of regular political institutions to the state. The Democratic party of the Golden Gate
City led the way, followed shortly thereafter by the local Whigs.[9]

The formal mechanisms of these reorganized political parties
were theoretically democratic, with popular primaries, conven-

tions, and ratification meetings. Offstage, however, the activists dominated and manipulated each detail of party life. Indirect primaries selected delegates to local conventions, who in turn made the nominations for city, county, and state offices and to state conventions, where candidates for national office were picked. Either direct primaries, ward club elections, or ward committee appointments made the ward and precinct nominations. The Democrats generally used the latter—or less democratic—method, and the Whigs, the former.[10] Whatever the procedure, it ended in a ratification meeting—a great gathering of the faithful, characterized by ample speechifying and a perfunctory acceptance of the list presented.

These mechanics often worked poorly. Therefore, in order to cure the ills of democracy which attended primaries and conventions, proposals were offered to make the selection both more and less democratic. The former involved elevating the mass meeting in importance, since the will of the majority supposedly could not be so easily thwarted nor worthless candidates named in this more public forum. The proponents of the more aristocratic caucus, however, had more success. Both the Know Nothings in 1854 and the reform People's party in 1856 adopted this device. This change seems retrogressive; yet it altered hardly anything. The primary-convention system boasted a little more color, but its choices were also made behind the scenes. This informal structure, therefore, determined how the formal arrangements would work.

The system is perhaps best seen by a description of the strongest political organization in the city, the "Tammany Democracy," dominated by David C. Broderick. From the moment this remarkable man arrived in California, he aimed for the Senate seat of William M. Gwin. This epic contest between two urban-based politicians was easily the most famous California political issue of the fifties.

Very early, the Democratic party in both city and state coalesced into two main factions around Broderick and Gwin. The differences between the men—one a Southern aristocrat and doctor, the other a plebian immigrant's son from New York City—were

many, but the one that concerned the Tammany chieftain most
was that Gwin held the Senatorship and the New Yorker did not.
After seven years of struggle, the low-born Northerner finally recti-
fied this glaring inequity.[11]

Broderick was born in Washington, D.C., the son of an Irish
stone carver. His family later moved to New York City, and David
grew up there in the sixth ward, which included the Five Points
District, a notorious center city slum. At an early age he received
valuable experience in the fire department, saloon keeping, and
political affairs. Hardly the stereotype Irishman of the metropolis's
newspapers, he was neither happy-go-lucky nor garrulous nor a
victim of the so-called "Irish disease"—alcoholism. Though probably corrupt, even his enemies admitted that he had none of the
personal vices so prevalent in California. He was cold, calculating,
imperious, determined, and learned. Relatively few people in the
city ever laid eyes on him, and on many important urban—*though
not statewide*—issues, he was usually reticent.[12] He kept his own
counsel; and when dealing with others, he often had no third party
in the room. Like many other Irishmen in both the Catholic Church
and politics, Broderick was an "organizer of victory," the best in
California.

In New York City, however, the dominant old-stock New Yorkers
who doled out lamplighters' jobs to the upsurging sons of Erin
considered the young man excessively ambitious. When Broderick
ran for Congress in 1846, a machine stalking horse, plus the American candidate and the general anti-Democratic backlash, defeated
him. Three years later the disappointed aspirant, tired of fighting
the prejudices against his class, set out for California with the in-
tention of returning only as U.S. Senator.[13]

Like everything else in California, the vehicle for realizing this
ambition was ever changing. This fluidity along with Broderick's
secretive nature makes it especially hard to recognize his friends
or enemies at any given time. However, the various power bases
of the organization reveal its essence, even if recounting its internal
history is a total impossibility.

The primary base of this pervasive alliance was Broderick himself. Once in San Francisco, he, like others, began drawing on his credit and associations from "home"—New Yorkers, Irishmen, and firemen. With the help of a loan from New Yorker Jonathan D. Stevenson, the future Senator went into the business of coining money. He and his partner and future political ally, Frederick D. Kohler, quickly increased their supply of cash, which, when reinvested in real estate, produced a moderate fortune.[14] By 1850 Broderick had collected enough allies to be elected to the state Senate; and by the fall of that year, he had established a city organization. In time, this faction of the Democracy, initially dubbed "Young Ireland" by its enemies, became the most powerful in San Francisco.

The banking house of Palmer, Cook and Company became one of Broderick's chief supporters around 1853. Most of the time the auction house of Selover and Sinton was an ally; and, periodically, that of John Middleton was, too. Broderick's ability to influence government wooed these and other businessmen. The bank received the city deposits as well as preferential treatment in cashing municipal warrants or scrip. Other creditors often found the corporation treasury empty; but Palmer, Cook and Company's warrants, purchased in large quantities on the market for 70¢ and redeemed for $1.00, generally were honored. As state treasurer, the bankers derived additional profits. The city and state auctioneers received a percentage of land sale prices and, just as importantly, the ability to get or give first chance at choice lots.

The New Yorker also gained substantial support from both city hall and the court house. County offices often proved very lucrative; and since the party sold nominations, it thereby derived considerable sums. The municipal authorities had numerous other favors to bestow. The Jenny Lind Theater, purchased from Broderick's friend Thomas Maguire, with whom he lived, involved $250,000; and wharf, street, plank road, and printing contracts added lesser but still impressive sums. Beyond these large plums were jobs as petty clerks, wharfingers, plaza keepers, and sextons as well as the "aldermanic tea room," run by the clerk of the common council. The aldermen had their meals sent in to them while at work on city business, and caterers eventually were paid several thousand dollars to sustain the politicians and "court house loafers." [15]

Other individual and institutional alliances abounded. Through William Shaw, elected in 1855 with Broderick's permission, the Tammany had an influence with the eighth ward squatters.[16] Paradoxically, Broderick also had strong associations with J. D. Stevenson, Palmer, Cook and Company, and other big real estate operators, who often claimed the same lots the squatters did. In addition, through officeholders James Grant and John McGlynn, the organization had a connection with the teamsters union; and Bill Lewis and Bill Carr gave it a line of communication to the boatmen.

Somewhat less reputable urban institutions were represented, too. Since the dispensation of alcohol was considered almost a part of the franchise, saloonkeepers and politicians were mutually dependent; and some Democratic barmen, such as Chris Lilly, also operated houses of prostitution. Ned McGowan, ex-bank robber and one of Broderick's chief lieutenants, provided another link to this business. Martin Gallagher did the same for the sailor boarding houses, or crimps; and William Walker, the "Grey Eyed Man of Destiny," bridged the gap between Tammany and the world of filibustering.[17] In the beginning, the gambling houses needed little protection; but with the arrival of females and families, hostile regulations gave the gamesters increasingly good reasons to follow the saloon and brothel keepers into the organization.

Another group, generally known as the "b'hoys," also belonged. Billy Mulligan, J. W. Bagley, Robert Cushing, Terrence Kelly, Moses Flanagan, "Wooley" Kearny, "Yankee" Sullivan, "Liverpool Jack," "Dutch Charley" Duane (a gunman and notorious bully), and J. Burke alias "Activity" provided a kind of power which the *Alta* described accurately when it referred to Gallagher as a "Hitite." In fact, Kearny, Lilly, and Sullivan all had been professional pugilists; and the latter had once fought Tom Hyer for the world championship.[18]

In addition, the Broderick coalition drew strong support from the Irish and Germans. The German Rangers, led by Frank Laumeister, provided much of this backing as did the German press. Tammany enjoyed even greater, though not undivided, loyalty from the Irish. Many sons of Erin allied with arch-rival Gwin, just as Southerners often stood with Broderick.[19] It was true, however, that few Irish or Germans supported any non-Democratic party, at least until 1856; and it was also the case that the Irish were disproportionately powerful in the ranks of Tammany.

So were the firemen. Broderick's comrades in this group, especially in the Empire Engine Company, one of his strongholds, regarded him well. Several other organization men, including fire chief "Dutch Charley" Duane and David Scannell, were long-time firemen as were most professional politicians. In addition, Sheriff Scannell, the former operator of the notorious Osceola Gambling Saloon, served as captain of the New York Guards, a volunteer military company.[20] In short, the politicians hovered anxiously around any recognizable group, hoping for new caches of strength.

When his allies were in office, the Tammany leader's party influence rose, which in turn enabled him to sally forth from his urban power base to dominate a large segment of the state organization. In 1853 Broderick and his big San Francisco delegation delivered the gubernatorial nomination to incumbent John Bigler. When that "worthy" was re-elected, "the State Land Commissioners, the Port Wardens, the Commissioner of Emigration, the Health Office, and the Hospital force, constituting altogether a very powerful combination of moneyed influence and voting strength, were entirely in Broderick's interest, as also were three fourths of the other state appointees, . . . who got their places . . . by the favor of . . . Governor Bigler." [21]

An 1855 investigation of the State Marine Hospital revealed that besides providing $166,000 in patronage money, the doctors, nurses, and patients all were expected to vote "the ticket" and apparently formed a mobile reserve that could be thrown into the fray wherever needed. Another important state plum was the printing contract, which in 1852 alone secured Broderick $270,000 and the services of the party press. Of course, power in the capital helped "the Tammany" in San Francisco. The relationship was reciprocal, but urban pre-eminence preceded state predominance and was the chief means to that end. Federal patronage, however—customs house, mint, port surveyor, and United States Marine Hospital—was the fief of the Chivalry Democracy or of one of Broderick's lesser rivals, though his allies did hold some customs jobs in 1853 and again in 1856 when the collector, Milton Latham, broke with Gwin.[22]

Despite its famous name, the Tammany coalition was not 100 per cent Democratic. Usually the New Yorker had one foot in the opposing camps; and this position gave him influence, or at the minimum a listening post.[23] For example, R. H. Sinton of the favored auction house was a Whig while partner Selover was a Broderickite.

Broderick's contemporaries—especially the reformers—largely exaggerated his power. In 1856, E. Gould Buffum, Know Nothing, pro-Vigilante editor of the *Alta,* argued in a typical essay that the Tammany chieftain had "so far succeeded in bending the whole party to his will—making them subservient to his ends." Yet the Democracy of San Francisco was never that pliant and could perhaps best be described as a war within a war. From September 1850, the "Young Ireland" faction usually dominated the organization, but only after a "regular Guelph and Ghibelline warfare in the ranks of the Democratic party." [24]

The Gwin wing fought bitterly for control; although with some exceptions, they usually closed ranks against the enemy. Nearly every year Tammany had to face formidable revolts, which were sometimes partly successful. So serious was this opposition that Broderick's famous election deal which allowed Gwin back in to the Senate required that Gwin acknowledge the sole authority of the local Broderick Central Committee.[25]

The actions and character of individual Democrats reveal the same lack of subserviency. Mayor Stephen R. Harris, a Gwin man in 1851, vetoed the Jenny Lind purchase; and when the all-Democratic city council reversed the veto, he refused to sign the city warrants issued to pay for the theater. When the same body tried to sanction the notoriously fraudulent Colton Grants, Harris again responded with a veto; and this time he was sustained by aldermen James Grant, Henry Meiggs, and others. Despite this aberration, all three remained important Democrats and office holders thereafter. Both Edmund Randolph and William Lent, Broderick intimates, helped defeat Tammany's ally Bigler and the county Democratic Central Committee on the extension bill. In 1855, James P. Casey stuffed his way into a supervisor's position over the Tammany leader's opposition; and in 1855–56, Democratic alderman Slocomb sided with four Know Nothing aldermen to block Broderick's choice for police captain. Apparently these were only the more open evidences of defiance. Frank Soulé, a colleague of Broderick in the legislature, claimed that the New Yorker did not vote for any of the thieving bills introduced there but was unable to prevent his own party from passing them anyway. The Irish-American himself, on the eve of his final victory, complained bitterly of the disloyalty of his followers despite the fact that he had "paid and paid." [26] Moreover, in 1856 the same reform press which attributed such tyrannical power to Broderick also admitted that he had been mercilessly blackmailed by his "tools" and that he was as glad as anyone when the Vigilantes "transported" them.

The personnel of the organization seemed as unstable as its control. Just as the Tammany, Gwin, McDougall, Weller, Latham, and Hammond forces allied, opposed, and reallied with one another, so did the men within the Broderick group.[27] The organization was no monolith. Like the pressure groups, it was fairly atomistic.

As the structure of Tammany indicates, Democratic practices largely nullified democratic forms. Insiders always dominated the primary, for example, often by notorious methods. Trick ballot boxes, bribes, stuffing, bullying, and similar devices were common. When these ploys failed, ballot boxes were stolen or smashed, necessitating a re-enactment of the whole process.

The convention in San Francisco had degenerated into something loathsome to the great majority of residents. In 1856 the *Alta* estimated that the county clerk, recorder, coroner, clerk of the Superior Court, and sheriff received yearly $325,000 in fees, of which $240,000 was profit.[28] The sheriff alone had an income of $100,000, about four times as much as the nation's president.

Understandably, these nominations came high. "Two of them [office seekers] came out openly and told me if I would vote for them, they would give me offices, with salaries of $2000 and $5000 per an[num]," noted a Whig convention delegate. The Democrats organized the operation thoroughly, selling nominations to raise party and personal funds. So venal had the practice become that the principles of the joint stock company were introduced. In one instance, James Grant sued John McGlynn for failure to share the profits of place. Yet the arrangement was one of "democratic venality": one could buy only the nomination, and once in office, the Jacksonian principle of rotation applied. Still the *Herald* was correct when it wondered if the current convention would "preserve from the clutches of the police a sufficient force to transact business during the sessions of the body."[29]

Violence in politics was not as widespread as corruption, but election rows, shootings, cow hidings, and canings took place frequently. When a candidate for county attorney accused the Tammany of fraud, "one of the Com[mittee] seeing him pass a gambling and drinking house, called him into the back room," wrote editor Jonas Winchester of "N. Y. 6th Ward Irish" methods of handling dissent. He "placed a tool of his own on each side of the door, and then fell upon and beat him most unmercifully. . . . He is a pitiable sight."[30]

Though perhaps more prone to rowdiness than other segments of the population, the politicos, Irish or otherwise, had no monopoly on violence. For example, the record shows that the representatives of higher culture were quite as sensitive to censure as the courthouse crowd. Theater people, stung by critical reviews, assaulted both Frank Soulé of the *Chronicle* and Etienne Derbec of the *Echo du Pacifique*. Newspapermen also fought each other, as did businessmen. Joseph L. Folsom, the real estate tycoon, had at least two such encounters; Winn, the operator of the city's most fashionable ice cream parlor, managed one; and Gregory Yale, a prominent lawyer, severely caned a grocery clerk who tried to collect a bill. Moreover, much of the politicians' violence was directed at members of their own class rather than at the citizenry at large.[31]

However prone to brutality and apt to turn criticism into an "affair of honor," the Vigilante charge that violence terrorized voters and editors into subservience is totally absurd. If anything, the papers bordered on too much freedom. Editorials were often scandalously unfair, irresponsible, venal, and self-interested. This often perplexed and misled public thinking, but it also guaranteed discussion of most important matters, if for no other reason than self-interest. Even in 1856 amidst the imperatives of a revolutionary situation, the *Herald* survived Vigilante opposition simply because of its support from the Tammany Democracy. And oddly enough, notwithstanding their frequent demagogy and conflicts of interest, such papers as the *Chronicle, Alta, Era, Pacific,* and even the *Herald* often did an excellent job of presenting issues and wise commentary.

Vote count irregularities probably thwarted popular will more than violence in the streets or press. Events often proved the current saying that after the polls were closed, "the election had just commenced." In 1855 fraud certainly gave the Democrats equal representation on the council, and in 1854 the same means carried the day in the first ward. Primaries, especially those of the Tammany, often featured ballot box tampering, which the nature and location of polling places encouraged. "The polls are always located at one extremity of the [First] Ward, upon the streets fronting on the bay," noted the *Pacific*. "The collection around these polls, will excel any for drunkenness, rowdyism, brawling, carousing, fighting, swearing, and each voting as often as he can crowd through." [32]

In addition, importing Sacramentans for election day and "colonization" (multi-ward voting with a change of clothes after each stop) were common, as were printing false tickets, bribing election judges, and flooding meetings with hostile toughs. In 1853 the latter nearly disrupted an independent labor rally; and packing the insurgents' gathering and carrying the resolutions against them quelled at least one incipient rebellion against the "unterrified" Democracy. On one occasion, Broderick and his "minions" actually broke up an indignation meeting against the Jenny Lind purchase; and in 1856, Vigilante supporters returned the compliment to a "law and order" conclave.[33]

The conduct of politicians in office was consistent with the means they used to get there. Horse trading, absenteeism, and stalling abounded. Conflict of interest and graft ran rampant regardless of which party won. "No one who has done business in the East can have an idea how things are managed here. The most unblushing rascality is practiced amongst those whose standing would seem to place them above it," a street contractor wrote in 1850. "Profitable contracts are given or sold by the officials who have the disposal of them or are given out at a large price and the two parties share the profits." Aldermen forged corporation warrants for their own use, purchased city lots with someone else as front men, or cornered all the municipal fire bonds for their clients.[34] In short, a lot of officials were simply "on the street."

Political manners, morals, and methods strongly emphasize the continuity in the city's experience. Malpractice was neither produced by the Gold Rush nor smuggled through the Golden Gate in the luggage of the Tammany. In the 1846 alcalde election, for example, sailors and soldiers from the American squadron voted to insure the success of Washington Bartlett over a supposedly pro-Mexican candidate. "There were no nice discriminations about the right of voting," the city's first public school teacher noted of the canvass that won him that job; "sailors and soldiers all voted." Nor were there any regarding conflict of interest. The Broadway Street Wharf, begun by the corporation in 1847, turned out to be on property claimed by Alderman William S. Clark, chairman of the town council wharf committee that recommended the project.[35] And town treasurer and alderman William Leidesdorff supplied much of the lumber purchased by the municipality.

The city council of 1849–50, elected before the organization of parties and made up mostly of businessmen—the natural leaders of the community—likewise could not have learned very much from Tammany regulars about "honest graft." In 1849, Alderman Rodman M. Price, real estate dealer, was granted a wharf franchise and land use privileges for the Central Wharf Joint Stock Company, of which he, Sam Brannan, William Heath Davis, and other aldermen were directors.[36] Furthermore, aldermen Price, Davis, G. B. Post, Aert Van Nostrand, and Brannan all were heavy purchasers at city land sales pushed by the council. It was subsequently discovered that Brannan, who helped hang John Jenkins for the theft of a safe and who led every drive against "lawlessness," had property located in the area to be benefited by the $100,000 council appropriation for Market Street Wharf. Post, Price, and Davis also were Vigilantes.

How much responsibility Broderick bore for the deplorable political condition of San Francisco is difficult to assess. His most recent biographer argues strenuously that he was a man of principle—democratic, tolerant, honest, antislavery, and so forth.[37] Perhaps this was true in state and national politics, but the conclusion seems much less applicable to the urban level. Almost every writer on the subject has noted that the Golden Gate City was Broderick's "bastion"; and if that were so, it is not too much to insist that the commander had some significant responsibility for the condition of his own fortress. The leadership qualities attributed to the Tammany chief are simply irreconcilable. If he was at the same time an unparalleled political tactician, the master of the metropolis, and man of integrity, then the city could not have had the political and governmental shortcomings it did. Given these, then he was either not boss or not all that dedicated to the public interest. It is true that he showed more concern for popular welfare than some of his critics and that there is hardly any direct evidence to connect him with a specific wrongdoing. Yet the circumstantial evidence is fairly damning.

The Vigilantes frequently charged that the corporation had been under a tyranny for many years, with "entrenched" politicians mocking a helpless people. As a Methodist minister and ardent Know Nothing party worker complained in 1855, "It was only by this corruption and fraud that the Democrats, as they ever have before, carried this last election." [38] Despite such claims, the Democrats neither carried the contest in which the preacher labored nor succeeded themselves in office a single time. San Francisco was consistently a two-party town.

In all, there were eight contests between 1850 and 1856. The first ended in something of a draw. Though party distinctions may not have been very important in this election, men calling themselves Democrats won the administration and Whigs held a majority on both boards of aldermen. Through resignations, the Whigs eventually dissipated their advantage; but in the spring of 1851 (by which time party lines were clearly drawn), they swept both the administration and councils. This time Broderick "chartered" them out of office by changing the date of elections in the new city charter from spring to fall. The Whigs argued that the next election should come in September of 1852 and refused to put up candidates. The Supreme Court accepted the Tammany date of September 1851, and their unopposed candidates assumed power. However, the next autumn the Whigs again captured both councils and the administration. The Democrats and Know Nothings successively duplicated that feat, and in the spring of 1855 they split both councils and the executive offices four and four.

(The Democrats won the mayoralty.) In 1856 the People's party blitz left Tammany with one supervisor and a few lesser officers.

Notwithstanding talk of "entrenchment," the one party that came closest to succeeding itself was not the party of Jefferson, Jackson, and Broderick, but that of the Know Nothings in 1855. The supposed "masters" of the city won the mayoralty four times in eight attempts. They captured both councils only twice, and one of these victories was that of the body known as "their accidency," elected in the fall of 1851 when the Whigs refused to run a ticket. Even if one considers the 1856 People's party victory as part of a new era, words like "entrenchment" and "tyranny" are inaccurate.

One can see the same nonpreponderance of the non-"juggernaut" by examining reformers' perennial complaints of voting malpractices in the eighth, first, and "Bloody Second" ward Tammany strongholds. Fraud or not, these districts were less reliable than the opposition third and fourth wards. The fourth did not elect one single Democratic alderman between 1851 and 1857, and the third and fifth produced only one each. These three wards were more reliable than the most regular Democrat ward, the eighth. The other two wards vacillated back and forth evenly. Therefore, neither Broderick nor the Democracy ushered in the one-party system in San Francisco. That honor belongs to the reform People's party.

Nevertheless, it was often argued that the nominations of the opposition were so "influenced" that even when the "New York" faction lost elections, men faithful to them held office. There is no doubt that Broderick had a foothold in the other parties; but to assert that he was a Democrat (both Tammany and Chivalry), Whig, Know Nothing, and Republican at the same time is a little far fetched. That would mean that all the bought conventions and the hoopla, the expensive election bargains and machinations were mere sham used to cover up Broderick's behind-the-scenes control of the entire drama. Anything was possible in Gold Rush San Francisco, but the evidence points to the conclusion that the local contests were just as serious as the statewide one between Broderick and Gwin. The "machine" was the most potent single group, but it had little resemblance to the absolutism that haunted reformers.

Yet if the same party or faction did not always rule, from 1850 on the same sort of people did—professional politicians. In that sense there was entrenchment in office, but of a large group of men pursuing divergent interests. And among these men, distinctions of principle were few and differences in morality and efficiency, fewer.

In national politics, as the *Herald* argued in 1851,

> The platform of the two parties, except in the matter of internal improvements and the Squatter question, is very similar. Both repudiate unequivocally the doctrine of the administration in regard to the disposition of the mines, and both, so far as appears by the resolutions, are equally opposed to the old dogmas of the Whig party. . . . All here are free traders by profession, and all are equally opposed to the banking system.[39]

By the next year, the *Alta* found them also in agreement on squatters and internal improvements, especially the Pacific Railroad, the Democrats apparently having abandoned what the *Courier* playfully called their "Strick" constructionism.[40]

Of course, some differences did arise, such as the Whig support of a tariff in 1850, the Know Nothing attempt to lengthen naturalization procedures in 1854, and the Republican "agitation" of the slavery issue in 1856. Yet even so, the Fremont men denied vociferously that they were Negrophile or even Abolitionist, and the Buchanan supporters just as forcefully opposed the extension of slavery to California.[41]

In municipal and county elections, reform remained the only important issue; and this question largely determined civic contests.[42] The familiar boss-reform duality had not quite emerged, since the San Francisco candidate for the former position did not yet qualify and reform was somewhat disorganized. Yet the situation was clearly evolving toward the dichotomy more well-known to later nineteenth century urban history.

The press frequently advised the uplifters to regenerate one of the established parties and make it fit to govern or to found a new party dedicated to the same ends. The fifties were spent working from the first of these suggestions to the second. In 1851 and 1852, the Whigs carried the hopes of the reformers to victory as the Know Nothings did in 1854. Yet the constructive results of these triumphs were slim; and by 1856 good-government forces, with a push from the political crisis of the summer, were ready to embrace the second alternative.

Despite the familiar reform plea that municipal and federal contests be separated so that national partisan passion would not determine civic issues, in 1852 and 1856 the local Whig and People's parties rode the reform issue into power in the face of Democratic presidential victories. The same local primacy appeared in the city's realignment of parties.

The fall of the Whigs is somewhat mysterious. Their election strength had been at least equal to that of their opponents, and in 1850 and 1851 the city was often considered Whig and not Democratic. The former were never well organized, though; and the loss of federal patronage in 1853 hurt them. Furthermore, California voted predominantly Democratic on the state and national levels, and the Whig municipal victories may have been largely a protest against the Democracy. The malodorous administration of 1852–53, however, largely exploded Whig pretensions to urban reform; and after 1853 the party of Webster and Clay declined. It staged a comeback in 1855 but finished third and thereafter disappeared as members deserted to the Americans, Republicans, and Democrats.[43]

The career of the Americans is more easily explained and more clearly urban. The California Know Nothings organized first in San Francisco; and there the new party was a combination of Whigs, the predominant element, and Democrats, subdivided into spoilsmen, reformers, and nativists. The politicians supplied the expertise and the other two factions, especially the reformers, the votes. "We presume . . . that the 'Know Nothing' party owe their success here . . . more to the promise of reform and the fact that their tickets have generally been made up of good men, than from the peculiar principle which is understood to be the basis of their organization," argued the *Alta* in 1854. That opinion reflected the consensus on the Americans.[44]

Equally broad disillusionment, however, followed the sweeping victory of 1854. Once it was clear that the Americans were not reformers, their *raison d'être* in the city disappeared. In 1855 they tied the Democrats; in 1856 they came in third in a race of three, and thereafter quietly withered away.

The nativist element in the party (one in four according to the *Alta*) was equally frustrated. Anti-Catholicism was rare, despite the strong priest-baiters in San Francisco. No doubt these men were sorely disappointed in 1855 with the state convention platform plank favoring "universal religious toleration." Worse still was the near nomination of Lucien Hermann, a Catholic German, as mayoral candidate in 1854. Apparently, however, that was too incongruous even for San Francisco, and the party dropped him, possibly at the behest of the nativists. Antiforeignism was probably more important than hostility to "Romanism." For the most part, this resentment grew out of the prominent political role played by foreigners, especially Irish-Democrats. The 1855 American convention resolved its "inflexible opposition to the appointment or election to offices of trust . . . of all who are not truly national in feeling, and especially all who acknowledge allegiance to any foreign government." Yet the party never went so far as to advocate immigration restriction. In San Francisco proscription did not get far, either. The charter reserved police jobs for citizens, but there was no wholesale purge of policemen, though the schools were shaken by this nationalism. The *Alta* questioned the entire nativist pose, however, in 1855 when it revealed that some of them "were coquetting with the foreigners a year ago, and would join Freedom's Phalanx tomorrow if the promise of spoils could be improved thereby." [45]

The Democratic response often seemed undistinguishable from the real or imagined xenophobia of the new party. It was advantageous to the "Unterrified" to hammer at the themes of anti-Catholicism, antiforeignism, and secret societies, and they did. Yet there was lots of hokum, insincerity, and hypocrisy in their stance. For example, when the French and Germans joined the Vigilantes in 1856, the Democratic *Herald* attacked them while McGowan's *Phoenix* contained denunciations of "Jew chokers" and "Frog chokers." Moreover, the Democrats falsely charged that the 1856 Vigilance rising was an anti-Irish movement; they established their own secret society called Freedom's Phalanx, which the *Alta* called more proscriptive than the American party; they ridiculed New Englanders; and they labeled the Know Nothings treasonable and "dangerous to the perpetuity of our institutions." And the accusations of discrimination against the Know Nothings matched similar ones leveled at the Democratic administration of the State Marine Hospital.[46]

Fortunately, nothing like the large-scale violence of antialien politics in the civilized East took place. One drunken killing scrape occurred; but that was not a bad record in the context of Gold Rush San Francisco. In short, the Know Nothings were no more irrational, conspiratorial, or intolerant than the Democrats and considerably less brutal.[47]

The Americans ran as the Citizens Reform party, but the first nonpartisan reform party to win and retain this character in office was the People's party. This group emerged in 1856 as rapidly as the Americans had. It lasted longer, however, ending only after many years in office.

The contests prior to the first charter of 1850 all were non-partisan, and similar tickets generally appeared in subsequent elections. Vigilantes, labor leaders, Maine Law advocates, license holders, jewelers, and the "Israelites" put up whole or partial

slates, usually to no avail. The Whigs and Know Nothings carried
the main hopes of nonaligned voters in 1851, 1852, and 1854; and
each of these elections revealed large bi-partisan strength. Even
when independent tickets did poorly, split ticket voting was
common.[48]

The nonaligned coalitions encountered several problems. They
usually got into the fray late and consequently had to endorse
the best candidates of the regulars; they never fielded much of
an organization. Moreover, independent efforts were suspect because weak regular candidates commonly raised the cry of "no
party" in order to draw off votes from their stronger opponents.[49]

Despite the widely prevalent nonpartisan ideology, split-ticket
voting, and uplift sentiment, it took the 1856 Vigilante crisis to
produce the necessary institution. That event fathered the final
realignment, which produced the People's Reform and the Republican parties.[50] The first of these organized to defend the program and members of the Vigilance Committee from Democratic
vengeance. These independents, interested primarily in municipal
power, consequently offered to support any state candidates who
promised protection for the Vigilantes and their "reforms." The
Republicans were quick to accept, and that, in large part, explains
the rise of the state party. In 1856, when "the People" overwhelmed
"the Tammany," the fledgling party of Free Soil, Free Men, and
Fremont rode to victory on the coattails of urban reform. Fremont
lost the county, but his local cohorts carried all the state offices
nevertheless—by majorities much smaller than their coalition
partners won in the city.

The first Republican meetings in California were in either the
metropolis or Sacramento; but, as the legislative roll showed, their
initial electoral success came in San Francisco. Nine of twelve
assemblymen and two of three senators hailed from the Golden
Gate. Moreover, their presence was not due to antislavery rhetoric.
"If it be a fact that the Republican legislative candidates have
been successful in this county," wrote the Bulletin, "it may be
attributed to the prevalent feeling in favor of men who are pledged

to sustain the action of the [Vigilance] Committee . . . (for Republicanism is virtually an abstraction in this State)." [51]

The overall issue upon which most *elections* turned, the omnibus category for all others, was reform. Yet the specifics of day to day politicking were more tangible and usually more economic. Periodically moral, ethnic, religious, and even class concerns arose; but these were ordinarily less important. So were nonlocal questions. Citizens may have been interested in international, national, and state matters, but their impact at the Golden Gate largely determined people's positions on these topics. [52]

This custom, in turn, explains the paucity of divisive issues and principles. Normally, whatever was thought to be for the community's well being—what was clearly the majority choice—was championed by Whig, Democrat, and Know Nothing alike. Voters expected politicians, especially state and national ones, to behave like city state diplomats, promoting urban self-interest. Sometimes leaders evaded this imperative and often they spoke of their "eternal" principles, yet the city's politics were democratic instead of dogmatic. Both parties sought to represent the constituency rather than impose ideologies upon it.

It would be impossible to classify all the strictly municipal issues; but real estate, services, franchises, spatial relationships, and government spending, corruption, and corporation mismanagement sparked most political battles. Writers nearly always argued that commerce was the city's chief economic activity, yet this this preponderance was not reflected in politics. Real estate remained the pre-eminent local issue, and that business had the strongest lobby. Men contested fiercely for land control, as Leavenworth and Colton grantees, squatters, Mexican grant holders, slip speculators, Peter Smith claimants, and extensionists fought each other at the ballot box, in the courts, in the press, and sometimes in the streets. The influence of this exhausting competition was pervasive. For example, the city councils from 1850 to 1853 operated under the spell of real estate men. The placement of every street, institution, plank road, or wharf affected the question, and even the Consolidation Act had a realty angle. So prevalent was the issue that in 1853 the *Alta* claimed that the municipal independent reform ticket was antiextensionist, that the Democrats were extensionists, and that the "controlling power of the Whig caucus was City Squatterism." Even seemingly unrelated questions touched land. Despite the talk about crime and inefficiency during the 1851 Vigilante rising, for instance, some of the wholesale condemnation of the courts was intended to undermine respect for certain judicial decisions regarding real estate. A similar furor had occurred in 1850 over the disreputable past of the aspirant to corporation auctioneer. In truth, several large realtors, including R. M. Price, Brannan, and possibly Broderick, used the background story to destroy the rival of their candidate, A. A. Selover.[53]

Franchises, though lucrative, never generated the same explosive excitement. Most privileges—the gas, street, wharf, water, and plank road contracts, for example—caused comparatively little uproar. Yet by the end of the period, these topics heated up. The depression sparked resentment at the excessive profits from unjustifiable flush times rates. The hospital franchise did not fit into this pattern; instead, there was often a considerable fight over the dispensation of that plum, particularly in the years 1849–51 and, due to the efforts of James King, again in 1855–56. A much greater controversy accompanied the famous "Bulkhead" question of 1856. This maneuver by speculators, wharf owners, and others to gain a monopoly over the entire waterfront followed the "classic" pattern for such things. The cove had been filled in rapidly, but nothing restrained the dirt from flowing into the water, making the landing too shallow for large ships and rendering insecure the foundations of buildings on land. As the seaward ooze continued, a crisis mounted. The city was financially unable to check this creeping bay fill; and if the need was made to seem imperative, private enterprise could drive a hard bargain for the job. The entrepreneurs offered to build a sea wall around the harbor to check the muck in return for a monopoly on wharfage for a number of years. Although everyone agreed that a wall was necessary, the town refused to be stampeded into building one before it could be done by the corporation or by private parties on better terms. It took several more years to lay the project to rest definitively, but the first round represented a victory for the popular side.

City services probably provided more excitement than franchises. Law and order became a volatile topic in 1851 and 1856; and even in non-Vigilante years, crime waves drew considerable verbal attention. So did the abominable condition of the streets and, between 1849 and 1851, fire protection. The increasing efficiency and popularity of the fire department deflated the issue until 1856, when the parsimonious provisions of the new charter revived the issue.

Government spending, corruption, and mismanagement drew major attention on occasion. Besides such major controversies as the "Salary Grab" and the Jenny Lind purchase, an almost ceaseless torrent of taxation protests went on, either in the courts, the council, or indignation meetings. This was supplemented by a steady stream of criticism about incompetence and corruption, culminating in public outrage over Meiggs.

The spatial relationships of the city also nurtured a variety of political problems growing out of competition for the use of urban land. Merchants objected to hackmen or vendors parked in front of their doors, while street vendors fought amongst themselves for favored downtown spots. The placement of brick kilns, candle and soap manufactories, hospitals, slaughterhouses, and other noxious activities generated additional protests, usually from outraged householders. The same physical proximity started controversies that were more moral than economic. Father Taylor occasionally got in trouble because his crowds congested Plaza saloonkeepers' doorways. The Methodist street preacher argued that he was only blocking up the entrance to Hell, but the bartenders saw the matter in considerably more secular terms. In a like fashion, the Baptist services and Turnverein parades could not coexist in the same neighborhood. Either the churchgoers had a right to silence or the gymnasts had a right to make noise. An even more explosive question was emerging in the fading days of 1855, as the rapidly accumulating population of "respectable" women found themselves forced to traverse the vice district on their way to town.[54]

An endless variety of combinations arose to pursue these controversies. These ephemeral alliances personified the atomism of the city as men entered and left and joined others in turn. Contests occurred between opposite sides of an avenue over sharing street assessments, between one thoroughfare and the next for planking or wharfing, or among city sections. During the Hoadly grades controversy, the political division went according to geographic elevation. When the city took the Pacific Street Plank Road franchise under consideration, adjacent suburban property holders formed the political coalition behind it; and when abolition of tolls became a demand, linear alliance of "property holders along the roads [successfully] remonstrated against making them free thoroughfares, for the reason that they would be compelled to keep them in repair." [55]

Economic self-interest explains the establishment of many other combinations. The funding question aligned the debt holders against the property owners whose taxes would have to redeem the indebtedness; the sale of the Central Wharf slips juxtaposed real estate dealers and wharf proprietors; the water lot controversies ranged two different land grantees against each other while the squatters defied both; and taxation leagued property holders against license payers. In addition, the bulkhead scheme matched the operators of most wharves and the remainder of the city; the attempt to tax foreign capital aligned those who wielded it against those whose extra burdens made up for the exemption; and the Pacific Street toll road eventually set omnibus operators after the toll gaters. Political ambition, ethnicity, religious conviction, class, and other factors fathered additional alliances. Though decidedly less important than economic ones, these were equally diverse. Therefore, in view of this pervasive pluralism, it is unrealistic to speak of a ruling class or élite in San Francisco. Economic interests dominated the political process; the only issue that could have united them was the defense of the capitalist system. But, of course, that question never arose.[56]

Politics revealed most clearly the developing civic consciousness and the attempt to reconcile the interests of the community and the individual. For example, in 1850 J. L. Stevenson, J. L. Folsom, and William C. Parker, "desiring to further the general and permanent interests of the city," petitioned to build a wharf at North Beach which would insure the commercial prosperity of San Francisco, enhance land values and thereby taxation, and help check the rise of commercial rivals elsewhere on the bay.[57] Much the same thing happened in electoral (as opposed to interest group) strife. Political aspirants invariably claimed a complete identification with the community, including permanent residency, since transiency was a reproach and transients, suspect. These assurances, of course, were sometimes insincere, as with Stevenson and Parker, who were themselves promoting a rival town, New York of the Pacific. Yet the fact that they felt called upon to justify their selfishness in terms of civic well-being strengthened the sense of community nevertheless.

The same communitarian approach that was applied to state and local topics was followed on national ones. "We have our own peculiar wants, demanding peculiar legislation, and we want our own man [for U.S. Senator], imbued with our own California ideas, who will advocate them, and leave the squabblers of the other side to their own sectional issues," commented a typical editorial. California problems, such as the admission of the state into the Union, the establishment of an assay office and mint at the Golden Gate, urban free delivery, cheap postage, internal improvements—lighthouses, improvements on the San Joaquin and Sacramento rivers, and fortifications in California and on the Pacific—a subsidy for a China Steamship line, a Pacific telegraph bill, and, above all, a wagon road and a railroad across the continent were taken very much to heart.[58] However, controversies over the banking system and the tariff seemed hardly important, and both parties ordinarily strove to represent the community majority on all these questions instead of providing choices.

Even the slavery morass, so central to the political life of the "States" and often in California politics as well, did not have a corresponding importance in the city. The peculiar institution was condemned and decidedly unwelcome in the Golden State; but the *Chronicle*, writing in 1855, spoke for the large majority when it asked, "What have we in California to do with slavery? Really nothing. Why then let its discussion enter as a question into our State policy, or into the relations of social life?" [59]

The debate was not entirely squelched, however. Both the *Evening Journal* and the *Christian Advocate* kept up antislavery drumfire in defiance of general editorial opinion. *Uncle Tom's Cabin* circulated in the city; and the French Theater even put on a stage production of it. In 1852 a Free Soil party entered the presidential election, and at least one meeting of Negro inhabitants denounced the institution. Union meetings had been held the year before, and articles denounced disunionists throughout the period. In addition, slavery was a live issue during the fight over California's admission into the Union as well as during attempts to divide the state (supposedly by slavery advocates). Finally, the question was agitated in the Presidential race of 1856, especially by the Republicans, who argued that slavery extension was a threat to free labor in California. Yet even in the aggregate, the activity regarding human bondage did not amount to much, and abolitionism had hardly any foothold.[60]

Of all nonlocal issues, foreign policy probably claimed the least attention. Yet the city was hardly isolationist. External affairs which engaged the interests of the metropolis generated considerable enthusiasm. When natives attacked travelers crossing the Isthmus—the city's lifeline—there were loud cries for retribution. In a similar vein, many demanded U.S. trading privileges in both China and Japan even if it took force to secure these "rights."

When it looked as if French or British power threatened Hawaii or the Hawaiian government maltreated Americans, the press was full of talk about annexation and manifest destiny. The various filibustering expeditions that departed from the metropolis also got some support, though a majority probably felt hostile or at best neutral about these episodes.[61]

In short, neither diplomacy nor national issues activated urban interests as often as "home" problems.[62] Squatterism, the extension scheme, the bulkhead project, the water lot bills, the vigilance risings, and the salary grab stirred the community to its very depths. When the People's party organized in 1856, 10,000 to 15,000 residents attended one of its mass meetings. No extra-local question, including the supposedly vital Pacific Railroad, ever drew this much attention.

The xenophobic side of the city came out in politics more than in any other activity. Just as in the economic arena there was continuous abuse of Eastern shippers for flooding the market, in politics San Franciscans complained constantly against Washington and Sacramento. Any supposedly hostile act by the state government they generally blamed upon the inveterate enmity of the interior or the legislature. There can be little doubt that much animosity existed and that events like the San Francisco flour monopoly of 1852 did nothing to allay it. Yet the local origin of most of the obnoxious state measures was well known, though the knowledge did not in any way hamper the growth of the myth that the interior was bent on systematically harassing the city.[63]

Neither did large federal expenditures discourage a comparable piece of folklore about national neglect. This conviction emerged during the delay over California's admission to the Union and remained through 1856. The federal government built a mint, a marine hospital, and a customs house in the city; fortified Fort Point and Alcatraz Island; established a navy yard at Mare Island; subsidized the Pacific Mail Steamship Company with a mail contract; built lighthouses on the coast; and purchased supplies for Indian wars in the state—all of which significantly helped San

Francisco. The customs house and the Alcatraz fortifications alone cost $1,216,000; and the U.S. Marine Hospital accounted for another $250,000. However, in 1854, after many of these projects were already underway, the *Chronicle* still grumbled that "a plethora of California's ore is now in the national treasury, and notwithstanding this, the Government has never expended anything on the Pacific Coast." [64]

Even if this was not an accurate analysis, the city's complaints against Washington, Sacramento, and Eastern shippers should be seen in another context—as part of a city-state "nationalism." Whether expressed in this way or as civic consciousness, xenophobia, anticolonialism, separatism, or community, this attitude largely exaggerated the sins of the outside world against the metropolis and minimized both the participation of the "natives" in those transgressions and the services rendered by outsiders. Eventually, these convictions developed into a full-blown urban anticolonialism which in its extreme form led to threats of independence. "California is virtually (in a commercial sense) a colony of the Eastern States, as much so as were the original thirteen States, colonies to Great Britain," argued the *Bulletin* in late 1856. "Our tribute semi monthly, amounts to millions of dollars, for which we receive nothing as a people but our subsistence in part, [and] our raiment." Moreover, the argument went, the state was overrun with political carpetbaggers, many of them representing the federal government, who exercised an undue influence on crucial municipal, state, and national issues. As this mentality matured, it began to lapse over into various degrees of separatism. [65]

A number of things encouraged this independence, including discord at home. "If the eastern thirty States must disagree and separate, let them not calculate upon transferring us like chattels to either the one or the other. . . . Our case is bad enough with Uncle Sam—but it would be intolerable with his two sons who murder him," warned the *Chronicle*. [66] The controversy in the East kept the possibility of disunion before the people, thus playing into the hands of those like Henry S. Foote and others who encouraged joyfully what that newspaper regarded as a last resort.

So did the rise of civic consciousness and the pervasive doctrine of local primacy. Since both Whig and Democratic administrations had been disappointments and since the issues that convulsed the East were considered irrelevant, San Franciscans came to the same conclusion on the national level that they had on the municipal—that party did not matter. The demand to sunder political ties—a major connection to the East—contributed to Western sectionalism. The remedies suggested by such men were essentially those advocated in municipal affairs—nonpartisanship. "Let us then, as a band of brothers, unite together for our common good, form ourselves into a California Party, determine to overthrow the old political hacks that have brought us to the verge of ruin," urged the *Bulletin*. "Let us send men of character and ability to represent our interest at Washington, so that California may command that respect which her geographical position and resources entitle her to *abroad*." [67]

Yet the strongest impetus to anticolonialism was economic. It seems also to have been urban, since such talk did not get far until the depression of 1855. But beginning in that year, complaints about the enormous revenues exacted from the state, the drain on its private capital, and the dependence upon outside goods multiplied. At the same time, long dormant or partly submerged topics like the wagon road across the country, the Pacific railroad, coast fortifications, internal improvements to foster California commerce, and similar projects took on a new urgency. The railway was especially significant. Of all the so-called national issues in the 1856 campaign, it was by far the most important; and, as usual, both parties favored it.

"Look at San Francisco, commercially in ruins," stormed Caxton in the *Bulletin*. "Her wharves deserted, her streets dilapidated, her storehouses untenanted, her treasury bankrupt . . . nineteen twentieths of the entire city is mortgaged to usurers and aliens." "There is but one thing which can save the commercial interests of this State from hopeless and irremediable bankruptcy," he continued. "IMMIGRATION. There is but one way by which immigrants can be induced, in any considerable numbers, to flock to our shores—A GRAND CONTINENTAL NATIONAL RAILWAY." Unless the federal government moved into this work, Caxton was ready to advocate secession.[68]

Paradoxically, most others were probably using the language of separatism in order to promote unity, since nearly all hoped that iron rails would alleviate the community's distress. "The threat that we will set ourselves apart from the Eastern states may set the wise but selfish politicians at the East to thinking," suggested the *Chronicle* as early as 1855. "They may be induced to consider and acknowledge how much the '*mother country*' owes to the child." [69] And it was no doubt the metropolis that was at the bottom of this anticolonialism. Polemicists usually talked of the state's economic difficulties; but in San Francisco, California was regarded as an economic hinterland. What they were really talking about was urban business misery, and they were also speaking of economic hegemony for the future. In the midst of its caterwauling about outside transgressions, the *Bulletin* revealed the city's real ambition.

> Those who come here now, if their hopes of success are properly based, must expect to make our shores their home, to break off the ties that bound them to their former dwelling places, and assume the position of pioneers in the land to which the entire range of countries on the western slope of America, and a portion of that region we have hitherto styled the "East" will, in time, become tributary.[70]

In both theory and practice, it was sometimes difficult to tell the colonized from the colonizers. The idea of dominance was inherent in the idea of community.

The Revolution of 1856

San Francisco's resentment at its status in the nation was matched by disenchantment with affairs in both the city and California.[1] The year 1856 was the peak of this outrage, as the Vigilance Committee argued that matters had deteriorated so badly that nothing but revolution could shake off Broderick's tyranny and restore the majesty of the law. Yet by any rational calculation, these "insoluble" problems were on the way to solution by 1856, especially if compared to the state of things in 1849 or 1850. Despite the reformers' contentions that the will of the people had been systematically defeated, the popular side had ordinarily prevailed on the more important issues facing the city.

On the perennial issue of government finances, for example, progress was perhaps too impressive. During 1855–56 municipal spending declined substantially, and the Consolidation Act of 1856 slashed outlays so drastically that the corporation could not replace the firemen's hose. Other "improvements" flowed from the new charter as well. "No more ruinous contracts can be entered into for the benefit of the men who get them and those who pass their bills," asserted the *Atla*. "The street contracts, these huge vampires who have sucked the very hearts blood from our city treasury, have received their death blow."[2]

The Consolidation Act diminished the tax load even more strikingly. City and county rates fell from $3.15 per one hundred dollars assessed valuation in 1855–56 to $1.60. This figure was lower than that of Louisville, Memphis, Brooklyn, St. Louis, and New Orleans, which suffered neither the inflation of a Gold Rush nor the unprecedented problems of an instant city. The amount collected plummeted along with the rates. Property charges which raised $592,240 in 1853–54 brought only $290,000 in 1856–57, and license revenue nearly disappeared. At their peak in 1852–53, these had provided $328,000; yet by 1855–56 this tax supplied $33,000, though it rose to nearly $60,000 the next year.[3]

The frequent outcries over real estate questions created similar results. It was the Peter Smith, Colton, extension, and squatter interests that were considered disreputable in San Francisco; and by 1856 these had either lost or were losing to their opponents. Though the Limantour fraud seemed successful, most of the land battles had been won by the popular side, and the Frenchman's victory before the U.S. Board of Land Commissioners would have to be defended all the way to the Supreme Court.

The most bitter realty fight prevented a $16,000,000 swindle and demonstrated just how powerful popular opinion could be when it took the trouble to be anything at all. The county Democratic Central Committee, with Broderick's lieutenant, Edward McGowan, at its head, supported a bill before the state legislature to extend the city front into the bay and thereby create much expensive new land. Five of seven San Francisco assemblymen resigned in protest against the bill and sought re-election in what amounted to a special referendum to fill the vacancies. The antiextensionist "slaves" (renegade Democrats and regular Whigs) carried the strongholds of their Tammany "masters" by four to one and the other wards by as much as ten to one.[4] Such was the extent of the tyranny!

The people followed this triumph with another, though less democratic success in the legislature. "The Extension Bill has been defeated in the Senate by the casting vote of the Lieut. Gov. Purdy," Thomas O. Larkin's lobbyist explained. "It took a good deal of the 'dust' to accomplish this result."[5]

This outcome conformed to the usual pattern of events when

strong adverse public opinion confronted something the politicians tried to foist upon the community. The "Salary Grab," the Bulkhead Bill, and the water lot controversies all fell before a vociferously expressed popular will. The most important exception to this rule was the Jenny Lind purchase, which mass outrage could not deter. Yet even here, it was later admitted that the building had been a better bargain than had been supposed. The passively accepted gas contract of 1852 also came under fire as another example of corruption; but most agreed that the pact, made at a time of prosperity, was not a bad one. The flight of good times as much as its inherent inequitability made the transaction seem intolerable.

The patterns of electoral violence and chicanery did not fit the deterioration-tyranny thesis, either. The year 1853 seemed to be the high point for such activity; and even James King admitted that the 1854 election, which resulted in a Know Nothing victory, was an advance over past ones.[6] "Yesterday was the proudest day . . . San Francisco . . . has ever seen," gloated the *Alta* over the orderly fall of 1855 canvass. "Truly a change has come over our city, and she is no longer open to the charge that she is at the mercy of rowdies and bullies." Yet even an improved election was not altogether tranquil; in this very contest, ballot box stuffing carried the day in the sixth ward.

Developments in 1856 made even this limited fraud less likely to recur. The Consolidation Act provided for honest contests, including the designation of upright election judges. This was a crucial matter, for it was always held that these positions were key links in the chain that shackled the city to the Broderick tyranny. Indeed, the fair election of 1856 was conducted by these new men. The Consolidation Act also eliminated overlapping offices, reduced fees, and set stringent financial standards; and the 1855 legislature had lowered justice of the peace and constable fees, those paid most often by poor people, by half. Finally, in 1856, according to two independent and pro-Vigilante papers, candidates were much improved.[7]

There was more protest against vice in 1855–56 but there were fewer practitioners.[8] In the wide-open boom town of the late forties and early fifties, the harlot and the gamester had been almost accepted members of society. But by 1856 family women were crowding out the prostitutes; and the theater, home, club, and church encroached upon the halls of chance.

The condition of the supposed tyrant's political fortunes provides further refutation of the tyranny thesis. In mid-year, Broderick was only six months away from the goal that had brought him to California, but the bases of his power had seen better times. His real estate was a drug on the market; and his banking ally, Palmer, Cook, and Company was under a withering attack from the reformers and not financially sound. Moreover, the "Boss" had many fewer offices than earlier. The Know Nothing defeat of Bigler in 1855 deprived Tammany of its state patronage. An investigation of the State Marine Hospital destroyed that institution during the same year, further depleting the supply of jobs. In 1854 the Americans had won the local elections and that, too, hit at Broderick's resources; and the next year, even with the help of fraud, the best the Democrats could do was a split of positions and spoils. And as usual, the "machine" was beset by rebels—called the Purifiers—within the ranks of the Democratic party. Therefore, to the extent that Broderick was the trouble, he was much less so than in 1853.

Nor was the New Yorker entirely a problem. Oddly enough, the same man who had a clear connection to gamblers, shoulder strikers, and speculators also had some uplift tendencies. Broderick's reformism may have been sham, an attempt to save himself from defeat, blackmail against disreputable elements, economically or politically self-serving, or an effort to satisfy all groups with some kind of tangible results. It may even have been sincere. Whatever his motives, he is on record for significant reform as well as rascality.

Broderick suggested consolidation several years before its passage, and to the same end he had urged the elimination of county

taxes. Moreover, the Democratic "Boss" specifically approved of
the 1856 election of Horace Hawes and William J. Shaw, knowing
that they were going to Sacramento to frame and pass a charter
that would reduce the number of jobs and the level of fees. As
Senator, Broderick himself had tried and failed to lower county
officers' charges. He was more successful with the 1851 charter,
which he guided through the legislature and which included the
important financial reform that established a Funded Debt Commission. In the same year, when pioneer educator John C. Pelton
came to San José seeking aid, it was the New York Irishman who
helped him secure the first state education law when most other
legislators were hostile or indifferent.[9] On the very eve of the
Vigilante rebellion, Broderick's close associate Franklin Tilford
sponsored a number of other legislative reforms. One would have
responded to the near universal complaint that the state bankruptcy laws made it ludicrously easy to defraud creditors and
still come out rich. Some even thought Tilford's proposed penalties
were too harsh. The second would have stiffened the punishment
for manslaughter and jury tampering, another clear response to
democratic pressures, in this case to eliminate flaws publicized
by the Cora trial of late 1855.

All these things suggest that Frank Soulé, a Whig politician and
long-time rival of Broderick, was partially right when he said, "We
have known Mr. Broderick long and intimately. In the Senate, this
city had no more ardent nor active defender and guardian of what
were considered her interests. And we have no reason to believe
that his interest in her welfare has changed." [10]

Writing four months before the Vigilante revolt, a religious newspaper summed up the overall improvement. "Morality is gaining
ground. A higher tone prevails with each year. Wealth cannot
now screen a man from public scrutiny. . . . Corrupt judges can
no longer sit on the benches," argued the editor. "Corrupt jurors
will soon be driven from the box and witnesses brought out of
gambling rooms and tippling places will scarcely be allowed a
place. . . . The lives of men of pure association are just as safe

now in San Francisco as they are in New York." The *Pacific*, a
religious journal, had been taking this line since 1853 and not
unilaterally. "A change has taken place within the last few years,
and that change has been for the better," the *Alta* said in 1855.
"The past year has been prolific of all the indications of an improved social organization," echoed the *Era* in January 1856.[11]
It is relatively clear, therefore, that the revolution of 1856 came on
the political upswing.

Other indicators are not quite so clear. Few accurate statistics
on employment, trade, manufacture, banking, and other business
matters remain to demonstrate whether the uprising came in a
period of economic decline or betterment. Yet at the time of King's
death, the panic of 1855 was over a year behind the community;
and though the number of failures in 1856 was greater than in
1855, the amount of money involved was much smaller. The sta-
tistical problem looms just as large in regard to crime. Though
two spectacular killings occurred, there certainly was no wave in
1855–56 comparable to that of 1851 which sparked the first Committee.

If the deterioration interpretation cannot explain the Revolution,
spouses, spatial relationships, and spurious sensationalism can.
The journalism was provided by James King of William, a pioneer
in the city who came to California in 1848 and remained as a
banker. For a time he did well, but the depression forced him to
suspend operations. He stayed in the same business, however,
with the house of Adams and Company, which assumed his liabilities and assets and put him in charge of banking. Soon after,
they, too, fell in the great run of 1855. After a temporary retirement, King assumed the editorship of a new paper, the *Evening
Bulletin*, and the leadership of a reform drive.

Once launched into his fresh career, the twice-ruined banker
created a sensation. No one else had ever attacked the forces of
evil quite as vehemently and directly. He called things by what
he fancied to be their real names and neglected few scoundrels
in his indictment. Though he did not consistently nor even fre-

quently advocate upsetting the constituted authorities, his language was often inflammatory in the extreme; but that merely strengthened his hold on the majority of San Franciscans.

Most of King's targets were in need of denunciation, and by and large he stood for the right ends. Yet his methods were morally much more ambiguous. In the words of one historian, he used a "bludgeon instead of a rapier" in his assaults.[12] He was not interested in fine distinctions; and as long as he was right over all, he did not worry about mistaken details. Nor did he scruple over the niceties of argument or fair play. He had a supreme contempt for the courts, who, according to him, let off criminals, quibbled, and perverted the law.

No one would have accused him of a legalistic approach himself. Whereas the courts operated on the principle that one was innocent until proven guilty, King worked on the opposite assumption. "Let us go back a little and review the case [of Father Gallagher and the hospital] as the records prove, and the charges not denied seem to indicate as also true," wrote the crusading editor in 1856. King was an expert at broadcasting unproven indictments while seeming not to make an open accusation. "The *Crime of Infanticide* might with some show of truth be charged . . . upon Father Gallagher," continued the journalist after repeating various complaints against the "priestly Shylock." "He has refused to admit us for the purpose of investigating their truth." [13]

Religious matters concerned King greatly, and here again he was none too subtle. Though the Tom Paine Club was an innocent debating society, this group of intellectuals was attacked as atheistic; and the rival *Chronicle* got a dose of the same medicine for employing John S. Hittell, a Paine Club member and one of the best minds in the city. On another occasion, King ostentatiously refused to place a notice of a Spiritualist meeting under "Religious Notices" in his paper; and on yet another, his heading for a letters to the editor debate between Baptists and Germans, on which he took no open stand, was headed with the suggestive title "TURN VEREINS VS. THE SABBATH." Still more outrageously, after first declaring it none of his business, he pompously pried into the initiation of a young girl into the Catholic Sisters of Presentation. "Her friends have been in conversation with her for several days on the subject of the step she was about to take," he piously reassured his correspondent who had urged him to take a stand against Catholic convents. "But she was firm in her determination to devote her days to the service of the church." [14]

Besides being morally overcommitted, King was also overbearing. He was not openly anti-Catholic, anti-Semitic, or anti-Quaker; but his language skirted these sentiments so closely that the adherents of those faiths must have been uneasy. When Father Gallagher's friends defended him in a published statement, King replied that these "liars" "by that act of fulsome adulation to an unworthy priest, proved themselves unworthy of the name of American Catholics or American citizens." [15] The reformer harped so vigorously on the fact that Dr. Gibbon (the hospital contractor) was a Quaker that one distraught member wrote in begging the editor not to refer to his sect so much.

King had even stronger language for other situations. "Hang Billy Mulligan" was one of his more colorful suggestions for dealing with the shoulder strikers in the county sheriff's office. His response to a tragedy on the Isthmus was equally heavy handed. One Jack Oliver had refused to pay for a purchase, whereupon the Panamanian vendor pulled a knife and the drunken New Yorker shot him. The ensuing riot cost twenty-five American lives, including women and children. King called for U.S. retaliation and noted further, "Our great regret is that the passengers were not armed, as they formerly were in '49 and '50. Had they been so," declared the reformer, "and every savage on that Isthmus from Panama to Aspinwall, in any way connected with the outrage, would have been shot down like brutes as they are, the civilized world would have justified the act." "As far as the rights of the natives or those of the New Granadian Government are concerned," he continued, "we should not hesitate a moment as to the seizure by our Government of the Isthmus, and if the Governments of England and France did not like it, let them make the most of it." [16] Fortunately, King thought the spot too expensive to hold.

His intemperance also led him to the scandalously unfair charge that his fellow journalists had been either too scared or too corrupt to reveal the true state of affairs in the city. There can be little doubt that the community knew exactly how bad conditions were despite the supposed dereliction or muzzling of the media, in which case the press was either not gagged or not necessary. Far from being mute, journalists actually helped distort the reality of affairs by exaggerating the seamy side of urban life, though not as much as King. He was surely the catalyst for the "Revolution of 1856," but his colleagues had just as certainly prepared the ground for him.

A number of other things about the "crusading" editor were puzzling. At one time he had been associated in business with Joseph C. Palmer, the morally questionable ally of Broderick; and at another he had been the patron of John Nugent of the *Herald*, both of whom his editorials assailed incessantly. Morality certainly motivated King in part, but competitive journalistic capitalism, that is, circulation, played an important role, too. It is possible that his strictures against Adams and Company were self-interested also. King, like others, had lost money in their collapse.

Yet none of these charges caused King any misgivings about his own moral rectitude. He continually challenged his critics to show that he was not blameless; and when they complied, he always had an explanation that satisfied himself and the community. His failure to warn his former customers who had followed him into the house of Adams and Company of its imminent collapse, for example, he put down to loyalty and a desire to work from within to rectify its financial situation. However persuasive these defenses were to King and his devotees, it is hard to escape the conclusion that along with being right about a host of things, he was less pure than he and his friends assumed. He was also, to employ a description used by his enemies, an "assassin of character" and a "moral peacock."

Yet to the majority of San Franciscans he was an unprecedentedly popular reform demagogue, and his political impact was devastating. He flayed the politicians, the prostitutes, the barbarous custom of dueling, the defaulting bankers, the gamblers, the toughs, the police, and just about everything else in sight while championing the home, the church, the school, and reform —and the city loved him for it. With unmatched skill, he cleverly communicated the tensions of the community and played upon its frustrations until his own interpretation of history, like bad money in Gresham's Law, had driven its competitors out of the marketplace. Despite the obvious improvements in the situation, despite the evident complexity, regardless of the apathy, indifference, and downright connivance of good citizens, King convinced San Franciscans that they were a band of innocents crushed by a steadily worsening tyranny. By presenting only the bad side of the story, he completely distorted the reality of urban life.

Many of the most significant political themes of the decade— the reconciliation of individual and community interests, anticolonialism, nonpartisanship, community consciousness, and local primacy—all came to the fore and coalesced around the reform crusade. At the same time, King drew together allies faster than anyone had imagined possible. Although he did not always agree with the sentiments expressed, he nevertheless opened his columns to a multitude of causes. Even though he sometimes allowed the "accused" to defend themselves, the *Bulletin* very quickly became the major forum for expressing nearly every frustration with the status quo as well as schemes for civic or individual betterment. Everything from night schools to new cures for corns was advocated from this reform pulpit, in some cases winning him over. For example, he came to see that women's economic opportunities in San Francisco were insufficient and that his initial suggestion that the unemployed should go to the mines often proved impractical.

Yet he made few such admissions about his enemies. They were the forces of malevolence for whose conduct, unlike his own, there were no adequate explanations and no mitigating circumstances. Very quickly the conviction developed that the defaulting bankers, the cheating politicians, the rouged women of the night, the brutal gunslingers and toughs, the impudent gamblers, the fraudulent land claimants, and the economic speculators were leagued together against the good people of the city. Broderick's organization included many from these groups, but it did not quite take in all the forces of evil. Nor was that element entirely lacking on the side of the reformers. Yet in the community's mind, the Emporium became increasingly polarized between good and evil.

King ignited a class struggle of sorts, though not the European variety involving the classic duality of working class and middle class. The reformers envisioned themselves as an all-embracing alliance of worthy citizens that cut across the categories of upper, middle, and lower orders. They were, in their own minds, *the* people; and that meant the respectable, useful, resident portion of San Francisco. The upheaval of 1856 was pre-eminently a revolution of the "legitimates."

If King was the hero and martyr of the rebellion, women were the shock troops, giving a distinctive character and much of the moral fervor to the struggle. Above all, King was their champion, the upholder of family and home interests in the metropolis against gamblers, prostitutes, and their allies. "I find you a [*sic*] especial favorite with the dear house-wives," wrote a correspondent. "Indeed, there is sometimes danger of our being minus tea when the *Bulletin* arrives." [17] The journalist's broadsides against vice were his best and most stirring.

From the beginning people argued that until women and families arrived in large numbers, the moral tone of urban life would be very unsatisfactory. Though feminists called themselves squaws and though women suffered discrimination, they also were depended upon to be the great civilizers of the community. They were "God's own Police"; and unlike the regular force, they worked for nothing and were a good deal more zealous.

As the ladies went about their task of eliminating barbarism, however, the barbarians and their powerful allies tenaciously resisted any further loss of status. The most sensational battle between the emerging and declining classes of women began one night, late in 1855, when Arabella Bryan decided to go to the theater. It ended soon thereafter in the street killing of United States Marshal William Richardson. That a gamester and lover of harlots should gun down a family man on a San Francisco street was outrageous; but what followed, or rather what did not follow, was horrifying. Cora was tried and his jury, hung amidst numerous charges of bribery, which added to the frustration of the indecisive result. Worse yet, Colonel Baker, the defense lawyer (a class itself none too highly regarded) argued that the bonds between the prostitute and the man of chance were as genuine as any other between men and women. "A tie which angels might not blush to approve," argued the Colonel. "Has the man who thus endorsed the sinful union between gambler and prostitute, a mother living?" answered a correspondent for a furious community. "Has he a wife or daughters, who can read his sentiments? Has he a son?" [18]

Yet the Cora-Richardson incident was a chance one, not likely to recur; and, therefore, the clash between women might have abated. It did not die down, however, largely because of the spatial relationships of the city. What could happen in a theater only rarely occurred in the streets often. As the middle class moved west, the separation of places of home and work unfolded. Men worked downtown and lived on the heights; but between these two areas and to an extent mixed in with them was a large concentration of sin, especially along Dupont and cross streets between there and Stockton. Many middle-class people still lived

on Dupont; and even those who did not were thrown into proximity with this vice district, whose inhabitants were entrenched
upon the access routes to downtown. A trip to the dentist, the
doctor, the milliner, the husband's office, and sometimes even to
church kept the situation explosive by renewing the contact between housewives and harlots.

"Is it not wonderful," stormed an angry lady, "that young men
should nightly spend their evenings, like dogs, smelling out all
these vile excrescences, peeking through the cracks and crevices
of doors, windows, and blinds in our crowded thoroughfares, in
the full face of ladies and gentlemen going and returning from
church?" Another wrote to denounce "the liberties of men, who
will pass the early part of the evening in the society of virtuous
females, discoursing upon the charms of domestic life, and the
solace of home, and virtuous associations! and directly upon leaving, *cross the street and enter a house of ill fame.*" Still another
woman, a foreigner, described her encounter, on the way to market, with two livery stable loafers. "As I passed up the streets
these creatures attracted my attention by giggling, laughing and
making impertinent remarks to each other, looking me in the face
and passing, and then allowing me to repass them under their
licentious stare and meaningless giggle." This same correspondent
urged her sisters "never to venture outside except under the care
of their natural protectors, who ought to be prepared with a
volume of Colt's practice, to teach those fellows . . . the respect
due to our sex"; and the *Era* recommended a "whipping post" for
the same purpose. Not every denunciation was this fervid, but
the "gentler" sex certainly did not intend to tolerate the vices they
passed on their way to town. "Let something be done . . . so
that a man may be able to walk through the streets with a virtuous
woman," commanded the *Fireman's Journal.*[19]

Although most housewives did not advocate "women's rights,"
this conflict between Pike Street and Powell was surely a feminist
uprising to remake the community. "The ladies of San Francisco
hold the power in their own hands . . . to purify this city," wrote

a woman. "To drive hence the gambler and the harlot, and restore the tone of moral health and purity, and make it a suitable residence for the virtuous and the good." [20] Thus, at a time when the regular police force was reduced in numbers and morale, "God's own" were ubiquitous and hyperactive.[21]

Denizens of Pacific Street presented a number of threats to women of the hills. Though not all of the latter felt personal hostility toward prostitutes, they were united in resenting contact with something that was certainly evil even if its practitioners were only unfortunate. The harlots also menaced the home, and respect for that institution was as close to absolute as the city's value system allowed. Too, women resented prostitution as male exploitation of both consort and courtesan and as an influence which degraded both the young in particular and society in general to its own vicious level.[22]

King urged the wives on; and even though he was no lover of women's rights, his paper afforded the ladies much greater influence than local feminists could have hoped for. He still believed that their place was in the home, but their defense of that institution profoundly influenced developments in the wider urban world.

Nevertheless, neither King nor the women had given any institutional form to the frustrations they nourished. It took the death of its champion to transform community anger into action. That event was hastened by the editor's insistence on exploiting every kind of conflict; and when the Democrats' annual party strife entered its 1856 phase, King was drawn into it. The "Purifier" wing of the party objected to the employment of several Broderickites in the customs house. King first denied this accusation but then backed down and demanded that the collector, who also employed King's brother, remove the Tammany men. In the course of this polemic, the editor publicized the biography (a frequent political ploy) of James P. Casey, the supervisor, brawler, and ballot box stuffer. This politician had served a stretch in Sing Sing for repossessing his gift of furniture from his mistress. Though this information had been printed previously in the *Chronicle,* Casey warned King that his reputation could not stand an encore; but King, stubborn and courageous as usual, printed one anyway.

That evening Casey accosted King in the street, pulled a pistol from his cloak, and fatally wounded him. The killer was taken into protective custody by the police, many of whom were probably his friends. San Francisco, supine to this moment, now rose in revolt; as the life ebbed from the stricken man, it seemed to flow into the community. There was no mob violence—no thanks to Sam Brannan and other hotheads—only a steady, determined drive to organize. With native merchants at its head and the great majority of everyone else in the ranks or in support, the Vigilance Committee began operations. And from North Beach to South Park to the hills in the west came a cry of outrage unparalleled in the city's history.[23]

In many ways King was both fool and fanatic; but he was a beloved one, and San Francisco could hardly find words to express its indignation at his injury. "Men flew to arms; Ladies threatened to punish the assassin, if their husbands permitted him to escape. The very school children urged their fathers on, and wept for their benefactor and friend," wrote Caxton. The women were especially grieved and angered. "Several of our carriers inform us that yesterday, at almost every door on their routes, the ladies were waiting to see them to enquire into the state of the health of Mr. King, and that the little girls ran half way across the street, asking the same question," the *Bulletin* wrote. "What is to be done with that villain, Casey?" demanded a furious female. "If the men don't hang him the ladies will!"[24]

They were spared the bother. The reformer soon died; and Casey and Cora, tried by the Vigilantes, were hanged on the day of the martyr's funeral. Before the episode closed, two others met a similar end. In the meantime, the Committee went about collecting evidence on the basis of which they added about twenty deportations, mostly Broderickite Irish and political toughs, to their triumphs, "not for punishment of specific crimes, but because

the safety of the State, the safety of this revolution . . . requires it." Even Broderick found this an expedient moment to be
out of town rounding up support in the interior for the 1857 legislative battle over the Senatorship, and many others suddenly discovered similar pressing business elsewhere. Yet the interior was
not necessarily more friendly to these tourists. Throughout the
state, military organizations arose to support the Vigilantes if necessary, and expressions of support poured into the city. For once,
the omnipresent rural-urban antagonism was largely drowned as
the shock waves of sympathy from the bay engulfed the state.[25]

The press was not exactly censored, but it received considerable
guidance. When John Nugent's *Herald* opposed the Committee,
merchants burned copies on the streets, withdrew ads, and stopped
subscriptions, thereby reducing a leading paper to secondary importance and dependence on Broderick to stay alive. The *Alta* at
first vacillated. Its staff prepared two articles, one calling the
shooting an affray, the other, a murder; but after a visit from the
Vigilantes, the latter version suddenly seemed more appropriate.
The *Chronicle* also hedged. Frank Soulé eventually came around,
but not before he had lost enough popular respect to ruin ultimately his excellent paper. Vigilante supporters always boasted
of the near unanimous newspaper support; but of the four leading
dailies, only the *Bulletin* went along willingly. The *Herald* refused; the *Chronicle* and the *Alta* were clearly coerced; the *Fireman's Journal* was only lukewarm; and others probably were, too.
Similar pressures were applied elsewhere. According to critic
William A. Scott, the foremost preacher in town, "it was the policy
of the . . . Committee to force every body into their ranks." He
himself was "requested" by the officers of his church to cease his
opposition. Scott refused and was burned in effigy. Even so, the
Pacific's traveling editor found that "ten in San Francisco dissent
where there is one in the mountains." [26]

Since men of means and property led the Vigilante uprising, it
is tempting to classify it as reactionary. Yet the event was much
more complex than that. The upheaval probably would not have

occurred without the death of James King, and revenge was its original *raison d'être*. But it gained its own imperatives and quickly became a species of urban revolution against the Gold Rush status quo and on behalf of typical nineteenth-century city reforms. The colorful, lawless metropolis had often been exciting, and many would remember it affectionately. Yet contemporaries had seen enough of it. They insisted that San Francisco now fall back into the line of march of urban progress; and that decision led them from punishment to politics. This in turn involved both backward- and forward-looking measures.

In many ways, the rebellion was both unfair and unreasonable, but it was not undemocratic. There was no small, conspiratorial clique which seized power. The use of terror was real enough, but it was supported by the mass of people and wielded by the acknowledged community leaders, the merchants. As the *Chronicle* put it, the Committee "was governed by a higher law—the law of self defence by an outraged community." [27]

As usual, the situation involved San Francisco in an ethical dilemma, this time between the will of the people and the demands of the law. Both community ideals obviously could not apply in this case; and as in any revolution, the choice was situational. "What law can bear against nine tenths of a self governing community?" demanded the *Pacific*. "Circumstances determine the duty of the Governor of a State, with regard to the enforcement of the letter of the law [against the Vigilantes]. *Not under all circumstances* does it rest on his conscience, to take up arms for the enforcement of law." [28] Though deploring the "LYNCH LAW," the *Era* admitted, "Cases there are, which set the ordinary rules of human conduct at defiance and seem to sanction the exclamation of the poet,

> When dishonor enters our hearths, law dies,
> And murder takes the angel shape of justice." [29]

In making this decision to take up arms, San Franciscans were also ruled by the same motives that led their ancestors to fight the British. In their own eyes, the rebels acted in the American tradition. "When men enter into the social compact, they delegate to society certain of their rights on condition that society shall protect them in others," wrote Caxton. The *Era* agreed: the "people" had only "taken back the power entrusted to the keeping and exercise of unworthy servants." "The whole struggle has been a strange and novel one. It has been called a revolution; and yet resembling only the one of our forefathers in 1776," the *Bulletin* argued in November. "Contrary to the general rule, the most active and the originators . . . were the established and most honest of our citizens and those who had the most to lose in case of defeat." [30]

Yet these words were more than just repetitions of what the community thought its forebears had said, for the rebellion was accompanied by an urban reform ideology. Earlier uplifters had a fund of doctrine and no party, but 1856 established their political institution and encouraged a more complete elaboration and wider acceptance of their thinking. The ideology of community that emerged drew together the most important political thoughts of the decade.

One thing upon which nearly everybody agreed was the malevolence of politicians. "The great lesson . . . that is to be learned from the result of the election," exulted the *Bulletin* in November, "is the fact that the People have demonstrated their entire independence of professional politicians." [31] They were not the only illegitimate order; but the gamblers, prostitutes, economic speculators, contractors, bullies, and shyster lawyers were part of the "wire puller's" set, leagued with him in infamy. Above all, the movement of 1856 rejected parties and the emergence and continued growth of a distinct caste of politicians. San Franciscans usually accepted urban specialization in other spheres, but they resisted the creation of a special class to deal with politics.

The indictment contained several counts. Parties, it was held, were not relevant to the city, whose needs were so obvious and simple that there need be no division of opinion on how to respond to them. Argued the *Town Talk*, "*There is no political principle involved in the contest for our local officers, and no party lines should be drawn.*" Moreover, parties had institutional interests that clashed with those of the metropolis. Political passions ran so deep that some men felt that "next to those [passions] of a religious character, none are so potent as these in influencing the actions of men." [32] Party ties encouraged straight ticket voting, which always included a multitude of bad men, rather than balloting for the best men to run city affairs.

With the independents local primacy was a cardinal principle. "Tomorrow the citizens will be called upon to decide one of the most important issues ever presented to them, in comparison with which even the election of the President . . . is of secondary importance," exhorted the *Bulletin* in November. It was part of the anticolonial psychology to regard regular organizations as alien intruders which undermined the principle of self-determination. "When it comes to local interests of San Francisco the citizens must settle their own affairs and no outside influence," Vox Populi wrote in urging the familiar panacea of separating the national and local elections. "The great majority of our fellow citizens are in favor of REFORM, and the only method of making that reform a permanent one . . . is to entirely divest our local elections of everything pertaining to politics and thus secure the choice of men for the various offices who are . . . qualified to fill them." [33]

If parties were in disrepute, professional politicians were beneath contempt; and here the independent, communitarian-class consciousness came out most clearly. The Revolution of 1856 pitted "the *People* against the office holder and political aspirant." The city needed a "transfer of the management of our political affairs from the hands of politicians to the masses." "How often . . . have the merchants ever been represented in the Legislative body?" demanded the reformers, identifying the masses. "Henceforth . . . the sober and industrious [may] be represented and have influence," the *Pacific* exulted after the election. In contra-

distinction, the politicians were invariably described as having no
"visible means of support" except the "new trade" of politics.
Complained the *Bulletin*, "The laboring and producing classes
have spent over one hundred millions of dollars" in the building
of the state. Yet they were "compelled to maintain in comparative
idleness . . . those idlers and drones." The politicians understood
and resented this thrust at their pre-eminence, as their counter-
blasts indicated.[34]

Moreover, the carpetbagging politicians never intended to
"identify themselves with the interests of the State or become permanent citizens," whereas the "industrial classes" were "anchored
here by family ties . . . and households."[35] This last was an especially important point, for residence was the prime test of one's
loyalty. There could be legitimate differences over the best interests of the community, but at least a man had to be willing to
live in it and be able to contribute something to it, in short, to be
a San Franciscan.

As this nascent civic consciousness grew, it encouraged demands
for an independent vehicle for regeneration; and the Vigilantes
added an even harsher imperative. They hanged four men without any shadow of legality; and since literally thousands were
implicated in these acts, seizing power became a necessity. Otherwise, a resurgent Tammany would "persecute" the Committee and
its supporters. Thus the desire for reform and the fear of retribution finally bore tangible results.

Hardly had James King been buried when demands for a People's party filled the air. But that remedy was not turned to
immediately. The first tactic called for the resignation of the
municipal authorities. Through the usual chartering maneuver,
the Consolidation Act had abolished the year-old city government
—divided between Know Nothings and Democrats—in the spring
and provided for the holdover of the solidly Democratic county
officers until the fall. That is why in mid-June, ten to fifteen thousand people gathered at an evening meeting to demand their
resignation and to return a thunderous ovation to the remark of

Colonel Baylie Peyton that "the Vigilance Committee [has] the prayers of the Churches and the smiles of the ladies, God bless them." [36]

However, this demand of "The People in Council"—even with the support of the Lord and the women—did not turn the rascals out. They clung resolutely to power and demanded proof of their rascality. Therefore, on August 11 another mass gathering listened to popular orators tell them that reform had been rebuffed by Democrats, Whigs, and Know Nothings alike. These repeated snubs by the regular parties dictated a third, and the "people" named a caucus of twenty-one men to select candidates for the fall election. Although the uplifters promised not to meddle in the national contests, they insisted upon making the local choices themselves. The politicians tried their standard tactic of infiltrating the reform movement in order to secure control; but this time the maneuver, apparently by Gwinite Democrats, was unsuccessful. [37] Caucus nominations were ratified, and the reformers began the battle to elect Tammany's successors in November.

Though preventing Tammany vengeance was undoubtedly the main motivation, urban reform was also an important consideration. And the abolition of the convention system was one of the foremost secondary concerns, for this Jacksonian reform, established to enhance the popular voice, had come to be an anti-democratic device, producing the hated class of politicians. Since no one but a professional had time for the electioneering that primaries and conventions required, the mass meeting, where the people, rather than the regulars, chose their own candidates, was proposed. A registry law to eliminate fraudulent voting became another part of the program, as did abolition of the fee system. Along with reduced rewards should come increased publicity, especially a registry of disreputable characters to protect the community from further impositions by these men and shame them out of additional chicanery.

Law enforcement reforms supplemented the recommendations. Beyond this, the regenerators wanted the resignation of corrupt

Justice Hugh Murray of the California Supreme Court, a jury system streamlined to allow a majority to convict, the foundation of
a house of refuge, the re-establishment of a chain gang, the improvement of the police, and the abolition of the state ban on Negro and Chinese testimony. This proscription, argued the *Bulletin*,
had been transferred from the South to California; but it did not
work, for criminals often went unwhipped because no white persons witnessed the crime. "It is a glaring injustice, one which, while
it oppresses a particular class of our inhabitants, does not benefit
any other." [38]

In addition, reformers demanded that the poorly enforced anti-
gambling and antiprostitution statutes be toughened to the point
of prohibition. Failing that, these businesses should be driven off
the public thoroughfares into an informally segregated vice district of the kind that they claimed was already common in Eastern
cities and of which the Storyville District of New Orleans and the
First Ward of Chicago were later famous examples. Moreover, the
gamesters and courtesans, along with the politicians and others who
patronized them, should be socially proscribed by polite society.
Some women even urged unsuccessfully that their frail sisters be
driven out of town entirely.

Suppression of vice and crime formed part of the rationale for
urban education, but it had other significant justifications as well
and was a major plank in the reform platform. Both before and
after the death of King, the *Bulletin* crusaded for a high school,
a night school, larger appropriations for the entire system, better
pay for teachers, and other improvements.[39] The middle-class
forces of civic betterment even began a timid approach to the problems of poverty and welfare. They resolutely opposed the mistreat-
ment of sailors by crimps, and King's paper constantly urged the
establishment of a sailors' home to deliver them from the boardinghouse monopolists who controlled marine labor. Discussions of unemployment abounded in the press, and the *Bulletin* served as a
partial labor exchange. Day nurseries for working mothers were

advocated; extreme cases of poverty, revealed; and institutions dealing with human suffering, encouraged. Treatment of prisoners became an issue; and King's brother Thomas, who inherited the editorship, visited the jail to inspect conditions. When he found that they were poor, the reform journal solicited private donations to humanize the jail. Even those at the bottom of society received a sympathetic hearing. When a crew of badly mistreated Indian sailors mutinied, the *Bulletin* described their leader as a hero and went on to state that "if their charges about provisions are true however, and if they really had nothing to eat but the fish and rice . . . it was an outrage upon humanity, which ought not to go uninvestigated; be the sufferers rich or poor, black or white." [40]

Nor did the operation of government go unexamined. City services were constantly discussed, especially the condition of the streets. So was budget slashing, which everybody seemed to favor. Yet the *Bulletin*, at least, did not demand the unreasonable and even fought against cuts for the fire department, schools, and other things. "If there is a point where outlay should stop, there is also one below which economy would become niggardliness— its operation an absurdity." [41]

Although it probably jeopardized some support, the reformers, in addition, angrily denounced tax evasion. Despite the fact that James King himself had led one of these efforts in 1855, King's successors complained "that *over five millions seven hundred and seventy thousand dollars* worth of property, in this country alone, has not contributed one cent towards State and county expenses, and this property owned, too, principally by the rich." Will the authorities "look quietly on, and allow the middle class alone to pay, as heretofore, all the expense of Government?" This "was not the fault of the old city government," argued the *True Californian*. "It is not the fault of the present government—but of the miserable, miserly, swindling tax delinquents—who, because they owe $300,000 and can afford to contest the assessments, refuse to pay, throw the whole burden of the government upon their poorer

neighbors." The *Bulletin* even published names of some of the
revenue dodgers, including Sam Brannan and Thomas O. Larkin,
two of the founders of the People's Reform party.[42]

Economic, along with governmental, wrongdoing claimed a
share of the reformers' attention. Those who had used the bankruptcy laws to defraud their creditors, including some among the
People's party, received heavy and frequent censure. A number of
remedies were suggested, but neither these nor the complaints
stemmed the flow of insolvencies or eventuated in effective legislation.

A number of other minor demands rounded out the program;
but above all, the reformers wanted power. This priority was well
advised, for their enemies intended to gain revenge. The opposition persuaded the governor to issue a proclamation declaring San
Francisco under martial law, thereby casting doubt on the legality
of the election. When the chief executive failed to raise the militia
to put down the rebellion, the United States government became
the next hope. Fortunately for the reformers, the federal authorities, with some exceptions, maintained an official neutrality. The
Broderickites unsuccessfully tried the old tactic of breaking up their
opponents' meetings, and the Law and Order party likewise cease-
lessly attempted to instigate a "reaction" against the reformers.
The *Herald* fanned every prejudice imaginable, particularly ethnic
and regional ones. This sheet assured Southerners that the Vigilantes were really abolitionists in disguise; reminded natives of the
prominent role played by French, Germans, and Jews; told the
Irish that the uprising was just another form of nativism; and
warned Democrats that the group was Republican, and vice versa.
These charges were largely untrue, though anti-Catholic feelings
probably tainted many reformers. The independents frequently
reiterated their friendship toward minorities, a pledge that their
unwillingness to agitate sectional, ethnic, and religious issues
largely redeemed.[43] The "respectables" wanted to overthrow the
politicians, not to harass the subgroups the *Herald* sought to terrify.

This class basis of the reform movement appeared in its nominations. Eight of the thirteen members of the caucus lived in middle-class areas, as did twenty-one of the thirty of the Vigilance executive committee whose addresses could be found. Yet the majority of all classes supported the People's party, which clearly represented a diverse coalition. Their ticket in 1856 was balanced politically, including Democrats, Republicans, and Americans, but not ethnically. The "natives" made up the bulk of aspirants, though the Irish had several representatives and the Jews, one. Vocational balance was much more important; and only those bona fide members of the producing, useful, nontransient, respectable elements made the slate. For example, in the Tammany first ward stronghold, the uplifters ran a lumber dealer, a warehouse keeper, a lawyer, a stevedore, a drayman, and a ship master.[44] Yet the middle class predominated by three to one, though workingmen made up about 61 per cent of the population.

Professional politicians comprised the one unwelcome bloc. In fact, the People's party made it a test of acceptability that no one be considered for office who seemed to want it. This was a sure sign of a pro; and, moreover, "true merit is modest, and never impudently thrusts itself forward." [45] The uplifters desired capable and honest servants; and to the politicians' euphemism of "principles not men," the reformers answered with one of their own: "Men not parties."

Certain pre-election promises loomed just as important as this proscription. Reformers demanded legislative support for an amnesty act for the Vigilantes and approval of the results that had grown out of the upheaval. Issues like the Pacific Railroad were significant also, but how one stood on the "Revolution of 1856" remained the crucial question in the campaign. A pledge of allegiance was an absolute necessity; and the Republican, Know Nothing and People's parties all made it.

So did the great majority on election day, as the People's party easily outdistanced both Know Nothings and Democrats for local offices, the only ones the reformers contested. The Republicans also prevailed for state offices, but by a margin of only about five to four. Since the People's party beat the Democrats two to one in a city that was half foreign and the Americans pulled 6 per cent of the vote, an ethnocultural explanation of reform rests on shaky ground.[46]

Moreover, the farther one went from downtown, the larger the popular victory became. The Broderickites carried only district one, a slightly enlarged version of their old first ward bailiwick. Crowded next to the waterfront and against Telegraph Hill, this section was more proverty-ridden, criminal, vice-filled, rough, lower-class, and Tammany than any other. The "people" did not war on the lower class, but the other things had long been their favorite targets. The rebellious citizenry carried a large part of the middle as well as the fringe and thus surrounded the last bastion of the Tammany status quo. Until this time the electoral maps had been rather confused, the center and periphery pattern only hinted at, with the Whig-Know Nothings entrenched outside the city, and the Democrats downtown. Yet the Democratic eighth at the mission and the volatility of the rest of the metropolis had always complicated the situation.

"This peaceable, joyous termination of the moral revolution through which we have passed is a sublime spectacle," beamed the *Bulletin* of the Vigilance Committee.[47] However, the electoral triumph of 1856, not the lynchings, constituted the main contribution of the Vigilante episode, a clearly political rather than moral victory. At the end of 1856, moral regeneration lay far ahead. The houses of prostitution and gambling still received patrons. Crime had not declined, as the reform paper itself shows, though a new police judge at least handed out stiffer sentences. The streets were not fixed; the gas company clung to its extortionist rates; the plank roads monopoly endured; and tax dodgers still refused to "come forward." In addition, the teachers remained unpaid; the police, undermanned; the firemen, without hose; the poor and unemployed, without jobs; and incendiarism and crimping, unsolved. More men resorted to the notorious bankruptcy laws in 1856 than in 1855, although their assets and liabilities were much less than those of their predecessors. Moreover, Broderick, symbol of villainy, retained enough power to elevate himself to the Senate within months of the Vigilante exit. Finally, many of the achievements that the Vigilantes took—or received—credit for, like the Consolidation Act, were none of their doing. Much of it had come through the normal, imperfect, evolutionary processes of democracy.

In short, no regeneration or purification occurred.[48] San Francisco in 1857 did not differ markedly from what it had been in 1855, except politically, and even that was only a partial victory. Yet this did represent a real break from past practice where politicians alternated among themselves in office. Now at least, officials "identified" with the interests of the community. Whether they would govern in accordance with them remained to be seen.

Although the victory at the polls was the reformers' most important contribution, they spent more of their time justifying their extralegal activities. And for this task, a revolutionary ideology supplemented that of reform. Throughout the period, two distinct interpretations of the city's history coexisted, one individual and the other social. Both admitted the bad state of affairs but disagreed on the causes.

James King and the more extreme reform-revolutionaries tended to blame certain individuals or groups. The politicians became the special target for this attack, and the tyranny thesis, its most important component. "The people have been slaves for six years, and if they do not now secure freedom from the most shameful oppression, they deserve to be slaves," stormed "An Observer" in the *Bulletin*. "The necessity of revolution is self-evident." All peaceful means had failed. "It is not the one act of assassinating Mr. King which has produced the Vigilance Committee," the *Chronicle* wrote after its change of heart. "It is the series of high-handed villainies which have existed here for years, growing worse all the time, until they could be borne no longer."[49]

Yet alongside this explanation of San Francisco's history was a broader one which explained community sins as social rather than individual. "Men whose acts are recorded are but representatives of the times and of the society in which they live," wrote "Cassius" to the *Bulletin* in regard to James Casey.[50] As the *Chronicle* put it, before the advent of James King's sensationalism hardened the tyranny thesis,

> A new country peopled from all sections of the United States, and from all the nations of the world, thrown together . . . by accident, strangers to each other, consequently without any general sympathy of feeling, any harmonious tone; beyond the restraints of their former society; and above all, every man in fierce pursuit of gold, or office; these and a thousand other considerations come into the account in settling the particular responsibility of the evils so prevalent.[51]

"An evil tree cannot bring forth good fruit—a poisoned fountain cannot pour forth pure water," the same paper contended earlier in the same year. "The moral tone of society may be changed, improved, elevated, purified. . . . But this is a work of time. It is a work in which all should join. It is a work in which each man should begin with himself." [52]

The meager results of the rebellion demonstrated the correctness of the *Chronicle's* evolutionary argument, and the political history of the city revealed the unwillingness of individuals to "begin with themselves." The amount of evidence regarding the normal political apathy of subsequently rebellious citizens is literally staggering, much of it coming from the revolutionaries themselves. The people had allowed King to be shot down on Montgomery Street despite their foreknowledge that an encounter was probable. In fact, a crowd gathered to watch it. On the day of the editor's death, even a supporter of extreme action against the crooks admitted that "we, fellow citizens, . . . think we have sufficiently discharged our duty to the city and State, if we can escape being victimized by these precious scoundrels." [53]

"It had been an undeniable and lamentable characteristic of the elections which have heretofore taken place in this city, that the men most active in endeavors to control them were the worst and most unscrupulous members of the community," conceded the *Bulletin* itself. "Those most interested in obtaining a good government, and who by their numbers are perfectly capable of obtaining that consummation in the constitutional manner, abstained from taking any part in the contest and allowed it to go by default." The mouthpiece of the revolution admitted that "it will not, however, be denied that we have been even more culpable here [regarding nonvoting] than elsewhere [in America]. We have not done our duty at primary or regular elections. We have permitted fraud and corruption to influence nominations and elect candidates," continued the *Bulletin*, "and we have in consequence been forced into a revolution, which while it has proved in its bloodless [!], triumphant course our capacity for self government, inflicts on us a stern rebuke that it should in such a community ever have become necessary." [54]

After listing various acts of chicanery, the *Alta* went on to agree with its contemporary: "The people, meanwhile, stood and looked on carelessly; sometimes a little amazed at the corruption which was exposed, but never doing anything to prevent its occurrence." "One cause of the great evils we have been laboring under," chimed in Vox Populi, "and in my opinion the chief cause—has been the apparent apathy evinced by our businessmen, and the industrious classes generally, in regard to the subject of elections. A reform is now demanded by the people," he continued, "but the people must first reform themselves." Rascally officials were the problem, noted the *Pacific* in 1852. "And we have to blame ourselves for their being where they are." [55]

Other men put the matter even more sharply. "Governing Patriotism, although something more than a mere name, like the Chinese spirit Gods, is sleeping, as a rule, and wakens only on great occasions, and at remote intervals," contended a correspondent. The men who organized the People's Reform party "realized that civic patriotism could be depended upon only for emergencies and could not be relied on to secure that constant watchfulness which is as much the price of municipal official integrity as eternal vigi-

lance is said to be that of liberty," Vigilance executive C. J. Dempster wrote in retrospect. That judgment admitted that the uprising
was a confession of the bankruptcy of community rather than an
expression of it.[56]

Now free and unfettered in the wake of the Vigilantes' retirement, the *Chronicle* penned the most accurate indictment of the
"good citizens." The politicians

> would be perfectly helpless, and their endeavors futile, were it
> not for that most impracticable of all classes in every com-
> munity—the well disposed, well meaning citizens, "who seldom
> meddle in politics." These good people, who, in the absorbing
> occupations of chasing the dollars by day, and retiring into
> dressing gowns and slippers at the end of the chase, think of
> nothing but their personal comforts and the prescribed formalities
> of a rigid faith, have no affinities with the practical workings of
> the political organization on which social good and individual
> repose depend. Such men let everything political alone until it
> becomes an aggregation of dangerous material, that threatens a
> combustion destructive to their favorite dollar occupations and
> social exclusiveness; they then rush out *en masse*, and, with
> vehement zeal, hurl indignation upon politicians, resolve upon
> a reform, and rush directly into the arms of the sympathetic
> crowd who have long been waiting to receive their embrace.[57]

"It is an attempt by a short spasmodic effort, to repair the damages
that have accrued by long neglect of political duties," the *Chronicle* wrote on a later occasion.

> The demoralization of public affairs consequent upon this neglect
> is taken into view and a wholesale slaughter of those who have
> taken advantage of such neglect is decreed, and up goes the
> usual ensign of reform, and in the end down comes the same
> flag, tattered and besoiled by the same old politicians who, true
> to their experience, knew that the reformers would abandon
> their bantling and give them the usual chances to work their
> depredations upon the public welfare.
>
> Thus these spasmodic revolutionists are the contrivers of their
> own revolutions. They perpetuate a state of public policy that

renders a new reform party necessary at the return of every
election period. They care not to preserve the element of reform,
by each laboring in his own party to keep the average of moral
sentiment up to the requirements of good government.[58]

A better summary of the weakness and crisis-mindedness of reform movements before 1856 could hardly be found. In 1856 it was
popular to plead hopelessly with opponents "to point out a way of
redress without resorting to the revolutionary measures," but even
the most obvious of these had been systematically ignored.[59] Anxious merchants and professionals never rushed forward eager to exchange their duties for the patrolman's low-paid privilege of arresting San Francisco's roaring and well-armed drunks or toughs. No
indignation meeting drew 10,000 to secure back pay for police or
teachers nor to protest about the many men who had fallen through
the streets and drowned; and no property owners were hanged for
this murderous neglect. The reformers, until 1856, had not seriously
tried to clean up one of the old parties or to found a new one. Nor
had the Vigilance Committee been established to protect the ballot box even though such preventive action could easily have
headed off any "need" for lynchings. And it is clear that terror did
not cause this indifference, as the words of the reformers themselves prove. The regenerators and broad masses of people were
quite naïve to think that evil and inefficient men would not take
in hand the work that good and capable ones neglected. They were
just as foolish to expect instant redress simply by requesting it.

Then, after a do-nothing policy of eight years, the independents
and good citizens piously turned to revolution with the lame justification that all legal means of protest had been used up. A higher
law covered the community now, they said; and to this statute the
"good citizens" appealed. Yet violence was not the last resort; it was
simply the most convenient and the easiest. Democracy had not
really failed; it had not been tried. The worst enemies of democracy in San Francisco were the people.

The Urban Context:
Social Life Outdoors and In

Everyone recognized that economic and political San Francisco was altogether too full of hard work, strife, and selfishness. Fortunately, a lively social life grew up to balance the intensity of the struggle for advancement. This dimension of the metropolis developed in a familiar way. In the beginning much was peculiar and even outlandish; much that was unique endured. In dozens of ways, however, the tumultuous, odd, Gold Rush town took on the appearance of its Eastern counterparts. In 1848–49 a typical description of the pastimes of the city dwelt on drinking, gambling, and carousing. In 1856 these diversions remained, but they had been surpassed. "Christmas was duly celebrated in San Francisco this year," mused the *Bulletin* happily in describing the change. "The time honored anniversary of family reunions, of feasting, fun and frolicking—the season of mince pies, egg nog, roast turkeys, and all the good things of life was kept up." [1]

Yet whether in the late forties or mid-fifties, most would have agreed that "in this fast town," as the *Era* put it, "there seems to be a . . . determination to enjoy life while it lasts." The city's pleasures were not uniformly decorous, but they were highly enjoyed nevertheless. A few, like the Reverend Timothy Dwight Hunt, might have qualified as puritans; but most would not have. [2]

Much of San Francisco's social life occurred publicly. The

metropolis was a "private city" in that personal rather than corporate decisions largely shaped its existence. Yet it was also a "public city" because to a striking extent its individual activities belonged to all.[3] Less isolated than in a modern city, men knew where their fellows lived and worked and what they looked, smelled, and sounded like. Urban variety, diversity, and complexity were available to everyone; and the city as a whole was easily grasped. All of this enriched the urban context and enhanced the city's understanding of itself. Partly economic and partly social, this public life concentrated mostly upon the streets.[4] As yet largely unspecialized, these served as media of urban culture rather than merely as traffic arteries, a function that arose out of several circumstances.

San Francisco became increasingly specialized and its activities segregated into particular districts. But this process was far from complete; and various phases of urban life spilled over onto each other. A fascinating, inefficient indistinctness multiplied contacts between persons and between people and things. Different occupations, nationalities, classes, religious groups, and races often lived close enough for frequent meetings; and even when proximity did not exist, they probably had to travel through each other's neighborhoods to get to their own. Moreover, buildings did not always fit their functions; and such isolating facilities as parade grounds, parks, clubs, and playgrounds were absent or scarce.

Therefore, the thoroughfares served as a meeting place for an early version of a "street corner society" and as a parade ground, promenade, amphitheater, zoo, surrogate recreation space, and antechamber for a dozen brothels. In a stroll past the Plaza in 1851, one could take in baseball as well as the furious economic chase. In the streets boys flew kites, fished through the holes in the planks over the water, tied tin cans to rats' tails, shot off fire crackers on the Fourth, or just off the avenues, sailed at high tide over the mud flat destined to become the new customs house. Nor was it unusual to encounter an engine trial between two fire companies or, occasionally, a balloon ascent or a grizzly bear being

led somewhere or other. The rougher element met in front of the
livery stables to talk of fire engines and boxing; the young Christian men gathered about the steps of the churches to see and be
seen by their female coreligionists; and little knots of men congregated outside the quarters of Sarah Livingston, Belle Cora, and
Jane Brooks, where "the inmates of several of the houses of ill
fame . . . make no concealment of their charms." Particularly
on Montgomery "men of all characters and grades gather to con-
verse the general topics of the day," observed the *Era* in 1855.
"There is a feeling of fraternity among those who congregate on
this street, which is astonishing to behold. Loungers and idlers are
as sure to meet on this street as the sun to give light." [5]

Inadequate business and domestic buildings further intensified
the use of the thoroughfares by forcing the human and material
contents of these structures onto the streets. During the day,
shovels, barrels of salt pork, building materials, clothing, and
harassed pedestrians cluttered sidewalk and street below Montgomery; and at night the gaming halls, theaters, and other establishments filled the avenues with lights, music, and mirth. Since
the stores and ware rooms overlapped the streets, a trip down the
avenues also meant a partial jaunt through rather than in front
of the shops. "Under the awnings extended over the side walks of
Commercial street are bristling canopies of every species of wearing apparel, suspended from poles," the *Era* noted in 1855. On
"some parts of Clay, Battery and Front streets . . . the goods are
piled so closely on the sidewalks, that the passers by are obliged
to fall into a single file—à la post office on mail days." [6]

Since the avenues were laid out for a town rather than a
metropolis, the instant city immediately outgrew them. In 1856
much of the economy and the broad culture of a seaport city of
around 50,000 still flowed through the streets of a hamlet. As a
foreign traveler observed in 1853, "You can hardly make your way
through for the throng of carts, carriages, horsemen, and pedestrians." [7]

Small dwellings probably conspired to effect the same end. "The low, narrow dwellings in which people live here appeared to me at first very oppressive and uncomfortable," wrote Ida Pfeiffer. "The largest apartments would scarcely allow of twelve or fifteen persons sitting down to table; and of the smaller ones I need not speak—they really seemed destined for Liliputians." Oddly enough, the public streets often provided more seclusion. Lovers of all ages sought Meiggs Wharf, which was to San Francisco what "'Union Park,' 'Washington Square' and the 'Battery' are to New York," the *Fireman's Journal* wrote in 1855, "combining as it does with all its surrounding beauties a sufficiency of privacy, romance and reality." On a Sunday "hundreds of [other] persons, mostly ladies and children," went past Meiggs Wharf and thence along the beach to Point San José. To the east "crowds of people" clambered up Telegraph Hill for a view "beautiful in the extreme, . . . a glance at the [Allied Crimean Fleet] lying off the North Beach," or one of the "good, generous, refreshing milk punches to be had in the room beneath the lookout" of the telegraph station.[8]

Customs guaranteed that this pedestrian throng would behold and hear a fantastic amount of urban ceremony and ritual besides the normal sights and sounds of traffic. People spilled out for almost any reason, quite often accompanied by a brass band. American, Californian, and a dozen or so ethnic holidays demanded a parade. Fire companies marching to the wharves to meet their counterparts from the interior, the green and gold clad Marion Rifles drilling, strikers advertising their cause, Sunday school picnickers tramping to the steamboat, school children with bouquets and garlands and the Turnverein parading on May Day, and the Sons of Temperance all beat their way through the streets. It even required a horse race to deliver the mails. "It is a custom," the *Era* wrote in 1855, to stop the steamers off North Beach to allow the expressmen to secure their bags. "When they obtain them . . . every nerve is strained. When the boat strikes the wharf, out they jump and spring on their horses, standing ready saddled and bridled, and away they dash. . . . They clatter over the planks at a fearful rate." The slightest urban occurrence often required an enormous amount of celebration and walking. The initiation of the new "truck" of the Lafayette Hook and Ladder Company in 1855 involved pulling the machinery through "the principal streets . . . attended by a fine band of music" and representatives of every company. "After passing the several engine houses," they went to the Polka Saloon and thence some two miles away at the mission to be entertained by the Young American Engine Company. After a "splendid dinner" and accompanying merriment, they walked back to town to attend the Fire Department Benefit at the Metropolitan Theater.[9]

Even when crowding did not force them onto the streets, women appeared there for fashionable display, lovers for serenading, and so forth. Stockton was the most chic promenade; and "on a beautiful afternoon hundreds of ladies in their carriages and afoot, may be seen shopping" on Montgomery.[10] The women's gaudy and colorful clothing further enhanced the visual image.

The instant city quality of the place reinforced the lively street life. A chronic shortage of families forced men into a greater dependence upon commercial, public institutions for food, lodgings, recreation, sex, and baths. Not centralized in the home, these necessitated more walking. In the early years, an acute housing shortage and a large transient population had the same effect.

Therefore, a crowd could be put together with ease. Yet the spontaneous, curious, and emotional nature of the people explains this phenomenon, too. A Vigilante hanging drew thousands, but the novelty of the scene counted more than the morbidity. In 1855, eight to twelve thousand people (perhaps a fifth of the city) thronged the streets to watch Signor and Signora Caroni, the parents of nine children, walk a tightrope 175 feet to the top of the International Hotel, a rise of sixty feet. When Kennovan, the pedestrian, finished his walking feat, over a thousand admirers waited to congratulate him. Even the weather drew spectators. "Yesterday . . . was a very exciting time in our city," wrote Stephen Woodin to his wife. "Night before last we had what the sailors call a Norther. . . . Thousands of people were crowded upon the wharves to witness the rage of the Elements." [11] The Isthmian steamers invariably attracted great numbers, and even such a common early entertainment as a bit of ratting collected considerable congregations to watch the city's famed rodent-hunting dogs and their equally notorious quarry.

The hills themselves added to the sense of urbanism, of living amongst a much larger number of humans, because they continually forced people to view more of the metropolis more often. The high ground lengthened each street vista, freeing the eye from the parochial limits of the immediate area and drawing it from the top of the hills to the crowded shipping. Every morning men could see the "volume of black smoke constantly" arising "from the making up of the fires for the day" in the "various mills in the Valley"; each night afforded the magnificent view of the flickering gaslights of a great city; and special occasions produced bonfires "on every prominent hill" to celebrate some political victory.[12] Each spectacle reminded San Franciscans of their larger urban world and confronted them once again with the remarkable achievement of their instant city.

The relatively low level of technology heightened the usefulness of the streets. Lack of telephones and modern business forms necessitated face to face contact in the economic world; and in social terms, this dictated more trips up and down the avenues by businessmen and messengers. The lack of refrigeration meant the same thing for wives and maids. Since mass transit was crude and private vehicles, few (even these were often open and usually slow), the journeys generally took place on foot, in closer contact with and less isolated from the variety of the urban world. This conveyed a more vivid sense of what the travelers were about. "During the whole evening [Christmas Eve]," wrote the *Bulletin* in 1856, "men and women were to be seen toiling through the streets loaded down with brown paper parcels, and big turkeys flung over their shoulders, with laurel branches and cedar, branches of parsley and sage, nice fresh eggs, and in fact everything that could furnish forth the holiday table." On New Year's Day "everyone calls upon every one, so the streets present a scene of incessant salutation," wrote an Englishman in 1852.[13]

These bustling, narrow streets added to the acoustical dimension of the city by filling the air with sounds; and the small overall size of the place made these noises more accessible. The din of traffic —swearing teamsters, creaking harness, rumbling planks—supplemented the omnipresent bands; and a thousand more sounds, sacred and secular, complemented these. As early as April 1849, residents noted church bells "almost nightly in use"; and throughout the years these continued to call men to worship. During the day one heard the clank of machinery or the sharp crack of pistols discharged in the many galleries; and in the evenings there were often serenades for famous actresses, returned fire company foremen, or someone's "inamorata" or a "lively chorus of some Bacchanalian party, after a night spent in . . . celebration." In the early morning, sometimes too early, water and milk wagons rumbled over the planks, and street merchants awakened the sleeping city with their cries. As the sun burned off the fog, these sounds multiplied. A fruit peddler sold his wares "with the assistance of a penny trumpet and a mammoth rattle," while a scissors grinder used a bugle. And at Christmastime, candy vendors "stationed at every street corner" bellowed out their sweets so loudly that they drowned out pedestrian conversation around them. A combination of wit and salesmanship floated out of the Jewish auction houses on Commercial, "where everything goes for a song," in contrast to "Montgomery street, where every thing dances to another tune."

An observer noted, "I went home as much amused as if I had been at a good theater." In short, whether one sauntered through the Plaza in the evening "listening to the cheerful strains of Winn's colored band on the balcony of the Union" ice cream saloon, or on a still summer night sat listening to "the hum of [beach-bound lovers'] buggy wheels and the sound of horses hoofs on the plank roads [which] could be heard for miles," or mingled at daybreak among the French market gardeners lounging around the all-night coffee stands on Commercial Street "chatting about their own affairs, or singing French songs that smack strongly of republicanism and detestation of tyrants in general, and of Louis Napoleon in particular," one was usually in the presence of diverse, interesting, entertaining city sounds.[14]

All these things added up to a "public city," an extraordinary, fascinating one, in many ways the antithesis of its twentieth-century counterparts. Oddly enough, most of its charm arose from its defects—of housing, planning, lack of women, architecture, site, technology. Yet how much this variety, diversity, and complexity reformed the habits of men—made them better able to exercise choice, more creative, more at home with conflict, more human, better able to handle alienation and so on—is debatable. In the long run, urban diversity may have promoted these virtues; but in the short run, people were more apt to try to suppress it than understand it, and failing that would flee to the suburbs. Critics accused teamsters of cruelty to their animals, damned street corner types for impertinence, attacked Turnvereins for violating the Sabbath, blasted hardware dealers for blocking the sidewalks, criticized vendors for the decibel rate, scored Sabbath music for disturbing services, and even questioned the men waiting before the church about their right to view the female exodus. Without a doubt, complexity did not promote any greater spirit of community. Yet even if it did not make San Franciscans love jury duty any more, the variety of the place did make them love their town. "A great city is San Francisco," glowed the *Era* in 1855. "People who have never been here don't know how much they are losing." [15] The Golden Gate community clearly had not yet emerged, but the legend of San Francisco already haunted the streets.

The compact, congested nature of the place allowed people to use the nearby country as a park. Very few areas of this metropolis of 50,000 were more than a few blocks from open space, a frequently exploited advantage which allowed residents to "exchange the noise of the city for . . . quietude and green glades" and loveliness. Despite their money-grubbing, San Franciscans repeatedly demonstrated a very strong aesthetic appreciation, especially of the city site and its surroundings. "On a clear day the beauty of the Bay of San Francisco, and of the hills and mountains which encompass it, are beyond my powers of description," wrote James Ward.[16]

Many others "improved upon the occasion" by picnicking, strawberrying, horseback riding, or hiking; and as early as 1849, residents had discovered the Seal Rocks. By 1855 something of a precursor of the forty-nine mile drive—a marked tourist route in modern San Francisco—already existed: out the road to the Presidio, then on to Seal Rocks, and south down the misty, lovely, windy ocean beach to Lake Merced. There the Lake House or Ocean House warmed and revived the traveler for his return trip with a meal, boating, swinging, bowling, or quoits. Closer by, the Sans Souci House between the mission and the Presidio offered nearly the same attractions.[17]

Transportation technology made these country pleasures more accessible. Trips to the Contra Costa were common; and on one occasion in 1854, the ferry proprietors offered two boats to accommodate "the public who [desire] to attend the camp meeting and the bull fight in Alameda," which to the *Alta* represented a "laudable disposition to please all parties."[18] Pleasure excursions plied the bay and even ventured as far as the Farallones, Sacramento, the mines, and spas like the sulphur springs at Napa.[19]

Sunday school excursions were especially festive, beginning with the march to the steamer. Once on board, "a polka was demanded, and soon fifty couples were tripping the light fantastic toe," observed a letter to the *Bulletin*. "What a change . . . in public opinion within the last ten or fifteen years. . . . Now, children and church members are permitted to pass through life enjoying it." The outing might terminate at Oakland, where oak groves provided a shelter for picnic tables, or the more hilly and open Martínez, with its striking vista of the Straits of Carquínez and plentiful play space. On departure, the citizens of Martínez on the wharf "hurraed and Young America sent back an answering shout that fairly shook the vessel." [20]

Some San Franciscans admired the country enough to ruralize the city itself. Citizens began planting greenery and demanded even more. The Plaza was beautified, but it was much too small to qualify as a park. Nor did the other public squares, which ordinarily served as junk and refuse areas. Therefore, as early as 1855 requests for a bona fide park appeared in the *Chronicle,* probably influenced by the example of Central Park, just then under consideration.[21]

Here again the aesthetic dimension appeared. Since the charcoal burners and the street graders had largely eliminated the trees and shrubbery, some compensation was demanded. "Every lover of the beautiful—and nature has nothing more beautiful than a fine Park —must have felt the absence of rural scenery . . . in and about San Francisco," argued the *Chronicle.* In addition, the woodland would provide lungs for the city; and like the suburb, club, and home, the park would be a refuge from urbanism. It offered "the citizen weary of six days of dust and dirty walls, the groves and scenery which are ever so grateful to all." Finally, the project would be a source of moral strength and civic defense to "keep away the poor and the young from the temptations scattered all around them, to do evil," the *Chronicle* stated. "A grand Park within the reach of every citizen would do more in preventing dissipation and vice than half the sermons preached, half the moral lectures and teachings given to children and to men." [22]

Sports and games, whether city or country, remained popular throughout the period.[23] Horse racing appeared before the Gold Rush; and here again the Mission Dolores, the principal suburban recreation resort in the early years, supplied the facilities. In 1856 a Jockey Club grew up to supervise racing, improve breeds, and keep records of registry; and by 1857 the city boasted two tracks. Steamboat racing also prospered. In the *New World-Confidence* race of 1851, "the passengers were excited to a high pitch, cheering lustily on each side." After 1854 such events declined, though other aquatic contests continued. So did a number of remarkable pedestrian and long-distance competitions. In 1856 James Kennovan attempted to pull a sulky six miles in fifty-eight minutes but lost to a heavy track. He had his triumphs, however, including an endurance walk of 106 consecutive hours. Various gyms accommodated those who preferred indoor exercise.[24]

Other favorites were not so gentle. During the cholera epidemic of 1850, "the road was completely thronged with persons . . . wending their way" to a boxing match. Eventually two thousand people paid five dollars apiece to watch Messrs. McGee and Kelly contend for a $500 purse, the nearer spectators sitting on the grass and those in the rear, on horseback. Despite inveterate press hostility, the fight game continued and even moved into the American Theater, where in April 1856, Yankee Sullivan fought Steve Simmons before a delighted packed house of "all classes of people, from the regular 'b'hoy' up to the most prominent citizens." Yet boxing was tame compared to the frequent bull and bear fights or the 1855 Adelphi spectacle between "a wild cat and a white bull terrier." [25]

As urban facilities and skills increased, many entertainments became professional and took place indoors. Thanksgiving, Christmas, and the various ethnic holidays usually called for some form of banquet. So did departures for the "States," a very entrenched Bay City custom which required an all-night spree. The traveler "generally wakes up to a consciousness of his identity somewhere in the vicinity of Acapulco," observed the *Herald*. He "devotes the remainder of the journey to getting sober." [26]

Dancing prospered even before the Gold Rush. The Mission Dolores hosted the Mexican fandangoes, but Yerba Buena had its own balls. The first general gathering after the conquest was at Leidesdorff's residence in September 1846, and the revelers did not stop till "the rising sun rendered the candlelight useless." By 1853 the custom so throve that the *Alta* wrote, "San Francisco is becoming a second Paris, in the fondness of its gay floating population for dashing, dressy public balls." [27] Various low dance halls furnished the same amusement for the working class; and in addition, military and fire companies, benevolent societies, groups of boardinghouse ladies, Young America, and many others held their own soirées.

Newly opened residences, hotels, businesses, firehouses, and even warehouses called for an urban housewarming; and almost anything prompted social visiting, especially on New Year's, when the ladies held open house for their gentlemen friends. This "old New York custom" survived even the disorganizing impact of the early Gold Rush. "For want of better vehicles, and for the sake of oddity, the gentlemen were drawn about by one horse in *hand carts!* thus paying their addresses to the few families who were in readiness to receive them," as Timothy D. Hunt described the first such occasion. "Each cart was *piled* full." However, social calling went on continuously, particularly by bachelors, who customarily spent considerable time in the salons of married women. Yet visiting between families also constituted an important, and sometimes taxing, "recreation." [28]

Ordinary home activities included parlor games, reading aloud, lunches, tea parties, gossiping, and music. Any melodically inclined visitor had to perform, and the hostess often provided some entertainment herself. Music remained one of the most popular and omnipresent pleasures in the city; and current favorites temporarily threatened to sweep everything else before them. "Have you ever heard 'The Old Folks at Home' . . . a negro song, sung and I believe composed by the Christy Minstrels?" McCrackan queried his sister. "It is a very sweet thing, but it is sung and whistled about our streets so much, it has become actually sickening." [29]

Serenading supplemented street whistling. The military or fire companies or the Turnverein always held forth beneath the window of someone upon their return from an outing. Editors got special attention because they kept late hours and could notice the merriment in print. In 1851 a group of Italian sailors gave

such an excellent impromptu concert in front of the customs house
that residents successfully insisted that they sing in different parts
of town.[30]

Other kinds of street music abounded. From the beginning,
strolling orchestras and organ-grinders offered their wares, sometimes stimulating considerable activity inside. "Our nightly visitor,
a man with a hand organ . . . made his appearance under our
window," McCrackan wrote.[31]

A thin line divided entertainment from advertising, particularly
in regard to music. The gaming halls employed it; and when prize
fights occurred nearby, competing steamers had rival bands wooing patrons. A musical procession preceded bullfights; and in
1850, "each night a company of boys parade/d/ the streets with an
illuminated advertisement of Rowe's Circus, accompanied by fife,
bass and tenor drum, rousing early sleepers from their dreams."
Even the "bootblacks who have squatted on the steps in front
of the California Exchange, daily pour forth their melodious strains
to a crowd of admiring listeners." [32]

Besides this "Concert for the Million," there were Cafés Chan-
tants that Friedrich Gerstacker described as "common drinking
rooms, especially kept by Frenchmen" which "exhibited in the
back part a sort of stage and piano." Other places featured louder
and much less agreeable sounds. In 1853 James Lamson, proprietor
of the Thistle Inn on Broadway, "listened hour after hour to the
scraping of a fiddle of twenty men, each succeeding one striving
to outdo the last in noise; and to the harsh dissonance of a squawk-
ing accordian, to which a dozen drunken voices chimed in, while
stamping feet kept time to the music." [33]

Classical and professional music complemented the democratic
variety that emanated from the Thistle Inn. In 1853 the German
population organized the Germania Society, which provided concerts for the rest of the period. Despite its criticism that the offerings were too heavy, the *Chronicle* admitted that "as usual the
large Hall [was] crowded in every part." A flourishing Philhar-
monic Society rounded out the amateur offerings and visiting pro-

fessionals supplemented both. Stephen C. Massett gave the first such musical concert; he was followed by numerous other artists.[34]

A series of professional female vocalists presented the best music. Signora Elisa Biscaccianti of Boston spent nearly all of 1855 in California; and for a time, she and Catherine Hayes of Ireland both resided in the city. That coincidence led to the usual rivalry, but raw and lawless San Francisco witnessed nothing comparable to the 1849 Astor Place riots of civilized New York. P. T. Barnum brought Hayes to town; others—Anna Thillon, Anna Bishop—came and received a warm welcome. Even opera did well for a time.[35]

The most popular entertainers of any kind were far less pretentious. Appearing as early as December 1848, minstrelsy prospered marvelously. The New Orleans Serenaders, the Backus Minstrels, and the Christy Minstrels succeeded each other in triumph; and by 1856 the *Alta* could claim that "the San Francisco Minstrels have accomplished what never has been equalled in San Francisco by any caterers of public amusements. For about four months they have performed almost nightly to crowded houses, and still they are as eagerly sought." [36]

The legitimate theater established a more modest record. Stevenson's Regiment put on the premier theatricals before the Gold Rush. In mid-January 1850, Atwater's Eagle Theater Company of Sacramento presented the first professional efforts at Washington Hall. Hailed as a milestone in the city's history, the plays closed in less than a week. The early productions were distinguished more than anything else by poor quality and bad acting; but eventually this situation improved. Several members of the Booth family, Julia Deane Hayne, James Stark, the Barney Williams, Lola Montez, Laura Keene, the Bateman children, and James E. Murdoch presented Shakespeare, local hits, stock Irishmen and Yankees, and panorama, often at considerable profit to themselves. Several imposing theaters were built to accommodate them—the Jenny Lind, the American, the American II, Maguire's Opera House, and the Metropolitan. These and other playhouses put on an impressive number of "pieces"—1,000 altogether (including 900 plays)—between 1850 and 1859.[37]

Yet the theater suffered numerous frustrations. The great names usually performed, collected, and left. After a time the public became distrustful of the press's puffing and angry about highly ballyhooed mediocrity. Lack of talent compounded this difficulty. Too little talent exacted too much money, and the consequent high admissions reduced the number of patrons. In addition, it proved impossible to establish good stock companies; therefore, prime supporting casts remained scarce.[38] Bad management, repetition in performances, and professional rows caused still more headaches.

The drama survived anyway, but often just barely. The Jenny Lind was sold to the corporation because it did not pay as a playhouse. Moreover, the community did not produce any original plays of merit. The advent of a star provided an occasional boost; but in between and sometimes during these visits, patrons made frequent complaints of its failure. Poverty was not the problem. "The theatres in San Francisco are doing a miserable business," wrote the *Alta* in the last depression, although no less than five minstrel troupes played to packed houses. "To some observers the success of the latter species of entertainment has been construed unfavorably to the tastes of the community," the *Bulletin* noted. "To our view it is simply an evidence that the popular taste prefers an inferior kind of diversion well conducted, to that of a first class character indifferently performed." The success of "horse opera," to which "the democracy and Young America" thronged despite the depression, and the concurrent failure of "Italian opera" merely reinforced the point. Obviously this was an era of building for the higher forms of entertainment. The city remained a "theatrical suburb of New York, London, and sometimes Paris." [39]

Opponents of the theater begrudged even this limited success. They felt it encouraged pleasure seeking, frivolity, and bad morality generally. The defenders retorted that the drama was "among the proudest and mightiest works of civilized man" and actually encouraged morality. "It is worthy of remark that those points of the play, where some noble, patriotic or magnanimous sentiment is uttered, invariably call down the heartiest applause of the audience," said the *Herald*. Moreover, its champions claimed that the theater served as a surrogate for and guardian of the home. The stage often portrayed that institution and therefore tended to strengthen its influence. Most importantly, especially to the homeless, the drama, like music, had the effect of "dissipating and annihilating . . . gross and demoralizing . . . places of amusement, and substituting those of society in its highest state of refinement," of replacing a corrupt with a pure or at least less corrupt environment.[40]

The dissenting minority of opponents, even though vocal, did not seriously hamper the drama. They did secure a law banning Sunday night theatricals; but for the most part, their efforts failed. Yet the opposition played an important role, since the theater aspired not only to freedom to perform but also to the dignity of a value-imparting institution. Therefore, the community had every right to question its credentials, especially in an age when prostitution, drinking, and riotous disorder frequently accompanied its art.[41] Moreover, the case of the drama was by no means unique. Citizens argued just as forcibly the roles of the church, home, public schools, and press and also forced each to develop, and to an extent live up to, its own peculiar ideology of justification, explaining its usefulness to the community.

Probably the most striking feature of San Francisco's early social life—particularly its manners and morals—was its peculiarity. "I am in an odd humor but in San Francisco one has an undoubted right to be," wrote a resident in 1849; "it is an odd place: unlike any other place in creation and so it should be; for it is not created in the ordinary way, but hatched like chickens by artificial heat." People marveled at the difference, but they largely approved. The city was novel, stimulating, fun, challenging, and above all, freer. "You cannot know the perfect freedom and independence that characterizes all our relations," wrote McCrackan in 1852. "Society if it exists at all is freed from the multitude of prejudices and embarrassments and exactions that control [sic] the Eastern cities." [42]

Personal dress strikingly revealed this liberty in the early years. The city may have had a commercial life equal to that of large Eastern ports, but one could not tell from the clothes. "But few persons wore coats"; and the general costume, the miners' garb, was the most popular style, which "consisted of a heavy woolen shirt, trousers held up by a sash or belt around the waist, and the legs inserted in a pair of high legged boots. A slouch hat covered the head." Beards frequently complemented this attire, and anyone wearing a silk hat was likely to be hooted and ridiculed.[43]

Fewer class distinctions and more egalitarian habits of association characterized the scene, especially in the dance halls and gaming houses, where merchants, doctors, lawyers, and just about everyone else spent quite a bit of time. "The invitations were general in those days," reminisced one of the city's early barkeepers. "There was no distinction as regards persons, Jack was considered as good as his master." [44]

Vocational mixing accompanied social, a habit that endlessly fascinated observers. "A French nobleman . . . who lost [his] fortunes in the revolution of 1848 . . . drive[s] a water cart. His lady takes in washing [sic] a most lucrative employment here," an emigrant letter noted. "An Italian Count of distinguished mind and manners, cleans shoes on the Plaza; his hands beautifully white, his demeanor aristocratic." [45]

Sundays had a different quality, too. Churches held services less frequently than in the East, and little community discipline existed to enforce attendance. "Society at home demands much," McCrackan wrote to his sister; "here we are left to indulge our own peculiar views, dont attend church but half a day, believing I can spend the ballance [sic] more profitably amid the beauties of nature." [46] The custom of Sabbath-breaking was well entrenched before the Gold Rush, but it was reinforced by the arrival of many Europeans accustomed to enjoying the pleasures of a "continental Sunday."

Gambling afforded many of these pleasures, especially right after the Gold Rush, when few recreations existed. As an argonaut wrote home in 1850, "The great vices here are gambling and drinking and wearing dirty shirts." The allied trade of prostitution also flourished, and its practitioners seemed to enjoy extraordinary liberty. "We must confess," said the *Alta* in 1850, "our regret at the perfect freedom and unseemly manner in which the abandoned females . . . are permitted to display themselves in our public saloons and streets." [47] In this year some even had the temerity to attend a ladies' church fair, causing a sensation.

The scarcity of women raised the status of all females, prostitutes included. "It is astonishing to see the class of men gathered [at a soirée thrown by the "Countess"] . . . —executive, legislative, judicial, commercial, ministerial all of what are commonly called the upper class of society," wrote a resident. "There were very few men who had brought their families to the state and when these girls appeared in the streets they were treated with the greatest respect and gallantry the same as would be extended to the most respectable women by men in general." Other women also benefited. "You have no idea how few women we have here and if one makes her appearance in the street, all stop, stand and look," McCrackan informed his sister. "The latest fashion is to carry them in the arms (the streets were incredibly muddy). This we see every day." [48]

The divorce mill reputation of the metropolis revealed another freedom. Any California court would willingly grant a separation, "but no court among them all has been more liberal . . . than the District Court of San Francisco," reported the *Chronicle*. "Marriage among us seems to be regarded as a pleasant farce—a sort of 'laughable afterpiece' to courtship." Publicity may have been some deterrent; but most would have agreed that "the divorces which are granted here will exceed in a tenfold ratio the number in any other part of the Union of equal population." [49]

Freedom to take life was also fairly common, and weapons toting prevailed to such an extent that it gave the population the look of a civilian army constantly mobilized. Guns were not used as often as carried, but affrays and duels happened frequently enough. Indeed, the duello was a highly institutionalized argument that escalated from some minor point to a question of honor. Various insults passed; the challenge was sent; and seconds (often important instigators) moved in to arrange the choice of weapons, site of combat, and rules.

Heavy drinking, whether in business or pleasure, did not lessen the danger inherent in these customs. All in all, the amount of imbibing exceeded anything the inhabitants had been accustomed to. Supposedly, an urban environment with few restraints and more risk, excitement, and stress explained this predilection.

So did the scarcity of wives for drinking men to go home to. Most "enjoyed" a bachelor life of considerable discomfort and crudity. As the city settled down, however, single living improved markedly. Men shifted from tents to boardinghouses, but many lived in offices and stores. Bachelor eating habits changed, too, as restaurants and boardinghouses increased. "We all get our meals together at a restaurant," William T. Sherman described the gentlemen's "mess." "This is my usual way and it suits very well indeed—." [50] McCrackan noted how, despite the transiency of the Gold Rush and the anonymity of the city, one could escape from the dangers of an impersonal existence.

> I dine with my mess at 6 1/2 p.M. We number four regular attendants, generally one or two invited guests, and far more agreeable gentlemanly persons, it has seldom been my good fortune to meet. All charming old bachelors, between the ages of thirty five and forty, men of exquisite manners, and very decided intelligence, all have passed a few years in England, and on the continent of Europe, which has secured to them many of the refinements and elegances of life. Full of wit and humor which you may imagine kills two or three hours at one dinner table in the kindest manner possible. They usually adjourn to my room where an hour, or the evening, is passed with music, after which we will often walk two or three miles before parting.[51]

San Franciscans had no monopoly on hard work; but even so, it is very likely that they worked harder than Easterners. The Gold Rush was a romantic event full of color and "derring do"; yet the urban end of this episode involved a remarkable amount of grinding, ceaseless toil. "We get to bed no night till midnight," editor Jonas Winchester informed his wife. "For the last two weeks I have been up on publication nights till 2 and 3 o'clock." A month later he told her, "I write today, almost used up, for I have no cessation, sleeping in my room and only going out to eat." Surveyor Robert Lammot's 1851 schedule found him up at six, and from that time until eight he wrote and read the papers. Then he breakfasted and toiled until his 4:30 "lunch" hour. After his meal, he labored until dark; and from that time he worked at the Vigilante headquarters until nine, unless he was on patrol, in which case he was up until the next morning. Nor were businessmen excused. "Nine o'clock finds us at the office," wrote W. D. M. Howard's agent, "where I am occupied until four at which hour we dine; back to the office at five, write until ten, sometimes much later—then home head still filled with business." [52]

In the late '40's and early '50's, very few comforts mitigated the toil. Iron houses which were too hot in the day and too cool at night, board shanties through which the wind whistled, or the backs of rude stores did not make for much ease. Life under canvas was particularly bleak in the winter season. "It rained all night and blowed," argonaut David Cosad noted wearily in his diary. "Sherman Kent and myself had to hold our tent to keep it from blowing down in the bay and we got verry [sic] wet and cold for we held it about three hours . . . the next morning most of the tents [in his area] had blown down." And some men lived an even ruder existence in crates, in boxes, and under woodpiles. Dirt and sand abounded, circulated by the constant breeze. "There was dust on the counter, on the shelves, on the seats, on the decanters, and in them; on the tables, in the salt, on my beef steak and in my coffee," lamented William Ryan of a restaurant in

1848–49.[53] Flies swarmed through the inside of houses and teamed with the infamous, unstoppable San Francisco fleas to make life miserable. Rodents, as diverse as the people, also found the dirty city a paradise.

If daily life had more discomforts than "home," San Franciscans thought it had more excitement, as future Supreme Court Justice Stephen J. Field noted:

> There was something exhilarating and exciting in the atmosphere which made everybody cheerful and buoyant. As I walked along the streets, I met a great many persons I had known in New York, and they all seemed to be in the highest spirits. Everyone in greeting me, said "It is a glorious country," or "Isn't it a glorious country?" or "Did you ever see a more glorious country?" or something to that effect. In every case the word "glorious" was sure to come out. There was something infectious in the use of the word, or rather in the feeling, which made its use natural. I had not been out many hours that morning before I caught the infection; and though I had but a single dollar in my pocket and no business whatever, and did not know where I was to get the next meal, I found myself saying to everybody I met, "It is a glorious country!" [54]

This feeling stemmed in large part from the presence of seemingly unlimited opportunity. That was an exaggeration, but in the early years it was still a very credible one. It was hard for Easterners to understand, wrote McCrackan, "the startling chances that are thrown open to confront the industrious, energetic and determined mind." San Francisco was a vast rumor mill, and that, too, stimulated the excitement. "I am as much in the dark as when I left home," declared argonaut R. R. Taylor in frustration. "Every man has a different opinion and I have heard so many different stories since I arrived that my mind is a perfect chaos." The extraordinary velocity of life in this instant city helped sustain the intensity. "The incidents of a day, I might say hour, attending a life in San Francisco, are so varied and not infrequently startling in their import and character, as to prompt one to look upon the

present only as secure," McCrackan wrote to his family. "Change
followed change insomuch that we became accustomed to change.
A new surprise was a usual morning experience," noted Albert
Williams. "The person who in the dark stumbled into a mortar
bed, . . . exclaiming, 'I wish San Francisco were finished,' expressed a common desire." [55]

All of this led to a different concept of time from that which
Easterners had. So many things happened so fast that men felt
keenly aware of having their lives compressed in time. Therefore,
it did not seem at all absurd for them to talk of "old timers" even
as early as 1850, when the Society of California Pioneers began.
Anyone who had lived a few years in San Francisco qualified as
a "pioneer," for that period was equal to many times as much elsewhere.

And finally, in the early days many found "a prevalence generally, of a kind [of] good feeling—less of selfishness and over-
reaching in business transactions; less of jarring discord; far less
of clannish divisions of society, than in our cities and villages of
the old states." [56] The Hounds disturbance upset this camaraderie
somewhat; yet before and after that event, a considerable number of people believed that more friendly sentiment existed there
than anywhere else.

Though not totally peculiar, the Emporium differed markedly
from Eastern cities; and greater liberty constituted the main explanation of this divergence. The ensuing years witnessed the decline of this uniqueness. San Francisco did not become a carbon
copy of Eastern communities, but its drift was unmistakable. Step
by step, society's bonds crept in where the freedom had been;
and as they did, the peculiarity of the instant city declined.

Clothing styles reflected this very soon. "The fashions of San
Francisco are very materially improved from last year, principally
because the weather has been clear and fine, as well as the streets
having been planked," Robert Lammot wrote in early 1851. "Patent
leather boots and beaver hats are quite as common this winter as
were 'cow hide extensions' and felt tiles, last." Despite poor streets

and bad weather, a transition from extreme simplicity to pronounced ostentation for both men and women continued. "I was
told by a Mr. Southworth formerly a jobbing merchant in New
York who has travelled over the Continent to make purchases, that
our merchants here have the richest and most extravagant goods
he ever saw," McCrackan explained. Other forms of prodigality
blossomed too. "We might have established a sensible society,"
moaned the *Chronicle* editorially in 1856; "but instead of that, instead of a quiet style of home life, a simple style of dress, a reasonable style of living, of house, of furniture, of life before the public,
all the vanities of the rotten customs of the older cities have been
introduced and doubled." [57]

Egalitarianism waned as fashion waxed. The city's first history
and James King might contend that society was still democratic
in 1854 or 1856; but very early, habits of indiscriminate association drastically declined.[58] The *Annals* itself chronicled the rich
gambling in the rear of the Parker House as early as 1849, and
clubs and social circles furthered the sorting out. "Every care has
been taken that no improper person shall be admitted," promised
an 1851 advertisement for the Atheneum Club. The rise of fashionable churches further separated rich from poor. Men also went
back to their old pursuits if they had abandoned them; and new
members joined the ranks of the hierarchy, as profession reasserted
itself. In short, the Gold Rush had leveled men socially and pro-
fessionally only to elevate them again in about the same fashion.

By the middle of 1850, a year of depression, the gaming "industry" began to decline. In this year the city council passed a
law forbidding Sabbath gambling, and later in the period the
legislature added another hostile statute. However, the habit
survived both attempts, though in a much abbreviated form. So
with prostitution. Prostitutes did not openly receive the mighty of
the city, if they received them at all, and men no longer paid them
public deference. In fact, each time one rode out on the street, it
strengthened the movement to remove or drive them out of sight.[59]

The importance of the virtuous female rose in proportion to the prostitutes' decline. "Instead of a woman being regarded as a natural curiosity, of which every man would stop to look," wrote one resident, "they are now seen in almost as great a number as they would anywhere else, and their influence is felt in Society—." [60] Joseph G. Eastland exaggerated their numbers, but not their impact on Gold Rush life styles.

Sabbath breaking, dueling, drinking, and divorce also came under increasingly sharp attack, especially from the religious. Yet none of these pioneer habits suffered a striking decline. Sabbath breaking abated somewhat, but the other customs seem to have been altered very little.[61]

Bachelor living, however, was in much more trouble. By 1857–58, people seldom lived in their offices or stores. The boardinghouse remained, though, as the city merely replaced one kind of peculiarity with another. In the beginning, numerous families adopted this style of life because it was more economical. In time, it became fashionable amongst married and single folk alike and prevailed to a degree unknown to San Franciscans before. Yet even this habit came in for sharp criticism because it supposedly did not promote wholesome family life. But boardinghouse living could on occasion be very charming. Ferdinand Ewer, journalist and future minister, roomed with a lawyer, two teachers, and two opera singers from the Anna Bishop troupe.

> With Mrs. Parker's brilliancy, wit and humor, . . . with Miss Congdon's satire and knowledge of the world generally and of literary men and literary life particularly, with Mr. Stebbins' rabid abolitionism, with his love of arguing and his rich genial humor, with Judge Lake's repartees, with Dr. Holmes for a butt etc. . . . we have a merry and instructive time, the wits of all being constantly kept in the highest condition of polish.[62]

The comforts of life also increased whether in the Tehama House, Rassette House, What Cheer House, a family dwelling on Powell, or at South Park. Few lived in tents anymore.

The city's concept of time and sense of excitement remained,

but it was born of economic and political frustration instead of
hope. Even optimists like James King realized by 1856 that if the
metropolis had ever possessed unlimited opportunity, it no longer
did. For, as the bankruptcy lists revealed, even the mighty fell.[63]
By 1856 all complained of the presence of too many lawyers, businessmen, and workingmen. Men were counseled to go to the mines,
take up farming, or do anything but stay in the city. This grudging
confession repudiated many boosters' words, but by 1856 the
golden dreams had flown and everyone knew it.

Even before the acknowledgment, poverty stalked the city in
force. "This is the most extraordinary place on earth," William T.
Sherman wrote his brother in 1853. "Amid all this business and
bustle there is more poverty than in New York. Not a day passes
without distressed individuals ask [sic] for money." In 1856 the
situation had apparently worsened. "Those whose walks are confined only to Stockton, or Montgomery, or Front Street," commented the Alta, "know but very little of the poverty and sickness,
and weary watching in the little bye streets and alleys." A week
later it conceded that "the amount of wretchedness and poverty
existing in some parts of this city is scarcely exceeded by that of
the purlieus of the larger Atlantic cities." [64] This sad admission
of the further decline of San Francisco's uniqueness would have
been impossible in the flush days of 1848–49. The challenge of the
city was no longer the same.

The "era of good feelings" retreated as pauperism advanced.
Business gouging and widespread indifference to suffering remained, and the Vigilantes created new bitterness. "We are no
longer brothers. We are no longer a community of friends, whom
like adventures and pursuits and a rather rough and checkered
life have united in a brotherhood," the Chronicle lamented in mid-
1856. "Distrust has succeeded confidence, coldness has come like
an unwelcome ghost between friends." [65]

The popular reaction to this loss of uniqueness was ambivalent.
The great majority in 1848–49 shared the sense of excitement that

Judge Field experienced. Moreover, in later years many looked back just as fondly on those "pioneer days," and it would be difficult to exaggerate retrospectively the charm of the place. What is more, most approved of the revolt from the Eastern tyranny in manners and morals. "Living as we do under a republican government, and in a new country, the greatest charm of whose society ought to consist in its freedom from the slavery of fashion and the restraint of conventional rules, we might naturally be expected to present models of simplicity, economy and all the domestic virtues," argued the *Chronicle* in 1856.[66]

Yet at the very same time that people praised the distinctness, their actions undermined it. Perhaps John McCrackan's career best reveals what happened. A broadminded, wise, and vivacious man, he particularly admired the absence of restraint in the peculiar city of San Francisco. Yet his personal conduct helped establish the ladies' salons; he hailed the advent of fashionable weddings though he disapproved of ostentatious dressing; he deplored the lack of manners that he had been used to; he joined a dining club made up of lawyers and other representatives of the local notability; and he was genuinely shocked when a Quaker girlfriend of his sat in the window of her own house in a dress that left her arms "entirely bare, quite up to the shoulder."

As if to deepen their spiritual and intellectual confusion, San Franciscans soon developed a very strong nostalgia for the distinctness they destroyed. Some of them even pined for a time before the Gold Rush. Thomas O. Larkin, promoter of Benicia, local capitalist, and former United States consul in Mexican California, whose career helped bring the progress-minded Yankee to the Pacific shores, expressed his yearning in an 1856 letter. "Times are hard here, becoming harder. I begin to yearn after the times prior to July 1846 and all their beautiful pleasures and the flesh pots of those days—halcyon days they were. We shall not enjoy the same again." The ex-consul may have been longing for '46 rather than '49, but his attitude typified many who had done so

much to build the present in San Francisco only to end up hankering wistfully after the past.[67]

As did most nineteenth-century Americans, San Franciscans believed in progress. They built a great city on a site that nature
had not intended for one and contemptuously turned back the
efforts of any and all to challenge their urban hegemony in California. Yet the same people who hailed the erection of the mint,
the customs house, the new wharves, the great brick cathedrals of
commerce, the churches, and the families also lamented the passing
of every landmark of the old days—each adobe, each hotel, or
each formerly prosperous gambling saloon. Thus progress and
primitivism coexisted in the minds and hearts of most men and
women and eternally warred for dominance.

Urban Institutions

Though clearly anarchic, San Franciscans valued institutions designed to serve society by mitigating and softening their individualism. Therefore, the city rejoiced at the reversion to family living that set in after '48. Both the ideology of community and its practice assigned the female and the fireside the key role in the social structure.[1]

Before 1848, women constituted about one-third of the population; but immediately after the Gold Rush, one rarely saw a woman in the streets. Virtuous ones were scarcer still. "There are some honest women in San Francisco," asserted Russailh in 1851, "but not many." Whether employed as dancers, dealers, demimondistes, or what the French called "bar keepeuses," these women added variety and color to the local scene. Their freedom from convention astonished witnesses. "Abandoned women visit these places openly," wrote an argonaut. "I saw one the other evening sitting quietly at the monte-table, dressed in white pants, blue coat, and cloth cap, curls dangling over her cheeks, cigar in her mouth and a glass of punch at her side," he continued. "She handled a pile of doubloons with her blue kid gloved hands, and bet most boldly." [2]

Since so many wives lived out of sight on ships in the early years, observers underestimated their numbers. Yet deterrents to family life remained throughout the decade. No one knew pre-

cisely how long the mineral deposits would last, and husbands
consequently did not send for their families. The trip out was
often long and costly and sometimes marred by steamboat disasters, shipwrecks, disease, and violence. The high cost of living
in San Francisco, of which rents and servants' wages were the two
principal ingredients, remained for most of the period. Finally,
the numerous fires, the high crime rate, and the generally bad
atmosphere for home life discouraged many men from sending for
their wives.[3]

Throughout, the press bemoaned this scarcity; and when ocean-
going vessels unloaded cargoes of women, the papers usually pre-
maturely predicted an inundation by them. The longing for female society revealed itself in other ways. "It was the custome [sic]
to rent a room or two no matter how rich you was [sic] for a room
in a Privit [sic] family was a treasure," wrote Mrs. Benjamin F.
Butler in her memoirs. "If they could only feal [sic] it was home
like." There were even schemes to import women in quantity. The
most famous of these was Mrs. Farnham's in 1848–49. News of
her departure from New York aroused intense excitement. When
it was learned that Mrs. Farnham's female cargo never got beyond
Valparaiso, however, more drunkenness and violence occurred in
a single night than had for a long time. Even as late as 1855 a
similar project by promoter George Gordon was received with
rapturous applause; but it fell through, too.[4]

The presence of women was pre-eminently a city concern as
well as an antidote to loneliness. Civic patriotism proclaimed that
all well-regulated communities center around the hearth. More
than any other single thing, the family would lend stability and
improve the quality of urban life, a prospect which appealed to
both the civic-minded and the self-interested.

In the domestic circle, the businessman found refuge from the
anarchic conflict of city existence and recuperated for another
round of struggle. As the *Alta* said, "The bustle, strife, and continual watchfulness required for a successful competition in any
business in this country keeps the mind strained up to a great

tension all day, and it becomes indispensable to health and happiness that some relaxation should be supplied." Moreover, as the home environment expanded, gambling and drinking would contract. Writing in 1853, the *Alta* recognized this potential for community discipline when it called women and children the "flowers and buds on the widespread desert of society—with all their happy, hopeful and restraining influences." The home likewise performed a positive function. There the more spiritual side of life—"the nobler and refining qualities of the heart"—could be encouraged at the expense of the materialism of downtown, thus bringing more balance into the lives of San Francisco's men of business.[5]

The drudgery of raising children, providing a retreat, and nurturing the ennobling qualities of menfolk often belied this theory. Even when servants became available at reasonable prices, supervising them properly tended to be difficult and sometimes frustrating. Either overwork or managing domestics could cause one to neglect her music or "bury her intellectual pursuits in a matrimonial grave." Hence "when the husband return[ed] home," he was often met by a "poor broken hearted, discouraged, burnt faced woman, whose petty grievances [had] well nigh ruined both mind and body." Yet some critics held that women were spoiled by too much time for literary and cultural pursuits and did not work half as hard as their grandmothers.[6]

If so, their ancestors must have been fearfully industrious. The diary of Chastina Rix records the lot of the majority of women. "Washed and baked and brewed and everything else today. Tired enough," she noted on August 22, 1853. "I know but very little that is going on here. Stay at home very close," she wrote ten days later. "Ironing I have to work pretty hard seven in the family most of the time I hope I shall not always have to work so hard." [7] She and Alfred did find time to get to the theater occasionally, to visit friends, to walk, and to read aloud; but hard work was the normal routine.

However, hard work did not necessarily defeat the "home ideal."

On the first of January 1854, Chastina listed the members of her family, enumerated their various functions, and told how well they got along in the world. "Bub's [the baby's] business is to laugh, play in the sand, run after his parents and bawl and eat victuals," she wrote.

> The old man is Justice of the Peace and spends nearly every hour of the day at his office. . . . Chastina does the house-work, sews and tinkers so as to make, by herself, some $30 per month.—She is up and has breakfast every morning before daylight and is perfectly healthy and full of contentment and fun. Clara teaches school at the Mission at $100 per month and rides back and forth every day—Dustan works at Wheelwrighting at $4.50 per day. We are all as happy as crickets and as healthy as pigs.[8]

As the "burnt faced woman," the many divorces, and the court record of beatings and desertions demonstrate, many marriages were not as happy. Yet the "home ideal" was a reality for many people.

Fortunately, society reserved this sphere for women, for not much else was. Certain vocations had large numbers of females; but for the most part, these did not make one rich or famous. Women made up a large proportion of the milliners and boarding-house operators in 1857–58. School teaching actually claimed more women than men. Washing and needlework were traditionally female professions, although laundry women faced the formidable competition of the Chinese and the American-run steam laundries. And nursing, music, and the theater provided a few other "opportunities." Moreover, like their jobs, "few enough" female amusements existed.[9]

In view of the other freedoms in San Francisco, the weakness of feminism is ironic. Women "never talk of 'women's rights'— never parade the streets in bloomers and high heeled boots— never mount the stump . . . telling of the tyranny of men," remarked the *Era* in 1855. "In this respect [they] are angels in contrast with their strong minded sisters in the East." The metropolis could not even tolerate this activity in other places. In 1854 the *Alta* described such reformers as masculine creatures and poked fun at conventions where "woman unsexes herself, disclaims the nursery, maternity and the delicacy of her nature by her forward, impudent and brawling conduct in public crowds of rowdies." Female lecturers at first received a cool reception and even ridicule. Everyone from the *Era* to the San Francisco Ministrels "artistically" burlesqued "Woman's Rights" activities. Bloomers fared about as badly. The costume generated a crowd in front of Mrs. Cole's millinery store window in July 1851, and a furor when she wore the garment into the streets. Defenders stressed its practicality for San Francisco; opponents fumed that if some women "can't have men's jobs, they'll take their pants." Despite this uproar, the city's females, by 1853, were "down on the Bloomers." [10]

Yet the prevalent styles were hardly conservative. In a running controversy, the press deplored ostentatious dress, but the town's women largely adored it. Denounced by critics as impractical for the dirty streets of San Francisco, the long, expensive, luxurious dresses (copied from the French and possibly the prostitutes) supposedly collected too much urban dust while revealing too much female charm.[11]

Other evidences of female assertiveness occasionally appeared in businesses. One of McCrackan's many lady friends had made large sums in realty despite the community's conviction that her place was in the home, and sometimes women exercised decisive economic influence behind the scenes. One resident had "set her husband up in business here, manufacturing Soda—and they are making money fast. She doesn't trust him with the profits 'nary time' but keeps the stuff in her own hands." [12]

Women also mingled in politics. One husband imported large quantities of *Uncle Tom's Cabin* as a business speculation. His wife took the book seriously, distributed a whole case of them among her intimates, and propagandized the work and its message to the point of jeopardizing her friendships. In 1855 San Francisco women lobbied for statewide prohibition; and in 1856 the "gentler

sex" played a key role in provoking an urban revolution featuring
lynchings, deportations, violations of press freedom, and other
"vigorous" acts. Female lecturers championed this and other political causes as early as Sarah Pellet's 1854 debut. In this year
female journalism made its bow in an East Bay paper; and in 1858
the *Hesperian,* edited by and written for women, appeared.[13]

Despite the "home ideal" and the general aversion to feminism,
the community displayed a growing willingness to admit in detail
what it denied in general. An 1852 state law authorized "married
women to transact business in their own name, as sole traders."
As early as 1854 the *Alta* argued that females should be allowed
to be postmistresses as in some Eastern states, and the *Chronicle*
suggested in 1856 that retail shops which catered to women should
become their exclusive business preserve. Even the "home-minded"
Bulletin admitted "the difficulty of getting employment for respectable females" and carried numerous letters urging the establishment of nurseries for children of working mothers and like reforms. The literary *Era,* the most consistent critic of women's
rights, advocated the abandonment of the "peculiarly American
prejudice" of not allowing women to attend horse races and
praised the lectures of Sarah Pellet.[14]

Divorce practices provided a much greater breakthrough, however. The majority regarded divorce as a terrible calamity because
marriage supposedly lay at "the very foundation of the social order." As usual, the value was not absolute, for the community did
not advocate "the unqualified immutability of the marriage vow."
Yet urban convictions heavily favored marriage because the well-
being of society took precedence over the convenience of individuals. "Let evils then be borne," argued the *Pacific,* "for the sake
of avoiding those which are greater." [15]

Still "society" did not have its way. The state legislature passed
a very permissive statute in 1851, introduced by San Francisco
legislator J. D. Carr, and the ease of parting seemed to feed upon
itself. The "extraordinary temptations that exist in our midst," the
long separation that San Francisco residence often involved, and

the scarcity of females, which enhanced their bargaining power, added social incentives to the legal. This situation, in turn, provoked a number of reform suggestions. Since a court-appointed referee decided the matter without trial, publicity, or thorough investigation, a more difficult and lengthy procedure, including a public trial, was suggested to encourage better initial "selections" of mates and more serious attempts at reconciliation. Reformers also encouraged men to send for their families immediately and later marriages between more mature people. Despite these proposals, divorce continued to be a mere formality. Without much ado, many women seemed to practice what feminists preached. In 1856 "two hundred and sixty marriages occurred in the city" and "seventy two applications for divorce. . . . Nearly all of these suits were commenced by the wives of the disagreeing pair." [16]

It is tempting to dismiss the whole subject with some simple phrase like "male chauvinism," "sexism," or "squawism." Opportunities for unmarried women were much too narrow; and in "shared" professions, such as teaching, women received less salary and rank. Moreover, male attitudes were often selfish and condescending. They described females as "God's best gift to men," denigrated "petticoat literature," and reminded women that they had produced no Shakespeares because they did not have the same innate capacity for reason as opposed to emotion. Overprotection added to the problem. Any wisecracks from the "livery stable democracy" directed at respectable females invariably brought cries for a horse whipping; and when the *Era* advocated allowing women to go to the races, it still insisted that they be given a section "separate from the crowd." Furthermore, the community considered wife beating the lowest form of human activity; heated argument with a woman could jeopardize one's standing as a gentleman; and often men unabashedly put women on a pedestal.[17]

In some respects, however, women held positions merely different or even superior. All admitted that the society's hopes depended upon the younger generation, and women raised the children and presided over the home. That institution possessed more

prestige than the "dingy marts of commerce." At the fireside society's values were imparted and partially sustained. Men produced titanic energy and feats of reason, business, and literature,
it was argued; but without women they were innately incapable of
anything but barbarism. Moreover, one could work as hard at a
job as in the home and just as easily lose one's taste for art, literature, and the nobler things among the boxes, bales, and prices
current of California Street as in a "matrimonial grave." [18]

The public school stood alongside the home as one of the defense institutions of society. Although public education provoked
hardly any dissent, there were many different reasons for supporting it. Some grew out of hope or fear, of a desire to maintain the
status quo or to innovate, of concern for the individual or the
community, of democratic convictions or fear of the people. "The
only way to secure the stability of our republic," the *Alta* argued
in 1856, "the only way to insure the patriotism of the next generation, is to make them well acquainted with our constitution"
through education. "No country has ever succeeded or become
great," urged the *Courier* in 1850, "unless they encouraged and
sustained the Common Schools. They are the bulwark of national
prosperity, of civil and religious liberty." [19]

For those who distrusted the masses, popular enlightenment was
a matter of self-defense; the adherents of the people supported
public education for less negative reasons. It was the "great social
leader and leveler—elevating the more humble and gently re-
pressing the austerity of the more exalted." "The free school is the
institution of the people," wrote the *Alta*, pre-eminently important
"because of its democratic tendency." The private seminary had
a role, too, but it encouraged "a contempt for those in less affluent
circumstances." "Between the rich and the poor too many separa-
tions and distinctions exist, all of which are unfavorable to Republicanism, and the stability of our institutions," said the *Bulletin*.
The public schools could contain this threat; for "acquaintances
there formed between the children of those who occupy the very
extremes of society, and these friendships are based upon an actual

knowledge . . . that under a ragged jacket may throb a nobler heart, or work a more gifted mind." Finally, public education compensated those with parents too poor, miserly, dissipated, or indifferent to send them to private schools.[20]

While breaking down class barriers, education would mitigate those between nationalities. "The largest portion of our foreign population are possessed of great intelligence and enterprise, and an ardent love of liberty," said the *Bulletin*. Still, they and the Americans were mutually ignorant of each other; and this could lead to "convulsion and strife." Schools provided the minimum consensus, particularly on republican democracy, necessary to the existence of so much ethnic and political diversity. They cemented the community by making masses of men "well acquainted with each other, and firmly knit together by the ties of friendship and similarity of feeling and education." [21]

Schooling also served as an instrument of urban aggrandizement. Because of the importance of education, schools became a favorite device to lure families to the Golden Gate. And families would, in turn, further stabilize and uplift the community.

The usual environmentalistic assumptions suffused this rhetoric of justification. "It may be unnecessary to say how much our surroundings have to do with the formation of character," the *Chronicle* noted in 1853, "especially in that early part of life when impressions are so easily received, and so lasting in their influence." Children must be "surrounded by the wholesome influences of such a state of society as Free Schools obtain." These should inculcate morals, knowledge, and practicality while providing a refuge "against the false and pernicious." Believing that "knowledge is power," "the nurse of freedom," and "the right hand of Christianity," education would promote individual and community prosperity, liberty, and spirituality. Moreover, Dr. Scott argued that the British experience had "conclusively shown" "that every guinea contributed for educational purposes saved the payment afterwards of ten for the support of Jails, Houses of Correction and Criminal Courts." [22]

Operating the system proved more difficult than delineating its virtues. The Mormons opened the first American school in April 1847, which featured bad instruction, poor attendance, and tuition. Following the familiar pattern of private and public cooperation, a town meeting initiated a search for a replacement, and late in the year a building stood expectantly on Portsmouth Plaza. Early 1848 produced a school board, the first school census, which revealed sixty children in need of enlightenment, and Mr. Thomas Douglas, A. M. of Yale, to provide it. The city council contributed enough to make up what private subscription failed to raise of the teacher's $1,000 salary, and the Portsmouth Square building opened its doors on April 3, 1848. The Gold Rush closed them again within two months as the scholars, apparently anxious to learn of the rough passes of life first hand rather than from their texts, departed en masse for the mines with their teacher, Mr. Thomas Douglas, A. M. of Yale, at their head.[23]

From 1848 to 1850, Reverend Albert Williams and several others conducted private classes in the "old" Plaza schoolhouse when it was not in service as a church, court, jail, or meeting hall. In 1850, John C. Pelton, a New Englander, received a municipal subsidy, thus in Pelton's mind—though not in his critics'—founding the public school system. Next year, the government appointed T. J. Nevins, the San Francisco agent of the American Tract Society, to draw up a school ordinance and organize a system, which he did by late 1851.

The structure that emerged borrowed heavily from New York and Boston rather than from frontier experience. It was coeducational, though with separate playgrounds and doors, and was divided into primary, intermediate, grammar, and high schools. Each had three classes, except the high, or Union Grammar School, which had four. The latter served the entire city, though each district had at least one of the others by 1856. In addition, a night school contained the three lowest departments, but the grammar school section claimed most of its 200 students.[24] This school charged two dollars per month; the rest were free.

The Union Grammar and night schools both appeared in 1856, and for the same reason. Without a high school, public education would be disadvantaged vis-à-vis private academies, which provided this grade level. "A popular system, which thus limited the poor, would be lamentably defective," argued the president of the Board of Education in 1856. "It would admit the necessity of an aristocracy of knowledge, incompatible with the very first principles of an American free educational system." Despite the opposition of private institutions, grammar school teachers who resented losing their best scholars, and economizers, the new department came into being in 1856, at least two decades before such institutions became popular elsewhere. The night school, which gave those who worked during the day a chance to complete their learning and allowed foreigners to master the English language, survived similar assaults of the savers as well as a chaotic beginning.[25]

Another significant reform of 1856 granted considerable autonomy. Previously, Board of Education actions required town council ratification. The Consolidation Act, however, granted wider jurisdiction, especially the power to set the school tax rate within limits.[26]

In the lower grades the three "R's" interspersed with recesses and singing dominated the curriculum. The top of the grammar school level brought a more varied fare, which was intensified in the high school. The latter featured history, both United States and world, languages (French, Spanish, and German—all well adapted to the city's needs), mathematics, geography, chemistry, agriculture (!), speech (declamation), hygiene, botany, grammar, astronomy, rhetoric, logic, moral philosophy, political economy, United States Constitution, physiology, and natural history. Physical education in some form or another had a foothold at all levels.

So did harsh discipline. The *Pacific* claimed that authorities "seldom resorted to" corporal punishment; but in a few schools, teachers frequently "sent up" students for a whipping. Many substitutes for the rod—"making the pupil 'sit on nothing' and causing

him to bend forward with his finger upon the floor, obliging him
to hold heavy weights at arms length, or keeping him an undue
length of time in any unnatural position"—were not much better.
Sometimes instructors ridiculed students before their peers or
singled out examples of bad conduct at the school examinations.
Youngsters had mischievous ways of retaliating, however. At a
public examination in 1856, the principal punished a pupil, but
"no sooner had Mr. Swett turned his back than the little scamp
'made a face' at him." [27]

The annual May Day Parade, in which all common school students participated amidst general praise, supplied one of the high-
lights of the academic year. The public examinations provided a
second climax. Spectators enjoyed a scholarly exhibition and an
exposition, appropriately, by the students themselves, of the value
of common schools.

Women ordinarily presided over these events and the everyday
chores of instruction, but males nearly always dominated the administration and received about one-third more pay. Under the
reorganized system of 1856, the Board of Education chose instructors by oral examination, thus supposedly eliminating political influence. A weekly Normal School, mandatory upon pain of dismissal, provided continuing education for teachers.[28] In addition,
a San Francisco Teachers' Association existed, and the instructors
threatened unsuccessfully in 1856 to strike for their back pay.

These various arrangements of the system generated considerable controversy. The successful proponents of coeducation urged
that it promoted a more realistic appreciation of the opposite sex
than seclusion and that as in the community at large, little women
were the domesticators of little men. The opposition reversed the
argument, holding that the ruder males lowered the academic and
behavioral record of all. Fortunately, private school, especially a
Catholic one of 200 girls, could accommodate the opponents of
coeducation.[29]

Since intellectual health was supposedly related to bodily condition, physical education became a popular reform. "Good boys

generally die in their fiftieth year," needled the *Chronicle,* "not because they are good, but because their quiet habits make them strangers to mud puddles, oxygen, dirt pies, and all out door exercise." A "sedentary" urban existence made this concern acute.[30] In the 1856 state teachers' convention debate on mandatory physical education, many argued that country lads exercised enough in their work and play; but most agreed that city children needed school exercises. These arguments won out, and schools began setting up gymnastic facilities, sometimes raising the money through exhibitions.

Discipline fared less well. San Franciscans tried to square the claims of liberty and control; but in theory at least, they agreed that "Order is Heaven's first law and without perfect discipline a school room must be a very chaos." Nevertheless, the use of corporal punishment to enforce this statute caused considerable controversy.

The question of practicality versus ornamentality added another. "We are a working people," argued the Reverend William A. Scott, "and education then must combine the practical and useful with the profound and ornamental." Mammon worship remained a constant concern for those who feared the practical. It was like too much competition or rusticity. "The totally uneducated man has precisely the same . . . capacity for enjoyment as . . . an intelligent horse, luxuriating over a peck of oats," remonstrated the *Californian* in 1848.[31]

These theoretical problems shared the stage with numerous practical ones. Transiency caused the *Annals* to note that "Few pupils are now in attendance who belonged to the schools a year ago." The well-entrenched custom of late rising or the need for older children to help with morning chores or evening meals meant that "these scholars must either be deprived of schooling or, as is generally the case, make a general confusion by constantly entering school late in the morning, and leaving before closing in the afternoon," the *Chronicle* complained in 1855. The minority who opposed the public schools and foreigners, who often confused the system with "Pauper Schools, Ragged Schools, and Parish Schools of other countries," created other difficulties. This non-patronage encouraged competing "private academies to which they have no repugnance." American boys already earning a living further curtailed attendance as did the rainy season. Furthermore, many parents took little interest in the schools, ignoring examinations and other public events. Often they viewed the system more as a baby-sitting service or "a local Botany Bay." Even when pupils had parental backing, poverty precluded the price of a textbook, thereby undermining the school's function as a social equalizer.[32]

Yet schools could hardly accommodate those who did attend. The system claimed 1,574 pupils in mid-1854; 2,075 one year later; 2,996 at the end of February 1856; and 3,606 in November of that year.[33] And this great increase coincided with a severe depression.

These burdens in turn complicated the two most critical problems of the decade—faith and finances. The long-range causes of the former dispute lay in irreconcilable nationalist, political, and religious views. Protestants feared that Catholic demands for public monies for parochial schools would damage public education. Catholics felt that parents should have the right to choose the kind of schools their offspring attended and that anything less represented discrimination against them and an infringement of conscience. They were willing to see others have the same privilege, but that concession merely deepened Protestant anxieties. The latter feared that separate education would encourage divisiveness and religious discords. Moreover, since Catholic clergy usually hailed from foreign monarchies, Protestants questioned their qualifications to impart democratic and republican principles; and as servants of a despotic church which was strongest where popular education was weakest, their interest in education of the masses was highly suspect. Protestants found Catholic demands for public monies doubly outrageous because most taxes came from Protestant pockets.[34] They also feared proselytizing and a union of church and state.

Yet their opposition was highly flexible. Many Protestants favored the use of the Bible and certain textbooks that the Catholics objected to; they demanded municipal realty for the American Missionary Association; they praised policemen who distributed religious tracts on the beat. Most Protestant spokesmen agreed that "it is in the power of the state to create a Sabbath." And outside of school they tried to win over the Catholic population. The slightest pretext could have pushed the holders of these contradictory views into conflict, and the Protestants seem to have supplied it. Superintendent Nevins insisted upon Bible-reading in classes; and in November 1852, a city council ordinance required "that schools shall be opened by reading a portion of scripture." [35] This practice apparently lasted only about eighteen months, but that was enough. Catholics considered mandatory Bible-reading an intolerable attempt at proselytizing; they withdrew en masse to establish their own schools.

In August 1854, the *Alta* reported 930 pupils in the county or Catholic institutions and 1,703 in the city Protestant ones. Though religious groups dominated both systems, neither was entirely private, for the Catholics persuaded the 1853 legislature to divide educational funds. The state provided about one-third of local school money and the town, two-thirds. The Catholics controlled the former, the Protestants, the latter; and neither would give any of the cash to the other. In 1853, the corporation attorney ruled that the Catholics were entitled to municipal money; but some time passed before they got it. Finally, in 1854 the Protestant Board discharged "every foreigner who occupied a post as a teacher." Know Nothingism exacerbated the whole episode, and the ensuing furor led to repeated calls for an abolition of all traces of sectarianism, whether Protestant Bibles or Catholic sisters.[36]

In 1855 the legislature began the process of adopting this settlement by prohibiting the division of the funds and any sectarianism and establishing a consolidated Board of Education. Legally, this action ended the schism, but it did not terminate the battle. The Catholic schools demanded an appropriation from the cor-

poration. The city council allowed this claim, but Protestant lay-
men secured an injunction forbidding the government to pay
Catholic teachers. Catholics then enjoined the use of city funds
to pay any teachers, and this impasse lasted for more than six
months in 1855–56.[37]

Finally, in 1855–56 the Board of Education imposed a settlement
based on the legislative prohibition of 1855 and the Consolidation
Act. The 1855 school board elections returned four Know Nothings and four Democrats, including two Catholics and two non-
nativist Protestants. The Romanists dominated one of the latter;
and the other, Ferdinand Ewer, resented the Know Nothing purge
of foreign teachers. Since the regular Democratic mayor, James
Van Ness, had the casting ballot, the Democrats held the whip
hand. However, the Democrats, with the exception of Ewer,
seemed as anxious as the Americans to rule or ruin. The Know
Nothings "were determined to Protestantize the schools" and "to
ostracize all R. Catholic teachers," and the "Catholics desired the
admission of the Sisters of Charity." Ewer favored a compromise,
and being a majority of one, eventually prevailed. He helped
examine the Sisters of Charity at their convent and passed favor-
ably upon them. Then he got them to withdraw voluntarily, thus
ending the schism between himself and the other Democrats. The
pupils received a holiday, and the board held teacher examinations for both Catholics and Protestants despite Know Nothing
protests. Only nine Catholics opposed to thirty-four Protestants
qualified, but all nine were hired. The board then created new
districts, integrated the instructors religiously by putting an "R. C.
teacher in what had been a Protestant district and a Protestant in
what had been a R. C. school," and banned sectarianism.[38]

Catholic schools did not die out, but they no longer enjoyed tax
support. From time to time, Catholic spokesmen demanded subsidies or the participation of the Catholic orders in the public
school; and Protestants periodically called for the reinstatement
of the Bible.[39] Nevertheless, the "Ewer settlement" gained increasing acceptance.

Sectarian battling compounded financial problems, but these would have been insoluble even if the Bible had not existed. Education gained first place in the 1856–57 budget largely because of ruthless cuts in everything else. Peak expenditures came in 1854–55, but the $157,000 spent on education amounted to just over half the individual outlay for fire prevention, police, and health and less than half the expense of streets and salaries.

Depression-born economizing threatened to reduce expenses further. The Grand Jury recommended the discontinuation of the newly established high school. The *Bulletin* urged eliminating the "infant school," reducing teachers' salaries, operating fewer buildings, and employing academic child labor, that is, "pupil teachers," at cheap rates. Despite drastic cuts, the refusal to pay taxes brought the system to the verge of collapse by 1857.[40]

This basic inadequacy produced several others. For most of the period, no good school buildings, nor even enough bad ones, existed. One school held sessions in a board structure with a set of tenants living upstairs, and overcrowding was commonplace. The pupil-teacher ratio was equally absurd—about seventy to one in 1855—and teachers' salaries were low. Often male instructors earned just a little more than a clerk. In mid-1855, the library contained 800 volumes for 2,100 children, compared to 3,700 books for 526 Mercantile Library Association members. In addition, the educational services, like those of the fire and police departments, were maldistributed.[41]

Given its many and vexatious difficulties, it is amazing that the system accomplished anything at all. Yet it made considerable progress. Enrollment burgeoned seven-fold from 485 in early 1852 to 3,606 in 1856, as did the proportion of eligible children in school. Some 500 attended in 1852, about one-third of those of school age. In 1856, the figure rose to 3,606 out of 4,751 or 76 per cent; and by that year competitive private facilities in the state and city had greatly increased. Moreover, bad as it seems, seventy to one constituted an improvement over the ninety to one pupil-teacher ratio of 1853. In addition, despite poverty, late rising, rain, and religion, daily attendance averaged about 75 per cent by 1856. The building crush also began to ease. In 1854, the city dedicated the first structure "permanently and properly built" for the purpose of education and floated a loan of $100,000 for further expansion.[42] Even the Negro population had a tax-supported, though segregated, school. In absolute terms, twice as many black children went to town schools as did white children in the rest of the county, and a much greater proportion of school-age Negro children actually attended.

Compared to the rest of the state, the metropolis's performance looks even better. The *Alta* noted in 1850 that "San Francisco is the only place in the State where able and competent teachers can be had"; and in December 1851, the state superintendent admitted that "only San Francisco has a Common School System." That pre-eminence did not disappear thereafter. "Probably one-fourth, if not more, of the public school interest, is in this city," wrote the *Bulletin* in 1856. The *Bulletin*'s estimate was probably very low. In early 1856 the state superintendent reported 26,170 youngsters of school age, of which only 6,422 had attended in the last year; and 3,000 of these were in the metropolis. At the same time that San Francisco city attendance approached three out of four, the county districts "had 45 only of 409 . . . in school"; and prosperous, stable Santa Clara County claimed only 255 of 1,751. Fully a year and a half after San Francisco founded its system, the state had not yet appropriated a dollar of its small educational fund to the schools. The nineteenth-century city is often pictured as the epitome of horrors, but even this instant city offered far more educational advantages than the surrounding countryside or the state as a whole. And as eminent a man as Horace Bushnell believed "the public schools of San Francisco are not inferior to those of our Eastern cities,—many think them superior." [43]

Numerous private schools added to the city's educational achievement. Like the public ones, they had important religious ties, though fewer students. John McCrackan estimated in 1853

that "we have nearly as many Select as free schools." The total
was probably exaggerated for 1853, and certainly for 1856; yet it
indicates a firm foothold. They had much the same educational
activities as the public schools but were often boarding as well
as day schools and frequently noncoeducational. Moreover, many
designed to serve the metropolis were located in nearby Oakland,
Sonoma, Benicia, San José, and Santa Clara.[44]

Higher education also took a tenuous hold in the bay area. The
establishment destined to become the nucleus of the University of
California opened its doors in 1853 in Oakland, in large part through
the work of San Franciscans. Other institutions located in the
metropolis itself. The Jesuits established one; another, called San
Francisco College, was launched in 1856. These were indicative
of the future; but neither they nor the University of the Pacific
and nearby Santa Clara College served many students by 1857.[45]

These education deficiencies heightened the importance of other
organizations and clubs such as the Mercantile Library Association, founded in late 1852. After a wobbly beginning, this institution grew to 600 members, about one-sixth as many as the New
York Association. Besides literature, it provided an intellectual
forum through lectures and debates, which reveal a wide-ranging
curiosity. In 1853–54, for example, the members debated whether
"the circumstances of education, habit, food, and climate" were
"sufficient to account for the varieties of the human race," whether
the indefinite extension of the American Republic would lead to
its downfall, whether the public school system should be designed
to impart education to all children of the state, "whether capital
punishment should be abolished," whether the victor should get
the spoils, and what ought to be done about the Kansas-Nebraska
Bill. The society was also one of the town's defense institutions,
a community anchor which "every man who is interested in the
permanency of our city" should support. While stimulating men's
minds, the Library would remove their bodies from the evil surroundings of the gambling hall, saloon, and flesh pot and provide
a refuge from urban life.[46]

Similar institutions performed most or all of these services for different social groups.[47] The Negro San Francisco Atheneum, the Historical Society of the State of California, and the California Academy of Natural Sciences, the oldest scientific body in the state, all date from 1853. The San Francisco Lyceum, the Young People's Society of Inquiry, the St. Mary's Library Association, the Society for Free Discussion, the Jeffersonian Club, and the Mechanic's Institute came later. Like other institutions not tied to the profit motive, these made a late and shaky start. Yet despite the depression, by late 1856 the *Alta* claimed that "debating societies, literary associations, and public lecturers on scientific subjects, are the desideratum which has long been wanted, and which we are now in a fair way of obtaining." [48]

The church stood alongside the school and home as one of the crucial defense institutions in the city, but in 1846 the settlement stood largely unprotected. Until 1848, the Mission of San Francisco was its only church. Protestant services were conducted by chaplains on ships in the harbor, through prayer meetings in the home, and by missionaries on the way to Oregon. The well-attended services of the Oregon-bound Methodist ministers highlighted the religious difficulties. The preachers used one part of Brown's Hotel—while others drank, gambled, and played billiards under the same roof. Sabbath-breaking was notorious and backsliding, frequent.[49] The Gold Rush intensified this irreligious quality, but it also brought the forces that eventually established Christian influence.

The Protestants moved first in November 1848. The town meeting appointed Timothy Dwight Hunt, the representative of the American Board of Foreign Missions, town chaplain to men of all "persuasions" at $2,500 per annum. This provided the first regular Protestant worship, and others soon followed. The Baptists erected the original Protestant church in the city and thus the first in the state; and the Congregationalists, Presbyterians, Catholics, Episcopalians, and Methodists also organized congregations in 1849. By 1856, at least two Jewish, six Catholic, and twenty-two Protestant houses of worship served the community. In '49, gold- and pleasure-seekers filled the avenues; but on a Sunday morning in 1856 "the streets were thronged with pedestrians threading their way through opposing crowds /to/ gather from the different parts of the city" to these churches.[50]

At first, several denominations worshipped in tents, coarse board shanties, the Plaza schoolhouse, or some government office. As late as 1856 the Mormons held services in the basement under Schueppert's Lager Bier Saloon, where the Germans celebrated their continental Sundays. However, by this year the increase of the faithful had wrought a $500,000 improvement in the architectural setting. St. Mary's Cathedral alone cost $85,000, and Calvary Presbyterian and Broadway Synagogue cost $69,000 and $35,000 respectively.[51]

Most of the money came from the houses of Mammon downtown, but the churches tended toward the periphery. Real estate prices, the fire hazard, and the need to be near parishioners caused this drift. Yet as early as 1850, the churches had located on the outskirts of town before many residents lived there. Initially, the houses followed the steeples; but once the people began moving out, other churches followed. Within the periphery, Catholic churches served a geographic area; but Protestant churches usually did not.

In the beginning, the same comradeship that united miners, merchants, and others found religious expression in a much-praised irenic spirit. "Protestants contributed one thousand dollars to subscription for the Vallejo Street [Catholic] Church," noted DeMassey. "Where, in old world annals, could one find such a similar instance of religious tolerance?" Father Langlois allowed Albert Williams to circulate a Spanish language Bible in the Jesuit's flock, and they attended temperance meetings together and cooperated in banning barbarous Sabbath amusements.[52] The first Protestant communion service in the country was interdenominational; and initially, many kinds of Jews shared one house of worship and diverse Catholics went to church together.

This friendly sentiment never quite faded out, but a very decided reversion to the old sectarian and dogmatic customs took place. Intolerance did not usually reach the point of denying the right of any denomination or sect to exist; yet hostility grew. As the only religion in the city torn by theological controversy, Judaism found itself divided over the rising question of reform versus orthodoxy and split again by ethnic enmities. Each Protestant denomination set up its own churches; and "high church"-"low church," "Old School"-"New School," and North-South cleavages further fragmented Episcopalians, Presbyterians, and Methodists. Cooperation continued in maintaining the *Pacific* newspaper, the American Board of Foreign Missions, and the "Presbytery and Association," an alliance of Presbyterians and Congregationalists; but for the most part, each group went its own way. Churches of the same sects did not always help each other, and often rivalries developed between ministers. Even the monolithic Catholic Church witnessed the emergence of at least two ethnic churches —Notre Dame des Victoires and St. Patrick's—and German discontent with Irish prominence in the hierarchy.

A more serious hostility developed between Protestants and Catholics, for which the former were primarily responsible. From the beginning they proselytized the rival flock, and that did not win them many Catholic friends. Each side took educational precautions, and eventually schools sprouted up next to churches all over the city while Protestant and Catholic orphan asylums guarded outcast children from contamination by the wrong religion. Further controversies raged over the division of school monies and the city hospital. The Sisters of Mercy seemingly were doing a good job of attending to the sick; but in doing so, "religious prejudices were excited, and a fierce religious war . . . was commenced." [53] This led to the Sisters' ouster in 1856, and the period ended as polemically as it had begun ironically.

Spiritualism apparently reached San Francisco in 1852 and caused considerable excitement, too. Despite a momentary check resulting from the "blunder of . . . predicting . . . the election of General Scott to the Presidency and . . . the States which had voted for him," the "Rappers" were still important in 1856. To the orthodox, Spiritualism was a travesty on religion; yet in 1852, John McCrackan reported some twenty Spiritualist circles, "and all have had some wonderful experiences of this mysterious agency." [54]

The main thrust of Christianity in San Francisco was directed toward reconciling the claims of the next world and this. Yet the demands of the here and now were clearly subordinate to those of the hereafter. "This life, beloved friends, is but a place of mist and shadows. Even while we seek to grasp them, they fade away," warned Episcopal Bishop Kip on New Year's Day, 1856. "Raise yourselves above the world, that you may be independent of its degrading trammels." The *Pacific* went so far as to denounce the worldly existence as an "unreal life." [55]

Christians resisted the inroads of the world at several points. The Scriptures did not oppose "cheerfulness and innocent recreation." Work must be balanced by play, but "whosoever . . . steps so far aside from the weighty duties of life, as to give himself more to amusements than to self improvement and usefulness, is dead." [56] The theater-goer obviously qualified as one of the latter, as did the gay young socialite and the fashionable churchgoers. The House of the Lord was dedicated to His glory; but increasingly it also hosted an interminable fashion show, renewed every seventh day despite the fulminations of press and pulpit.

The same otherworldliness led many to shun an active role in government. In 1856 the ministers thundered their support for the Vigilantes; but ordinarily, numerous clergymen agreed with the Reverend Dr. Anderson that ministers should be "free from all party ties and the influence of party strife, never to be an active participant in the civil commotions of the day." Nor were most interested in reforming basic economic conditions. They might establish Sabbath schools as a "powerful instrumentality in drawing the young from the streets and from desecrating the Sabbath," but the underlying causes of social distress usually passed unnoticed. In fact, some Christian views stood in the way. "One hundred years hence . . . it will be nothing to us that our life on earth has been one of ease or penury," warned the Bush Street Baptist minister; "but it will be everything to us then that we have made God and heaven our own." The Reverend Cummings even went so far as to argue "that poverty was sometimes a real blessing, while wealth was rather a curse than the reverse." On one occasion Dr. Scott stated that the key to unemployment was to "have the gospel preached" to the poor; and in 1858, during the depression, the Catholic *Monitor* argued that the "greatest moral and social evil" of the day was obscene literature, novels, and antireligious books.[57]

It is not true, however, that ministers scorned reform entirely. Not all their protests would please the modern critic; but active Christians, especially Protestants, had more social conscience than any other single group. They were among the most likely to speak out against slavery and among the first to attack dueling (many years before James King did). They condemned the barbarities practiced against Indians; led in establishing the schools, libraries, orphan asylums, and sailors' home; and denounced gambling, wanton destruction of forests, divorce, intemperance, prostitution, adultery, the publication of Sunday papers, and Sabbath-breaking. The work of Catholics is not as well documented; but they, too, were active, caring for the sick, founding schools, establishing Magdalen Homes, and so forth. Yet the inroads of Mammon and atheism, particularly the former, worried the clergy most.

Whether churches reflect the world or mold it is often debatable, but Christianity did not reflect one of the mores of its urban context. Honest industry was a necessary concession to the world, yet the prevalent money grubbing was invariably condemned by the ministers. Pointing out the difficulty of reconciling the worldly and other-worldly, a Baptist minister noted that he had never "seen a harder task than to get a man to look through a lump of gold into eternity." The high priority of the struggle against Mammon caused the *Pacific* to declare in 1853 that the most heartening improvement in San Francisco "social life is, the moderation to be

rich." Despite financial dependence upon wealthier members, fulminations against the excessive pursuit of money and "overreach-
ing among merchants and traders" and exhortations to the laborer
to "work diligently, the employer /to/ act liberally, and the
merchants /to/ deal honestly" substantially increased.[58]

Next to Mammon, the drift toward skepticism and atheism provided most anxiety, though these hardly reached epidemic proportions. The Gold Rush made life very harsh, and some men felt
unable to combine a Christian existence and a business career.
Some simply stopped believing, and one ingenious man declared
a two-year moratorium on faith while he accumulated his fortune.
The Thomas Paine Club revealed the extent of church concern
over this drift. This group dedicated itself to the consideration of
any question on rational grounds, whether that course led to a
loss of faith or not. One of their leading lights, John S. Hittell, a
journalist and early historian of the city, even wrote a book sub-
jecting Christianity to a rationalist criticism. Church representatives denounced both the Paine Club and Hittell and vigorously
defended their own faith in God.[59]

Sermons, lectures, Sunday school classes, outings, sick visitations,
prison visitations, temperance meetings, discussion groups, Ragged
Sabbath Schools, religious newspapers, prayer sessions, Bible societies, pamphlets, tracts, and clubs put forward in this world the
claims of the next. These activities changed but did not revolution-
ize the condition of society. Sabbath-breaking declined; theatricals
and barbarous amusements were banned on the Lord's Day; some
Sunday steamer travel stopped; a few papers ceased publication;
and some businesses stayed closed on the Sabbath. With materialism, prostitution, drinking, dancing, and the "enormous oaths"
heard so frequently in the streets, the churches succeeded less
well.

If the churches were successful in blunting some of the demands
of this world, the process also worked the other way. To demonstrate the glory of the Lord, they spent vast amounts of money
upon their buildings and lots. Yet this otherworldly aim was the

very one that most often raised financial problems, which led the faithful still further into the realm of the here and now. Ministers, trained to convey the word of God, found themselves and their wives carrying hats in hand down to the arena of Mammon on the flatlands; and buildings designed to be houses of worship came also to be used for fairs, raffles, sacred concerts, and other fund-raising activities.

These worldly adjustments proved painful. The *Chronicle* denounced raffles as gambling; and the Reverend Ver Mehr argued that the church was strictly a House of God, off limits to either sacred concerts or fairs. Yet he was forced to allow both lest the Lord's house become the sheriff's. Protestants and Catholics frequently depended upon pew rents, despite the widespread conviction that a church should not be open just to those who had paid admission. Fittingly enough, the system provoked a rash of "pew squatting," with outsiders crowding into popular churches as others had crowded onto city lots. The expense both deterred people, including James King, from attending worship and destroyed the north end Protestant church of William Pond and the seamen's bethel established in 1850.[60]

Financial necessities also encouraged a search for "name" pastors and some rather harsh, and possibly un-Christian, consequences. The recruitment in 1853 of Dr. William Scott of New Orleans ushered in the "cult of personality." His advent rapidly siphoned off money and members of rival congregations. Pioneer T. D. Hunt's dismissal came directly from his inability to compete with Scott for parishioners to pay off his church's mortgage, and Reverend Pond also lost precious middle-class worshippers to the dynamic newcomer.

This worldly and spiritual duality involved expression as well as expenses. "O for wisdom to tell me just how far and when no farther to go," worried Hunt over his temperance sermons.[61] It is difficult to determine how widespread this problem was; but Hunt, Ver Mehr, and Scott all received pressure to alter their messages, though none did. Despite spiritual compromises, however, churches never had enough money. Several folded; another fell to the sheriff's hammer. Both St. Mary's Cathedral and Grace Episcopal Church stood for several years with uncompleted spires.

The same sequential colonialism that made San Francisco an economic appendage and a theatrical suburb of Eastern cities operated in the field of religion. Until the local denominations built up their strength, they were to a very considerable extent religious dependencies of their outside allies. By 1854, the American Home Missionary Society had provided $40,000 to its cohorts ($80,000 by 1856); and the Catholic Paris Society for the Propagation of the Faith sent $45,000.[62] Yet by the end of the period, both Catholics and Protestants had become increasingly self-sufficient.

As the papers often reminded their readers, there was a qualitative difference between city and country. Services attracted more people in cities; churches organized there first; and the Sabbath fared better in town. A similar gulf separated San Francisco and the interior towns. Through the pages of the Christian press—the *Pacific, California Christian Advocate,* and *Catholic Standard*—urban religion had a voice in the remotest villages and mountain hamlets. The *Pacific* compared a pulpit without a newspaper to an "army with a trumpet and sword only, but without artillery," and Isaac Owen rated the *Christian Advocate* (saved by a San Francisco merchant) more important to the Methodists than additional ministers. San Francisco was also the headquarters of the Catholic Archdiocese of San Francisco (Northern California where most of its people lived) and the American Board of Foreign Missions on the West Coast, the main operating base for most of the other churches, and the matrix and dominating influence in the Pacific Tract Society. The best ministers resided there, too. "San Francisco is not only the first city," but it is "a city that controls, to some extent the whole country," wrote Methodist minister Isaac Owen. "Now the other churches . . . are doing all they can to fully supply every part of the city, and with their most talented men too." And just as the size of the urban ethnic market helped prolong national diversity, the same factor fostered religious variety. For example, many places in California had no Jewish services at all; yet the metropolitan concentration supported four or five different congregations ranging from Beth El, on the verge of adopting the Minhag America, to Shomre Shabas, "consisting of Russian Jews" and extremely orthodox. Some Jews actually moved from the frontier to the city in order to maintain their faith, while others did the same by joining the "numerous concourse of strangers, coming here for the purpose of keeping the holidays." [63]

Religion overlapped urban benevolence. "The citizens of San Francisco are proverbial for being the most liberal, public spirited people in the world," wrote the *Bulletin* in 1856, echoing the majority sentiment.[64] To what extent they deserved this reputation is impossible to determine, yet philanthropic contributions never caught up with this rhetoric. Benevolent societies shared the late start, shortage of money, and heavy indebtedness of other nonprofit organizations. Moreover, self-interest and good works were often very closely connected.

For example, in 1852 the Bay City subscribed $29,000 in money and over $40,000 in breadstuffs for flood-stricken Sacramento. "Is it too much to say we are liberal?" McCrackan queried triumphantly. Yet it was notorious that more money was pledged than collected in any fund-raising venture in San Francisco. In addition, much of the city's trade went to Sacramento as the main northern supply depot for the mines. Too, San Franciscans owned some of Sacramento's business, just as New Yorkers owned much of the bay metropolis. And while encouraging donations, the flood also sent the price of flour, the main staple in the trade, skyrocketing to a near record fifty-five dollars a barrel. The same "motives of interest as well as charity" even touched a "mariner's home." The sponsors hoped such an institution would help regain some of the whaling trade that bypassed the port because of the crimps and shanghaiiers. On the other hand, there is considerable evidence of unambiguous open-handedness, as in 1853 when the city raised $10,000 for epidemic victims in New Orleans.[65]

Part of the difficulty in measuring generosity lies in the system of press reporting. Deeds of philanthropy were "not so intensely interesting to the readers of daily news, and hence they [did] not stand a fair chance of being noticed." A regular police reporter sought all the failings and selfishness of the city, but no one specialized in finding society's strengths.[66] Nor did any central place, like the police station or the Recorder's Court, harbor the data of good works. Moreover, the personal or familial nature of much benevolence further veiled its true extent.

Even if the city did not merit some of its reputation for liberality, there can be no doubt that its population gloried in it. Warmheartedness characterized philanthropic thinking, and benevolence did not appear as an unwise subsidy to the unfit. Here as elsewhere the social ideology of San Francisco was communitarian as much or more than individualistic. "The poor have ye always with you" was a popular dictum; but the responsibility, sometimes of the "entire community," for ameliorating misfortune was universally accepted. The "idlers who are constantly to be found about the lunch rooms of Montgomery street," who "would not work if they could," did not qualify for benevolence; but men could be unemployed "either from faults of their own or defects in the operation of our social system." [67]

Several ethnic benevolent societies, two orphan asylums, the full complement of temperance groups, a Ladies' Protection and Relief Society, a Seamen's Friends Society, a YMCA, Masons, Odd Fellows, and a Magdalen Asylum stood ready to implement these principles. Even the temperance movement featured Protestant, Catholic, adult, and teenage sections. However, the functions performed were often not as sharply distinguished; many undertakings overlapped. Each association was a multipurpose aid society for a special social group. Businessmen usually financed these works and sometimes ran them; but women, ministers, and other religious persons more often directed them.

Since it was believed that "in a country like our own, efficiency and consequent self reliance are *almost* complete antidotes to pov-

erty and despair," the YMCA and ethnic, Ladies' Protection, and
Seamen's Friends societies each had an employment agency or
were planning one.[68] The ethnic organizations, the Odd Fellows,
the Masons, and the YMCA furnished pocket money for those in
need or passage money home or to the mines. The German and
French groups had or planned hospitals; the YMCA made sick
visitations; and the Odd Fellows and Masons dispensed medical
care to members. The latter two and the Jewish associations also
provided funeral money and cemetery plots.

For those not requiring ultimate aid, the societies offered a refuge from the "evil influences" of the streets. "It is in vain that you
build Bethels for seamen until you throw around them some moral
influences outside of the church," the *Alta* argued. And as the term
"Mariner's Home" implies, the "kindly influences" radiated from
the ever-civilizing female and the domestic hearth. Ironically, Father Taylor's wharf-side seamen's bethel was relocated toward
California Street Hill because middle-class ladies would not ordinarily go to the waterfront. The Ladies Aid and Protection Society
for Seamen also secured the Mercantile Hotel on Front Street as
an alternative to the ruinous places mariners usually stayed in. The
same environmentalism underlay the YMCA boardinghouse and
hotel committee's "white list" of suitable lodgings, the YMCA
Ragged Sabbath School established so that newsboys and other
children "might be gathered in from the streets," the Protestant
and Catholic orphan asylums, the Ladies' Protection and Relief
Society, the Sisters of Mercy's House of Mercy, and several "dry"
boardinghouses.[69]

Yet these buildings were more than just urban havens. The
YMCA sponsored lectures, debates, and religious exercises and
collected a library designed to promote "the moral and intellectual
improvement of young men." [70] The Y excelled in this respect, but
the propagation of the "right values" concerned all groups.

Despite creditable work, each encountered beguiling competition from "the streets." "There are the horse races, processions with
martial music, whose tones ever charm them, excursions on steam-

boats and to Russ's Gardens, exhibitions of flying horses, etc.," noted a Ragged Sabbath School report ruefully of its newsboys. "All these have attractions of such magnitude that it requires no ordinary Sabbath school and teachers to induce them to attend regularly." [71]

Following patterns familiar to other nonprofit endeavors, several groups appeared only after 1853 and most experienced difficult beginnings. Money was generally scarce, and they usually demanded public aid, since elsewhere governments had done some of the work carried on by San Francisco philanthropists. In 1855 the Protestant Orphan Asylum received a $5,000 state subsidy for taking in children from all over California. However, that grant and one intended for the Catholic asylum ended in 1856. In one year, a Catholic asylum subsidy actually survived the Know Nothing council but fell to a mayoral veto.[72] Yet the municipality helped operate the town's largest and most broadly based philanthropic institution, the city hospital, which also served as a poorhouse.

Substantial personal, family, or ad hoc philanthropy supplemented institutional. One was supposed to fall back upon family and friends in case of trouble; and sometimes such special benevolence efforts—occurring constantly on behalf of overland immigrants, flood, epidemic, and shipwreck victims, the fire department, and others—were bigger than the organized ones. The aid could be more personal and unpublicized, too. After the murder of the editor of the *Police Gazette* in 1854, T. D. Hunt recorded that friends of the widow "had raised her quite a sum of money for her relief." [73]

Sometimes the amounts were quite large, but not ordinarily. The entire Protestant Orphan Asylum budget was $12,000 in 1855, an extraordinary year because of the expense of a new building and a state subsidy. In the same year, the Catholic Asylum spent just under $900 a month and had a $15,000 debt, twice as large as the Protestants'. The Ladies' Protection and Relief Society expended a little more than $2,000 for 1855; the Hebrew Benevolent

Society spent $4,500 between 1849 and 1855; the Eureka Benevolent Society disbursed $200 a month from 1850; the expenses of the German Benevolent Society for fifteen months in 1854–55 were $3,812; and in ten months in 1853–54 the French Benevolent Society spent $20,000, half of which purchased a lot and building.[74]

The number of people aided by these expenditures varied. In 1855 the two orphan asylums sheltered close to 200 children, about 10 per cent of the number in public schools. The Catholics cared for at least three-fourths of this number. The Sisters of Mercy helped 500 and provided jobs for 1,100 more in 1856; and in 1855 the Ladies' Protection and Relief Society placed seventy-five persons.[75] The ethnic societies and the YMCA also found employment for a large number of people. Still, many remained in need.

Although the press did not share all the duties of the other urban institutions, it did help them impose and support the accepted values of society. Despite fierce competition, disastrous fires, depressions, duels, and other discouragements, the communications business grew remarkably. Edward Kemble, a pioneer journalist, claimed that in 1858, one thousand San Franciscans had either a current or former connection with the press. In 1856 the *Bulletin* and *Alta* split a hundred. At the same time, no less than one monthly, ten weekly, and fifteen daily newssheets served the instant city of 50,000. In spite of hard times, that figure represented a high for the decade; and from 3,000 to 6,000 copies of each paper daily passed through the newsstands, bookstores, and newsboys' hands to the public. "By far" the most important reading matter in the city, the newspaper was universally acknowledged "the great instrument of power in this age and country." [76]

Again that potency was disproportionately urban and, more precisely, San Franciscan. In 1853, the Bay City claimed sixteen of thirty-eight papers in the state. (Sacramento had four.) Yet even this figure does not accurately gauge the influence of the metropolitan press, for a large portion of its output went to the "mountain and valley villages" "before sundown" of the day it appeared. Most of these places had no paper of their own and therefore got

more news of San Francisco and the world than of their own surrounding area. Just as the telephone largely broke down the need
for face to face contact within the metropolis, the urban-domi-
nated means of transportation and communication—steamboats,
"steam presses and printing telegraphs"—partially eliminated the
necessity for face to face contact between city and country; and
as the case of the Christian press showed, this in turn widened the
outreach of metropolitan influence. "When the infidel could only
speak and write, . . . Christianity could spread and triumph by
the lips and pens only of its advocates," noted the *Pacific*. "But
now religion must bring to its aid all the power and facilities of
modern influence. For Voltaire and Paine, and the English infidels,
though dead, yet speak . . . and their voice is still heard wherever the printed sheet can find a reader." [77] Christianity, therefore,
was a city export; and a sophisticated, urban press could preach in
the frontier village "to those who have no preacher."

As the producer and manager of the state's reputation, the power
of the city press extended in the other direction as well. "The opinion of the rest of the world regarding California, is chiefly derived
from the San Francisco press," wrote the *Era* in 1855. And its
"image" was disproportionately urban. As the *Era* noted, "Great
cities are the centres of political and social depravity . . . [and]
the first duty of the journalist . . . is to cure the evil nearest
home." Therefore, a muckrakers' picture of San Francisco came to
represent all of California.[78]

Mormon leader Sam Brannan founded the pioneer newspaper,
the *California Star*, in January 1847. The next year Robert Semple
moved his *Californian* up from Monterey to enjoy a more progressive atmosphere as well as proximity to his town speculation of
Benicia. Suspended when the Gold Rush cleaned out their help-
ers and patrons, they resumed jointly as the *Star and Californian*
in the fall of '48. Renamed the *Alta California* in 1849, it remained
one of the foremost journals, first as a weekly and after 1850 as the
first daily.

Until at least 1850, the *Alta* and its proliferating imitators had

many troubles. Before 1848 little news occurred in the frontier
state, and comparatively few ships stopped with any. The Gold
Rush eliminated these problems; but slow periods remained, particularly during the rainy winter months, when essays replaced
scarce news items. The steamboat greatly increased the amount of
local, national, and international news. Most items that arrived via
the Isthmus came from the "States," notably from New York and
New Orleans. After the New York telegraph reached New Orleans, the Southern port could transmit information even before
the Eastern metropolis. In addition, news reached San Francisco
from all over the world, often through regular correspondents in
other news centers. The telegraph likewise quickened the flow of
information from the interior. In the beginning, too, the technical
levels were low. Until the advent of the Hoe and Napier presses in
1850, hand presses were the rule; and before the large paper shipments, shortages frequently necessitated the use of wrapping paper and other bizarre substitutes.

The early press business was very lucrative. From 1848 until
well into 1850, the profession could not handle the demand for
papers and well-paid job work. However, high profits attracted
crippling competition, which sent several papers into oblivion.
Journals continued to proliferate, but the flush times did not last
beyond 1851.

Newssheets specialized as they multiplied. Political papers existed year round on political patronage, usually printing contracts
from the federal, state, or city governments; and presidential election years increased their numbers. Other papers represented religious, ethnic, fireman, agricultural, labor, and other interests. The
so-called independents, like the *Alta*, the *Evening Bulletin*, the
California Chronicle, and the *Herald*, were generally the best and
biggest. Independent meant not affiliated with any political party,
a description which did not always apply.

Since each sheet tried to be all things to all men, the subject
matter ranged far and wide. Foreign and American, California and
San Francisco items all figured largely. Special columns on the

city covered the police, courts, theater, entertainment, merchants, market, Protestant churches, and city government. In addition, Macaulay, Gibbon, and Genesis marched side by side with "Squibob" and other local literati, as did homilies, sermons, lectures, political speeches, editorials, letters to the editor, and all kinds of proceedings.

The experience of the newspapers reveals the usual dilemma. The press and public, in trying to define the best code of conduct, laid great stress upon liberty and the avoidance of censorship. Yet no one wanted unfettered freedom. Therefore, nearly every paper began by assuring its readers that it would avoid either extreme.[79] The boundary lay in a murky no man's land, but closer to license than to control.

In justifying this freedom, the press attempted to identify its own interests with those of the community. In fact, citizens touted newspapers almost as highly as the home, school, and church as an instrument of civic betterment and feared them more as a weapon of destruction. The press was an "index of the times," the defender of republican institutions, "conservator of public morals and directors and controller of an enlightened public sentiment," promoter of the city, and the inculcator of taste and intelligence as well as a business.[80] Newspapers were, therefore, a private institution with public functions.

The tension between these roles caused endless troubles. The *Picayune* and many others stood for "the fullest exhibition of truth or events affecting the public weel [sic] and for the frankest discussion of all topics." However, that public function could and did often run counter to the private business interests of newspapermen and sometimes to their physical welfare. Newsmen were caned, shot at, punched, and intimidated into some compromises of press freedom. Infringements took other forms as well. In 1855 the *Alta* sustained advertising losses and severe criticism for undermining business confidence when it correctly and publicly doubted the stability of Page, Bacon, and Company during its initial troubles. The *Californian* had suffered a similar advertising loss in 1847 over its political stance; and in 1856 the *Herald, Alta,* and *Chronicle* encountered Vigilante coercion. Less overt pressure came from free tickets to public entertainments and free passage for newsmen and newsboys on stages, steamers, and other public conveyances. As the frequent "puffing" indicates, these little services did not go entirely unrewarded.[81] In addition, certain sheets, while independent of parties, allied closely with particular businesses, as the *Herald* did with the powerful auctioneers. The wider public compromised the liberty of the press, too. Early in the period, editors muted their trumpets on such questions as bull- and bear-baiting, gaming, and Sabbatarianism out of fear of the public. And during the rising of 1856, the majority of citizens supported the businessmen who terrified the journalists.

The apprehensions of editors were well grounded, for while nearly everyone subscribed to freedom of expression, numerous situations seemed to demand suspension of the rule; and editors as well as ordinary people sometimes called for something approaching censorship. The *Bulletin* and *Pacific* denounced the *Chronicle* for describing the Tom Paine dinner; the *Pacific* objected to publication of Mormon communications; and the *Fireman's Journal* demanded that a customs house employee be fired for publicly insulting the fire department. In the French community, every paper that opposed Consul Dillon and his editorial ally Derbec "was usually taken care of in one way or another." "A journal cannot be honestly conducted and live, without being . . . able to . . . breast the hurricane of adversity which an independent expression of opinion continually subjects them to," complained the *Era*.[82]

Competition further exacerbated the tension between public and private imperatives. Too many journalists competing for the same clientele seems to have lowered the independence of some. Others were driven to questionable practices in order to succeed financially.[83]

The press tried to regulate itself by establishing rules of conduct. It condemned prejudicial comment on a trial pending before the courts, puffing as opposed to legitimate advertisement or praise, dealing in personalities, putting self-interest over public concern, and reporting such events as steamboat racing and dueling. The desire to serve the public interest sometimes led to a kind of censorship. For example, the *Chronicle* for a time refused communications on abolitionism and slavery; and it tried to discourage and even ignore sectarian controversy. Both public demand and private interest often got in the way of the rules, however, as the frequent discussions of duels, trials, personalities ("character killings"), and steamboat racing and the puffing indicate. Sensationalism—"blood items"—prevailed to such an extent that the *Pacific* compared the press to a cannibal in the Donner Party who "was with difficulty persuaded to turn from the human flesh [to] healthy fare." [84]

Some newsmen, like Jonas Winchester, merely clothed their own greed in an idealistic garb. When the city's journalists agreed to a day off for a holiday, Winchester scooped them with an "extra" graphically chronicling the gruesome explosion of the *Sagamore*. After the state press rate bargain, Winchester broke the pact and pushed prices down again. He also used his influence to promote Yuba City, Stockton, and the infamous Colton Grants in return for real estate bribes. Enemies could easily be taken care of. "It cannot be possible," he wrote in 1850, "that Bailey would deceive me, for I could kill him deader than Julius Caesar in the news, [*Pacific*] (*News*), *and would too*." As he summed up his journalistic philosophy to his wife, "I now see nothing to prevent me from making a half a million dollars in the next five or ten years. I have got the position and shall not fail to use it for my own advancement." Most newspapers admitted that many others were, as Winchester so admirably put it, propagating the "right views." [85]

In an embarrassingly large number of cases, James King's charges of venality, cowardice, and subservience were correct. Yet despite its shortcomings, journalism made many significant contributions. Most topics of public interest, whether political questions, public school discipline, matters of church and state, Spiritualism, unionism, firemen's rights, business chicanery, and wrongdoing all found their way into print. Moreover, press dissent was widespread and proved instrumental in defeating several unpopular schemes. In fact, as the *Era* noted in late 1855, "Newspapers devote too much space to the revelation and reproof of wickedness, when they find little or none left for the record of . . . good deeds." [86]

Excessive competition explains some of this sensationalism, but so does the press's public functions. A journal played the roles of both muckraker and booster, ironically for the same end, that is, urban promotion. This duality partly explains the seeming ambivalence of San Franciscans toward urbanization, for the concurrent need to ballyhoo and reform led to simultaneous censure and praise of their urban condition. The advent of James King in late 1855 temporarily gave the muckraker the upper hand over the booster and that in turn led to revolution.[87]

The attempt to exercise personal liberty of expression within certain broad civic guidelines forms a part of a larger topic in the city's history. The press, the school, the home, the church, and the benevolent societies were vitally concerned with the eternal effort to reconcile the rights of the individual and the community. Each had certain peculiar roles to play, but each was allotted a series of crucial urban jobs which justified its presence in San Francisco. "The theory of our institutions is that every man is competent to govern himself—," wrote the *Chronicle* in 1854.[88] Yet the urban institutions supposedly imparted the proper values before one ventured out into the individualistic strife of the big city. At the same time, several supplied a refuge from this conflict, a place where a man could forget about the latest commercial intelligence from New York or the weather report from the mines. Here also the values—originally inculcated by the home, church, and school—could be protected, sustained, and nourished. For those who could not make it, a community institution was again the recommended cure, a kind of spiritual bandaging station in the battle of life. The orphan asylums, the House of Refuge (should it ever be built), the Ladies' Relief and Protection Association, the Magdalen Home, the Mariners' Home, or the benevolent societies took in the fallen and unsuccessful for rehabilitation and another try at the individual world.

Conclusion

As the United States moves toward an ever more urbanized existence in the 1970's, the chorus of disapproval of its cities has increased proportionately. Simultaneously, there has been a growing interest in "new towns" and "instant cities" as the answer to the American "urban problem." The federal government, with its massive powers of eminent domain, and huge corporations have become involved in this field. Between fifty and one hundred such projects are already under way, and some schemes for building these communities involve tens of millions of human beings. Since San Francisco increased its population from almost 1,000 to nearly 50,000 in eight years, it, along with Chicago, must have strong claims to the title of America's first "instant city." Yet it bore a very small resemblance to the modern American communities that have claimed that name.

Its supposed modern counterparts have been neither instant nor urban, nor have they even been towns. With few exceptions, their development has been quite modest and has been linked to an already existing metropolitan area. They have been suburbs rather than cities. Moreover, these suburbs have been highly and even rigidly planned, with considerable backing. The federal government has guaranteed mortgages; and corporate giants such as Connecticut General Life Insurance, Gulf Oil, and Goodyear Tire and Rubber have been deeply involved along with lesser, but still sizable, operators. All kinds of "urban" specialists have helped plan these noncities; free inspection tours have shepherded people through them; market analyses have gauged the public demand for them; psychologists have predicted their impact upon the human personality; and such thoroughly urban names as "Leisure World," "California Rancho," and "Irvine Ranch" have been applied to them to attract the metropolitan American. Yet most have been only moderately successful, and many have a bad case of what the British call the "New City Blues."

In most respects, San Francisco was the antithesis of these modern instant cities. It was both instant and urban and detached from other metropolitan areas by thousands of miles. It was full of risk; it was unplanned; it had no large corporate backers, no studies, and no free tours. And there was a still more important difference. Anarchic, mis-sited, miserably planned, full of chaos, conflict, hope and greed, oft burnt and oft rebuilt, alternately a source of despair and extravagant expectations, San Francisco succeeded in a very short time in becoming the wonder of almost all who encountered it. And it has never stopped being just that.

Though the pace of life seems to belie the possibility, San Franciscans pondered their experience seriously, trying to think their way through their problems as they went about homemaking, entertaining, working, and worshiping. Thrown up on the shores of San Francisco Bay with little or no organization, residents sought, in a strange environment, to establish what was desirable in this new urban situation. The answers were usually not absolute nor very legalistic.[1]

People had come to the Golden Gate with heads full of general rules, yet few of these regulations were always applicable. Generally they were merely a starting point for the solution of a problem. Residents often sounded absolutist and legalistic; but more often than not, men attempted to reconcile the claims of different and contrary values. Some things, like the belief in the home, found little dissent; yet most canons had to share the ground with others. Each case had to be hammered out on its merits, depending upon the time, place, and interests—the situation—involved. San Franciscans constantly kept in mind the general welfare of the community as the ultimate end, but the means—democracy, liberty, or progress—varied. There was a constant reconciliation of things, a continuous renegotiation of the social contract. This was not necessarily a quest for a middle ground between two extremes; it was a search for proportion, a pursuit of the right amount rather than a via media.

This attempt penetrated many spheres of urban existence. In the realm of economics, the effort seemed to be the avoidance of either unrestrained competition or untrammeled monopoly. And the press which carried this argument had its own adjustment as it tried to avoid both too much and too little liberty. The pulpit, too, hoped to compromise the demands of this world and the next and to hold public favor without sacrificing Christian principles. Even the city's social reform and criminological thinking wrestled with opposites. The individual was responsible for his own behavior and theoretically granted the right to act as he pleased, but the very great importance of his surroundings in determining conduct was also recognized. Nor was local opinion about crime much more certain where punishment should leave off and rehabilitation begin. Likewise, educators sought the proper proportion of the practical and ornamental, of the physical and intellectual, of conformity and diversity; and the public schools themselves were an attempt to balance the aristocratizing tendencies of wealth by democratizing opportunity. The field of immigrant-native relations faced at least as great a dilemma. How much each nationality should maintain of its own individuality was the problem; and, as the editor of the *German Journal* put it, "The attempt to draw the line [between Americanism and foreignism] necessarily created difficulty." [2] Finally, the uprising of 1856 found the community wrestling with the claims of order versus the right of revolution.

The intellectual and emotional adjustment to urbanization presented a similar dilemma. The city was praised, but suburban attractions continued to populate the hills away from downtown. The same reconciliation of progress and primitivism emerged from the disappearance of the Gold Rush town and its predecessor. The new buildings, streets, and wharves were welcomed at the same time that the loss of old landmarks was deplored. All of this was,

in turn, part of an increasing awareness of the urban dimension—
a recognition that cities were special places where life was quite
different from that in any other form of settlement. This perception
was revealed in a series of questions which were amplifications of
the city-country debate. Did cities cause more crime, more election
frauds, more sophistication, and worse health than the country?
Did cities or small towns represent the real America? Did the cut-
throat competition of the urban press make it more servile or
sensational, or did the city press harbor more dissent than that of
the mountains? Were urban areas the natural leaders in things like
the re-establishment of public schools and churches? How many
country jobs were necessary to support a city? How big did a
place have to be before urban anonymity began to protect one
from small town-style gossip? Was the city or the country the
best place for black men to make an economic stand? Did not
cities need special kinds of ministerial talent? And did the cities
have a comparable qualitative difference in politics? The answers
were often contradictory and were never spun together into a
grandiose theory of urbanism; but the questions indicated that
mental adjustment to urbanization accompanied the building of
wharves, docks, and city halls.

The most significant dilemma was the attempt to reconcile the
rights and interests of the individual and the community. "You
must have lived long enough," wrote Samuel Ward in 1854, "to
know that there are two lines in every man's history—the Chess
game of interest and the interchange of personal regards and
social sympathies." [3] The continual convergence and divergence
of these "two lines"—"the Chess game of interest" and the "social
sympathies"—was probably the single most important thread in
the fabric of urban life in San Francisco during the years 1846
through 1856.

There is abundant evidence that the "Chess game of interest"
got most attention. A Methodist minister described the prevailing
ethic very accurately. "In all old settled communities, each member, however humble, is a link in a chain of association, which

runs through the whole community," wrote William Taylor. "Cut one link, and it affects the whole chain. But here the links are nearly all separated, and where there is a connection it is generally by *open* links, which can be slipped at pleasure." [4] German immigrant Frank Lecouvreur was even more forceful.

> In California one does not as a rule become intimate with anybody. You combine with others, whenever you find that to do so is in your interest, and that it enables you to accomplish a certain purpose. The moment this is accomplished, perhaps without saying as much as "good bye," you follow your own way and pay no more attention to the other fellow than you would to an old tool, which you have thrown aside, not having any further use for it.[5]

However, the other "line" was not entirely neglected. It played a considerable part in what people said and a lesser but still visible role in what they did. Men did owe some allegiance to society beyond self-interest, and the sense of community gradually increased. Yet this growth was a slow and painful process and, on the whole, was undertaken with great reluctance and considerable compulsion. It is hardly fair to call this evolution a "search for community." That phrase makes the event sound voluntary and conscious. In San Francisco, the development of civic spirit and the notion of mutual obligations between men was not a quest; it was a "forced march."

Paradoxically, despite the prevalent individualism and regardless of the fact that people within the metropolis were very reluctant to act as a community, there was a strong tendency to feel like one, to talk of it even though it did not exist, and to judge things by its standards. As far as ideology is concerned, there was actually much more stress upon the community than upon the individual; and there certainly was not the same glorification of the latter that existed in post-Civil War America. Moreover, each institution, each group, and each practice in the city justified itself in terms of its value to the generality and was identified by its function within it. Everything, from the length of women's skirts to the function of the home, church, school, club, and gaming hall, was evaluated in terms of the community. This ideology appears strange, for if there was ever a city of nonaltruistic individuals—of men whose sympathy and regard for each other was scant—it was San Francisco during the Gold Rush. Part of this paradox can be explained by cynicism and hypocrisy, which led the self-interested to speak of society's welfare in order to benefit themselves. Yet there seems little doubt that most believed the rhetoric. If they did not, there would have been little point or advantage in repeating it over and over and clothing their self-interests in it. The freedom-loving social atoms went their own ways; yet in doing so, they had to feel, and to convince others, that their individual actions somehow or other coincided with the purposes and best interests of the community. They were a horde of individuals parading in a communitarian guise, but that guise seemed just as important as the individualism that belied it.

They were also very much under the influence of the outside world. To a considerable extent, San Francisco was an urban colonial outpost which imported and planted the cultural forms of older, more settled areas. Its businesses were anchored in the East; its capital market depended upon Boston, New York, and London; its schools were patterned after Boston and New York; its fire companies, after half a dozen cities; and its architecture, after half a hundred. Its clothing styles hailed from Paris; its theater was fed by the "States"; its charters drew upon the experience of older cities; its water system was inspired by the Croton Water Works; its efforts to build parks were influenced by Central Park; its clothing outlets were called "New York Stores"; its big-name preachers were drawn from abroad; its customs were imported; and its theaters acquired names like the "Dramatic Museum" and the "Jenny Lind."

A smoldering, anticolonial resentment of this dependent status existed throughout the period. It came to the surface in barbed remarks about the "tyranny" of Eastern fashions and the domi-

CONCLUSION 347

nance of outside literary tastes, in complaints about the outflow
of specie, in the denunciation of carpetbagging politicians and
businessmen, and in the strictures against transient actors who
came to exploit the resources of the city and carried away their
riches to the "States." Yet in every sphere the dependence upon
the outside world was being eroded by the development of local
experience and traditions. The reappearance of older customs was
a continuing theme in San Francisco's history, but that only went
so far. A local culture was developing; even as it imported some
of the old ways, it discarded many others.

While the city struggled against the Eastern yoke, it was imposing its own dominance on a vast hinterland; for San Francisco
was a main link in a chain of urban sequential colonialism that
stretched the length and breadth of California. As Hubert Howe
Bancroft put it, "To Greeks, Delphi was the centre of the earth;
to Jews and Christians, Jerusalem; to Californians, San Francisco." [6]

To exaggerate the importance of the Bay City in the Eureka
State would be unfortunate, but it would also be difficult to do.
Not every farmer, miner, or trapper in the state danced to the
metropolis's tune; but it influenced, directed, and dominated California to an extraordinary degree. Though only 14 per cent of the
population, San Francisco had a pre-eminence very disproportionate to its numbers. Richard Hofstadter has written that America
was born in the countryside and moved to town. That is correct,
but misleading in the case of the Golden State. What happened,
in addition, was that the characteristic institutions of modern California were born in or transplanted to the town and nurtured by
city people; the ruralites either appropriated these institutions or
moved to town to occupy, enjoy, or fight against them.

It was from the metropolis that party organization proceeded
and party realignment progressed. The dominant political factions
made the city their headquarters and base of power. Moreover,
California "politics of the period [1849–60] were centered in, and
for the most part were expressed through, the rivalry for leader-

ship and control between . . . [San Franciscans] William Mc-
Kendree Gwin and David C. Broderick." [7] In education, the city's
weight was equally out of proportion, for it claimed about half
the public education pupils in California. The first public school
was set up there, and what became the University of California was
established in the metropolis's hinterland. Oakland's Henry Durant
was its first principal, but Samuel H. Willey and other San Franciscans played a significant and perhaps crucial role in the movement
from 1849 on.[8] Certainly in the religious, entertainment, journalistic, and intellectual life of the state, the city claimed more than its
share. In the words of Josiah Royce, "Here from the first was the
centre of the State's mental life." [9] The history of the Gold Rush
theater is largely the history of San Francisco; the state's first
literary journals grew up there; nearly half its newspapers spoke
from there, beaming their influence to areas with no press of their
own; and the best preachers thundered from its pulpits. In addition, the state historical society was founded there; California's
first scientific association commenced there; the pioneer society
began there and in the fifties half its members were San Franciscans. Here also "soonest of all places in the growing parts of the
country, there were to be found numerous families; and where the
most justly influential men were not wanderers only, but often
merchants of high character, of conservative aims, and of extraordinary ability." [10] When these men undertook to restore order
in 1851, the impact was much like that of the panic of 1855. San
Francisco led and the rest of the state followed, as the waves of
vigilantism spread from the bay to the mountains.[11] The 1856 Committee showed leadership of another kind, for "this formal vigilance
organization was not to be compared with the rash, vindictive,
mob-like risings which had so often disgraced the mining region." [12]

In the economic realm, the city's pre-eminence was even more
apparent. The instruments of commercial dominance for the entire
state were usually headquartered there. The major banks, the express companies, the foremost money market, the transportation
facilities, both rail and water, the main manufacturing interests,

the Chinese Six Companies, which supplied labor all over the state, the telegraph, the biggest importers and exporters, and the Mint all resided in San Francisco and projected their influence from that spot throughout the entire economy. When California labor unions began the long and painful process of eroding the businessman's dominance, they began that effort on the shores of the bay. And the first steps toward the modernization of California agriculture were taken by San Franciscans rather than farmers. In short, the city played much the same role that its counterparts on the Atlantic seaboard and in the Ohio-Mississippi valleys did in the eighteenth and nineteenth centuries respectively.[13] The metropolis served as the entrepôt of civilization where its institutions and customs were transplanted. Arthur M. Schlesinger, Sr., has written of the period 1878–98 that "underlying all the varied developments that made American life was the momentous shift of the center of national equilibrium from the countryside to the city." [14] In most respects, this was already true in California.

Notes

INTRODUCTION

1. Letter of John B. Montgomery to William A. Leidesdorff, Yerba Buena, July 8, 1846, in William A. Leidesdorff Papers (Huntington Library, San Marino, Cal.).
2. Lt. Henry Wise, *Los Gringos, or An Inside View of Mexico and California* . . . (New York: Baker and Scribner, 1850), pp. 73–75.
3. *Ibid.*, p. 70.
4. Ernest DeMassey, *A Frenchman in the Gold Rush: The Journal of Ernest DeMassey, Argonaut of 1849*, trans. Marguerite Eyer Wilbur (San Francisco: California Historical Society, 1927), p. 12.
5. Richard Van Orman, "The First Ten Years," a paper delivered to the Western Historical Association Convention, Oct. 1970, p. 11.
6. Patrice Dillon, quoted in A. P. Nasatir, *French Activities in California* (Stanford, Cal.: Stanford University Press, 1945), p. 544.
7. Letter of Etienne Derbec to Sir, San Francisco, Dec. 1, 1850, in *A French Journalist in the California Gold Rush: The Letters of Etienne Derbec*, ed. A. P. Nasatir (Georgetown, Cal.: The Talisman Press, 1964), pp. 163–64.
8. *Golden Era*, Aug. 26, 1855; Nov. 30, 1856.
9. Horace Bushnell, *Characteristics and Prospects of California* (San Francisco: Whitton, Towne and Company's Steam Presses, 1858), p. 29.
10. Ida Pfeiffer, *A Lady's Visit to California, 1853* (Oakland, Cal.: Biobooks, 1950), p. 11.
11. See Daniel Boorstin, *The Image* (New York: Atheneum, 1962), pp. 45–77, for the distinction between hero and celebrity.

CHAPTER I

1. For a description of the Panama crossing, see John Haskell Kemble, *The Panama Route, 1849–1869* (Berkeley and Los Angeles: University of California Press, 1943), xxix, pp. 1–95.
2. Levi Stowell, "Bound for the Land of Caanan, Ho! The Diary of Levi Stowell," ed. Marco G. Thorne, *California Historical Society Quarterly*, XXVII, No. 1 (Mar. 1941), 45.
3. John Dwinelle, "Diary. From Panama to San Francisco in 1849," ed. W. F. Chipman, *Quarterly of the Society of California Pioneers*, VIII, No. 3 (Sept. 1931), 174.
4. Journal of Henry L. Abbott, entry for May 30, 1855, in Henry L. Abbott Collection (Oregon Historical Society); Zoeth S. Eldredge, *The Beginnings of San Francisco . . . 1774–1850*, II (San Francisco: 1912), 504, 612–14.
5. Peter Thomas Conmy, *The Beginnings of Oakland, California* (Oakland, Cal.: Oakland Public Library, 1961), pp. 7–9.
6. Hubert Howe Bancroft, *The History of California*, IV (San Francisco: The History Company Publishers, 1888), 664.
7. Frank Soulé, John H. Gihon, and James Nisbet, *The Annals of San Francisco* (New York: D. Appleton and Company, 1855), p. 163.
8. William T. Sherman, *Memoirs of William T. Sherman*, ed. Rachel and Sherman Thorndike (1894 ed.; New York: Scribner's, 1894), pp. 83–84. Sherman, whose memoirs are often criticized for faulty memory, nevertheless was exactly right in this matter.
9. Quoted in Lawrence Kinnaird, *History of the Greater San Francisco Bay Region*, I (New York: Lewis Historical Publishing Company, 1966), 413.
10. Jane Jacobs, *The Economy of Cities* (New York: Random House, 1969), pp. 32–34.
11. J. Wieland, Biographical Sketch, Bancroft Library Mss; *The Alta California*, Dec. 21, 1853. Cited hereafter as *Alta*.
12. *Golden Era*, Dec. 18, 1853; Jan. 8, 1854. Cited hereafter as *Era*.
13. *Alta*, Nov. 13, 1855; *California Chronicle*, Nov. 13, 1855. Cited hereafter as *Chronicle*.
14. Market Street exemplifies this point. It may have made good sense in 1847 to point that future artery toward the Mission Dolores instead of working it into the street plat already in existence. Rapid growth, however, quickly brought the settled area down that far and the inability to cross straight over from the north to the south part of town because of the Market Street "angle" produced for the future a traffic nightmare.
15. Rev. Albert Williams, *A Pioneer Pastorate and Times* (San Francisco: Bacon and Company Printers, 1882), p. 61.
16. *Alta*, Sept. 9, 1851.
17. See United States Coast Survey maps for 1853 and 1857 (Bancroft Library, University of California).

18. These and other conclusions about land use have been largely drawn from residential and economic maps made by the author and based upon the various city directories: Charles P. Kimball (comp.), *San Francisco Directory for 1850* (San Francisco: Charles P. Kimball, 1850); J. M. Parker (comp.), *San Francisco Directory for 1852* (San Francisco: J. M. Parker, 1852); S. Colville (comp.), *San Francisco Directory for 1856* (San Francisco: S. Colville, 1856); Henry G. Langley (comp.), *San Francisco Directory for 1857–58* (San Francisco: H. G. Langley, 1857–58).

19. Letter of Albert Dibblee to John N. Hicks, San Francisco, Apr. 16, 1853, pp. 1–2, in Albert Dibblee Correspondence and Papers (Bancroft Library, University of California); *Picayune*, Nov. 1, 1851; *San Francisco Daily Herald*, Sept. 25, 1853. Cited hereafter as *Herald*.

20. *Picayune*, Sept. 24, 1851.

21. *Ibid.*, Dec. 14, 1850; Oct. 15, 1851.

22. *Ibid.*, Aug. 7, 1850.

23. *Daily California Courier*, July 20, 1850. Cited hereafter as *Courier*. Theodore A. Barry and B. W. Patten, *Men and Memories of San Francisco in the Spring of '50* (San Francisco, 1876), p. 25; *Picayune*, Aug. 23, 1851; *Herald*, Oct. 28, 1853; *Chronicle*, May 10, 1856.

24. *Herald*, Oct. 28, 1853. Other wharves had their own specific functions also. Pacific Street Wharf was the terminus of the river steamers which would take the goods away from the city to the interior; Jackson Street Wharf was the host for the Nicaragua steamers; and Vallejo Street Wharf performed the same function for the Pacific Mail steamers. *Chronicle*, May 10, 1856.

25. *Picayune*, Sept. 8, 1851.

26. Letter of David Fay to his brother, San Francisco, Mar. 31, 1853, p. 2, and Logan Fay to Patrick Fay, San Francisco, May 16, 1853, p. 1, in Fay Collection (California State Library at Sacramento); *Chronicle*, Apr. 25, 1856.

27. Alfred L. Tubbs, *Recollections of Events in California* (Bancroft Library Mss.)

28. These conclusions are also based on random and other samples of the various city directories as well as on maps based upon them and upon land use maps made in 1853, 1857, and 1869 by the United States Coast Survey, plus verbal comments of contemporaries; Barry and Patten, *Men and Memories . . .* , p. 94.

29. My definition of class is rather a catalog of the groups which would have been considered in one group or another rather than a list of supposed characteristics of a social stratum. For the most part, I have tried to let the contemporaries of the Gold Rush do their own defining; I merely list the results. Artisans, laborers, sailors, longshoremen, etc., were considered working class; merchants, clerks, lawyers, middle.

30. These estimates are based upon a 10 per cent sample of the 1857–58 city directory compiled by Langley.

31. An 1867–68 demographic map revealed about the same configuration as the 1857–58 one. In some places the middle class was on the periphery and in some places the working class was, but nowhere was a ring and core pattern very clear. The transportation facilities definitely affected the city but seem to have had their largest impact on the working-class district south of Market, which was stretched far to the west of the car lines. The map was based on a 3 per cent sampling of Langley's *Directory* for 1867–68. For 1857–58, the presence of the Chinese neighborhood at Dupont and Sacramento further skews the pattern, but it is hard to tell how much, since they were hardly represented in the *Directory*. Possibly the four square blocks bounded by Dupont, Montgomery, Clay, and California would have been working class if the Chinese were included. The year 1857–58 map was based on a 10 per cent sampling of Langley's *Directory* for that year.

32. *Daily Morning Call*, Dec. 5, 1856. Cited hereafter as *Call;* William Redmond Ryan, *Personal Adventures in Upper and Lower California, 1848–49* . . . (London: William Shoberl Publishers, 1851), pp. 271–75.

33. See U.S. Coast Survey maps for 1853 and 1857 (Bancroft Library, University of California); *Annals,* p. 298.

34. See Bache map for 1857, Bancroft Library, University of California.

35. Roy S. Cameron, *History of Public Transit in San Francisco, 1850–1948* (mimeo copy, San Francisco: San Francisco Transportation and Technical Commission, 1948), pp. 1–2; Barry and Patten, *Men and Memories* . . . , p. 26; *Pacific,* Oct. 21, 1853; Sept. 16, 1853. There was no correlation between class and the plank roads south of Market either. For a view which stresses the role of the omnibus in promoting differentiation of land uses, see Charles N. Glaab and A. Theodore Brown, *A History of Urban America* (New York: The Macmillan Co., 1967), p. 147.

36. *Annals,* p. 452; Benjamin Franklin Butler Papers (California Historical Society); *Chronicle,* Apr. 25, 1856.

37. *Alta,* June 9, 1852; *Annals,* p. 254. The complaints thereafter in the press about exorbitant rents were quite frequent.

38. *Alta,* June 9, 1852.

39. *Ibid.,* Aug. 29, 1852; *Chronicle,* Oct. 23, 1854; Letter of George Howard to Agnes Howard, San Francisco, July 14, 1855, Feb. 11, 1855, Feb. 25, 1855, in W. D. M. Howard Papers (California Historical Society); see also *Alta,* Feb. 23, 1853; July 1, 1856.

40. *Chronicle,* Apr. 10, 1854; Letter of William K. Weston to his aunt, San Francisco, Mar. 30, 1851, in William K. Weston Papers (California Historical Society).

41. Glaab and Brown, *History of Urban America,* p. 154; *Alta,* June 9, 1852; Feb. 5, 1855; Aug. 28, 1856; *Picayune,* Nov. 8, 1851; *Pacific,* Jan. 19, 1853.

42. *Era,* Apr. 24, 1853; Sept. 4, 1853; Sept. 12, 1854; Apr. 3, 1853; *Pacific,* June 30, 1854.

43. The ropewalk, powder magazine, and brick makers also were situated to take advantage of transportation gains by water. See U.S. Coast Survey map for 1857.

44. See, for example, the 1857 U.S. Coast Survey map for the impact of the plank roads to the Mission, the Brannan Street plank road and bridge, and the road to the Presidio.

45. Roger Lane, *Policing Boston* (Cambridge, Mass.: Harvard University Press, 1967), p. 14; Adna F. Weber, *The Growth of Cities in the Nineteenth Century* (Ithaca, N.Y.: Cornell University Press, 1965), p. 21; Ida Pfeiffer, *A Lady's Visit to California, 1853,* p. 11.

CHAPTER II

1. *Alta,* Aug. 10, 1852. See chapter on economics.

2. Wise, *Los Gringos.* . . , pp. 126–27.

3. *California Star,* Jan. 30, 1847; see also Bancroft, *History of California,* V, 671–74; *Annals,* pp. 178–79, 188; Letter of William H. Davis to Capt. Spaulding, San Francisco, Nov. 17, 1846, in William Heath Davis Letterbook (Bancroft Library, University of California); the city's most recent history, Oscar Lewis, *San Francisco: Mission to Metropolis* (Berkeley, California: Howell-North Books, 1966), pp. 41–43, is among those which give the traditional date. John Young, *San Francisco: A History of the Pacific Coast Metropolis* (San Francisco and Chicago, 1912), I, 119.

4. *Alta,* Oct. 25, 1850; see also *Alta,* July 27, 1850; Sept. 3, 1850.

5. San Francisco, of course, had its own version of the doctrine, as several of the foregoing quotes indicate. See Glaab and Brown, *A History of Urban America,* p. 72.

6. "Extracts from the Diary of James C. Ward," printed in *The Argonaut,* 96:2516, 3. Entry for July 22, 1848; *Californian,* June 18, 1847; Letter of R. B. Semple to Larkin, Benicia, July 29, 1848, in *The Larkin Papers,* ed. George B. Hammond (9 vols.; Berkeley and Los Angeles; University of California Press, 1960), VII, 326; Letter of Charles F. Winslow to a friend, San Francisco, June 19, 1849, and same to Chas. G. and H. Coffin, San Francisco, June 3, 1849, in Charles F. Winslow Letterbook (California Historical Society).

7. Larkin to Semple, Monterey, Sept. 14, 1847, *The Larkin Papers,* VI, 339.

8. *Alta,* July 2, 1849; quoted in Rev. Samuel C. Damon, *A Journey to Lower Oregon and Upper California, 1848–49* (San Francisco: John C. Newbegin, 1927), p. 56; Bancroft, *History of California,* VI, 473.

9. Eleutheros Cooke to Larkin, Washington, Aug. 6, 1850, *The Larkin Papers,* VIII, 333; see also Kinnard, *History of the Greater San Francisco Bay Region,* II, 413.

10. Semple to Larkin, Benicia, July 29, 1848, *The Larkin Papers,* VII, 326.

11. Eleutheros Cooke to Larkin, Washington, Aug. 6, 1850, *The Larkin Papers,* VIII, 340.

12. Wm. Steuart to Larkin, Aug. 25, 1850, *The Larkin Papers,* VIII, 340;

Same to same, Georgetown, Delaware, Aug. 5, 1850, *The Larkin Papers*, VIII, p. 330; *Alta*, Oct. 25, 1850; Nov. 9, 1850; Nov. 11, 1850; *Picayune*, Oct. 25, 1850; Nov. 7, 1850.

13. Bancroft, *History of California*, VI, 472–75; Peter Thomas Conmy, *Benicia, Intended Metropolis* (San Francisco: Grand Parlor Native Sons of the Golden West, 1958), p. 12.

14. *Chronicle*, Mar. 7, 1856.

15. *Ibid.*, Mar. 2, 1856; Mar. 18, 1856; Mar. 12, 1856.

16. *Alta*, Nov. 19, 1854; Apr. 22, 1856; Apr. 23, 1856; Apr. 30, 1856; *Chronicle*, Dec. 6, 1854; Mar. 31, 1856; Apr. 16, 1856; Apr. 18, 1856.

17. *Alta*, Sept. 10, 1850. Wm. J. Eames to Larkin, San Francisco, Feb. 15, 1853, *The Larkin Papers*, IX, pp. 223–24.

18. Conmy, *Benicia, Intended Metropolis*, pp. 12–13; *Alta*, Oct. 7, 1850; Dec. 29, 1850; Feb. 5, 1853; Sept. 18, 1854; *Courier*, Dec. 28, 1850; *Picayune*, Dec. 27, 1850; *Herald*, Mar. 12, 1852; Jan. 16, 1853; *Chronicle*, Sept. 26, 1854; Sept. 29, 1854.

19. *Alta*, Oct. 7, 1850; Dec. 29, 1850; Feb. 5, 1853; Sept. 18, 1854; *Courier*, Dec. 28, 1850; *Picayune*, Dec. 27, 1850; Oct. 13, 1851; *Herald*, Mar. 12, 1852; Jan. 16, 1853; *Chronicle*, Sept. 26, 1854; Sept. 29, 1854.

20. *Picayune*, Oct. 13, 1851.

21. T. Butler King to Secretary of the Treasury Corwin, San Francisco, April 30, 1851, in U.S. National Archives Correspondence . . . (microfilm in Bancroft Library, University of California).

22. William S. Clark, Biographical Sketch in *Chronicles of the Builders*, comp., Edwin Fowler, Bancroft Library Mss, pp. 20–30.

23. *Alta*, Dec. 14, 1856.

24. *Ibid.*, Feb. 5, 1851.

25. San Francisco, *Manual of the Corporation*, 1853–54, pp. 31–33, 82–83, 115–16; *Alta*, Dec. 29, 1853; Feb. 4, 1854; *Chronicle*, Jan. 7, 1854.

26. *Alta*, Apr. 19, 1855; *Chronicle*, July 21, 1854; San Francisco, *Manual of the Corporation*, 1853–54, pp. 366–70, passed September 4, 1854.

27. Letter of Aert Van Nostrand to Rodman Price, San Francisco, May 14, 1850, pp. 1–2, and July 2, 1850, pp. 1–2, in Rodman Price Correspondence and Papers (Bancroft Library, University of California).

28. Albert Dibblee to Chas. W. Crosby, San Francisco, Mar. 8, 1855, p. 5, in Albert Dibblee Correspondence and Papers.

CHAPTER III

1. Robert Greenhalgh Albion, *The Rise of New York Port* (New York: Scribner's, 1936), pp. 392–93, appendix on p. 392.

2. Letter of William Heath Davis to Charles W. Flugge, San Francisco, Mar. 18, 1847; Davis to Starkey, Jannion and Company, San Francisco, Oct. 27, 1847, in William Heath Davis Letterbook. See also pp. 1–9 of the same source; and *California Star*, May 1, 1847; Aug. 21, 1847; Sept.

19, 1847; Sept. 25, 1847; Oct. 22, 1847; Oct. 9, 1847; Oct. 13, 1847; Nov. 20, 1847; Dec. 11, 1847; Feb. 5, 1848; Feb. 26, 1848.

3. *Alta*, Nov. 15, 1855.

4. John Walton Caughey, *California* (2d ed.; Englewood Cliffs, Prentice-Hall, 1953), p. 257; Andrew F. Rolle, *California: A History*, based in part on *A Short History of California*, 1929, by Rockwell D. Hunt and Nellie Van De Grift Sanchez (New York: Thomas Y. Crowell Company, 1963), p. 225; *Chronicle*, Jan. 1, 1856.

5. *Chronicle*, Jan. 1, 1856.

6. *Ibid.*, Sept. 9, 1854; *Alta*, July 23, 1850; letter of John McCrackan to Family, San Francisco, June 21, 1854, pp. 4–7, in John McCrackan Letters (Bancroft Library, University of California).

7. *Alta*, Oct. 21, 1853; *Chronicle*, Oct. 3, 1854.

8. *Chronicle*, Oct. 3, 1854; Jan. 1, 1856.

9. *Alta*, May 12, 1854; June 2, 1854; July 7, 1854; Sept. 23, 1854; Mar. 15, 1855; *Chronicle*, June 8, 1855; Mar. 14, 1856.

10. Davis to R. M. Sherman, Monterey, Jan. 19, 1846; Sherman to E. and H. Grimes, San Francisco, Jan. 18, 1847; Davis to Grimes, Feb. 28, 1847; Davis to Fitch, San Francisco, July 27, 1846, and Oct. 25, 1846, pp. 11, 25, in William Heath Davis Letterbook; Mr. Thompson to Henry F. Teschemacher, San Francisco, Sept. 18, 1847, in W. D. M. Howard Papers; see also R. M. Sherman to E. and H. Grimes, Yerba Buena, Jan. 18, 1847, pp. 61–62, in William Heath Davis Letterbook.

11. Ira B. Cross, *A History of the Labor Movement in California* (Berkeley, Cal.: University of California Press, 1935), p. 26.

12. *Ibid.*, pp. 19–20. Cross saw only the scarcity as a cause of bad times. However, the reverse was also true. See Goddefroy and Sillem to Ward and Price, June 30, 1850, in Rodman Price Correspondence and Papers. See also Eldredge, *The Beginnings* . . . , II, p. 610; *Alta*, May 8, 1850.

13. Jacques Antoine Moerenhout, *The Inside Story of the Gold Rush*, A. P. Nasatir, ed. (San Francisco: California Historical Society, 1935, Special Publication #8), p. 60.

14. *Era*, July 30, 1854.

15. Letter of Alexander Grogan to Faxon D. Atherton, Aug. 31, 1849, in Faxon D. Atherton Papers (California Historical Society); *Alta*, Feb. 1, 1849; Dec. 4, 1852; Nov. 1, 1854; Aug. 14, 1855; Nov. 14, 1855; Feb. 1, 1852; Jan. 8, 1854; Jan. 2, 1856; *Courier*, Mar. 15, 1851.

16. Albert Dibblee to Harbeck and Company, San Francisco, Dec. 15, 1852, p. 3; Dibblee to Harbeck and Company, San Francisco, Apr. 22, 1853, p. 1, in Albert Dibblee Correspondence and Papers; Goddefroy and Sillem to Ward and Price, San Francisco, Jan. 21, 1850, p. 2, in Rodman Price Correspondence and Papers; Moerenhout, *Inside Story* . . . , pp. 45–46; letter of Wm. T. Coleman to Wm. Barnhart Co., San Francisco, Sept. 30, 1853, p. 1, in William Barnhart Collection (Oregon Historical Society).

17. *Alta*, Oct. 9, 1855.

18. *Ibid.*, Mar. 5, 1856.

19. *Ibid.*, Aug. 6, 1855.

20. *The Christian Advocate*, July 1852, quoted in Ira Cross, *Financing an Empire* (Chicago: S. J. Clarke Publishing Co., 1927), p. 153.

21. *Alta*, Aug. 15, 1853; July 20, 1854.

22. *Ibid.*, Sept. 20, 1856.

23. *California Star*, Apr. 8, 1848; *Chronicle*, Jan. 1, 1856; Benjamin C. Wright, *San Francisco's Ocean Trade Past and Future* (San Francisco: A. Carlisle and Co., 1911), appendix.

24. *Alta*, Jan. 10, 1853; letter of J. K. Osgood to George Strang, June 10, 1850, in J. K. Osgood Letters (Bancroft Library, University of California); Dibblee to Crosby, Dec. 4, 1855, p. 9, in Albert Dibblee Correspondence and Papers.

25. William T. Coleman, Statement, p. 46 (Bancroft Library, University of California). A ship manifest was an inventory of the cargo it carried.

26. William H. Davis to R. M. Sherman, Monterey, Dec. 11, 1846; see also Davis to David Carter, San Francisco, Dec. 6, 1848, in William Heath Davis Letterbook; *Chronicle*, Feb. 7, 1856; Feb. 22, 1856.

27. *Alta*, Apr. 1, 1854; Jan. 5, 1855; Apr. 9, 1855; *Chronicle*, Dec. 18, 1855; Jan. 1, 1856.

28. *Chronicle*, Mar. 18, 1856; *Pacific*, Nov. 20, 1856; *Annals*, p. 200; Albert Dibblee to Crosby, San Francisco, Dec. 18, 1855, in Albert Dibblee Correspondence and Papers.

29. *Alta*, Oct. 31, 1853; *Era*, July 30, 1854; Cross, *Financing an Empire*, p. 171; Albert Dibblee to Crosby, San Francisco, Feb. 4, 1856, in Albert Dibblee Correspondence and Papers (italics his); Albert Dibblee to Harbeck and Co., San Francisco, May 17, 1853, in Albert Dibblee Correspondence and Papers; see also McGowan, "San Francisco-Sacramento Shipping" (unpublished dissertation, Dept. of History, University of California), p. 127.

30. "Prices Current," quoted in *Chronicle*, Feb. 5, 1856; *Chronicle*, Feb. 7, 1856.

31. Editorial by James King of William in *Evening Bulletin*, Dec. 29, 1855. Cited hereafter as *Bulletin*; Cross, *Financing an Empire*, p. 165.

32. Editorial by James King of William in *Bulletin*, Dec. 29, 1855.

33. *Era*, June 5, 1853.

34. *Ibid.*, Nov. 11, 1855.

35. Rev. T. D. Hunt, Diary, IV, pp. 170–71 (Bancroft Library, University of California); Cross, *Financing an Empire*, p. 184.

36. *Alta*, Oct. 2, 1855.

37. *Chronicle*, Aug. 28, 1854.

38. *Ibid.*, Aug. 8, 1854.

39. *Annals*, p. 500.

40. Davis to Capt. H. D. Fitch, San Francisco, Oct. 25, 1846, in William

Heath Davis Letterbook; Larkin to Moses Yale Beach or James Gorden Bennett, California, Aug. 4, 1847, in *The Larkin Papers*, VI, p. 256; Larkin and wife to Charles L. Ross, Dec. 1, 1849, in *The Larkin Papers*, VIII, pp. 262–65.

41. *Alta*, Oct. 9, 1855; Apr. 16, 1856; *Herald*, Nov. 13, 1853; McCrackan to his sister Mary, San Francisco, Feb. 14, 1853, p. 1, in John McCrackan Letters, II; John W. Geary, Account Book, in John Geary Papers (California Historical Society). Geary was mayor of San Francisco at this time. See also miscellaneous records of tax sales, John Coffee Hays Papers (California Historical Society).

42. Letter of William S. Jewett, Oct. 28, 1850, William S. Jewett, "Some Letters . . . ," ed. Elliott Evans, *California Historical Society Quarterly*, XXIII (June 1944), 161.

43. Edwin W. Fowler, Mss Biography of William S. Clark in H. H. Bancroft, *Chronicles of the Kings* series, pp. 37–38, in William S. Clark Papers (Bancroft Library, University of California); *Alta*, Apr. 17, 1855; June 20, 1850.

44. Alfred Lovering Tubbs, *Recollections of Events in California*, Bancroft Mss; *Alta*, Nov. 14, 1855; William Lent to Faxon D. Atherton, San Francisco, Jan. 26, 1855, in Faxon D. Atherton Papers.

45. Alexander Grogan to Faxon D. Atherton, San Francisco, July 30, 1853; William Lent to Atherton, San Francisco, Jan. 26, 1855, in Faxon D. Atherton Papers.

46. *Herald*, Nov. 13, 1853; Edwin W. Fowler, pp. 20–30; see also Alexander Grogan to Faxon D. Atherton, Nov. 5, 1856, in Faxon D. Atherton Papers; John McCrackan to his family, San Francisco, Jan. 31, 1851, p. 3, in John McCrackan Letters, I; Aert Van Nostrand to Rodman Price, San Francisco, June 18, 1851, p. 4, in Rodman Price Correspondence and Papers; Charles F. Winslow to Charles G. and H. Coffin, San Francisco, June 3, 1849, in Charles F. Winslow Letterbook.

47. *Alta*, Dec. 2, 1855; Robert G. Cleland, *March of Industry* (Los Angeles and San Francisco: Powell Publishing Co., 1929), pp. 133–34; *Chronicle*, Dec. 9, 1856; letter of Stott to Freeman Wilcox, San Francisco, May 17, 1852, in Stott and Company Letterbook (Bancroft Library, University of California).

48. Joseph G. Eastland, Mss Statement, p. 6 (Bancroft Library, University of California); Mss Biographical Sketch of Peter Donohue, p. 10, and Mss Biographical Sketch of James Donohue, pp. 1–10 (Bancroft Library, University of California).

49. *Herald*, June 9, 1853; Sept. 23, 1853; Bancroft, *History of California*, VI, 782–83, note 62; *Alta*, Aug. 14, 1850; Feb. 1, 1852.

50. *Alta*, Dec. 27, 1850; Aug. 6, 1851; May 4, 1852; Apr. 25, 1853; Oct. 7, 1854; *Chronicle*, Apr. 15, 1854; McGowan, "San Francisco-Sacramento Shipping," p. 85.

51. *Alta*, Oct. 9, 1852; Dec. 8, 1856; *Courier*, Oct. 8, 1851; Mar. 14, 1851;

Nov. 20, 1855; *Chronicle*, Dec. 12, 1854; Dec. 16, 1854; May 15, 1855; Bancroft, *History of California*, VI, 782–83, note 62.

52. *Alta*, Mar. 26, 1854; Nov. 3, 1854; Oct. 28, 1855; Oct. 31, 1855; Dec. 2, 1855; Jan. 30, 1856; June 18, 1856; Sept. 23, 1856.

53. *Herald*, Aug. 16, 1851; Feb. 9, 1853; Feb. 18, 1853; Bancroft, *History of California*, VI, pp. 782–83, note 62.

54. *Chronicle*, Apr. 10, 1854; Jan. 9, 1855; May 15, 1855; *Courier*, July 9, 1854; *Alta*, Jan. 9, 1854.

55. McGowan, "San Francisco-Sacramento Shipping," pp. 25 and 97; *Alta*, Mar. 1, 1849; Feb. 14, 1855; John O. Earll, Mss Statement, p. 3 (Bancroft Library, University of California); *Herald*, Sept. 4, 1850.

56. Rockwell D. Hunt, *California Firsts* (San Francisco: Fearon Publishers, 1957), pp. 39–40; Albion, *Rise of New York Port*, pp. 357–64.

57. *Alta*, Jan. 28, 1855.

58. *Ibid.*

59. Lewis Mumford, *The Highway and the City* (New York: Harcourt, Brace & World, 1953), pp. 234–46.

60. *Era*, July 6, 1856.

61. *Chronicle*, Jan. 1, 1855. This figure includes handcarts, wagons, drays, and carts.

62. Davis to E. and H. Grimes, Monterey, Feb. 28, 1847, pp. 55–58, in William Heath Davis Letterbook.

63. *Chronicle*, Nov. 9, 1855; Jan. 18, 1856; Nov. 13, 1856; Dec. 11, 1856; *Alta*, Dec. 23, 1850; Nov. 12, 1852; May 29, 1853; Oct. 19, 1853; Aug. 10, 1853; Mar. 21, 1854; Mar. 3, 1854; Feb. 9, 1854; Nov. 3, 1854; July 30, 1854; June 8, 1854; July 20, 1855; Aug. 23, 1855; *Herald*, Oct. 1, 1852.

64. William K. Weston to his father, San Francisco, Apr. 17, 1852, in William K. Weston Papers. This was written some months after he and his associates had lost their deposits in the failure of Wells and Company, a local bank.

65. *Chronicle*, July 21, 1854; *Herald*, Sept. 22, 1852; July 12, 1852. In regard to overcrowding, see also the *Herald*, May 21, 1852; Milton S. Latham, Collector of the Port, to James Guthrie, Secretary of the Treasury, San Francisco, May 3, 1856, pp. 1–3, and Hart Fellows, Surveyor of the Port, to Collector T. Butler King, San Francisco, Apr. 14, 1852, pp. 1–7, in U.S. National Archives Correspondence . . . ; *Alta*, May 4, 1851; July 15, 1852; Oct. 14, 1852; Mar. 15, 1853; Rev. William Taylor, *Seven Years' Street Preaching in San Francisco* (New York: Carlton and Porter, 1857), p. 207; Alexander Stott to Engles, San Francisco, Dec. 31, 1854, and Stott to Engles, San Francisco, Jan. 8, 1855, in Stott and Company Letterbook.

66. *Herald*, July 3, 1852; *Courier*, Jan. 17, 1850; Milton S. Latham, Collector of the Port of San Francisco, to James Guthrie, Secretary of the Treasury, San Francisco, Jan. 19, 1856, pp. 2–3, in U.S. National Archives Correspondence . . . ; *Chronicle*, Mar. 27, 1855; *Alta*, Apr. 18, 1855; H. D.

Hunter of the U.S. Revenue Cutter of San Francisco to Collector King, San Francisco, Aug. 24, 1852, pp. 1–2, and S. Lamb, Inspector, to King, San Francisco, Mar. 29, 1851, in U.S. National Archives Correspondence . . . ; on smuggling, see also the letters of Feb. 27, 1850; Apr. 13, 1851; Apr. 15, 1851; Apr. 30, 1851; Aug. 27, 1851; Aug. 29, 1851; Nov. 30, 1852, in the Correspondence . . . ; and the *Herald,* Apr. 26, 1853.

67. Dibblee to John Hicks, San Francisco, Apr. 16, 1853, p. 1, in Albert Dibblee Correspondence and Papers. On packing of good flour with bad, see also *Bulletin,* Nov. 5, 1855; *Chronicle,* Dec. 14, 1853; *Alta,* June 22, 1853; Nov. 8, 1853; Feb. 8, 1854; Sept. 19, 1854.

68. William T. Coleman, Statement, pp. 44–48; *Alta,* Apr. 2, 1850; Alexander Grogan to Faxon D. Atherton, San Francisco, May 20, 1856, in Faxon D. Atherton Papers.

69. *Alta,* Jan. 13, 1856; *Chronicle,* Feb. 7, 1856. "Sydney Duck" was the term given to the criminal population during the Vigilante uprising of 1851. See also *Era,* Sept. 10, 1854.

70. Dibblee to Crosby, San Francisco, May 8, 1855, p. 1, in Albert Dibblee Correspondence and Papers.

71. *Pacific,* Mar. 2, 1855.

72. Green to Larkin, San Francisco, Jan. 23, 1848, in *The Larkin Papers,* VIII, 124. The same thing can be seen in the struggle between rival newspapers and competing sections of the town going on in 1847–48; *Alta,* Aug. 8, 1852.

73. *Chronicle,* July 24, 1854.

74. *Ibid.,* July 24, 1854; *Alta,* Jan. 15, 1853; May 15, 1854; June 8, 1854; July 16, 1854; Crogan to Atherton, San Francisco, Apr. 4, 1856, in Faxon D. Atherton Papers; Goddefroy and Sillem to Ward and Price, San Francisco, May 30, 1850, p. 8, in Rodman Price Correspondence and Papers; Dibblee to Alpheus Forbes, San Francisco, Sept. 30, 1852, and Dibblee to Messinger, San Francisco, Sept. 30, 1852, in Albert Dibblee Correspondence and Papers; *Herald,* Dec. 15, 1852; Rev. Albert Williams, *A Pioneer Pastorate and Times* . . . , p. 148; Dibblee to James Lee and Company of Boston, San Francisco, Nov. 15, 1852, p. 2, in Albert Dibblee Correspondence and Papers; *Chronicle,* Apr. 9, 1856.

75. McGowan, "San Francisco-Sacramento Shipping," pp. 23–24.

76. *Chronicle,* Aug. 28, 1854; *Era,* Nov. 30, 1856.

77. *Herald,* Dec. 15, 1852; *Era,* Nov. 30, 1856.

78. Thomas C. Cochran and William Miller, *The Age of Enterprise* (rev. ed., New York: Harper and Brothers, 1961), pp. 82–84; Cross, *Financing an Empire,* p. 230; *Alta,* Dec. 31, 1856. In 1855 there were 197 bankruptcies, with liabilities of $8,377,827 and assets of $1,519,175, leaving a balance of failure of $6,858,652. In 1856 there were 146 bankruptcies, with liabilities of $3,401,042 and assets of $657,908, leaving a balance of failure of $2,743,134.

79. *Chronicle,* Aug. 8, 1854; Mar. 18, 1856; *Alta,* July 8, 1852.

80. John W. Caughey, *Gold Is the Cornerstone* (Berkeley and Los Angeles: University of California Press, 1948); James Vance, *Geography and Urban Evolution in the San Francisco Bay Area* (Berkeley: Institute of Governmental Studies, 1964), pp. 9–14.

81. Wilbur Thompson, *A Preface to Urban Economics* (Baltimore: The Johns Hopkins Press, 1965), pp. 18–21.

82. *Era,* Jan. 20, 1856; *Pacific,* July 27, 1855; *Fireman's Journal,* Nov. 22, 1856.

83. Walton Bean, "James Warren and the Beginnings of Agricultural Institutitutions in California," *Pacific Historical Review,* XIII (Dec. 1944), 361–75. R. W. Paul, "The Beginnings of Agriculture in California," *California Historical Quarterly,* XLII (Feb. 1973).

84. *Era,* Apr. 1, 1855; Oct. 21, 1855; Dec. 30, 1855.

85. The first telegraph in the state stretched from San Francisco to the western side of the peninsula and was built to receive news of ship arrivals in order to speed up commercial transactions. This new communications system was built in 1851 and in 1853 was supplemented by another which reached from the city into the interior as far as Marysville. Hunt, *California Firsts,* pp. 51–52.

86. U.S. Office of the Census, 1860 Census, pp. 28–33 (microfilm in Bancroft Library, University of California).

CHAPTER IV

1. John McCrackan to his sister Mary, San Francisco, Dec. 9, 1849, pp. 2–3, in John McCrackan Letters, I.

2. J. Collier to W. M. Meredith, Secretary of the Treasury, San Francisco, Nov. 29, 1849, pp. 304, in U.S. National Archives, *Correspondence . . .* (italics his); *Herald,* Mar. 6, 1852; *Californian,* Oct. 7, 1848; Letter of Joseph Folsom to Thomas S. Jessup, San Francisco, Sept. 18, 1848, pp. 12–13, in Joseph Folsom Correspondence and Papers (Bancroft Library, University of California).

3. Letter from Rinaldo R. Taylor, San Francisco, Jan. 14, 1850, in Rinaldo R. Taylor, *Seeing the Elephant: Letters of R. R. Taylor, Forty-Niner,* ed. John W. Caughey (The Ward Ritchie Press, 1951), p. 87; Letter from T. Kerr, San Francisco, May 1, 1850, in "T. Kerr; an Irishman in the Gold Rush," *California Historical Society Quarterly,* VII, No. 4 (Dec. 1928), 401; see also E. Morrison Woodward, *Diary,* 1849–1850, entry for Dec. 20, 1849 (Bancroft Library, University of California); Letter of Stephen Woodin to his wife, San Francisco, Sept. 10, 1852, p. 3, in Stephen Woodin Papers (Huntington Library); *Herald,* Mar. 3, 1853.

4. *Chronicle,* Aug. 4, 1854; *Alta,* Sept. 13, 1856; Sept. 28, 1856; *Era,* Apr. 2, 1854.

5. A. P. Nasatir, "Guillaume Patrice Dillon," *California Historical Society Quarterly,* XXXV, No. 4 (Dec. 1956), 315; Andrew Rolle, *The Immigrant Upraised* (Norman, Okla.: The University of Oklahoma Press, 1968), p.

254; *Alta,* July 21, 1853; May 27, 1854; Lucile Eaves, A *History of California Labor Legislation with an Introductory Sketch of the San Francisco Labor Movement* ("University of California Publications in Economics," Vol. II; Berkeley: University of California Press, 1910).

6. Alexander Stott to an unknown correspondent, San Francisco, Sept. 20, 1853, p. 2, in Stott and Company Letterbook; Letter of Levi Stowell, San Francisco, Oct. 2, 1849, in "Bound for the Land of Caanan Ho . . . ," ed. Marco G. Thorne, *California Historical Society Quarterly,* XXVII, No. 4 (Dec. 1948), 365.

7. Letter of John B. Quinton to his brother, San Francisco, July 31, 1853, in J. B. Quinton Letters (Bancroft Library, University of California). (Italics his.) Frank Lecouvreur, *From East Prussia to the Golden Gate: Letters and Diary of a California Pioneer,* ed. Mrs. Josephine Lecouvreur, comp. and trans. Julium C. Behnke (Leipzig, Germany: Buchhandlung G. Foch, 1906), pp. 198–99; letter of Henry D. Lammot to his father, San Francisco, Jan. 26, 1850, p. 3, in Lammot Family Papers (Bancroft Library, University of California); letter of Montes Jean to his father, San Francisco, Dec. 25, 1849, in A. P. Nasatir, *French Activities in California* (Stanford: Stanford University Press, 1945), pp. 393–96.

8. T. Butler King to Thomas Corwin, Secretary of State, San Francisco, May 31, 1851, in U.S. National Archives *Correspondence* . . . .

9. *Alta,* Dec. 5, 1850; *Chronicle,* July 14, 1853; *Californian,* July 15, 1848; Folsom to Thomas S. Jessup, San Francisco, Sept. 18, 1848, pp. 12–13, in Joseph L. Folsom Correspondence and Papers; letter of Edward Austin to George, San Francisco, June 18, 1849, p. 4, in Edward Austin Letters (Bancroft Library, University of California); McCrackan to sister Mary, San Francisco, Jan. 9, 1849, pp. 2–3, in John McCrackan Letters, I; letter of James S. Barnes to his friends, San Francisco, Feb. 28, 1850, p. 3, in James S. Barnes Letters (Bancroft Library, University of California); *Chronicle,* Jan. 7, 1856.

10. *Alta,* July 1, 1851; Jan. 13, 1853; Nov. 16, 1853; Mar. 23, 1854; Mar. 28, 1854; Nov. 2, 1854; *Daily True Standard,* Mar. 6, 1851; Mrs. Ann W. Booth, *Journal of a Voyage from Baltimore to San Francisco, 1849,* entry for Oct. 25, 1849, p. 241 (Bancroft Library, University of California); *Era,* May 1, 1853.

11. Eaves, *History of California Labor Legislation* . . . , p. 197; *Alta,* July 25, 1853; *Chronicle,* Aug. 29, 1855; July 26, 1853; *Manual of the Corporation of the City of San Francisco* (San Francisco: C. K. Fitch and Company, 1852), p. 55.

12. Quinton to his brother, San Francisco, Sept. 30, 1852, pp. 1–2, in John B. Quinton Letters. (Italics his.)

13. *Alta,* Oct. 2, 1851; Oct. 5, 1851; Oct. 18, 1851; Apr. 23, 1853; May 1, 1853; May 29, 1853; July 9, 1853; July 10, 1853; Aug. 31, 1854; Nov. 3, 1855.

14. *Ibid.,* Aug. 3, 1853; Nov. 20, 1853.

15. Letter of Sophia Eastman to her family, San Francisco, July 30, 1854, in Sophia Eastman, Letters to Her Family, p. 56 (Bancroft Library, University of California).

16. Chastina Rix, *Diary*, p. 206 (California Historical Society); see also letter of Mrs. Theo. H. Stevens to Ellen, San Francisco, Oct. 29, 1848, in Mrs. T. H. Stevens Papers (California Historical Society) and the almost continual clamor in letters to the editor in the local press against high servants' wages.

17. *Alta*, Dec. 20, 1851; Mar. 10, 1852; Apr. 9, 1853; *Call*, Dec. 12, 1856; Cross, *A History of the Labor Movement in California*, pp. 28, 302.

18. *Chronicle*, July 12, 1855; Rev. William Taylor, *Seven Years' Street Preaching* . . . , pp. 224–25.

19. William Martin Camp, *San Francisco: Port of Gold* (New York and Garden City: Doubleday and Company, 1948), p. 206. For protests against shanghaiing, see the *Alta*, Nov. 28, 1853; May 7, 1855; July 13, 1855; *Herald*, Nov. 29, 1853; *Era*, Oct. 29, 1854. Protests about sailor thieving were too numerous to mention. Letter of Consul Aiken to the British Government, San Francisco, Feb. 18, 1856, p. 10, in British Foreign Office Consular Correspondence (microfilm, Bancroft Library, University of California).

20. *Herald*, July 30, 1853; *Alta*, May 18, 1851; Sept. 28, 1853; *Chronicle*, Nov. 24, 1853; June 10, 1854; Aug. 4, 1854; Oct. 9, 1854; Nov. 9, 1854; *Annals*, pp. 459–60; *Californian*, May 22, 1847.

21. *Herald*, Aug. 11, 1852; July 28, 1853; *Alta*, Aug. 5, 1853; Chronicle, June 10, 1854; *Call*, Dec. 27, 1856; *Pacific*, Aug. 5, 1852.

22. *Herald*, July 28, 1853; Eureka Typographical Union, San Francisco, Minutes, Dec. 19, 1854 (Bancroft Library, University of California).

23. Cross, *A History of the Labor Movement in California*, pp. 10–28.

24. *Ibid.*, pp. 14–15; *Alta*, Nov. 22, 1849; July 27, 1850; Aug. 6, 1850; Aug. 8, 1850; Oct. 26, 1850; Apr. 13, 1852; July 1, 1852; Nov. 8, 1852; Feb. 24, 1853; July 14, 1853; July 19, 1853; July 25, 1853; July 26, 1853; July 27, 1853; July 29, 1853; July 30, 1853; Aug. 1, 1853; Aug. 3, 1853; Aug. 14, 1853; Aug. 18, 1853; *Herald*, Aug. 19, 1853.

25. Cross, *A History of the Labor Movement* . . . , pp. 24–28; Robert Coleman Francis, "A History of Labor on the San Francisco Waterfront" (unpublished dissertation, University of California, 1934), p. 16; Eureka Typographical Union, Minutes, Oct. 31, 1853; *Call*, Dec. 27, 1856; *Alta*, July 26, 1854; Eureka Typographical Union, Minutes, June 4, 1854.

26. *Herald*, July 28, 1853; *Chronicle*, June 10, 1854; *Call*, Dec. 27, 1856.

27. Cross, *A History of the Labor Movement* . . . , pp. 10–28. The police force comprised anywhere from forty to seventy men, depending on the presence or absence of an economy craze in the government. Eaves, *A History of California Labor Legislation* . . . , p. 394. Eaves says 1889–1891 marked the first period of widespread use of "judicial restraint" in California labor disputes. I found no examples of it in the city, 1846–56.

28. *Herald,* July 14, 1853; July 17, 1853; Eureka Typographical Union, Minutes, pp. 3–13.

29. Eureka Typographical Union, Minutes, Dec. 19, 1854; Aug. 17, 1856; Nov. 16, 1856; *Alta,* Aug. 10, 1850; Apr. 13, 1852.

30. Francis, "A History of Labor . . . ," p. 18; Robert M. Robinson, "A History of the Teamsters in the San Francisco Bay Area, 1850–1950" (unpublished dissertation, University of California, 1951), pp. 1–2.

31. *Chronicle,* Apr. 7, 1854.

32. *Daily True Standard,* Mar. 6, 1851; *Alta,* Aug. 1, 1850; July 30, 1853; Aug. 3, 1853; Aug. 14, 1853; Sept. 7, 1854; *Herald,* Oct. 13, 1852; Mar. 25, 1853.

33. *Ibid.,* Aug. 14, 1853; Mar. 5, 1855.

34. *Ibid.,* Sept. 4, 1853; Sept. 3, 1854; *Herald,* Sept. 5, 1853.

35. Cross, *A History of the Labor Movement* . . . , pp. 14–15; *Alta,* June 28, 1851; Mar. 2, 1854.

36. *Fireman's Journal,* Oct. 20, 1855; Nov. 10, 1855; May 19, 1856; *Call,* Dec. 4, 1856; Dec. 9, 1856; Dec. 11, 1856; Dec. 14, 1856; Dec. 18, 1856; Dec. 23, 1856; Jan. 21, 1857.

37. *Ibid.,* Dec. 19, 1856; see also *Chronicle,* Aug. 2, 1855; *Call,* Dec. 22, 1857.

38. *Alta,* July 1, 1851.

39. *Ibid.,* July 26, 1853.

40. *Call,* Dec. 28, 1856; see also *Alta,* Aug. 3, 1853.

41. *Call,* Jan. 21, 1857; *Alta,* Aug. 3, 1853.

42. *Call,* Jan. 21, 1857; see also *Call,* Dec. 28, 1856.

43. *Chronicle,* June 10, 1854; Aug. 4, 1854.

CHAPTER V

1. *Californian,* Oct. 7, 1848; John B. Quinton to his brother, San Francisco, Aug. 28, 1850, p. 2, in John Boyd Quinton Letters; John McCrackan to his family, San Francisco, Mar. 13, 1851, p. 2, in John McCrackan Letters, I; *Alta,* Oct. 7, 1854. For an excellent quantified approach to the problem of transiency in an American city, see Howard P. Chudacoff, *Mobile Americans: Residential and Social Mobility in Omaha, 1880–1920* (New York: Oxford University Press, 1972).

2. Charles F. Winslow to Lingren, San Francisco, Aug. 20, 1849, in Charles F. Winslow Letterbook; Mrs. Ann W. Booth, *Journal* . . . , entry for Oct. 17, 1849, p. 230; George Howard to Agnes Howard, San Francisco, Apr. 11, 1855, in W. D. M. Howard Papers; William K. Weston to his father, San Francisco, Apr. 28, 1851, in William K. Weston Papers.

3. Diary of James Lamson, entry for June 19, 1853, pp. 222–23 (California Historical Society).

4. In part, this post office crush was due to the poor distribution services of the local mail handlers; but much more, it was the result of the deep loneliness of city life.

5. McCrackan to his sister Lottie, San Francisco, May 30, 1850, p. 1, and McCrackan to his family, San Francisco, Mar. 13, 1851, p. 2, in John McCrackan Letters, I.

6. *Californian*, Apr. 26, 1848; *California Star*, Mar. 18, 1847; Bancroft, *History of California*, IV, 664.

7. Abstract of the Census of 1852 of the State of California, pp. 41–43; United States Census for 1860, p. 31. The *Annals* considered the census figure of 1852 too low and estimated the population at 42,000. See *Annals*, p. 413, 484. *Alta*, Aug. 22, 1856. Kemble, *The Panama Route*, p. 254. Halving the increase between 1852 and 1860 would give a population of 45,000, but the ratio of arrivals for the first 4 years was 9 to 6 over the second 4, thus the 50,000 figure.

8. Letter of Feb. 26, 1850, p. 96, in R. R. Taylor, *Seeing the Elephant . . .*

9. *Annals*, p. 505. Jessy Quinn Thornton, *Oregon and California in 1848* (2 vols.; New York: Harper and Brothers Publishers, 1849), II, pp. 75–79; United States Census for 1860, xxxi–xxxii; California State Census Abstract, pp. 41–43. For 1852 a similar figure seems warranted; but this is not as certain, since that census was rather haphazard. U.S. Census for 1860, p. 33.

10. Thornton, *Oregon and California . . .*, II, pp. 75–79; abstract of the California State Census of 1852, pp. 41–43. There are no reliable figures for this latter period.

11. U.S. Census for 1860, p. 28.

12. At least 30 per cent of American San Franciscans came from urban areas and probably more. Estimates for proportions of urbanites, ruralites, foreigners, natives, etc. are based on samplings of the 1852 state census. McCrackan to Lottie, San Francisco, Mar. 21, 1851, p. p. 2, and Sept. 23, 1851, p. 2, in John McCrackan Letters, I.

13. Lecouvreur, *From East Prussia . . .*, pp. 182–83; *Alta*, Dec. 14, 1850.

14. Milton M. Gordon, *Assimilation in American Life: The Role of Race, Religion, and National Origins* (New York: Oxford University Press, 1964), pp. 84–88.

15. *Picayune*, Aug. 18, 1851; *Chronicle*, July 10, 1854; *Herald*, May 26, 1851; June 6, 1853; Lecouvreur, *From East Prussia . . .*, pp. 194–95; *Annals*, p. 446 and elsewhere; *Bulletin*, July 8, 1856.

16. *Herald*, Jan. 6, 1851; *Bulletin*, July 8, 1856; *Chronicle*, Dec. 25, 1854; *Annals*, pp. 368, 464.

17. *Chronicle*, Dec. 25, 1854.

18. *Alta*, Feb. 13, 1851.

19. *Annals*, p. 412 and elsewhere.

20. Quoted in Charles Wollenberg, ed., *Ethnic Conflict in California History* (Los Angeles: Tinnon-Brown, 1970), p. 49; *Era*, May 29, 1853; *Pacific*, Aug. 1, 1851; Sept. 12, 1851.

21. William Hagan, *American Indians* (Chicago: University of Chicago Press,

1961), p. 98; *Pacific*, June 11, 1852; see also the issues of Feb. 11, 1853; Nov. 21, 1851; *Era*, Jan. 1, 1854; Feb. 12, 1854; Mar. 5, 1854; Aug. 20, 1854; Oct. 1, 1854; Oct. 8, 1854; Feb. 11, 1855; Jan. 20, 1856; July 20, 1856.

22. *Chronicle*, Dec. 25, 1854; Sept. 19, 1855.

23. Editorial from the *Echo du Pacifique*, reprinted in *Alta*, Nov. 30, 1853.

24. Patrice Dillon, "La Californie Dans Les Derniers Mois de 1849," written in San Francisco, October 2, 1849, in Nasatir, *French Activities . . . ,* pp. 545, 555–56.

25. The distinction is Milton Gordon's. Structural assimilation involves association in clubs, churches, work, and so forth. Behavioral assimilation implies that though still separate structurally, the different groups exemplify the same conduct, customs, or behavior. Milton M. Gordon, "Assimilation in America: Theory and Reality," *The Shaping of Twentieth Century America*, ed. Richard M. Abrams and Lawrence W. Levine (Boston: Little, Brown and Co., 1965), pp. 312–16; *Israelite*, Jan. 11, 1856; Dec. 26, 1856; Lecouvreur, *From East Prussia . . . ,* pp. 182–83; Reuben R. Rinder, *A Century of Music in Emanu-El*, no date, p. 2 (American Jewish Archives, Cincinnati, Ohio).

26. McCrackan to Lottie, San Francisco, Nov. 25, 1850, pp. 2–4, and Mc-Crackan to Mary, Apr. 13, 1852, p. 2, in John McCrackan Letters, I; see also *Chronicle*, Oct. 28, 1854.

27. Quoted in George Rupert MacMinn, *The Theater of the Golden Era in California* (Caldwell, Idaho: The Caxton Printers, Ltd., 1941), p. 304.

28. *Herald,* June 5, 1853; *Fireman's Journal,* Aug. 4, 1855; Mar. 29, 1856; *Alta,* Apr. 6, 1856.

29. *Annals,* p. 463.

30. *Ibid.,* pp. 411, 446. For an opposite view of the Germans, see Andrew Rolle, *A History of California,* p. 386. Rolle argues that in California as a whole the Germans were outstanding for their unwillingness to assimilate. That was not true in San Francisco for the ten years under review.

31. *Alta,* Feb. 7, 1851.

32. *Bulletin,* Apr. 10, 1856; Oct. 8, 1856; see also *Bulletin,* Feb. 5, 1856; Apr. 10, 1856; for pieces by "Betsy Honeycomb" and "John Scroggins." (Italics his.) MacMinn, *Theater . . . ,* pp. 165, 441; Horace Bushnell, "Characteristics and Prospects of California," published originally in the *New Englander* (San Francisco: Whitton, Towne and Co.'s Steam Presses, 1858), p. 22.

33. *Era,* May 15, 1853; July 9, 1854; *Daily Evening News,* Mar. 19, 1855; Mar. 23, 1855; *Herald,* Mar. 21, 1855; Mar. 23, 1855; Henry J. Labatt, "Jewish Business Interests in California, 1861," *A Documentary History of the Jews in the United States, 1654–1875,* ed. Morris U. Schappes (New York: Citadel Press, 1952), pp. 441–44; I. J. Benjamin, *Three Years in America, 1859–62,* trans. Charles Reznikoff (Philadelphia: The Jewish Publication Society of America, 1956), I, p. 232.

34. Albert Bernard de Russailh, *Last Adventure: San Francisco in 1851* (from his journal), trans., Clarkson Crane (San Francisco: The Westgate Press, 1931), pp. 77–79. *Le Messager,* and after it, *Le Phare,* both favored naturalization, while the *Echo du Pacifique* opposed it. Editorial in *Echo du Pacifique,* reprinted in *Chronicle,* May 26, 1855.

35. *Bulletin,* July 12, 1856, quoted from *Le Phare.*

36. *Ibid.*

37. *Annals,* p. 464.

38. *Chronicle,* May 26, 1855

39. *Monitor,* Mar. 20, 1858; *Herald,* Dec. 14, 1851; *Chronicle,* Sept. 23, 1854; *The Weekly Gleaner,* Jan. 16, 1857, p. 2, reprinted from *The Philadelphia Ledger; Alta,* Oct. 22, 1854; *Frederick Douglass' Paper,* Sept. 22, 1854, Apr. 6, 1855, quoted in Leon Litwack, *North of Slavery* (Chicago: University of Chicago Press, 1961), pp. 167–68.

40. "China Boys" was the early appellation for the Chinese before they fell from grace in the city; letter of Tasheira to his daughter, San Francisco, Nov. 19, 1854, p. 2, in Tasheira Collection (State Library at Sacramento); *Alta,* Aug. 29, 1850; Heinrich Schliemann, *Schliemann's First Visit to America,* ed. Shirley H. Weber (Cambridge, Mass.: Harvard University Press, 1942), p. 56; Henry D. Lammot to Alfred, San Francisco, Feb. 24, 1850, in Lammot Family Papers.

41. *Annals,* p. 462; *Alta,* June 29, 1856.

42. Eureka Benevolent Society, Ladies United Hebrew Benevolent Society, and Young Men's Relief and Literary Society. The Germans had an immigrant aid society as well as a general benevolent society.

43. Yet even Chinatown itself was not entirely given over to Chinese. A residential map of the city indicates non-Orientals living there and the *Annals* noted the same. *Annals,* p. 381. These neighborhoods were located by both literary sources and ethnic residential maps plotted by the author from city directories.

44. A. P. Nasatir, *A French Journalist in the California Gold Rush: The Letters of Etienne Derbec* (Georgetown, Cal.: The Talisman Press, 1964), p. 32. The Italian press of Chicago had a similar impact, and I am indebted to Humbert Nelli for suggesting the possibility for San Francisco. Nelli, *The Italians in Chicago, 1880–1930* (New York: Oxford University Press, 1970), pp. 158–70.

45. *Israelite,* Nov. 16, 1855; Dec. 7, 1855; Nov. 21, 1856; Rev. Albert Williams, *A Pioneer Pastorate . . . ,* pp. 135–36.

46. See Oscar Handlin, *The Uprooted* (Boston: Little, Brown and Company, 1951), pp. 117ff.

47. *Chronicle,* Feb. 24, 1855; Raymond Stevenson Dondero, "The Italian Settlement of San Francisco . . ." (unpublished master's thesis, University of California, Berkeley, 1953), p. 35.

48. *Alta,* Dec. 1, 1850; Jan. 4, 1853; Dec. 2, 1853; Dec. 15, 1853.

49. *Ibid.,* Dec. 10, 1850; Nov. 14, 1852.

50. *Ibid.*, Nov. 3, 1850; *Chronicle,* Jan. 9, 1855.

51. *Bulletin,* Dec. 23, 1856.

52. Unless otherwise indicated by specific footnote references, the remainder of this discussion of the Chinese leans heavily upon the study of the Chinese in America by Gunther Barth. Gunther Barth, *Bitter Strength* (Cambridge, Mass.: Harvard University Press, 1964).

53. *Annals,* pp. 382, 387.

54. Barth discusses the same phenomena in Southeast Asia among the Chinese who emigrated there.

55. The system was very much like that described by Dan Wakefield in Spanish Harlem, where the residents were terrorized into silence by fear of reprisals from the gangs that harassed the neighborhood. Dan Wakefield, *Island in the City: Puerto Ricans in New York* (New York: Houghton Mifflin, Corinth Books, 1959), pp. 117ff.

56. *Chronicle,* June 6, 1854; Aug. 19, 1854; *Alta,* June 4, 1853.

57. According to Barth, these defenders were both commercial and humanitarian.

58. For a similar phenomenon for Southern California, see Robert Fogelson, *The Fragmented Metropolis: Los Angeles, 1850–1930* (Cambridge, Mass.: Harvard University Press, 1967), p. 196; and Joseph Boskin, "Associations and Picnics as Stabilizing Forces in Southern California," *California Historical Society Quarterly,* XLIV, No. 1 (Mar. 1965), 17–26.

59. Thomas Reid, Diary, entry for the year 1849 (Bancroft Library, University of California).

60. R. R. Taylor, letter of Feb. 26, 1850, in Taylor, *Seeing the Elephant,* p. 97. (Italics his.)

61. *Ibid.* It is possible that a number of other such boardinghouses existed, since there were many places bearing names like the New Orleans House, the Manhattan House, the New England House, etc. Wm. Herrick, Statement (Bancroft Library, University of California): Mary Prag, "Early Days," p. 2 (typescript, Western Jewish History Center at the Judah Magnus Museum, Berkeley, California).

62. T. A. Barry and B. A. Patten, *Men and Memories of San Francisco in the 'Spring of '50'* (San Francisco: A. L. Bancroft and Company, 1873), pp. 107, 206–8.

63. *Pacific,* Nov. 19, 1852; Dec. 3, 1853; Dec. 29, 1854; June 8, 1855; July 27, 1855; Nov. 20, 1856; Rev. Timothy Dwight Hunt, "Address Delivered before the New England Society of San Francisco at the American Theater on the Twenty-second Day of December, 1852" (San Francisco: Cooke, Kenny and Co., 1853), p. 20.

64. *Alta,* Dec. 8, 1851.

65. *Picayune,* Oct. 3, 1850.

66. *Ibid.,* Sept. 28, 1850; *Alta,* Mar. 16, 1853.

67. McCrackan to Mary, San Francisco, Sept. 15, 1853, p. 34, in John McCrackan Letters, II.

68. Hunt, "Address . . . ," p. 20.

69. *Alta*, Apr. 6, 1850.

70. I am indebted to Professors Rudolph Lapp and Phil Montesano for many valuable insights into the lives of Black Americans in San Francisco. *Alta*, Aug. 8, 1852; June 25, 1853; Dec. 30, 1853; Aug. 2, 1855.

71. *Californian*, June 19, 1847; John Henry Brown, *Early Days in San Francisco* (Oakland, 1949), p. 125; *Alta*, Nov. 30, 1852; Aug. 24, 1856; MacMinn, *Theater* . . . , p. 44; *Herald*, Oct. 2, 1856.

72. *Alta*, Mar. 22, 1850; Aug. 12, 1851.

73. For use of this term, see Velesta Jenkins, "White Racism and Black Response in California History," *Ethnic Conflict in California*, ed. Charles Woolenberg (Los Angeles: Tinnon-Brown, 1970), p. 123. "Proceedings of the First State Convention of the Colored Citizens of the State of California, 1855" (November 20–22) (Sacramento: Democratic State Journal Printer, 1855), pp. 18–19; letter of Jacques A. Moerenhout to Minister of Foreign Affairs, Monterey, July 30, 1856, in A. P. Nasatir, ed., "The Second Incumbency of Jacques A. Moerenhout," *California Historical Society Quarterly*, XXVIII, No. 1 (Mar. 1949), 77; see also Moerenhout, *Inside Story of the Gold Rush*, entry for July 17, 1848, p. 21; *Chronicle*, Sept. 23, 1854; *Alta*, Sept. 22, 1854.

74. *Chronicle*, Dec. 16, 1855; *Alta*, Feb. 7, 1854; Apr. 1, 1855; Leon F. Litwack, *North of Slavery* (Chicago and London: University of Chicago Press, 1961), pp. 115–17; "Proceedings of the First State Convention of the Colored Citizens . . . ," p. 27.

75. *Alta*, Dec. 9, 1853; Mar. 26, 1854; Nov. 7, 1855; Nov. 30, 1856; *Call*, Feb. 13, 1857; *Pacific*, Nov. 21, 1851; Mar. 10, 1854; *Chronicle*, Oct. 6, 1854.

76. *Alta*, July 23, 1853; Apr. 7, 1854; *Herald*, May 1, 1852; *Era*, Nov. 30, 1856.

77. For a different explanation of black leadership which stresses the quality of the slaves brought to California rather than the urban origin of the leaders, see Rudolph Lapp, "The Negro in Gold Rush California," *Journal of Negro History*, XLIX, No. 2 (Apr. 1964), 84–85; see also Litwack, *North of Slavery*.

78. "Proceedings of the First State Convention of the Colored Citizens . . . ," p. 26.

79. See Nelli, *The Italians in Chicago*.

80. For the argument that the melting pot did not work in America, see Nathan Glazer and Daniel P. Moynihan, *Beyond the Melting Pot* (Cambridge, Mass.: MIT Press, 1963), p. v.

CHAPTER VI

1. The activities it could regulate included the price and quality of bread, rates of wharfage, and transportation in the city, and the storage of gun-

powder and other combustibles. San Francisco, Charter of 1850 (Bancroft Library, University of California), p. 6.

2. This clause, however, was not repeated in the 1855 and 1856 acts. San Francisco, Charter of 1851, p. 24 (Bancroft Library, University of California).

3. After 1856, however, the evolution seems to have been the same as in other United States cities.

4. *Alta*, Mar. 21, 1851; Peter T. Conmy, San Francisco City and County Consolidation Act, p. 1; *Daily Evening News*, Jan. 12, 1856; Feb. 16, 1856; Feb. 25, 1856; Apr. 18, 1856; *Pacific*, Apr. 27, 1855.

5. *Chronicle*, Apr. 17, 1855.

6. For a similar device used by modern cities to "reserve" room for expansion, see Mitchell Gordon, *Sick Cities* (New York: The Macmillan Co., 1965), p. 359.

7. Lawrence Kinnaird, *History of the Greater San Francisco Bay Region* (New York and West Palm Beach, Fla.: Lewis Historical Publishing Co., 1966), I, p. 278.

8. See below. Throughout the period, the Eighth Ward, which included the Mission, was the stronghold of the Squatters, as those people who wanted the pre-emption laws applied to land grants were called; *Alta*, Feb. 25, 1850; Clement Humphreys, Map of the Northern Portion of San Francisco County, 1853 (Bancroft Library, University of California).

9. *Chronicle*, Oct. 9, 1854; *Herald*, Aug. 21, 1852; *Call*, Dec. 11, 1856; *Alta*, Nov. 7, 1854; May 31, 1855. Most of the volunteer military companies' members deserted to the Vigilantes in 1856.

10. *Alta*, May 3, 1854.

11. Letter of Henry H. Haight to his father, San Francisco, July 17, 1850, pp. 3–4, in Henry Haight Papers (California State Library at Sacramento).

12. McCrackan to his mother, San Francisco, May 24, 1850, p. 2, in John McCrackan Letters, I.

13. *Alta*, Jan. 18, 1851; Jan. 29, 1851.

14. *Ibid.*, June 10, 1854; Sept. 19, 1854.

15. *Ibid.*, Oct. 19, 1851; Oct. 14, 1853; Oct. 15, 1853; Oct. 7, 1854.

16. *Ibid.*, Apr. 4, 1855; John Young, *San Francisco: A History of the Pacific Coast Metropolis* . . . (San Francisco and Chicago, 1912), p. 319.

17. *Chronicle*, June 24, 1856; *Alta*, Apr. 4, 1855.

18. Eldredge, *The Beginnings* . . . , II, 570; *Alta*, Jan. 23, 1856; Dec. 13, 1856.

19. S. W. Holladay, City and County Attorney, *Report of City Litigation*, pp. 65–66 (Bancroft Library, University of California).

20. *Alta*, Jan. 13, 1852; Sept. 7, 1852; June 22, 1854; Mar. 24, 1855; June 22, 1855; *Herald*, Aug. 17, 1852.

21. *Herald*, June 1, 1851; *Courier*, Aug. 23, 1850; *Alta*, Mar. 29, 1852; San Francisco, *Ordinances and Joint Resolutions of the City of San Francisco* . . . (San Francisco: no printer, 1852), pp. 217–24.

22. In 1856, with William Ralston and others, Garrison cofounded the banking house of Garrison, Ralston, and Fretz, and later operated the more famous Bank of California. See *Alta*, Nov. 16, 1853. The tax rate for the county, including state taxes which averaged about fifty cents, was $2.00, $4.10, $4.41½, $3.88½, $3.85½, $3.85⅝, and $2.30 per one hundred dollars assessed valuation for the years 1850–51 through 1856–57. See also *Alta*, June 29, 1853.

23. *Alta*, Mar. 12, 1852.

24. *Ibid.*, Aug. 9, 1855.

25. *Chronicle*, Jan. 25, 1856. See also, *Chronicle*, Apr. 27, 1855; Dec. 21, 1855; Jan. 25, 1856; Apr. 26, 1856; *Alta*, June 10, 1852; May 15, 1856; *Bulletin*, Jan. 16, 1856; *Fireman's Journal*, Jan. 26, 1856.

26. *Annals*, pp. 278–81; *Alta*, July 2, 1850.

27. *Alta*, July 17, 1850.

28. *Annals*, pp. 280–81; *Chronicle*, Nov. 7, 1855; *Alta*, July 18, 1854; Oct. 24, 1854; Nov. 6, 1855.

29. Letter of James F. to C. B. Houghton, San Francisco, Apr. 15, 1853, pp. 1–2, in Houghton Collection (California State Library at Sacramento).

30. Bancroft, *History of California*, VI, 775.

31. Eldredge, *The Beginnings* . . . , II, 568; *Alta*, Oct. 16, 1856; William J. Shaw, Dictation, pp. 43–50 (Bancroft Library, University of California).

32. *Alta*, Nov. 7, 1854; Nov. 9, 1854. See chapter on Urban Problems.

33. *Chronicle*, Nov. 7, 1855; Bancroft, *History of California*, VI, 615.

34. *Alta*, May 8, 1856.

35. *Chronicle*, Oct. 24, 1855; *Pacific*, Jan. 13, 1854.

36. See chapter on Urban Problems.

37. *Chronicle*, Aug. 10, 1855.

CHAPTER VII

1. *California Star*, Nov. 13, 1847.

2. Letter of Washington A. Bartlett to Jasper O'Farrell, San Francisco, Nov. 26, 1846, in Jasper O'Farrell Papers (California Historical Society); *Alta*, May 12, 1851; Neal Harlow, ed., *The Maps of San Francisco Bay from the Spanish Discovery . . . to the American Occupation* (San Francisco: Grabhorn Press, 1950), p. 102.

3. *Alta*, May 12, 1851; May 4, 1853; *Annals*, p. 490; Kinnaird, *History* . . . , I, 433.

4. Milo Hoadley, Diary, entries for Mar. 11, 1850, and Mar. 17, 1850 (Bancroft Library, University of California).

5. *California Star*, Dec. 4, 1847; Dec. 18, 1847; Jan. 8, 1848.

6. William S. Jewett, "Some Letters of William S. Jewett, California Artist," ed. Elliot Evans, *California Historical Society Quarterly*, XXIII, No. 2 (June 1944), 156.

7. *Alta*, Dec. 29, 1849.

8. Letter of Joseph G. Eastland to his Uncle Alfred, San Francisco, Jan. 15, 1851, in Joseph G. Eastland Papers (California Historical Society).

9. *Alta,* Apr. 25, 1850; Aug. 31, 1850.

10. Bancroft, *History of California,* VI, 199.

11. *Chronicle,* July 26, 1855; Oct. 13, 1855; *Alta,* May 14, 1851; July 22, 1851; Sept. 29, 1851; June 10, 1852.

12. Letter of Lydia R. Prevaux to Mrs. Prevaux, San Francisco, Feb. 14, 1854, in Francis Prevaux Letters (Bancroft Library, University of California); *Herald,* Nov. 24, 1853; *Alta,* June 23, 1854; May 13, 1854.

13. *Era,* Dec. 26, 1852; *Alta,* Dec. 28, 1852; Aug. 9, 1852; *Chronicle,* Aug. 10, 1855; Oct. 19, 1855; Jan. 9, 1856; Feb. 27, 1856; *Herald,* Sept. 21, 1852.

14. *Chronicle,* Aug. 10, 1855; Jan. 9, 1856; *Bulletin,* Feb. 4, 1856.

15. *Herald,* Apr. 15, 1852 (Italics his); Sept. 21, 1852; Sept. 24, 1856; *Chronicle,* Aug. 10, 1855; Feb. 27, 1856; July 31, 1856; *Call,* Feb. 3, 1857; *Bulletin,* Feb. 8, 1856; Aug. 21, 1856; Dec. 3, 1856; Dec. 10, 1856.

16. This assessment is based upon a map of the street improvements, drawn by the author, showing the date of improvement. These maps were overlaid on the residential maps previously mentioned.

17. *Manual of the Corporation* . . . , pp. 108–9.

18. San Francisco, *Ordinances and Joint Resolutions of the City of San Francisco* . . . (San Francisco: no printer, 1852), pp. 31–33, 82–83, 115–16.

19. See Clement Humphreys, County Surveyor, Map of the Northern Portion of San Francisco County, June 1, 1852, published Jan. 1853 (Bancroft Library, University of California).

20. *Alta,* Oct. 25, 1850; Nov. 9, 1850; Oct. 10, 1856.

21. *Chronicle,* Oct. 20, 1854; Nov. 1, 1855; Feb. 25, 1856; Feb. 29, 1856.

22. *Alta,* Oct. 18, 1850; Dec. 9, 1850; June 11, 1851; June 12, 1851; June 13, 1851; Sept. 21, 1851; *Chronicle,* Oct. 19, 1854.

23. *Annals,* p. 518; *Alta,* Apr. 1, 1851.

24. *Alta,* Dec. 31, 1852; Mar. 3, 1853; *Herald,* Oct. 13, 1853.

25. *Herald,* June 9, 1853.

26. *Alta,* Aug. 17, 1852; Stott to Freeman Wilcox, San Francisco, May 17, 1852, pp. 2–3, in Alexander Stott Letterbook; see also *Annals,* pp. 517–18.

27. *Era,* July 29, 1855; *Chronicle,* Jan. 21, 1856.

28. *Alta,* Apr. 19, 1855; Dec. 3, 1854; Dec. 22, 1856; *Fireman's Journal,* Aug. 18, 1855.

29. *Bulletin,* Nov. 12, 1856.

30. Larkin to Gov. Robert F. Stockton, Oct. 6, 1846, in *The Larkin Papers,* V, 257–58; Sherman, *Memoirs* . . . , p. 62; Harlow, *Maps of San Francisco Bay* . . . , p. 102; *California Star,* Dec. 18, 1847; *Californian,* July 24, 1847; Jan. 19, 1848; Sept. 30, 1848; *Alta,* July 7, 1852.

31. *Alta,* Apr. 19, 1849; Aug. 31, 1849.

32. *Ibid.,* June 10, 1850; Feb. 11, 1851; Feb. 12, 1851; Oct. 12, 1851; Map of San Francisco by Surveyor William Eddy, in Mary F. Williams, *Papers*

of the San Francisco Committee of Vigilance, "Publications of the Academy of Pacific Coast History," IV (Berkeley: University of California Press, 1919), xvi; Map of the U.S. Coast Survey, 1857 (Bancroft Library, University of California).

33. *Alta,* Jan. 27, 1851; Feb. 11, 1853; *Bulletin,* Apr. 16, 1856; Dec. 10, 1856; Dec. 30, 1856.

34. *Alta,* Jan. 30, 1852.

35. *Ibid.,* June 23, 1852.

36. *Ibid.,* June 25, 1851; June 26, 1851.

37. *Californian,* May 17, 1848; *California Star,* June 12, 1847; *Alta,* Jan. 18, 1849; Mar. 2, 1849; Mar. 29, 1849; June 28, 1849. The "Shades" Tavern fire is often referred to as the first fire in San Francisco, but it was not. *Alta,* Dec. 25, 1849; May 6, 1850; June 15, 1850; June 24, 1851; May 4, 1852; Nov. 10, 1852; *Courier,* Sept. 18, 1850; *Annals,* pp. 274-75, 329-33.

38. Schliemann, *Schliemann's First Visit to America,* pp. 63-65.

39. *Alta,* June 11, 1851.

40. *Ibid.,* Mar. 29, 1850; Apr. 17, 1850; June 23, 1851; July 1, 1851; July 6, 1851; Dec. 2, 1851; May 2, 1852.

41. See, for example, Allen Valentine, *Vigilante Justice* (New York: Reynal, 1956), p. 72. From Jan. 23, 1851, to Apr. 9, 1853, there was a total of 83 fires: arson—27; unknown—19; chimneys—9; stove pipes—7; accidental —4; candles—4; smoking—3; carelessness—3; lamps—2; mattress—1; spontaneous combustion—1; shavings—1; tar—1; cooking fat—1. The question of incendiarism is an intriguing one. The papers often thought incendiarism was present, but gave very unconvincing reasons for believing so. It is quite possible, therefore, that arson was exaggerated. Yet the papers are about the only source available, and until a better one turns up, must be believed.

42. San Francisco Fire Department, *Records of Fires and Alarms, 1856-61* (California Historical Society).

43. *Alta,* Apr. 6, 1850.

44. *Ibid.,* Dec. 26, 1849; Dec. 28, 1849; June 18, 1850; Oct. 2, 1850; Oct. 10, 1850; Dec. 16, 1850; June 6, 1851; June 30, 1851; Feb. 26, 1851; July 18, 1851; May 2, 1852; Sept. 22, 1852; Nov. 24, 1852; Mar. 28, 1853; Dec. 12, 1855; *Annals,* p. 616.

45. San Francisco, *Manual . . . ,* pp. 70-71, 156-57; *Alta,* June 19, 1850; *Annals,* pp. 614-25.

46. McCrackan to his sister Lottie, San Francisco, Feb. 20, 1850, p. 1, in John McCrackan Letters; J. D. Farwell, Statement, p. 4 (Bancroft Library, University of California); letter of Jonas Winchester to his wife, San Francisco, May 14, 1851, in Jonas Winchester Papers (California Historical Society); Daniel W. Coit, *An Artist in Eldorado: The Drawings and Letters of Daniel W. Coit,* ed. Edith M. Colter (San Francisco: Grabhorn Press for the Book Club of California, 1937), p. 22; Bernard de

Russailh, *The Last Adventure* . . . , p. 70; Weston to his father, San Francisco, June 15, 1851, in William K. Weston Papers.

47. *Alta*, May 3, 1853; May 19, 1855; May 31, 1855; Oct. 17, 1855; Oct. 10, 1856; *Chronicle*, Aug. 4, 1854; *Herald*, May 1, 1853.

48. *Alta*, Dec. 12, 1855; Apr. 22, 1856; June 17, 1856; Aug. 27, 1856; Nov. 10, 1856; *Fireman's Journal*, July 21, 1855; Nov. 17, 1855; Sept. 7, 1856; *Era*, July 30, 1854.

49. *Chronicle*, Nov. 1, 1855; *Fireman's Journal*, Oct. 11, 1856; Nov. 29, 1856.

50. *Chronicle*, July 20, 1855; *Alta*, Jan. 28, 1855; Apr. 30, 1856; Oct. 9, 1856.

51. *Alta*, Apr. 12, 1855; July 15, 1855.

52. *Ibid.*, Apr. 6, 1856.

53. Robert S. Lammot to Dan, San Francisco, Mar. 2, 1851, in Lammot Family Correspondence; see also *Bulletin*, Feb. 18, 1856; Sept. 4, 1856. (Italics his.) *Annals*, pp. 432–33, 115–16; *Bulletin*, Aug. 7, 1856; *Era*, Nov. 13, 1853.

54. *Alta*, May 5, 1850; Stott to Andrews & Wilcox, San Francisco, Feb. 18, 1852, in Alexander Stott Letterbook; Winchester to his wife Susan, San Francisco, Oct. 1, 1850, in Jonas Winchester Papers.

55. *Annals*, pp. 449–50; *Alta*, Feb. 1, 1851; Oct. 25, 1852; *Chronicle*, July 26, 1855; letter of June 2, 1855, in H. L. Abbot Collection (Oregon Historical Society); Barton Harvey Knowles, "The Early History of San Francisco's Water Supply" (unpublished Master's thesis, University of California, Berkeley, Cal.).

56. *Alta*, July 25, 1855.

57. *Ibid.*, Mar. 3, 1851; May 5, 1851; June 10, 1851; June 12, 1851; June 14, 1851; June 21, 1851; Oct. 25, 1852.

58. *Ibid.*, June 1, 1852; San Francisco, *Manual* . . . , pp. 117–19, 125–26; James Lamson, Diary, I, 225–26; *Alta*, Mar. 18, 1851.

59. *Alta*, Oct. 11, 1851; May 15, 1852; June 15, 1852; May 13, 1853; June 20, 1854; July 25, 1855; *Chronicle*, July 13, 1854; Dec. 4, 1855.

60. Knowles, "Early History of San Francisco's Water Supply; pp. 87, 94–95.

61. Nelson M. Blake, *Water for the Cities* (Syracuse: Syracuse University Press, 1956).

62. J. P. Leonard, "Medical Observations of J. P. Leonard, M.D.," ed. Robert T. Legge, *California Historical Society Quarterly*, XXIX, No. 3 (Sept. 1950), 213–16; Bayard Taylor, *Eldorado* (1892 ed.; New York: G. P. Putnam's Sons, 1892), pp. 106–7; *Alta*, Oct. 23, 1850; Jan. 22, 1851.

63. Leontina Murphy, "Public Care of the Dependent Sick in San Francisco, 1847–1936 . . ." (unpublished master's thesis, University of California, Berkeley, Cal.), pp. 7–8, 9–10.

64. It was wrongly claimed at the time of the organization of the French Benevolent Society that poverty-stricken foreigners were excluded from the State Marine Hospital. The surviving statistics indicate that immigrants were generally a majority; and at one time, aliens outnumbered

Americans by nearly four to one. Thomas N. Bonner, *The Kansas Doctor* (Lawrence: University of Kansas Press, 1959), p. 90. See also his *Medicine in Chicago*.

65. *Alta*, Oct. 1, 1853.

66. Letter of Sylvia A. Eastman to her sister, San Francisco, July 18, 1850, and same to same, San Francisco, Nov. 14, 1850, in Maria M. Child Letters (Bancroft Library, University of California); Rev. William Taylor, *Seven Years' Street Preaching* . . . , pp. 66–67.

67. Pfeiffer, *A Lady's Visit to California, 1853*, p. 20; *Era*, Mar. 27, 1853; *Pacific*, Oct. 2, 1856.

68. *Alta*, May 20, 1851; San Francisco, *Ordinances* . . . , p. 144.

69. *California Star*, Nov. 13, 1847; *Alta*, Oct. 23, 1850; Nov. 5, 1850; San Francisco, *Ordinances* . . . , pp. 210, 213–15, 249, 356–57, 386–87; San Francisco, *Manual* . . . , pp. 41–42.

70. *Herald*, Oct. 20, 1852.

71. For further discussions of contemporary medical practice, see Richard H. Shryock, *Medicine in America: Historical Essays* (Baltimore: The Johns Hopkins Press, 1966); Donald Fleming, *William Henry Welch and the Rise of Modern Medicine* (Boston: Little, Brown & Co., 1954).

72. Letter of Edward Anthony to his mother, San Francisco, Dec. 23, 1849, in Edward G. H. Anthony Papers (California Historical Society); *Star and Californian*, Nov. 25, 1848; David Cosad, Diary, entry for December 7, 1848 (California Historical Society).

73. For the argument that there was peace and quiet before the Gold Rush, see Stanton A. Coblentz, *Villains and Vigilantes: The Story of James King of William and Pioneer Justice in California* (New York: Wilson-Erickson, 1936), p. 20. "It is one of the tragedies of history that the reign of Arcadian simplicity and honesty should have been dissipated for all time by the incursion of the gold-seekers." *California Star*, June 12, 1847; July 24, 1847; Aug. 21, 1847; Nov. 20, 1847; Kimball H. Dimmick, Diary, entry for May 2, 1848 (California Historical Society); John H. Merrill to Thomas O. Larkin, Jan. 22, 1848, in *The Larkin Papers*, VII; *California Star*, Dec. 25, 1847.

74. Francis E. Prevaux to his parents, San Francisco, Mar. 2, 1851, p. 2, in Francis E. Prevaux Letters.

75. *Alta*, Aug. 3, 1855.

76. Hubert Howe Bancroft, *Popular Tribunals*, I, *Works*, XXXVI (San Francisco: The History Publishing Co., 1887), p. 78; John Henry Brown, pp. 102–4. H. H. Bancroft also agreed on the original nonmalicious intent of the Hounds; he said that Alcalde Leavenworth occasionally used them as agents of the law. Other accounts claim the Hounds were intent on creating mischief from the start. See Coblentz, *Villains and Vigilantes*, p. 34. Brown was an old resident and intimately acquainted with the merchants who had employed the Hounds (he had been a partner of one of the merchants), and his testimony should bear more weight. Whatever the exact nature of the origin of the Hounds, it seems clear that they had

connections to the business community and to the inchoate politics and government of the city at that time. Francis J. Lippitt, prosecutor at the Hounds' trial; Jonas Winchester, future publisher of the *Pacific News*; the *Annals*, San Francisco's first history; and argonault Charles F. Winslow each attest to this fact. Winchester even submitted that the Hounds exercised police powers. *Alta*, July 2, 1849; Jonas Winchester to E. Winchester, July 8, 1849, in Winchester Papers; *Annals*, pp. 553–61; Charles F. Winslow to Lydia Winslow, July 19, 1849, in Charles F. Winslow Letterbook.

77. Isaac Bluxome, Statement, pp. 4–7 (Bancroft Library, University of California); Charles Winslow to Lydia Winslow, July 19, 1849, in Charles F. Winslow Letterbook; *Alta*, July 19, 1849; Aug. 2, 1849.

78. Charles Winslow to a friend, Aug. 29, 1849, in Charles F. Winslow Letterbook.

79. *Alta*, Feb. 20, 1851; Feb. 22, 1851; Feb. 23, 1851; Feb. 24, 1851; Mar. 19, 1851.

80. George R. Stewart, the most recent historian of the Vigilantes, contends that Coleman was a moderate. If so, he seems to have been only a part-time moderate.

81. *Alta*, Apr. 27, 1851; May 5, 1851. Oscar Lewis thought that crime soared again. Lewis, *San Francisco* . . . , p. 60.

82. *Ibid.*, June 11, 1851.

83. Rev. Albert Williams, *A Pioneer Pastorate* . . . , pp. 1–3.

84. George R. Stewart, *Committee of Vigilance: Revolution in San Francisco* (Boston: Houghton Mifflin and Co., 1964), p. 330.

85. Certain kinds of robbery were punishable by death under California law.

86. *Alta*, Feb. 16, 1853.

87. For a more detailed discussion of the 1856 Committee, see Bancroft, *Popular Tribunals*, II; Valentine, *Vigilante Justice*; Coblentz, *Villains and Vigilantes*; and various other works.

88. So do many historians, though their defense varies in stridency and is not without considerable ambivalence. H. H. Bancroft, Josiah Royce, George R. Stewart, Allen Valentine, Stanton Coblentz, John S. Hittell, Oscar Lewis, and the triumvirate that authored the *Annals* have agreed upon the rectitude of the Vigilantes' course. See also Mary F. Williams, *The History of the San Francisco Vigilance Committee of 1851: A Study of Social Control on the California Frontier in the Days of the Gold Rush* (Berkeley: University of California Press, 1921); John S. Hittell, *A History of the City of San Francisco* . . . (San Francisco: A. L. Bancroft and Co., 1878); Josiah Royce, *California, American Commonwealth Series* (Boston and New York: Houghton, Mifflin and Co., 1886).

89. *Herald*, Oct. 10, 1851. *Alta*, Oct. 21, 1851; Oct. 22, 1856. Even the *Bulletin*, the great champion of the Vigilance Committee of 1856, carried numerous examples of lawlessness after the Committee disbanded. See that paper for the second half of 1856.

90. *Herald*, June 23, 1851.

91. *Era,* Sept. 21, 1856.

92. The 1856 group declared against this eventuality as had that of 1851, but in both cases these searches occurred.

93. *Bulletin,* Jan. 17, 1856.

94. *Alta,* Nov. 10, 1851; Jan. 31, 1852; Mar. 4, 1852; Jan. 21, 1853.

95. *Ibid.,* July 2, 1851; McCrackan to his family, San Francisco, Sept 14, 1852, in John McCrackan Letters, I.

96. *Alta,* June 4, 1851.

97. *Fireman's Journal,* Aug. 4, 1855. Up to this point the San Francisco experience paralleled the experience of other urban areas which were creating modern police forces to combat disorder. Thereafter, however, the city reverted back to vigilantism to effect the cure.

98. *Pacific,* Oct. 28, 1853; *Era,* Oct. 29, 1854; San Francisco, Charter of 1856, p. 9 (Bancroft Library, University of California), The *Annals* estimated the late 1849 population at 20,000 to 25,000. *Annals,* p. 244.

99. *Call,* Feb. 4, 1857; *Alta,* Mar. 27, 1854; May 25, 1854; May 29, 1854; Mar. 5, 1856; *Era,* Dec. 11, 1853; *Herald,* Feb. 28, 1852; *Chronicle,* June 3, 1854; Sept. 29, 1854.

100. *Bulletin,* Sept. 2, 1856.

101. *Herald,* June 6, 1851.

102. *Era,* Sept. 30, 1855; *Bulletin,* Nov. 10, 1856.

103. *Era,* Dec. 26, 1852; Aug. 24, 1856.

104. All the Recorder's statistics were compiled from monthly reports in the various newspapers.

105. *Chronicle,* Dec. 15, 1853.

106. *Chronicle,* June 14, 1854; *Alta,* Feb. 5, 1854; *Pacific,* Mar. 3, 1854; May 15, 1856; *Era,* Oct. 30, 1852.

107. *Herald,* Nov. 14, 1852; *Bulletin,* Jan. 29, 1856; *Courier,* Aug. 23, 1850.

108. *Alta,* Feb. 15, 1856.

109. *Ibid.,* June 13, 1854; July 13, 1854; Nov. 27, 1855; Oct. 1, 1856; *Era,* Dec. 18, 1853.

110. *Alta,* Mar. 31, 1854; *Chronicle,* Nov. 24, 1856.

111. *Ibid.,* Nov. 24, 1856; *Alta,* Oct. 1, 1856; *Bulletin,* Nov. 22, 1855; Mar. 7, 1856.

112. *Chronicle,* Dec. 4, 1856.

113. *Ibid.,* Dec. 4, 1856; *Era,* Apr. 9, 1854.

114. *Chronicle,* Dec. 4, 1856. See also *Pacific,* Oct. 16, 1856; *Era,* Nov. 16, 1856; and the *Chronicle,* 1853.

115. *Chronicle,* Dec. 4, 1856; *Herald,* Jan. 6, 1851; *Era,* Nov. 2, 1856.

116. *Pacific,* Nov. 16, 1855; *Alta,* Apr. 10, 1850; Dec. 10, 1853; July 28, 1854; Oct. 13, 1854; Feb. 2, 1856; Dec. 24, 1856; *Courier,* Dec. 7, 1850; *Herald,* Jan. 6, 1851; June 27, 1851; *Chronicle,* Oct. 13, 1852; Nov. 28, 1853; Dec. 21, 1853; June 2, 1854; Nov. 16, 1855; Feb. 6, 1856; Feb. 25, 1856; Feb. 28, 1856; Dec. 10, 1856; Dec. 12, 1856.

117. For a dissent from the prevailing view, see *Era,* Feb. 9, 1856.

118. *Bulletin*, Aug. 29, 1856; *Alta*, Nov. 22, 1853; June 14, 1855; Oct. 10, 1856; Nov. 8, 1856; Nov. 12, 1856.
119. Brown, *Early Days in San Francisco*, p. 35; *Alta*, Aug. 5, 1850; Feb. 8, 1849; see also Sept. 23, 1850; *Bulletin*, Aug. 29, 1856; *Courier*, Aug. 6, 1850.
120. *Alta*, Oct. 23, 1851; May 31, 1853; Oct. 1, 1853; June 1, 1856; Aug. 1, 1856; Oct. 1, 1856; Nov. 30, 1856; Dec. 2, 1856.

CHAPTER VIII

1. *Herald*, June 26, 1852; May 2, 1853; *Alta*, Nov. 16, 1855; Dec. 3, 1855; *Chronicle*, May 28, 1855.
2. *Bulletin*, Feb. 12, 1856.
3. *Chronicle*, Sept. 6, 1854; Aug. 17, 1855. (Italics theirs.)
4. McCrackan to Lottie, San Francisco, Mar. 3, 1850, pp. 2–3; same to same. San Francisco, Dec. 12, 1852, pp. 1–2, in John McCrackan Letters; Milo Hoadly, Diary, entry for Mar. 30, 1850, p. 23.
5. *Alta*, Mar. 21, 1850; Hoadley, Diary, entry for Mar. 30, 1850, p. 23; see also McCrackan to Lottie, San Francisco, Mar. 30, 1850, pp. 2–3, in John McCrackan Letters.
6. Willam Weston to his father, San Francisco, Apr. 28, 1851, in William K. Weston Papers.
7. *Alta*, Sept. 1, 1851; Oct. 26, 1856; Aug. 30, 1856. (Italics theirs.) Weston to his father, San Francisco, Apr. 28, 1851, in William K. Weston Papers. (Italics his.)
8. *Alta*, Mar. 26, 1850.
9. *Ibid.*, Jan. 15, 1849; Nov. 1, 1849; Dec. 31, 1849; Feb. 11, 1850; Mar. 4, 1850; Aug. 17, 1852; Aug. 6, 1854; *Bulletin*, Nov. 29, 1856; *Herald*, Apr. 8, 1851.
10. *Alta*, Oct. 13, 1852; Sept. 20, 1852; Aug. 24, 1856.
11. Since so much has been written about the competition and because it was more of a statewide rather than a San Francisco matter, this story will be neglected for a greater concentration on the local scene, i.e., the power base and locus of Broderick's operation, and on the impact of his organization on the metropolis. For a solid, spirited defense of Broderick's state political career, see David Williams, *David C. Broderick: A Political Portrait* (San Marino, Cal.: The Huntington Library, 1969).
12. Williams vigorously disputes the charge that he was probably corrupt. Broderick did occasionally declare himself publicly, notably on the Vigilante movements and the Jenny Lind Theater purchase; but one can search the prints in vain for his stand on many other important issues.
13. James O'Meara, *Broderick and Gwin* (San Francisco: Bacon and Co. Printers, 1881), pp. 20–21; Williams, *David C. Broderick . . .*, pp. 22–26.

14. O'Meara, *Broderick and Gwin*, pp. 22–23; *Chronicle*, Oct. 25, 1854.

15. Maguire is called the "Napoleon of the Theater" by Andrew Rolle; *Herald*, Nov. 18, 1853.

16. *Ibid.*, Nov. 1, 1852; *Alta*, Aug. 10, 1855; Aug. 27, 1855; Feb. 25, 1852.

17. *Chronicle*, Nov. 8, 1854; Thomas Reid, Diary, 1849, no page; Confession of Martin Gallagher in 1856 Vigilance Committee Papers (Huntington Library, San Marino).

18. *Alta*, Oct. 19, 1856; July 9, 1856.

19. *Chronicle*, June 2, 1855; Feb. 25, 1856; *Herald*, Oct. 2, 1852; Nov. 1, 1852.

20. *Alta*, May 22, 1855; O'Meara, *Broderick and Gwin*, p. 28; *Herald*, Apr. 29, 1853.

21. O'Meara, *Broderick and Gwin*, p. 84.

22. *Alta*, Mar. 30, 1855; Aug. 15, 1853; O'Meara, *Broderick and Gwin*, pp. 41–43, 136.

23. *Ibid.*, pp. 111, 116. There is a large and growing literature on bossism and city politics, including works by Callow, Stave, Zane Miller, Mandelbaum, Hays, Merton, Calvert, Tarr, Mann, Levine, Allswang, Holli, William Miller, Gottfried, Dorsett, and many others. These have raised very interesting questions about city politics, but the material on David C. Broderick is so limited that it is next to impossible to address the many suggestions recently put out by urban political historians. It is possible to connect Broderick with certain specific acts in the city; but until much more evidence appears, his role in meeting urban problems, in holding the city together with an informal system of control, in being the "great communicator," in assimilating and uplifting immigrants, etc. must remain somewhat unclear.

24. *Alta*, Oct. 24, 1856; *Bulletin*, Dec. 18, 1856; *Herald*, June 17, 1852; *Courier*, Sept. 20, 1850; *Chronicle*, June 16, 1855.

25. *Chronicle*, May 26, 1855; *Herald*, Feb. 26, 1852; June 17, 1852; *Alta*, Dec. 31, 1851; Feb. 27, 1852; June 28, 1852; July 19, 1854; Aug. 19, 1854; May 28, 1855; Sept. 8, 1856; O'Meara, *Broderick and Gwin*, pp. 31, 130.

26. *Alta*, Nov. 11, 1852; *Herald*, Aug. 17, 1852; O'Meara, *Broderick and Gwin*, pp. 31, 154; *Herald*, Mar. 18, 1852; *Alta*, Apr. 13, 1853; Confession of Terrence Kelly in 1856 Vigilance Committee Papers; *Bulletin*, Dec. 19, 1855; *Chronicle*, Sept. 10, 1855; O'Meara, *Broderick and Gwin*, pp. 1–192.

27. *Ibid.*, pp. 92, 97–102; *Alta*, Feb. 27, 1852; June 29, 1855.

28. *Alta*, Dec. 31, 1856.

29. Robert S. Lammot to his mother, San Francisco, May 15, 1851, in Lammot Family Correspondence; *Alta*, Sept. 25, 1851; Oct. 25, 1852; Apr. 18, 1855; *Herald*, Oct. 14, 1852.

30. Jonas Winchester to Ebenezer, San Francisco, Mar. 31, 1850, in Jonas Winchester Papers.

31. *Alta*, June 19, 1856. For the prevalence of violence among all classes, see chapter on Urban Problems.

32. *Pacific*, Dec. 11, 1856; see also *Chronicle*, Sept. 6, 1855. The Vigilance Committee of 1856 held investigations into the electoral fraud and, among other things, came up with a ballot box, apparently used only in Democratic primaries, whose trick sides allowed stuffing. *Alta*, May 30, 1856; letter of William T. Sherman to his brother, San Francisco, Aug. 19, 1856, in William T. Sherman Papers (California Historical Society). This and the other evidence scraped up by the Vigilance Committee does not substantiate the thesis that fraud carried the day in San Francisco elections. See Vigilance Committee Papers of 1856 in the Huntington Library, San Marino, California.

33. *Alta*, Sept. 4, 1853; Oct. 25, 1856; O'Meara, *Broderick and Gwin*, p. 85.

34. *Alta*, June 26, 1855; June 24, 1856; Robert S. Lammot to his sister, San Francisco, Sept. 23, 1850, pp. 1–2, in Lammot Family Correspondence; *Chronicle*, Nov. 4, 1854.

35. Thomas Douglas in *The Overland Monthly* for Dec. 1884, quoted in W. W. Ferrier, *Ninety Years of Education in California* (Berkeley, Cal.: Sather Gate Book Shop, 1937), p. 25; *Alta*, Sept. 7, 1852.

36. *Ibid.*, Jan. 4, 1850; *Annals*, p. 228; Bancroft, *History of California*, VI, 196.

37. Williams, *David C. Broderick*. . . .

38. Francis Edward Prevaux to his parents, San Francisco, Sept. 18, 1855, pp. 1–2, in Francis Edward Prevaux Letters; see also Jeremiah Lynch, *The Life of David C. Broderick* (New York: Baker and Taylor Co., 1911), pp. 70–71, who calls Broderick "the dictator of the municipality."

39. *Herald*, May 31, 1851.

40. *Alta*, July 27, 1852; *Courier*, Aug. 5, 1850.

41. Both practised representative "constituency politics." See below.

42. *Pacific*, July 17, 1856.

43. Coit, *An Artist in Eldorado* . . . , p. 31; *Chronicle*, Dec. 20, 1853; Oct. 23, 1854; McCrackan to Lottie, San Francisco, Sept. 14, 1853, pp. 1–3, in John McCrackan Letters; *Alta*, Aug. 24, 1855.

44. *Alta*, May 23, 1855; June 20, 1855; Aug. 10, 1855; Aug. 14, 1855; Sept. 3, 1855; Sept. 13, 1854; *Bulletin*, Oct. 13, 1855; Dec. 28, 1855; *Chronicle*, Aug. 23, 1854; Sept. 20, 1854; *Pacific*, Oct. 27, 1854.

45. *Alta*, Aug. 10, 1855; *Chronicle*, Sept. 14, 1854; Peyton Hurt, "The Rise and Fall of the Know Nothings," *California Historical Society Quarterly*, IX (March–June 1930), 16–49; *Alta*, July 17, 1854; May 10, 1855; June 20, 1855; Aug. 9, 1855; May 23, 1855.

46. *Phoenix*, see selected issues for 1856 and 1857 extant at California Historical Society; see also Ned McGowan, *The Narrative of Ned McGowan* . . . (San Francisco: Published by the author, 1857), pp. 229–30; *Alta*, Mar. 31, 1855; May 12, 1855; May 28, 1855.

47. *Chronicle*, Dec. 11, 1854. For a fuller discussion, see Peyton Hurt, "The Rise and Fall of the Know Nothings."

48. Letter no. 1, Aug. 1, 1849, Osgood Church Wheeler, "Selected Letters of Osgood C. Wheeler," ed. Sandford Fleming, *California Historical Society Quarterly*, XXVII (Mar. 1948), 16; *Herald*, Sept. 26, 1856; *Alta*, Sept. 7, 1854.

49. *Alta*, Apr. 18, 1855; Owen P. Sutton, Statement, p. 9 (Bancroft Library, University of California).

50. For a full discussion of 1856, see chapter on the Revolution of 1856.

51. *Bulletin*, Nov. 29, 1856. San Francisco had about 14 per cent of the entire population of the state. See also *Alta*, Nov. 8, 1856; *Bulletin*, Oct. 20, 1856; Oct. 25, 1856; Nov. 6, 1856; Dec. 3, 1856. For a fuller discussion of ante-bellum urban Republican politics which also lays heavy emphasis upon local factors in explaining the rise of the G.O.P., see Michael Holt, *Forging a Majority: The Formation of the Republican Party in Pittsburgh, 1848–1860* (New Haven: Yale University Press, 1969).

52. There is a growing body of literature that stresses the primacy of religious, ethnic, and ethno-cultural factors in political history. For a good summary of the literature, see Robert Swierenga, "Ethno-Cultural Political Analysis," *American Studies*, V, No. 1 (Apr. 1971), 59–79. Specific applications of this approach to American cities have been made by John Allswang, *A House for All Peoples: Ethnic Politics in Chicago, 1890–1896* (Lexington: University of Kentucky Press, 1971); Edward M. Levine, *The Irish and Irish Politicians: A Study of Cultural and Social Alienation* (Notre Dame: University of Notre Dame Press, 1966); Joel A. Tarr, *A Study in Boss Politics: William Lorimer of Chicago* (Urbana: University of Illinois Press, 1971).

53. See chapter on Government for the details. William J. Shaw, Dictation, pp. 50–60 (Bancroft Library, University of California); *Alta*, Sept. 1, 1853; Sept. 3, 1853; Aert Van Nostrand to Rodman M. Price, San Francisco, Feb. 2, 1850, p. 13, in Rodman Price Correspondence and Papers.

54. *Alta*, Nov. 29, 1852; Dec. 12, 1853; Dec. 16, 1853; *Bulletin*, Jan. 25, 1856; Feb. 2, 1856; Apr. 22, 1856; Sept. 20, 1856. See chapter on the Revolution of 1856.

55. William J. Eames to Thomas O. Larkin, Feb. 28, 1853, in *The Larkin Papers*, IX, 254; *Alta*, June 23, 1854; July 17, 1854; *Chronicle*, Jan. 7, 1854; *Herald*, Nov. 24, 1853; *Era*, Oct. 19, 1856.

56. For further discussion of the "power structure" question, see Edward Banfield, *Political Influence* (New York: The Free Press, 1961); Robert A. Dahl, *Who Governs?* (New Haven: Yale University Press, 1961); Edward C. Hayes, *Power Structure and Urban Policy* (New York: McGraw-Hill, 1972); Floyd Hunter, *Community Power Structure* (Chapel Hill: University of North Carolina Press, 1953).

57. *Fireman's Journal*, July 28, 1855; *Courier*, July 6, 1850.

58. *Chronicle*, Dec. 27, 1855; *Herald*, Dec. 19, 1850; Dec. 24, 1850; Aug. 18, 1852; *Courier*, Aug. 5, 1850; *Alta*, Feb. 17, 1854.

59. *Chronicle*, July 27, 1855; see also *Chronicle*, Apr. 3, 1854; *Alta*, Feb. 22, 1849; Aug. 8, 1850; *Californian*, Mar. 15, 1848; May 24, 1848.
60. *California Christian Advocate*, Apr. 7, 1854; Edward Kemble, *A History of California Newspapers, 1846–1858*, ed. Helen Bretnor (Los Gatos, Cal.: The Talisman Press, 1962), pp. 110–11; *Alta*, Oct. 15, 1850; Feb. 20, 1852; Oct. 19, 1852; Apr. 25, 1853; McCrackan to his family, San Francisco, May 22, 1853, pp. 1–6, in John McCrackan Letters; *Herald*, May 1, 1852; Sept. 24, 1856; *Chronicle*, Sept. 5, 1856; Sept. 24, 1856; *Pacific*, Oct. 2, 1856; *Pacific*, Nov. 5, 1852; Nov. 12, 1852; June 23, 1854; Aug. 4, 1854; Oct. 12, 1855; *Era*, June 5, 1853.
61. *Pacific*, Dec. 23, 1853; *Era*, Oct. 9, 1853; May 11, 1856.
62. *Pacific*, July 22, 1853.
63. *Herald*, May 3, 1851; March 17, 1852; June 26, 1852; Feb. 11, 1853; Feb. 19, 1853; Feb. 25, 1853; May 14, 1853; May 20, 1853; *Alta*, Dec. 3, 1855.
64. *Chronicle*, Oct. 12, 1855; Jan. 6, 1854 (italics theirs); see also *Chronicle*, Apr. 16, 1855; *Alta*, Dec. 17, 1850; Dec. 23, 1850; Apr. 12, 1852; Apr. 20, 1852; June 19, 1853; Mar. 14, 1856; *Herald*, Oct. 17, 1853.
65. *Bulletin*, Dec. 8, 1856; *Chronicle*, Jan. 4, 1856.
66. *Ibid.*
67. *Bulletin*, July 9, 1856; July 16, 1856. (Italics theirs.)
68. *Ibid.*, Apr. 9, 1856. Caxton was the pseudonym for William Henry Rhodes, a resident Southerner in the city. He supported both the Vigilance Committee and the reform movement and probably gave the most direct expression to threats of disunionism.
69. *Chronicle*, Apr. 16, 1855. (Italics theirs.)
70. *Bulletin*, Nov. 29, 1856.

CHAPTER IX

1. This chapter has leaned heavily on the *Bulletin* for documentation. Because of its leading role in the Vigilante uprising and reform crusade, I thought it important to stress the voice of these movements. However, the resource base is much broader, as the previous chapter and entire study indicate.
2. *Alta*, July 1, 1856.
3. Bancroft, *History of California*, VI, 774–75; *Bulletin*, Nov. 19, 1856. On a table of tax rates which included fourteen cities, San Francisco was ninth. The county and state tax rates were subtracted from my calculation because county and state taxes were not given for the other cities. The San Francisco figure was given in the table as $2.33, but only $1.60 was city taxes. Obviously there is no necessary correlation between reduced expenditures and urban well-being. Yet the people did demand reductions all along the line; and, whether sensible or not, they at least were democratic and therefore refute the charge of tyranny.
4. *Herald*, Apr. 15, 1853.

5. William J. Eames to Thomas O. Larkin, San Francisco, Apr. 29, 1853, in *The Larkin Papers*, IX, 252.

6. *Bulletin*, Oct. 13, 1855.

7. *Era*, Sept. 10, 1854; *Bulletin*, Feb. 9, 1856; *Alta*, May 29, 1855; Aug. 29, 1855; Sept. 5, 1855; Sept. 6, 1855; *Chronicle*, May 23, 1855; May 28, 1855; May 29, 1855; Sept. 13, 1855.

8. *Era*, July 1, 1855.

9. *Alta*, Mar. 8, 1851; Mar. 15, 1851, Mar. 23, 1851; William J. Shaw, Dictation, pp. 50–60; John C. Pelton, *Life's Sunbeams and Shadows* (San Francisco: The Bancroft Company, 1893), pp. 229–30.

10. *Chronicle*, Mar. 28, 1855.

11. *Pacific*, Apr. 23, 1853; July 29, 1853; Jan. 24, 1856; *Alta*, Aug. 29, 1855; *Era*, Jan. 6, 1856.

12. John Denton Carter, "The San Francisco *Bulletin*, 1855–1865: A Study in the Beginnings of Pacific Coast Journalism" (unpublished Ph. D. dissertation, University of California at Berkeley, 1941).

13. *Bulletin*, Apr. 26, 1856. (Italics his.)

14. *Ibid.*, Apr. 22, 1856; Apr. 30, 1856.

15. *Ibid.*, Apr. 26, 1856.

16. Mulligan was a functionary under Sheriff Scannell. *Bulletin*, May 2, 1856; May 3, 1856.

17. *Ibid.*, Jan. 5, 1856.

18. Various spellings are given for Belle Cora's real name, including both Ryan and Bryan. *Bulletin*, Jan. 22, 1856.

19. *Bulletin*, Jan. 16, 1856; Jan. 22, 1856. (Italics hers.) Feb. 16, 1856; *Era*, Oct. 9, 1853; *Fireman's Journal*, Nov. 10, 1855.

20. *Bulletin*, Jan. 24, 1856.

21. Page Smith has argued that antislavery agitation provided "the means of entry into American political life of a vast number of women." *Daughters of the Promised Land: Women in American History* (Boston: Little, Brown & Co., 1970), p. 111. In San Francisco, antisalvery did not provide a similar means; but the "Revolution of 1856" certainly did, as female influence was very strong before and during the episode and King's political journalism was surely calculated to appeal to women.

22. *Bulletin*, Jan. 16, 1856; Jan. 22, 1856; Jan. 24, 1856.

23. A recent interpretation of the Vigilantes by Richard Maxwell Brown stresses the fiscal-ethnic dimension of the story. According to Brown, the uprising was an attempt to smash the Broderick machine in order to restore the credit of the city with Eastern financiers. He feels the Viligantes did not confront the question of how to finance large-scale urban works without corruption and also ignored the question of whether "newcomers of minority groups status . . . should be fully absorbed into American life." Brown, "Pivot of American Vigilantism: The San Francisco Vigilance Committee of 1856," *Reflections of Western Historians*, John Carroll, ed. (Tucson: University of Arizona Press, 1969), pp. 105–19. I found no such evidence. This argument discounts the intense emotionalism generated by

James King of William; it ignores the fact that the Consolidation Act of 1856 had already laid the basis for restoring the city's finances *before* the Vigilantes arose; and it ignores the fact that the credit of the community was much more damaged by the merchant class than by the politicians. If lynching and deportations automatically flowed from the city's financial necessities, then the lamp posts would have been overwhelmed with the defaulting bankers, merchants, and retailers. (See above.) Moreover, in regard to the supposed inability of cities to finance large improvements without graft, one should note that the reform government did preside over a considerable growth in the many years they ruled the city. Finally, the ethnic thesis of Brown's is very hard to support. The Irish did make up a large number of the Broderick side, but contemporaries saw his machine as having many non-Irish allies. In addition, it is difficult to defend the argument that the "minorities" were being left out because the Germans and French played an important role in the 1856 committee, and the committee went to great lengths to assure minorities that they were not nativist. And, too, the law and order side also clearly tried to whip up ethnic tensions.

24. *Bulletin*, May 16, 1856.
25. *Pacific*, July 31, 1856; Bancroft, *Popular Tribunals*, II, 196–97, 202–3, 344–45, 653–62.
26. *Fireman's Journal*, May 17, 1856; *Era*, Oct. 28, 1855; May 25, 1856; William A. Scott to "My Dear Friend," San Francisco, Dec. 1856, pp. 1–2, in William A. Scott Correspondence and Papers (Bancroft Library, University of California); letter of William A. Scott to *True Californian*, Oct. 4, 1856, in William A. Scott Correspondence and Papers; *Pacific*, June 12, 1856.
27. *Chronicle*, May 19, 1856.
28. *Pacific*, June 12, 1856; June 19, 1856. (Italics theirs.)
29. *Era*, Oct. 28, 1856; see also Owen Wister Gibbs, *Shadow and Light*, pp. 51–56.
30. *Bulletin*, May 17, 1856; Nov. 7, 1856; *Era*, Aug. 10, 1856.
31. *Ibid.*, Nov. 7, 1856.
32. Reprint in the *Bulletin*, Sept. 2, 1856. (Italics theirs.) *Bulletin*, Sept. 19, 1856.
33. *Bulletin*, Oct. 29, 1856; Nov. 3, 1856.
34. *Ibid.*, June 5, 1856; Aug. 9, 1856; Aug. 12, 1856; *Pacific*, Nov. 13, 1856; reprint from the *Herald* in the *Bulletin* for Aug. 30, 1856.
35. *Bulletin*, Aug. 27, 1856; Oct. 9, 1856.
36. *Ibid.*, May 20, 1856; June 14, 1856; *Alta*, June 13, 1856; *Pacific*, July 10, 1856.
37. *Alta*, Aug. 11, 1856; *Chronicle*, Aug. 12, 1856.
38. *Bulletin*, Dec. 2, 1856.
39. See Chapter XI on the rationale for public education.
40. *Bulletin*, July 15, 1856.
41. *Ibid.*, Oct. 28, 1856.

42. *Ibid.*, May 31, 1856. (Italics theirs.) For a thorough discussion of the overtaxation of the middle classes, see C. Yearley, *The Money Machines: The Breakdown and Reform of Governmental and Party Finance in the North, 1860–1920* (Albany: State University of New York Press, 1970). Reprint in the *Bulletin* for Aug. 26, 1856; *Bulletin*, Aug. 27, 1856.

43. *Era*, June 1, 1856; *Bulletin*, Aug. 12, 1856.

44. *Alta*, Aug. 9, 1856; *Israelite*, Dec. 26, 1856; *Bulletin*, Oct. 30, 1856.

45. *Bulletin*, June 10, 1856.

46. Election returns printed in the *Bulletin* for Nov. 25, 1856.

47. *Bulletin*, Aug. 18, 1856.

48. Royce, *California*, p. 438, speaks of "regenerating the social order."

49. *Bulletin*, May 28, 1856; *Chronicle*, June 14, 1856.

50. *Bulletin*, May 28, 1856.

51. *Chronicle*, Aug. 31, 1856.

52. *Ibid.*, Aug. 24, 1856.

53. *Bulletin*, May 20, 1856.

54. *Ibid.*, Sept. 16, 1856; Oct. 21, 1856.

55. *Alta*, Oct. 25, 1856; *Bulletin*, Oct. 27, 1856; *Pacific*, July 9, 1852; *Fireman's Journal*, May 17, 1856.

56. C. J. Dempster, Statement, pp. 17–18 (Bancroft Library, University of California).

57. *Chronicle*, Sept. 22, 1856.

58. *Ibid.*, Nov. 8, 1856. For other admissions of the popular indifference to civic corruption through the period, see the following: *Alta*, June 28, 1850; *Bulletin*, May 20, 1856; *Call*, Feb. 4, 1857; *Chronicle*, Nov. 24, 1853; *Herald*, Mar. 4, 1851; *Courier*, July 23, 1850; *Picayune*, Jan. 17, 1851; J. K. Osgood to George Strang, San Francisco, June 10, 1850, pp. 2–4, in J. K. Osgood Letters; McCrackan to Lottie, San Francisco, Feb. 26, 1853, p. 1, in John McCrackan Letters, II. Many similar citations could be given from these same sources.

59. William A. Scott to Rev. Dr. McKinney, San Francisco, Oct. 18, 1856, in William A. Scott Correspondence and Papers.

CHAPTER X

1. *Bulletin*, Dec. 26, 1856.

2. *Era*, Oct. 28, 1855. "Puritan" in this case is being used in the pejorative and not necessarily in the accurate, historical sense, since many would argue that the Puritans were not "puritanical."

3. For a discussion of the "private city" and its opposite, see Sam B. Warner, *The Private City* (Philadelphia: University of Pennsylvania Press, 1968).

4. Contemporary New Orleans had a fascinating street life. Harry Kmen, *Music in New Orleans: The Formative Years, 1791–1841* (Baton Rouge: Louisiana State University Press, 1966), pp. 201–12, 226–47.

5. *Bulletin*, July 3, 1856; *Alta*, June 28, 1852; Feb. 23, 1856; *Fireman's Journal*, Nov. 10, 1855; *Era*, Jan. 21, 1855; Aug. 26, 1855.

6. *Era*, June 18, 1853; July 15, 1855.

7. Pfeiffer, *A Lady's Visit to California* . . . , p. 13.

8. *Ibid.*, pp. 6–7; Nasatir, *A Frenchman in the Gold Rush*, p. 86, letter of March 1, 1850; *Alta*, Oct. 30, 1854; Oct. 27, 1856; Barry and Patten, *Men and Memories* . . . , pp. 142–43.

9. *Era*, Feb. 11, 1855; *Fireman's Journal*, July 7, 1855.

10. *Era*, Aug. 26, 1855.

11. *Alta*, Oct. 26, 1855; Woodin to his wife, San Francisco, Oct. 5, 1852, p. 1, in Stephen Woodin Papers.

12. *Fireman's Journal*, July 21, 1855; June 23, 1855; *Era*, July 9, 1855.

13. *Bulletin*, Dec. 26, 1856; Sir Henry Vere Huntley, *California, Its Gold and Its Inhabitants* (London: T. C. Newby, 1856), I, 2.

14. Letter of John W. Geary to his brother, San Francisco, April 15, 1849, p. 4, in John W. Geary Letters (Oregon Historical Society); Kimball, City Directory for 1850, p. 130; *Era*, Sept. 25, 1853; Sept. 3, 1854; *Fireman's Journal*, Apr. 5, 1856; Sept. 27, 1856; *Era*, May 4, 1856; Dec. 26, 1852; Oct. 14, 1855; Apr. 9, 1854; July 22, 1855; Sept. 30, 1855; letters of June 15, 1855, and June 16, 1855, in Henry Larcom Abbot Collection (Oregon Historical Society).

15. For the argument that diversity does these things in a modern city, see Dorothy Lee, "Suburbia Reconsidered: Diversity and the Creative Life," in Elizabeth Geen et. al., ed., *Man and the Modern City* (Pittsburgh: University of Pittsburgh Press, 1963), pp. 122–34; *Pacific*, Feb. 11, 1853; *Era*, Oct. 28, 1855.

16. *Era*, Mar. 8, 1853. For the proximity of the country to the city, see the U.S. Coast Survey maps for 1853 and 1857 (Bancroft Library, University of California); James C. Ward, Diary, entry for 1847, reprinted in "Extracts from the Diary of James C. Ward," *The Argonaut* (Bancroft Library, University of California); *Bulletin*, Feb. 20, 1856.

17. Rev. Samuel C. Damon, *A Journey to Lower Oregon and Upper California, 1848–49* (San Francisco: John C. Newbegin, 1927), p. 84; *Alta*, Nov. 30, 1853; Aug. 30, 1854; June 8, 1855.

18. *Alta*, June 12, 1854.

19. *Ibid.*, June 4, 1850; May 1, 1854; Sept. 24, 1856.

20. *Bulletin*, Aug. 16, 1856.

21. *Pacific*, June 22, 1855; *Era*, Mar. 8, 1853; Apr. 13, 1856; *Chronicle*, Nov. 17, 1855; Glaab and Brown, *History of Urban America*, pp. 254–55.

22. *Chronicle*, June 10, 1855.

23. For a good discussion of the impact of urbanism on sports, see Dale Somers, *The Rise of Sports in New Orleans, 1850–1900* (Baton Rouge: Louisiana State University Press, 1972) and David Quentin Voigt, *American Baseball* (Norman, Okla.: University of Oklahoma Press, 1966).

24. *Californian*, Mar. 15, 1848; *Chronicle*, Jan. 19, 1856; *Picayune*, Sept. 23,

1851; *Alta*, Oct. 27, 1851; Sept. 12, 1852; Sept. 17, 1854; Dec. 27, 1856; Nov. 7, 1853.

25. *Alta*, Oct. 17, 1850; Feb. 5, 1855; June 7, 1856.

26. *Herald*, Feb. 2, 1853.

27. *Alta*, Aug. 27, 1853.

28. Hunt, Diaries, I, entry for Jan. 1, 1849. (Italics his.) Prevaux to his parents, San Francisco, April 30, 1855, p. 2, in Francis Prevaux Letters.

29. *Era*, Mar. 4, 1855; McCrackan to his family, San Francisco, June 16, 1850, p. 2, in John McCrackan Letters, I; McCrackan to Mary, San Francisco, June 6, 1852, pp. 7–8, in John McCrackan Letters, II.

30. *Alta*, Sept. 29, 1851.

31. McCrackan to Lottie, San Francisco, May 30, 1850, pp. 2–4, in John McCrackan Letters, I.

32. *Alta*, Oct. 18, 1850; Jan. 27, 1851; *Era*, Aug. 19, 1855.

33. Friedrich Gerstacker, *Gerstacker's Travels* (London: T. Nelson and Sons, 1854), pp. 271–72; James Lamson, *Diary*, entry for July 2, 1853, I, 30.

34. *Alta*, July 12, 1849; Sept. 10, 1855; *Fireman's Journal*, Sept. 29, 1855; McCrackan to Lottie, San Francisco, May 15, 1853, p. 1, in John Mc-Crackan Letters, II; George R. MacMinn, *The Theater of the Golden Era in California* (Caldwell, Idaho: Caxton Printers Limited, 1941), p. 402.

35. Glaab and Brown, *A History of Urban America*, pp. 99–100; MacMinn, *Theater* . . . , p. 402.

36. *Alta*, May 25, 1856; see also *Alta*, Dec. 10, 1856; Dec. 28, 1856; *Chronicle*, Dec. 2, 1856; *Herald*, Sept. 16, 1856.

37. Edmond McAdoo Gagey, *The San Francisco Stage: A History* (New York: Columbia University Press, 1950), p. 4; *Alta*, Jan. 18, 1850; Jan. 25, 1850; Oct. 24, 1851; MacMinn, *Theater* . . . , pp. 143, 197; Andrew F. Rolle, *California: A History* (New York: Thomas Y. Crowell Co., 1963), pp. 271–72.

38. *Era*, Mar. 18, 1855; Aug. 5, 1855; *Fireman's Journal*, Aug. 11, 1855; Sept. 6, 1856; *Bulletin*, Dec. 19, 1856.

39. *Era*, Aug. 5, 1855; Aug. 19, 1856; *Fireman's Journal*, Aug. 23, 1856. For the argument that Californians had an "insatiable appetite for every kind of theatrical entertainment" and "seldom had too much" of Shakespeare, etc., see MacMinn, *Theater* . . . , p. 109; *Alta*, Apr. 19, 1852; Feb. 15, 1855; *Bulletin*, Dec. 19, 1856; Gagey, *San Francisco Stage*, p. 3.

40. *The Pacific*, quoted in the *Herald*, 1851, exact date missing; *Alta*, May 23, 1853; Dec. 25, 1856; *Herald*, 1851, exact date missing; *Fireman's Journal*, Sept. 1, 1855; *Era*, Nov. 27, 1853.

41. MacMinn, *Theater* . . . , pp. 270–82, 301; Barry and Patten, *Men and Memories* . . . , p. 34.

42. J. K. Osgood to George Strang, San Francisco, Aug. 23, 1849, p. 2, in J. K. Osgood Letters; McCrackan to Mary, San Francisco, Feb. 13, 1852, pp. 1–2, in John McCrackan Letters, I; see also William Ingraham Kip, *Early Days of My Episcopate* (New York, no publisher, 1892), p. 29.

43. Col. James J. Ayers, *Gold and Sunshine: Reminiscences of Early California* (Boston: The Gorham Press, 1922), pp. 35–37.

44. Brown, *Early Days* . . . , p. 110.

45. Letter of Oct. 10, 1851, in *California Emigrant Letters,* ed. Walker D. Wyman (New York: Bookman Associates, 1952), pp. 169–70. See also McCrackan to Mary, San Francisco, Dec. 9, 1849, p. 2, in John McCrackan Letters, I; Chester L. Lyman, *Around the Horn to the Sandwich Islands and California, 1845–1850,* ed. Frederick J. Taggart (New Haven; Yale University Press, 1924), p. 214; and *Le Phare,* quoted in *Chronicle,* Nov. 10, 1855.

46. McCrackan to his sister, San Francisco, Feb. 27, 1852, p. 4, in John McCrackan Letters, I.

47. William S. Jewett, "Some Letters of William S. Jewett, California Artist," ed. Elliot Evans, *California Historical Society Quarterly,* XXIII, No. 2 (June 1944), 162; *Alta,* Sept. 11, 1850.

48. *Picayune,* Dec. 21, 1850; Elisha O. Crosby, *Memoirs* . . . , ed. Charles Albro Barker (San Marino: The Ward Ritchie Press, 1945), pp. 107–9; *Alta,* Aug. 12, 1850; McCrackan to Mary, San Francisco, Jan. 28, 1850, p. 4, in John McCrackan Letters, I.

49. *Chronicle,* Feb. 2, 1854; see also *Chronicle,* Nov. 8, 1856; *Alta,* June 12, 1854.

50. Levi Stowell, "Bound for the Land of Canaan, Ho! . . . ," Diary entry for July 28, 1849; William Tecumseh Sherman to Miss Ewing, San Francisco, June 30, 1853, in *Home Letters of General William Tecumseh Sherman,* ed. Mark A. DeWolfe Howe (New York: Charles Scribner's Sons, 1909).

51. McCrackan to his family, San Francisco, Feb. 13, 1851, pp. 1–2, in John McCrackan Letters, I; Stowell, Diary entry for July 22, 1849.

52. Winchester to his wife, San Francisco, Feb. 28, 1850, in Jonas Winchester Papers; see also Winchester to his wife, San Francisco, Mar. 31, 1850, in Jonas Winchester Papers; J. K. Osgood to George Strang, San Francisco, June 10, 1850, p. 4, in J. K. Osgood Letters; Robert Lammot to his father, San Francisco, July 22, 1851, in Lammot Family Correspondence; George Howard to Agnes Howard, San Francisco, Apr. 11, 1855, in W. D. M. Howard Papers.

53. David Cosad, Diary, entry for Nov. 2, 1849; Ryan, *Personal Adventures* . . . , pp. 269–70.

54. Stephen J. Field, *California Alcalde* (Washington, D.C., 1880), p. 17, entry for Dec. 28, 1849.

55. McCrackan to Mary, San Francisco, Feb. 13, 1852, pp. 1–2, in John McCrackan Letters, I; McCrackan to his family, San Francisco, June 23, 1851, in John McCrackan Letters, I; J. D. Borthwick, *Three Years in California* (Edinburgh, 1857), p. 59; Taylor, *Seeing the Elephant* . . . , pp. 59–60, entry for Aug. 22, 1849; Williams, *A Pioneer Pastorate,* p. 99.

56. William S. M'Collum, M. D., *California as I Saw It: Its New Cities and*

Villages . . . , (Buffalo, N.Y.; George H. Derby and Company, 1850), p. 62.

57. Robert S. Lammot to his mother, San Francisco, Feb. 21, 1851, p. 2, in Lammot Family Correspondence; see also Eastland to his uncle, San Francisco, Jan. 15, 1851, in Joseph G. Eastland Papers; McCrackan to his family, San Francisco, July 17, 1853, in John McCrackan Letters, II; see also *Chronicle*, Feb. 2, 1856; Jan. 26, 1856; Feb. 4, 1856; Nov. 10, 1856; Nov. 11, 1856; *Chronicle*, Feb. 5, 1856.

58. *Bulletin*, Jan. 21, 1856; Jan. 22, 1856; *Annals*, p. 630.

59. *Chronicle*, Sept. 5, 1854; Sherman to Miss Ewing, San Francisco, June 30, 1853, in *Home Letters* . . . ; *Chronicle*, Nov. 24, 1856; *Bulletin*, Sept. 30, 1856; Dec. 4, 1856.

60. Eastland to Uncle Alfred, San Francisco, Jan. 15, 1851, in Joseph G. Eastland Papers.

61. *Alta*, Dec. 3, 1855.

62. Ferdinand C. Ewer, Diary, entry for Dec. 1, 1854, p. 217; see also Barry and Patten, *Men and Memories* . . . , p. 128.

63. Alexander Grogan to Faxon D. Atherton, San Francisco, Aug. 19, 1856, in Faxon D. Atherton Papers.

64. *Alta*, Dec. 16, 1856; Dec. 20, 1856.

65. *Chronicle*, June 25, 1856; see also J. D. Farwell, Statement (Bancroft Library, University of California).

66. See also *Herald*, Jan. 3, 1853; *Alta*, Aug. 29, 1853.

67. When Hubert Howe Bancroft began collecting the personal reminiscences of Californians, those who wrote on the metropolis almost invariably devoted an inordinantly large part of their account to the San Francisco of 1848 and 1849; Thomas O. Larkin to Stearnes, San Francisco, Apr. 24, 1856, in *The Larkin Papers*, X, 263. Nor was the depression in which Larkin wrote the only cause of this attitude. The same nostalgia was expressed in good times and bad, before and after the year 1856 and its economic and political troubles.

CHAPTER XI

1. *Bulletin*, Jan. 23, 1856; For works on the history of women, see Page Smith, *Daughters of the Promised Land* . . . ; William L. O'Neill, *Everyone Was Brave: A History of Feminism in America* (Chicago: Quadrangle Books, 1971); David Kennedy, *Birth Control in America: The Career of Margaret Sanger* (New Haven: Yale University Press, 1970); Robert Riegel, *American Women: A Story of Social Change* (Rutherford, N.J.: Farleigh Dickenson University Press, 1970); Aileen S. Kraditor, *The Ideas of the Woman Suffrage Movement, 1890–1920* (New York: Columbia University Press, 1965).

2. de Russailh, *Last Adventure* . . . , pp. 27–30; *California Emigrant Letters*, ed. Walker D. Wyman (New York: Bookman Associates, 1952), letter of Oct. 10, 1849, p. 169.

3. Booth, entry for Oct. 18, 1849, p. 234; Winchester to Susan, San Francisco, July 16, 1850, in Jonas Winchester Papers; *Courier*, Oct. 17, 1850; *Herald*, May 30, 1853; *Alta*, Nov. 30, 1854.

4. Mrs. Benjamin F. Butler, *Memoirs* (California Historical Society); Wm. R. Ryan, *Personal Adventures* . . . , pp. 28–85; *Alta*, July 22, 1855.

5. *Picayune*, Sept. 27, 1850; *Alta*, Jan. 13, 1853; Mar. 4, 1853; May 3, 1853; *Pacific*, Oct. 31, 1851; *Oct.* 20, 1854; *Picayune*, Sept. 27, 1850.

6. *Herald*, May 30, 1853; June 4, 1853.

7. Alfred and Chastina Rix, Diary, pp. 198–99, in Alfred Rix Papers.

8. *Ibid.*, entry for Jan. 1, 1854.

9. Langley, City Directory for 1858. Women were 35 per cent of the boardinghouse operators in 1857–58; *Era*, May 6, 1855.

10. *Chronicle*, Sept. 28, 1854; MacMinn, *Theater* . . . , p. 172; *Alta*, Dec. 14, 1850; Aug. 7, 1851; July 9, 1851; July 14, 1851; July 15, 1851; Aug. 10, 1851; Sept. 23, 1854; *Era*, Oct. 1, 1854; Nov. 12, 1854; June 3, 1855; July 8, 1855; Woodin to his wife, San Francisco, May 13, 1853, in Stephen Woodin Papers.

11. *Chronicle*, Feb. 11, 1856.

12. McCrackan to Lottie, San Francisco, July 13, 1852, pp. 1–2, in John McCrackan Letters, II; letter of Sylvester Mowry to Edward Bicknall, San Francisco, May 30, 1853, p. 4, in Sylvester Mowry Letters (Bancroft Library, University of California).

13. McCrackan to his family, San Francisco, May 22, 1853, pp. 1–6, in John McCrackan Letters, II; *Daily Evening News*, Mar. 28, 1855; *Chronicle*, Oct. 2, 1854; *Era*, May 13, 1855; *Alta*, Oct. 2, 1854; MacMinn, *Theater* . . . , p. 287.

14. *Herald*, June 1, 1852; *Alta*, June 3, 1854; *Chronicle*, Nov. 26, 1856; *Bulletin*, Jan. 25, 1856; Mar. 8, 1856; *Era*, Dec. 31, 1854; May 6, 1855; May 13, 1855; Sept. 9, 1855.

15. *Era*, Feb. 3, 1856; *Pacific*, Sept. 4, 1856.

16. *Chronicle*, Nov. 8, 1856; *Era*, Mar. 23, 1856; Nov. 2, 1856; Huntley, *California, Its Gold and Its Inhabitants*, II, 28; *Pacific*, Dec. 4, 1856; June 19, 1856; Colville, *City Directory for 1856*. Liberalized divorce procedures were among the contemporary feminists' demands. See Page Smith, *Daughters of the Promised Land* . . . , pp. 163ff.

17. *Alta*, Sept. 30, 1854 (steamer edition, p. 7); *Era*, Oct. 9, 1853; May 6, 1855; Nov. 9, 1856; Nov. 23, 1856; *Chronicle*, Dec. 30, 1854; McCrackan to his family, San Francisco, May 22, 1853, pp. 2–7, in John McCrackan Letters, II.

18. *Pacific*, Oct. 31, 1851.

19. *Alta*, Nov. 13, 1856; *Courier*, Sept. 17, 1850.

20. John Cotter Pelton, *Life's Sunbeams and Shadows*, p. 200; *Alta*, Apr. 25, 1855; *Bulletin*, July 22, 1856; *Pacific*, Jan. 8, 1852.

21. *Pacific*, Aug. 1, 1851; *Bulletin*, July 22, 1856.

22. *Chronicle*, Dec. 5, 1853; Dec. 23, 1853; June 12, 1854; *Bulletin*, Mar. 8,

1856; May 12, 1856; Aug. 23, 1856; July 22, 1856, quoting Rev. Scott of Calvary Presbyterian Church. For the complete range of opinions on the matter of educational philosophy, see *Alta,* Oct. 4, 1850; *Courier,* Sept. 17, 1850; *Picayune,* Aug. 5, 1851; *Herald,* Mar. 13, 1852; Oct. 28, 1854; *Bulletin,* Oct. 28, 1854; *Pacific,* Apr. 29, 1853; William A. Scott, *Oration Delivered at the First Anniversary of the College of California,* pp. 1, 5, 7, 8, 11, 12, 15 (pamphlet, Bancroft Library, University of California); Rev. E. S. Lacy, *The Schools Demanded by Our Times,* pp. 8–9, 10–15, and many other citations from these same sources.

23. *Annals,* pp. 187–88, 200, 677.

24. *Era,* Oct. 28, 1855; *Pacific,* Aug. 17, 1855; *Bulletin,* July 19, 1856; July 26, 1856; Aug. 6, 1856.

25. President of the San Francisco School Board, quoted in the *Alta,* Nov. 18, 1856; Arthur M. Schlesinger, Sr., *The Rise of the City* (New York: The Macmillan Co., 1933), p. 162; *Alta,* Nov. 18, 1856; *Fireman's Journal,* July 12, 1856.

26. *Alta,* Nov. 18, 1856; City Charter of 1856, p. 12 (Bancroft Library, University of California).

27. *Bulletin,* Apr. 12, 1856; Apr. 16, 1856; Apr. 30, 1856; Aug. 20, 1856.

28. *Ibid.,* Sept. 22, 1856.

29. *Pacific,* Aug. 17, 1855; *Bulletin,* Nov. 27, 1855; Jan. 24, 1856; Jan. 28, 1856; Feb. 1, 1856; Feb. 4, 1856; *Alta,* Aug. 1, 1855; *Chronicle,* Nov. 28, 1855.

30. *Era,* Jan. 23, 1853; *Fireman's Journal,* Aug. 23, 1856; on physical education, see also *Bulletin,* Aug. 13, 1856; Aug. 18, 1856 (italics theirs); Aug. 14, 1856; Oct. 13, 1856; Oct. 23, 1856; *Chronicle,* Mar. 27, 1856; June 12, 1856; Aug. 25, 1856.

31. *Bulletin,* Apr. 30, 1856; *Pacific,* Aug. 3, 1855; Aug. 17, 1855; Scott, *Oration Delivered at the First Anniversary . . . ;* see also Bishop Kip, lecture delivered to the San Francisco YMCA, quoted in the *Chronicle,* Apr. 7, 1854; *Pacific,* July 16, 1852; *Weekly Gleaner,* Jan. 23, 1857; *Californian,* Sept. 30, 1848; *Star and Californian,* Nov. 18, 1848; *Chronicle,* Apr. 7, 1854, quoting Bishop Kip.

32. *Chronicle,* Nov. 28, 1854; Oct. 23, 1855; Nov. 28, 1855; quoted in *Alta,* Mar. 22, 1852; *Herald,* Mar. 12, 1852; Prevaux to his parents, San Francisco, July 30, 1853, p. 2, in Francis Edward Prevaux Letters.

33. *Alta,* May 18, 1855; Feb. 28, 1856; June 1, 1856; Nov. 18, 1856; *Bulletin,* Dec. 12, 1856.

34. California Correspondence of the *New York Freeman's Journal,* May 6, 1854; Aug. 7, 1852; *Pacific,* Aug. 6, 1852; June 3, 1853; Dec. 27, 1855; John Bernard McGloin, *California's First Archbishop: The Life of Joseph Sadoc Alemany, O. P., 1814–1888* (New York: Herder and Herder, 1966), p. 167.

35. *Pacific,* Nov. 3, 1854; Mar. 20, 1856; Dec. 25, 1856; see also California Correspondence of the *New York Freeman's Journal,* Aug. 7, 1852; June 4, 1853; June 18, 1853; July 14, 1853; Sept. 17, 1853; May 6, 1854;

June 3, 1854; *Pacific,* Aug. 1, 1851; Jan. 8, 1852; Feb. 27, 1852; July 16, 1852; June 3, 1853; June 17, 1853; Mar. 24, 1854; Apr. 27, 1855; May 4, 1855; May 11, 1855; Nov. 30, 1855; Dec. 27, 1855; Jan. 31, 1856; *Bulletin,* May 14, 1856.

36. Ferdinand C. Ewer, Diary, pp. 246–50 (California Historical Society); *Chronicle,* Jan. 17, 1856; *Alta,* June 4, 1854; Aug. 5, 1854; Aug. 23, 1854; *Era,* May 13, 1855.

37. *Bulletin,* Apr. 24, 1856; Apr. 25, 1856.

38. Ewer, Diary, pp. 248–49 (italics his); see also *Era,* Dec. 9, 1855. The *Era's* figures on numbers qualified and hired were considerably higher than Ewer's.

39. *Bulletin,* Nov. 27, 1855; Edgar S. Lacy, *The Schools Demanded by the Present Age* (San Francisco: Whittier Press, 1856), pp. 5–15.

40. *Bulletin,* Oct. 16, 1856; Oct. 21, 1856; Dec. 11, 1856.

41. Until the end of the period, pay was usually in scrip, often depreciated up to one-third of its face value. *Alta,* May 12, 1855; May 18, 1855; Oct. 16, 1855; *Chronicle,* Feb. 1, 1855.

42. *Bulletin,* Dec. 12, 1856; *Alta,* June 13, 1854; June 29, 1854; Feb. 4, 1855; Feb. 28, 1856; Mar. 22, 1856; Nov. 18, 1856.

43. *Alta,* Apr. 3, 1850; *Pacific,* Dec. 19, 1851; Apr. 29, 1853; July 29, 1853; May 1, 1856; Aug. 7, 1856; *Bulletin,* Aug. 13, 1856; Aug. 30, 1856; *Era,* Oct. 28, 1855; Jan. 27, 1856; May 11, 1856; *Chronicle,* Jan. 24, 1856; Bushnell, *Characteristics and Prospects . . . ,* p. 28.

44. McCrackan to his family, San Francisco, May 15, 1853, p. 5, in John McCrackan Letters, II; *Alta,* Nov. 8, 1852; Mar. 25, 1854; Jan. 1, 1855; *Chronicle,* Aug. 9, 1854; Sept. 27, 1855.

45. *Alta,* Nov. 20, 1853; Nov. 2, 1855; June 8, 1856; Aug. 27, 1856; Nov. 8, 1856; Hunt, *California Firsts,* pp. 145–46.

46. *Herald,* Dec. 31, 1852; *Alta,* Dec. 23, 1852; Hunt, *California Firsts,* pp. 145–47. The Vigilante claim to having founded this organization in the wake of the 1851 uprising is not substantiated. The organizational meetings were held in December of 1852, and in January the group was launched by the election of officers and the adoption of a constitution. *Chronicle,* Dec. 16, 1856; *Alta,* July 9, 1855; Dec. 10, 1856; and many other months before and after; *Bulletin,* Jan. 16, 1853; Nov. 18, 1856.

This San Francisco institution filled an important role with its library, which eventually reached a total of 6000 volumes, the largest such collection in the city. By far the most popular reading was the novel, which usually approached 50 per cent of the books checked out, with travels, biography, and history following in that order. This preoccupation with what many considered light and trivial reading was often deplored, but nothing was done about it since it was clearly a democratic matter. Novels made up only about 10 per cent of the volumes in the collection, but were much more used. The agency also provided other kinds of reading and subscribed to as many newspapers, religious and otherwise, as it could. *Alta*, Mar. 2, 1853; Apr. 16, 1853; May 21, 1853; May 27, 1853; June 11, 1853; July 14, 1853; Aug. 20, 1853; Apr. 8, 1854; *Herald*, Dec. 31, 1852; *Pacific*, Dec. 17, 1852; *Bulletin*, Jan. 2, 1856; Jan. 7, 1856; Jan. 8, 1856.

47. *Chronicle*, Mar. 21, 1856; *Bulletin*, Feb. 15, 1856; June 30, 1856; Aug. 6, 1856; Nov. 28, 1856.

48. *Alta*, Jan. 3, 1853; Jan. 22, 1853; Jan. 30, 1853; May 16, 1853; July 13, 1854; Jan. 11, 1855; Mar. 2, 1855; Feb. 1, 1856; Dec. 12, 1856; *Chronicle*, Mar. 8, 1856; *Bulletin*, Nov. 1, 1855; Jan. 9, 1856; Jan. 14, 1856; Jan. 24, 1856.

49. *San Francisco Catholic Standard*, reprinted in the *New York Freeman's Journal*, June 3, 1854; Lyman, *Around the Horn . . .* , p. 206; Brown, *Early Days in San Francisco*, pp. 68–69, 200ff; Rev. Timothy Dwight Hunt, Diaries, I, entry for late 1848, pp. 85–86. (Italics his.)

50. *Alta*, Aug. 16, 1849; *Bulletin*, Mar. 10, 1856.

51. *Bulletin*, July 29, 1856; *Pacific*, Nov. 16, 1856; Colville, *City Directory for 1856–57*, p. 250.

52. J. L. Ver Mehr, *Checkered Life in the Old and New World* (San Francisco, 1877), p. 358; DeMassey, *A Frenchman in the Gold Rush . . .* , pp. 47–48; see also *New York Freeman's Journal*, July 14, 1853. On the lack of intolerance, see also Alexandre Holinski, *La Californie et les Routes Interocéaniques* (Bruxelles: Meline, Cans, et Cie, 1853), p. 130; Williams, *A Pioneer Pastorate . . .* , pp. 61, 70–71.

53. *Alta*, Dec. 29, 1856.

54. *Alta*, May 30, 1853; *Herald*, Aug. 16, 1852; May 18, 1853; *Chronicle*, Apr. 26, 1856; McCrackan to Lottie, San Francisco, Sept. 14, 1852, in John McCrackan Letters, II; Woodin to his wife, San Francisco, Sept. 10, 1852, p. 4, in Stephen Woodin Papers.

55. *Bulletin*, Jan. 2, 1856; *Pacific*, June 4, 1852, July 23, 1852.

56. *Bulletin*, Feb. 25, 1856; see also *Pacific*, July 21, 1854.

57. *Bulletin*, Feb. 11, 1856; Feb. 18, 1856; *Pacific*, June 29, 1855; *San Francisco Monitor*, Mar. 20, 1858, pp. 3–4.

58. *Pacific*, Oct. 8, 1852; July 29, 1853; Wheeler, "Selected Letters . . . ," *California Historical Society Quarterly*, XXVII, No. 1 (Mar. 1948), 216, letter of Aug. 1, 1849; Coit, *Artist in Eldorado . . .* , pp. 20–21; *Bulletin*, Feb. 18, 1856. The *Bulletin* is a particularly good source on Christian opinion because it printed many sermons almost verbatim.

59. *Pacific*, Sept. 9, 1855; *Bulletin*, Feb. 11, 1856.

60. Ver Mehr, *Checkered Life . . .* , pp. 372–73; Rix, Diary, entry for Aug. 28, 1853, p. 198.

61. Hunt, Diaries, I, entry for Feb. 9, 1849, p. 226. (Italics his.)

62. McGloin, *California's First Archbishop*, p. 167; letter of Isaac Owen to Bishop E. S. Janes, Santa Clara, Feb. 19, 1852, p. 2, and Owen to D. M. Simpson, San Francisco, Feb. 5, 1852, pp. 1–3, and Owen to Simpson, San Francisco, Mar. 5, 1852, in Isaac Owen Correspondence and

Papers (Bancroft Library, University of California); Dr. Wm. A. Scott to Dr. Van Rensalaer, San Francisco, Mar. 4, 1856, in William A. Scott Correspondence and Papers; *Pacific*, July 23, 1852; Report of the Committee Appointed at a Convention of Israelites at San Francisco, Mar. 16, 1851, Report for Mar. 20, 1851, p. 1 (Western Jewish History Center at Judah Magnus Museum, Berkeley, California).

63. *Pacific*, Aug. 1, 1851; Aug. 29, 1851; Apr. 15, 1853; Dec. 22, 1854; Mar. 20, 1856; Bushnell, *Characteristics and Prospects* . . . , p. 28; *New York Freeman's Journal*, Dec. 20, 1856; Owen to Bishop E. S. Janes, San Francisco, July 29, 1851, p. 1; Owen to E. R. Ames, Grass Valley, Sept. 7, 1852, and Owen to J. P. Durbin, San Francisco, Oct. 20, 1852, in Isaac Owen Correspondence and Papers; *Israelite*, Nov. 21, 1856.

64. *Bulletin*, Nov. 21, 1856.

65. McCrackan to his family, San Francisco, Nov. 14, 1852, p. 3, in John McCrackan Letters, II; *Bulletin*, Aug. 5, 1856; *Alta*, Sept. 29, 1853; California Correspondence of the *New York Freeman's Journal*, Dec. 18, 1852.

66. *Chronicle*, Oct. 19, 1855.

67. *Alta*, Dec. 22, 1856; *Bulletin*, Sept. 16, 1856; Sept. 17, 1856; Nov. 18, 1856.

68. *Chronicle*, June 2, 1854. (Italics his.)

69. *Alta*, Dec. 22, 1856; *Chronicle*, Aug. 6, 1856; *Bulletin*, June 21, 1856; Sept. 17, 1856; Clifford M. Drury, *San Francisco YMCA: 100 Years by the Golden Gate* (Glendale, California: A. H. Clark and Company, 1963), pp. 27, 34; *Alta*, Apr. 7, 1856; July 19, 1856.

70. Drury, *San Francisco YMCA* . . . , p. 24; *Chronicle*, Nov. 3, 1855.

71. *Bulletin*, Apr. 7, 1856

72. *Alta*, Jan. 31, 1855; Feb. 19, 1855; Feb. 6, 1856; Apr. 23, 1856.

73. Hunt, Diaries, II, entries for March 1, 1854, May 15, 1854.

74. *Chronicle*, Feb. 6, 1856; *Alta*, Feb. 29, 1854; Apr. 22, 1855; July 11, 1855; letter of William S. Moses to his father, San Francisco, Feb. 23, 1853, pp. 1–2, in Letters of William S. Moses (Miscellaneous Collection, California State Library, Sacramento, California). (Italics his.)

75. *Alta*, July 11, 1855; Dec. 3, 1855; May 6, 1856; July 19, 1856.

76. *Ibid.*, Dec. 4, 1856; *Pacific*, Aug. 1, 1851; Aug. 10, 1855; Kemble, *A History* . . . , 43–44; Carter, "The San Francisco *Bulletin*. . . ."

77. *Era*, Aug. 7, 1853; July 2, 1854; *Pacific*, Aug. 1, 1851.

78. *Era*, July 8, 1855.

79. *Picayune*, Aug. 3, 1850.

80. *Call*, Feb. 4, 1857.

81. *Picayune*, Aug. 3, 1850; *Alta*, May 4, 1855; *Fireman's Journal*, Mar. 22, 1856; *Era*, Mar. 4, 1855.

82. *Fireman's Journal*, Mar. 22, 1856; *Pacific*, Feb. 9, 1854; Feb. 2, 1855; *Era*, May 25, 1856; Oct. 12, 1836; Nasatir, *Guillaume Patrice Dillon*, pp. 312–13; Nasatir, *A French Journalist* . . . , p. 32.

83. *Era*, June 1, 1856; Oct. 12, 1856.
84. *Pacific*, July 2, 1852; Dec. 16, 1853; Dec. 23, 1853; Dec. 8, 1854; Nov. 23, 1855; Sept. 18, 1856; *Era*, Aug. 31, 1856; Oct. 12, 1856.
85. Winchester to his brother Ebenezer, San Francisco, Jan. 30, 1850, in Jonas Winchester Papers. (Italics his.) Winchester to his wife, San Francisco, Apr. 16, 1850, in Jonas Winchester Papers; *Era*, Aug. 12, 1855; June 1, 1856; Oct. 12, 1856.
86. *Era*, Dec. 2, 1855.
87. *Ibid.*, July 8, 1855; Dec. 2, 1855; June 22, 1856; *Pacific*, Dec. 16, 1853; *Fireman's Journal*, Oct. 20, 1855.
88. *Chronicle*, June 12, 1854.

CONCLUSION

1. Joseph Fletcher, *Situation Ethics* (Philadelphia: The Westminster Press, 1966), pp. 1–40, calls this a "new morality."
2. *Chronicle*, Sept. 19, 1855.
3. Samuel Ward to E. D. Keyes, San Francisco, Feb. 1, 1854, in Rodman Price Correspondence and Papers.
4. Rev. William Taylor, p. 2, sermon preached July 1856.
5. Lecouvreur, *From East Prussia* . . . , p. 273.
6. Hubert Howe Bancroft, *California Inter Pocula* (San Francisco: The History Company Publishers, 1888), p. 260.
7. William Henry Ellison, *A Self-Governing Dominion: California, 1849–60* (Berkeley and Los Angeles: University of California Press, 1950), p. 269. For a comment on the political pre-eminence of San Francisco, see Chapter IX, page 1, quote from *Chronicle*, May 28, 1855.
8. Robert Cleland, *A History of California* (New York: The Macmillan Co., 1922), p. 462. William W. Ferrier, *Origin and Development of the University of California* (Berkeley, Cal.: The Bathergate Bookshop, 1930), pp. 81–222. Samuel H. Willey, *A History of the College of California* (San Francisco: Samuel Carson and Co., 1887).
9. Josiah Royce, *California, A Study of American Character* (Boston and New York: Houghton Mifflin and Co., 1886), p. 377.
10. *Ibid.*, p. 378.
11. Bancroft, *History of California*, II, 745.
12. *Ibid.*, p. 754.
13. For this role, see Richard C. Wade, *The Urban Frontier* (Chicago: The University of Chicago Press, 1964) and Carl Bridenbaugh, *Cities in the Wilderness* (New York: Capricorn Books, 1964).
14. Arthur M. Schlesinger, Sr., *The Rise of the City* (New York: The Macmillan Co., 1933), p. 435.

Index

397